Transnational Protests
and the Media

Simon Cottle
General Editor

Vol. 10

The Global Crises and the Media series is part of the Peter Lang Media
and Communication list. Every volume is peer reviewed and meets
the highest quality standards for content and production.

PETER LANG
New York • Washington, D.C./Baltimore • Bern
Frankfurt • Berlin • Brussels • Vienna • Oxford

Transnational Protests and the Media

EDITED BY Simon Cottle & Libby Lester

PETER LANG
New York • Washington, D.C./Baltimore • Bern
Frankfurt • Berlin • Brussels • Vienna • Oxford

Library of Congress Cataloging-in-Publication Data

Transnational protests and the media / edited by Simon Cottle, Libby Lester.
p. cm. — (Global crises and the media, ISSN 1947-2587 ; v. 10)
Includes bibliographical references and index.
1. Protest movements in mass media. I. Cottle, Simon. II. Lester, Libby.
P96.S63T73 2011   302.23—dc22   2011013897
ISBN 978-1-4331-0986-7 (hardcover)
ISBN 978-1-4331-0985-0 (paperback)
ISSN 1947-2587

Bibliographic information published by **Die Deutsche Nationalbibliothek**.
Die Deutsche Nationalbibliothek lists this publication in the "Deutsche
Nationalbibliografie"; detailed bibliographic data is available
on the Internet at http://dnb.d-nb.de/.

Cover image by David Rose/Panos Pictures.

The paper in this book meets the guidelines for permanence and durability
of the Committee on Production Guidelines for Book Longevity
of the Council of Library Resources.

Table of Contents

Part Three: Protesting Economy and Trade

Part Four: Protesting Ecology and Climate

Part Five: Protesting Human Rights and Civil Rights

Part Six: Transnational Protests and the Media: Toward Global Civil Society?

Series Editor's Preface

We live in a global age. We inhabit a world that has become radically interconnected, interdependent, and communicated in the formations and flows of the media. This same world also spawns proliferating, often interpenetrating, "global crises."

From climate change to the war on terror, financial meltdowns to forced migrations, pandemics to world poverty, and humanitarian disasters to the denial of human rights, these and other crises represent the dark side of our globalized planet. Their origins and outcomes are not confined behind national borders, and they are not best conceived through national prisms of understanding. The impacts of global crises register across "sovereign" national territories, surrounding regions, and beyond, and they can also become subject to systems of governance and forms of civil society response that are no less encompassing or transnational in scope. In today's interdependent world, global crises cannot be regarded as exceptional or aberrant events only, erupting without rhyme or reason or dislocated from the contemporary world (dis)order. They are endemic to the contemporary global world, deeply enmeshed within it. And so too are they highly dependent on the world's media.

How global crises are signaled and defined, staged and elaborated in the world's media proves critical to wider processes of recognition and response, entering into their future course and conduct. In exercising their symbolic and communicative power, the world's media variously inform processes of public understanding, but so too can they dissimulate the nature of the threats that confront us and marginalize those voices that seek to mobilize forces for change. The scale of death and destruction involved or the potentially catastrophic nature of different global threats is no guarantee that they will register prominently, if at all, in the world's media, much less that they will be defined therein as "global crises." So-called hidden wars and forgotten disasters still abound in the world today and, because of their media invisibility, go unnoticed, commanding neither recognition nor wider response.

The series *Global Crises and the Media* sets out, therefore, to examine not only the media's role in the *communication* of global threats and crises but also how the media can enter into their *constitution,* enacting them on the public stage and thereby helping to shape their future trajectory around the world. More specifically, the volumes in this series seek to: (1) contextualize the study of global crisis reporting in relation to wider debates about the changing flows and formations of world media communication; (2) address how global crises become variously communicated and contested in the media around the world; (3) consider the possible impacts of global crisis reporting on public awareness, political action, and policy responses; (4) showcase the very latest research findings and discussion from leading authorities in their respective fields of inquiry; and (5) contribute to the development of positions of theory and debate that deliberately move beyond national parochialisms and/or geographically disaggregated research agendas. In these ways the specially commissioned books in the *Global Crises and the Media* series aim to provide a sophisticated and empirically engaged understanding of the media's role in global crises and thereby contribute to academic and public debate about some of the most significant global threats, conflicts, and contentions in the world today.

Transnational Protests and the Media, edited by Simon Cottle and Libby Lester, addresses all the series themes above and does so by examining major protests around the world that are focused on issues and conflicts of transnational concern. Protests and demonstrations today increasingly register wider forces of global change and express grievances spawned by a radically interconnected and inegalitarian world. Crucially, as the editors and contributors to this book both argue and document, media and communications are at their core. It is in and through today's enveloping media ecology and complex of communication networks that protests and demonstrations taking place in particular locales or national contexts become effectively transnationalized. And it is here too that they register more widely and maximize their impacts. This is so whether in respect of wider publics and supporters, national and international political elites, authorities charged with their control (or suppression) and indeed, increasingly, the protesters and activists themselves who now seek to challenge mainstream media representations and communicate alternatives of their own. And it is also by these communication means that some of the world's foremost injustices and threats to humanity including war, weapons of mass destruction, inequalities of trade, ecological degradation, climate change, human rights abuses and humanitarian catastrophe become part of a new global awareness and, potentially, prompt new forms of transnational solidarity.

This volume provides an accessible and authoritative entrée to some of the differences of approach and debates currently informing the study of media, protests and demonstrations when approached in transnational and global contexts. The approaches and arguments in play draw on different disciplines and theoretical outlooks that range across the humanities and social sciences. What they share, however, is a general recognition of the *constitutive* nature of communications and media representation in the conduct and enactment of contemporary transnational protests and a preparedness to engage conceptually, theoretically and empirically with this fast-changing field. When protests and demonstrations are coordinated, mobilized and transacted around the world, moving above and beyond frames of national self-interest and political opportunity structures, is it conceivable, they ask, that a more complex dynamic of media-protest interactions, cultural frames and public responses can come into play? What are the principal forces, contingencies and complexities now at work in mediated transnational protests? How are these being played out across different global issues and concerns and in the communication networks and formations of today's global media? And to what extent and in what senses can mediated transnational protests express if only emergently or imperfectly "global civil society" and "global citizenship"? How, in an increasingly fragmented and multilayered communications environment, can they contribute to a "global public sphere"?

Transnational Protests and the Media seeks answers to these and other questions whilst incisively engaging with different substantive global issues focused through transnational protests. With contributions from leading theorists and researchers working in the field today, this cutting-edge collection explores transnational protests directed at issues of war and peace, economy and trade, ecology and climate change as well as political struggles for civil and human rights. At its core is the concerted attempt to better understand the pivotal role and creative uses of media and communications by transnational activists and how today's rapidly changing media environment is altering relations of communication power from the local to the global. In such ways we may also become better equipped to understand how both protests and media can help to instantiate transnational awareness and action.

Simon Cottle, Series Editor

PART ONE

Transnational Protests

Approaches and Agendas

CHAPTER ONE

Transnational Protests and the Media

An Introduction

SIMON COTTLE AND LIBBY LESTER

Across recent decades protests and demonstrations have increasingly sought to highlight issues of global scope and transnational concern. Global justice and inequalities of trade, war and peace, human rights and humanitarian catastrophes as well as ecology and climate change have all, for example, become the focus of major protests in recent years. The contradictions, conflicts and crises spawned by today's interconnected, globalizing late modernity, it seems, can also summon into being new social movements, coalitions of opposition and voices of dissent world-wide. These can sometimes be no less globalizing in their communicative intent or forms of transnational political action, lending weight and substance perhaps to claims about emergent "global civil society" and "global citizenship." *Transnational Protests and the Media* sets out to examine how the mobilizing and democratizing promise of transnational protests critically inheres within today's interpenetrating communication networks and encompassing worldwide media ecology.

Mass protests, coordinated and conducted simultaneously on different conti-nents, in different countries and across major cities have proved capable of mobi-lizing hundreds of thousands of people, sometimes millions of people, around the globe. Over 36 million took to the streets to protest against the invasion of Iraq in 2003, and 31 million people from 84 national coalitions united in a "Global Call to Action Against Poverty" (GCAP) including the UK's Make Poverty History campaign in 2005. So-called "summit sieges," following the "Battle of Seattle" in

1999, have also become a regular if not annual event with protesters from different countries taking up counter-positions outside the meetings of heads of state and high-ranking officials such as those of the World Trade Organization (WTO), the International Monetary Fund (IMF) the G8, now G20, and the Copenhagen summit on climate change in late 2009. Such protests are designed to challenge elite decision-making and the deliberation of polices behind closed doors, policies that if implemented will have profound impacts on populations internationally or even globally. And some protests, though involving a handful of protesters only, can also now resonate nationally, internationally and transnationally—whether, for example, local environmentalists chaining themselves to trees in ancient Tasmanian forests threatened by the logging industry or activists aboard the *Sea Shepherd* attempting to disrupt the industrialized slaughter of whales in the "global commons" of the Southern Ocean.

In these and other ways, transnational protests today both engage with but can also themselves instantiate global forces of change—even when locally enacted or directed against national institutions and governments (della Porta & Tarrow, 2005b; Tarrow, 2006). Through creative repertoires of protest they seek to bring recognition to issues of global concern, secure legitimacy for their cause and mobilize identities and voices of support worldwide. The "transnational" in the contemporary politics of protest, however, is not only characterized by political reach, motivating ethics or geographical scale—all of which invariably extend beyond sovereign national borders and parochial frames of national understanding. And there is certainly more to the "transnational" in transnational protests than the narrowly conceived terms of international relations and how national interests become pursued inter-*nationally*. Crucially the "transnational" in transnational protests and demonstrations, we argue, fundamentally inheres within *how* they become communicated and mediated around the globe.

It is in and through the flows and formations of worldwide media and communication networks that transnational demonstrations today principally become *transacted* around the planet. Though physically enacted in particular locales, cities, countries or indeed on different continents, it is by means of contemporary communication networks and media systems that they effectively become coordinated, staged for wider audiences and disseminated around the world. And it is here too that they often discharge their affect and effects on supporters, wider publics and different decision makers; whether by redefining the terms of public discourse, bolstering solidarities and identities of opposition, mobilizing supporters or shifting cultural horizons as well as seeking to influence political elites and government policies.

Through the Internet and new social media, protests and demonstrations today can be coordinated and communicated internationally, and it is by these same means that some also become exclusively conducted—whether for example, through online petitions, the mobilization of consumer boycotts or digital *hacktivism*. New digital means of recording, storing and disseminating images of protest have also eased the practical, if not ideological, cross-over of scenes of dissent into wider communication flows and mainstream media. And traditional print and broadcasting media continue to perform a critical role in defining, framing and dramatizing protests and demonstrations and, thereby, helping to publicly legitimize or de-legitimize them for mass audiences and readerships. It is in and through this fast-evolving complex of interpenetrating communication networks and media systems, then, that protests and demonstrations today principally become transacted around the world.

The transnational, as ethico-political imaginary (of what should be) and as collective political action (the struggle to bring this about), becomes *instantiated* within and through the communicative enactments of protest and demonstration—if only momentarily or imperfectly. Consider, for example, the following.

- Between 3 January and 12 April 2003, following the invasion of Iraq, an estimated 36 million people across the globe took part in almost 3000 protests. Many of these mass protests were coordinated simultaneously in cities around the world. After the biggest series of demonstrations, on 15 February 2003, *New York Times* writer Peter Tyler claimed that they showed that there were two superpowers on the planet: the United States and worldwide public opinion.

- In September 2007, coordinated demonstrations took place simultaneously in over 35 capitals protesting against the continuing genocide in Darfur, Sudan. Campaigners including media celebrities wore blindfolds in a call to world leaders to "Protect Darfur: don't look away." The day was organized by a coalition of over 50 organizations including Aegis Trust, Amnesty International, Human Rights Watch, the Save Darfur Coalition, the Darfur Consortium and many others. The events coincided with the second anniversary of the "responsibility to protect" agreement, when world governments vowed to act to stop genocide and mass atrocities.

- Also in September 2007 Burmese monks dressed in traditional saffron robes defied the Burmese authorities and led mass protests against the poverty and human rights abuses in their country. When a similar popular uprising had been attempted in 1988 it was brutally suppressed by the Burmese junta with the loss of nearly 3000 lives. Little was then known outside Burma of this crushed revolt. In 2007 the so-called "saffron revolution" registered around the world: graphic scenes and testimonies were conveyed by the latest communication technologies, including mobile phone cameras, weblogs and the Internet. Over the course of the first few days the world witnessed the progress of the revolt and then its brutal repression via smuggled videos distributed to news agencies and television networks and by online blogs (weblogs) written by dissidents in Rangoon and Mandalay. The power of these and other images, as well as the graphic testimonies of the protesters posted on the Internet and picked up by the mainstream Western news media, summoned condemnation from the UN, political leaders and different publics around the world.

- On 21 October 2008, in Tasmania's Upper Florentine Valley, two environmentalists from the unaligned and poorly resourced group, "Still Wild, Still Threatened," blockaded a logging road with a car body, in which they lay with their arms chained to a concrete block embedded in the ground. Logging contractors responded by allegedly attacking the car with sledgehammers. No journalists were present. Hiding in the bush, a third protester filmed the encounter and posted it on the group's MySpace profile (www.myspace.com/stillwildstillthreatened). Within hours the incident was available for viewing around the world. News media organizations in Tasmania and interstate soon began to cover the story. This prominence forced—among others—the premier of Tasmania, David Bartlett, to defend his environmental policies and views on forestry practices. The environmental campaign gathered momentum as the publicity and debate triggered by the incident in broadcast, print and online news media traveled throughout an international network of activist and news websites.

- In June 2009, the social networking site Twitter and the BBC's new Persian language satellite channel both played an important part in communicating mass demonstrations in Iran, prompted by the re-election of President Ahmadinejad amid calls of a rigged election. Twitter helped to bring the protests to a global audience and the BBC's Persian new service broadcast information and images back into Iran (at its peak it was receiving 10,000 emails a day and 10 videos a minute). Bypassing the restrictions imposed by the Iranian authorities on foreign journalists (who were not permitted to report unauthorized gatherings), web users and owners of mobile phones in Iran passed on a continuing torrent of images and updates of the demonstrations and their increasing repression to audiences worldwide. Such was the perceived power of Twitter, the US State Department persuaded the Californian company not to take the service offline for routine maintenance at this critical juncture—seeking to ensure worldwide opinion could pressure the Tehranian regime to accept change.

As these examples help to illustrate, protests and demonstrations today increasingly serve to focus political and public opinion on crises and issues of international and global concern. Their impacts, courtesy of global media and communication networks, can now also register internationally and transnationally. Whether the "scale shift" is upwards from the local/national to the transnational and global or downwards from the transnational to the national/local (Tarrow & McAdam, 2005), it is in and through communication networks and the pervasive and overlapping media ecology that oppositional currents and movements for change are principally conveyed. And it is here too that protests effectively become publicly known and register more widely. Their political efficacy need not always be measured in terms of exerting measurable, direct and radical effects on political elites or power structures. Such moments of decisive impact though not without historical and more recent precedents are in fact rare (see: Afterword: Media and the Arab Uprisings of 2011). But transnational protests, like protests more generally, can be deeply implicated in processes of change nonetheless: building and mobilizing support, redrawing cultural and political horizons, or even helping to create a prefigurative politics based on participatory practices and ethical norms of equality and justice. In the context of authoritarian states, protest and demonstration can sometimes help to usher in radical change and transform systems of political power—as we have seen across recent years. But they often run the risk of brutal suppression, as we have also witnessed in recent times around the world.

Lest we should succumb to either blanket pessimism about the power of protests and demonstrations or naïve celebration of the same, we need to situate them in relation to wider historical forces of change, contextualizing their mobilizing force within civil society and attending to the permeability of surrounding political structures and institutions to the voices of dissent. It would be simplistic therefore to approach, much less seek to explain or theorize, transnational protests as a simple reflex of available media technologies. Contemporary communication and delivery systems can certainly facilitate and shape the communicative forms and enactments of protests and demonstration as we have heard, but this should not be interpreted as a straightforward causality, much less media and communications determinism. Composed of different and overlapping media formations, both old and new, accelerating, horizontal and vertical communications flows and new virtual, interactional and user-generated capabilities, today's complex media and communications ecology offers unprecedented opportunities for the wider enactment and diffusion of political protest—from the local to the global. But how these opportunities become realized, negotiated, challenged and contested in practice and with what repercussions on protest movements and coalitions, on their goals and tactics, supporters, publics and relevant elites, clearly demands detailed empirical exploration and careful theorization.

The complex and evolving interplay between transnational protests and media and communications cannot be reduced to one size fits all. Coordinated, networked actions spearheaded by new transnational movements and loosely affiliated campaign groups, such as the global justice movement, can deliberately stage summit-sieges and spectacular "image events" (DeLuca, 1999; Opel & Pompper, 2003; de Jong, Shaw & Stammers, 2005). These are often deliberately performed in front of the world's media or uploaded to them shortly thereafter on the basis of a media-savvy understanding of journalist news values and news organizations' predilections toward the dramatic, spectacular and revelatory. But mass actions can now also be recorded and communicated directly by protesters, supporters via new social media and alternative news sites such as Indymedia (Independent Media Centres), as well as by members of the general public who "bear witness" via everyday communication technologies: mobile phones, digital cameras or pocket videocams. When uploaded and circulated via the Internet, these new forms of "citizen journalism" can play a part in altering the balance of communicative power (McNair, 2006; Allan & Thorsen, 2009; Gowing, 2009).

Though political demonstrations and their informing politics continue to be "symbolically annihilated" in some national media given their perceived assault on institutions of governance and the legitimacy of authorities, they nonetheless often "leak out" into the wider circuits of global communications and information flows when recorded and communicated clandestinely, as in our examples from Burma, Iran and Tasmania above. First-hand accounts and incriminating images of repressive state actions, corporate violence or individual acts of police brutality can now all be captured and communicated almost instantaneously via the Internet. These, moreover, can be circulated to émigré communities, publics and political leaders around the globe and, importantly, can also re-enter the communications environment of the country from whence they secretly came, documenting the latest events on the ground and contributing to processes of protest diffusion and the mass mobilization of civil societies. In such ways local and global communications can interpenetrate, conditioning each other and intensifying political pressures for change. They facilitate the new "civilian surge" (Gowing, 2009) and the wider "transformation of visibility" (Thompson, 1995) of late modern, mediated, societies, and by these means they can seemingly empower the formerly communications disenfranchized.

The power relations that constitute the foundation of all societies, argues Manuel Castells, "are increasingly shaped and decided in the communications field" (Castells, 2007: 239; 2009). The conflicts and crises that have become characteristic of our global age—climate change, the "war on terror," nuclear proliferation, human rights abuses, humanitarian emergencies, Third-World debt and inequalities of trade, financial meltdowns—can all become the focal point of transnational protests. These often seek to move beyond and above "the national" and register transnationally. But how exactly they become transacted from the local to the global through media and communications, and how these register and reverberate transnationally, demands detailed and theoretically informed examination.

Transnational Protests and the Media sets out, then, to explore and theorize the changing nature of transnational protests and their transactions within and through the complex circuits of contemporary communications and media but without collapsing into simplistic media centrism or communications determinism. With contributions from leading theorists and researchers working in the field of transnational protests and communications today, we consider a wide array of pertinent themes and issues. These are addressed while examining transnational protests focusing on war and peace, economy and trade, climate and ecology, and struggles for human rights and civil rights. We explore the creative uses of different but invariably media-reflexive protest repertoires and the new political opportunity structure(s) opened up by transnational communication flows and how the latter may be altering relations of communication power. We consider how both old and new media become infused in the wider enactments and diffusion of mediated protests as well as their scaling-up to the transnational and scaling down to the local levels. Competing ideas of political mediation conceptualized in terms of the "public sphere" and "public screens" as well as the rise of celebrity and spectacle in demonstrations and the performative and dramaturgical staging of global protest events also feature prominently, as do the differing emphases granted to the "politics of connectivity" and the "politics of representation" by those focusing, respectively, on the Net and mainstream media in the coordination and communication of transnational protests. And so too do many of our contributors address and help to deepen our understanding of how mediated transnational protests serve to constitute a "global public sphere" of "global citizenship" notwithstanding the fragmentary nature of the former and underdeveloped institutionalization of the latter.

As editors we have deliberately sought contributions from authors and researchers from around the world and with differing disciplinary and theoretical allegiances but all working on different transnational issues and protests whether in respect of war and peace, economy and trade, ecology and climate, or political oppression and human rights. We have also sought to represent new theoretical, conceptual and methodological approaches to the study of mediated protests, approaches that are now invigorating the field of academic debate. Recent developments, for example, in new media studies, the sociology of media sources, audience reception studies, social movement studies and contentious politics, cultural geography and anthropology as well as media approaches now generally attuned to both the *strategic dynamics* of communication power as well as the *cultural forms* of their mediation including the dramaturgical, performative and spectacular, all hold promise for in-depth analyses and improved understanding. Together these and other recent infusions into the field of media and protest studies prompt new research questions and new research agendas and do so in a context that must now address the increasingly globalized nature of mediated transnational protests and dissent.

When protests and demonstrations are coordinated, mobilized and transacted transnationally, moving above and beyond frames of national-interest and political opportunity structures, is it now conceivable that a more complex dynamic of media-protest interactions, cultural frames and public responses can come into play? What are the principal determinants and dynamics, contingencies and complexities at work in mediated transnational protests today? How are these being played out across different global issues and concerns and in the communication networks and formations of today's global media? To what extent and in what senses can mediated transnational protests be seen to express if only emergently or imperfectly "global civil society" and "global citizenship," and how, in an increasingly fragmented and multilayered communications environment, can they contribute to a "global public sphere"? In what ways can today's media and communication networks constitute a political opportunity structure of potentially transnational significance when put to work in the service of protests focused on issues of global consequence and transnational concern? These are the principal questions that this collection seeks to grapple with–conceptually, theoretically, empirically, politically. The book's architecture reflects these broad pedagogic ambitions.

Plan of book

In Chapter 2, "Transnational Protests and the Media: New Departures, Challenging Debates," Simon Cottle discourses on some of the introductory remarks above. With reference to established work in the field as well as positions advanced by the contributors across this volume, differences of approach and six key debates are highlighted. This opening chapter aims to map some of the main theoretical perspectives and debates in play and to plot some of the key theoretical and conceptual coordinates of use when approaching the research field of transnational protests and the media.

Part Two: Protesting War and Peace, provides three contrasting contributions to the field of war and protest studies. Chapter 3: "Scales of Activism: New Media and Transnational Connections in Anti-War Movements," by Jenny Pickerill, Kevin Gillan and Frank Webster, explores how new media have been put to use in anti-war movements. Based on five case studies of British anti-war and peace organizations, the authors demonstrate how new information communication technologies (ICTs) can help to make anti-war activists feel global and interconnected while also noting some of the limitations of these different transnational forms. Importantly they also invite us to rethink "scale" in the context of transnational protests as not simply linear (and thus scaled-up from the local to global) but as relational and mutually constituted—a theme that is echoed across some of the chapters that follow.

Chapter 4: "'Not in Our Name': British Press, the Anti-war Movement and the Iraq Crisis 2002–2009," by Craig Murray, Piers Robinson, Peter Goddard and Katy Parry, examines how the transnational protest movement against the Iraq war, one of history's largest-ever global anti-war movements, was represented in Britain's national press. Notwithstanding claims about the increased capacity of protest groups to mobilize support through new forms of communication technology and a brief window of opportunity in the period prior to the invasion when dissenting voices were heard, the British press are generally found to have worked against the potential transnationalism of the anti-war movements and quickly succumbed to elite political opinion and the national default position in times of war, national patriotism.

Chapter 5: "On Anti-Iraq War Protests and the Global News Sphere," by Stephen Reese, considerably broadens the media lens when considering national and global media in respect of anti-war protests. As social protests have become transnationalized, argues Reese, so too have the media platforms on which they play out. In this context, the globalized anti-war movement demonstrates an important development in the flow of political influence through transnational networks. Transnational links help invigorate the global public sphere, where the military policy of superpowers becomes subject to critique more than ever before and where mediated protest events can help to shift the boundaries of communication power.

Part Three: Protesting Economy and Trade examines global activism broadly conceived in terms of global justice and focused on economics and international trade. Chapter 6: "Leaderless Crowds, Self-Organizing Publics, and Virtual Masses: The New Media Politics of Dissent," by Andrew Rojecki, follows up on his earlier influential analysis of the so-called "Battle of Seattle" (2002) and how protesters were able to secure improved and sometimes even sympathetic media coverage. Here he provides a thoughtful reflection on how new web-based technologies post-Seattle as well as the changing political opportunity structure of a post-9/11 world now inform transnational movement tactics as well as the continuing role of mainstream media in certifying legitimacy on new transnational protests.

Chapter 7: "Mediating and Embodying Transnational Protest: Internal and External Effects of Mass Global Justice Actions" is by Jeffrey Juris. He argues that mass counter-summit actions incorporate a tension between the emotional and media dimensions of protest. Externally, they are powerful "image events" (DeLuca, 1999), where diverse activist networks communicate their messages to an audience by "hijacking" the global media space afforded by multilateral summits. Internally, identities are expressed and emotions are generated through ritual conflict and the experience of lived, prefigured utopias. Juris brings a welcome anthropological sensitivity (as well as first-hand experience) to the complex relations between the mediated and affective dimensions of social movement practice and the performance of mediated protests.

Two chapters follow, both based on an analysis of the London G20 protests in 2009. Each provides usefully contrasting insights into the possibly changing nature of transnational protest reporting, attending respectively to news sources and visual images–two key dimensions of protest reporting. Chapter 8: "Protest and Public Relations: A New Era for Non-institutional Sources?" by Adam Bowers, considers whether news media savvy non-governmental organizations (NGOs) can now challenge institutional source dominance in media reporting on global issues–bucking the trend established in earlier studies of primary definition, elite indexing and elite news dominance. Findings are presented that suggest non-institutional sources remain systematically and politically disadvantaged in their ongoing struggle to get their voices heard, whether through public relations or protests. Chapter 9: "Photography, the Police and Protest: Images of the G20, London 2009," by David Archibald, provides a contrasting discussion focused specifically on the increased circulation and changing nature of visual images in mediated protests. Following the death of an innocent bystander, Ian Tomlinson, in the G20 protests in London that was caught on camera, Archibald sees this recorded incident as emblematic of how ease of recording and transmitting of visual images has led to growing unease on the part of the police and government. Archibald argues that such images now demonstrably and significantly alter the media narratives of protest.

Part Four: Protesting Ecology and Climate comprises five chapters. Chapter 10: "Wild Public Screens and Image Events from Seattle to China: Using Social Media to Broadcast Activism," by Kevin Michael DeLuca, Ye Sun and Jennifer Peeples, updates DeLuca and Peeples's earlier and influential disquisition on "image events" and the "public screen" (2002), and does so in the contemporary context of environmental politics. Their starting premise is that television, digital cameras, the computer, the Internet, Web 2.0, and smartphones have together fundamentally transformed the media matrix and produced new forms of social organization and modes of perception. In today's imagistic and visceral mediated environment, traditional notions of the "public sphere" as a common realm of rationality that leads to democratic consensus or closure are found severely impaired for the task of better understanding and intervening within mediated protests centered on ecology and environment.

Chapter 11: "Politics, Power and Online Protest in an Age of Environmental Conflict," by Brett Hutchins and Libby Lester, offers a detailed analysis and theorization of how Tasmanian environmental protests became projected nationally and globally. The pressure that can be brought to bear by such communication flows, they argue, is now well understood by today's transnational constellation of activists and NGOs. Developing on Manuel Castells's recent theorization of communications power in the global network society (Castells, 2009), Hutchins and Lester document and argue that it is the capacity to control and/or influence how these networks connect and interact that determines which actors possess most power in environmental conflicts.

Chapter 12: "Amazon Struggles in the Global Media Age," by Conny Davidson, also explores how local and regionalized struggles centered on environment and ecology, identity and democracy are currently being played out in and through local-global circuits of communications. The Amazon rainforest has become one of the foremost frontiers of clashing economic and environmental interests in the world and indigenous rights movements are increasingly using media channels to strengthen their voice in this clamor of competing public discourses. This chapter analyzes the interface of socio-environmental protests and the media in the Amazon Protests 2008–2009.

Chapter 13: "Piracy Up-Linked: *Sea Shepherd* and the Spectacle of Protest on the High Seas," by David Crouch and Katarina Damjanov, turns to a different "global commons": the Southern Ocean and a direct action campaign aimed at disrupting the industrialized killing of whales. The actions of the *Sea Shepherd* in the Southern Ocean are recorded by its crew and are then broadcast back to the world via the Internet and blogosphere, replete with broadcast-quality images and a barrage of news releases, twitters, and updates of events. Here the authors argue that the environmental activism of the *Sea Shepherd* uses new forms of communication technology in culturally crafted ways that both enhance the idea of a global society and encourage a nascent transnational public sphere of eco-citizens.

Chapter 14: "Climate Change and International Protest at Copenhagen: Reflections on British Television and the Web," by Neil Gavin and Tom Marshall, analyses how these media reflected and refracted internationally organized protest activities at the Copenhagen summit on climate change in December 2009. The authors ask what the nature of the TV coverage was and what contribution it could have made to British public understanding of the protesters and their political aims. They also pursue whether the web possibly changed the wider contours of the mediated landscape and, if so, how. On both counts the authors conclude that television and the web provided limited opportunities for the protesters' views and voices to come to the fore: the former often reverting to "the protest paradigm" delegitimizing the voices of dissent and the latter providing relatively few spaces for oppositional accounts and voices though noticeable infusions from the traditional mainstream media.

Part Five: Protesting Human Rights and Civil Rights provides four cutting-edge analyses of protests that register communicatively and transnationally. Chapter 15: "Open Source Protest: Human Rights, Online Activism and the Beijing 2008 Olympic Games," by Ana Adi and Andy Miah, explores the potential of the Internet to promote human rights activism and awareness. The authors address how international human rights advocacy groups, such as Amnesty International and Human Rights Watch, coordinated their Internet presence to reach the mass media, members of the public, critics and supporters on the occasion of the Beijing Olympic Games. Their findings and discussion suggest that transnational activism, including Olympic-targeted activism, has now entered a new stage based on con-vergent media processes and characterized by integrated offline and online strategies.

Chapter 16: "The 2008 Tibet Riots: Competing Perspectives, Divided Group Protests and Divergent Media Narratives," by Chen Li and Lucy Montgomery, pro-vides a rare analysis of the complexities of audience reception and sense-making in respect of mediated accounts of political protest as they register across geo-politi-cal borders and through different political and national outlooks. Their in-depth study of contending responses to the Tibet riots of 2008 serves as a case study of how global diasporas make sense of the competing claims presented by news out-lets when reporting on trans-national protest movements and how, inevitably, this became a point of potential tension. News coverage of the riots, in turn, became the catalyst for transnational protests against "western media bias" in which Chinese stu-dents studying overseas played a key role. The chapter skillfully recovers the com-plexities of audience sense-making and response to transnationally mediated news reports of political protests.

Chapter 17: "'Resistanbul': An Analysis of Mediated Communication in Transnational Activism," by Ilke Sanlier Yüksel and Murat Yüksel, explores the ways in which a transnational activist network based in Turkey communicates among its active members and with the public it seeks to influence. This includes attending to how the Internet has been used to mobilize supporters and organize protest actions as well as its efforts to attract mass media attention. Based on their analy-sis of *Resistanbul* the authors also analyze and reflect on how the local and transna-tional now often interpenetrate and mutually condition each other in contemporary forms of mediated protests.

Chapter 18: "Political Protest and the Persian Blogosphere: The Iranian Election," by Nazanin Ghanavizi, examines the integral role played by the Internet and the blogosphere in the protests for civil and political rights following the result of the presidential election on 12 June 2009–the biggest demonstrations held since the 1979 Islamic Revolution. In a country like Iran, argues Ghanavizi, the Internet and blogging in particular have contributed greatly to the formation of public opinion, and her analysis of the Iranian presidential election demonstrates how these new media helped in the struggle for political and civil rights. The specific history and shape of the Internet in Iran provides an example of an embryonic public sphere through which we can consider the association among blogs, free speech and protest and the new salience of the Internet in relation to public reasoning and social protest.

Chapter 19: "The Global Human Rights Regime and the Internet: Non-Democratic States and the Hypervisibility of Evidence of Oppression," by James Stanyer and Scott Davidson, argues that human rights abuses have never been so globally visible. Whereas once repressive acts in distant places were exposed to a mass audience intermittently or not at all, now such material is routinely posted online and made visible to a global audience of Internet users. What is emerging, the authors suggest, is a new interconnected online space where a wide range of activists, media and civil society organizations continually uncover, raise awareness and campaign for action on human rights abuses. Based on a discussion of websites documenting human rights abuses in Burma and Zimbabwe, the authors address the important question of how these help to underpin campaigns to pressurize liberal democratic states and International Governmental Organizations (IGOs), such as the United Nations, to take action.

Finally, Part Six: Transnational Protests and the Media: Toward Global Civil Society? provides some concluding reflections by the editors. Pulling together different arguments and drawing on some of the different approaches as well as empirical findings offered by the different contributors to this volume, Chapter 20 by Libby Lester and Simon Cottle reflects on the contentious nature and no less contested academic claims that surround transnational mediated protests and their possible contribution to emergent global civil society and global citizenship. As the contributing authors and their chapters variously argue new forms of transnational protest and their enactment in and through today's media and communications ecology exhibit considerable complexity including forces of media containment as well as progressive opportunities. Steering a course between the "one eye open" celebration of new digital media on the one hand, and the "one eye closed" skepticism based on a view of old media as "business as usual," this concluding chapter seeks to keep both eyes wide open on the evolving cultural power and political efficacy of transnational protest when enacted within and through today's interpenetrating media ecology and communication networks.

The need for steering a course between celebration and skepticism in respect of the role(s) performed by media and communications in protests was further demonstrated when this book was about to go to press. The wave of Arab uprisings that surged through countries in the Middle East and North Africa in the early months of 2011 challenged autocratic and repressive regimes in the region and called for democracy and social justice. Quickly dubbed the 'Twitter Revolutions' or

'Facebook Revolutions' by some, the role of media and communications in these popular revolts demands close inspection. A necessarily brief and preliminary audit of the complex ways in which media and communications entered into these pro-democracy struggles and their reverberation around the world is provided in Simon Cottle's 'Afterword: Media and the Uprisings of 2011.' In keeping with the findings and discussion presented in this book, media systems and communication networks are found to have been powerfully involved and deeply enmeshed within these momentous historical events.

CHAPTER TWO

Transnational Protests and the Media

New Departures, Challenging Debates

SIMON COTTLE

The world of protests is changing. Increasingly, as we have heard, protests and demonstrations register wider forces of global change and transnational concern; they express grievances spawned by a radically interconnected and inegalitarian world. This is not to suggest that all transnational protests and demonstrations today can be theorised simply as a direct reflex of "globalization," however we may want to conceive this, or that they necessarily seek to bypass local, national or regional forms of engagement. And neither is it to imply that demonstrations of international solidarity are without historical precedence. It is to recognize, however, that new forms of transnational activism increasingly give expression to deeper processes of social transformation and the wider political opportunities thrown up by globalizing, late modernity. And, crucially, media and communications are at their core, facilitating and shaping repertoires of protest and transacting their impacts around the world.

It is in and through today's enveloping media ecology and complex of communication networks that protests and demonstrations taking place in particular locales or national contexts can effectively become transnationalized. It is principally by these means that they register more widely and maximise their possible impacts. Whether in respect of wider publics and potential supporters, national political elites and tiers of international governance, authorities charged with their control (or suppression), or indeed the protesters and activists themselves who increasingly seek to challenge the media's frames and narratives or communicate directly a few of their own. In such ways the field of transnational protests today becomes complexly enacted, communicatively expanded and reflexively conditioned. And it is by these same means also that some of the world's foremost injustices and threats to humanity including war, weapons of mass destruction, inequalities of trade, ecological degradation, climate change, human rights abuses and humanitarian catastrophe become part of a new global awareness and, possibly, prompt forms of transnational solidarity.

This chapter sets out some of the differences of approach and debates currently informing the study of media, protests and demonstrations when approached in transnational and global contexts. It builds on the author's earlier discussion of the changing media politics of dissent (Cottle, 2008) and addresses the mediated nature of transnational protests and their possibly shifting relations of communicative power. Written as a prelude to the chapters that follow, the discussion deliberately interweaves positions and arguments advanced by the contributors to this volume as well as those of other notable voices in the academic field. It does so with the aim of providing a guide to some of the main theoretical departures and debates currently informing the latest research agendas and their relevance for the study of mediated transnational protests. Specifically, six new departures and critical debates are discerned, and each has direct bearing on the contemporary study and theorization of mediated transnational protests. These are discussed, respectively, in terms of: i) politically mediated control and transnational communication flows; ii) delegitimizing framing and political dramaturgy; iii) the public sphere and public screen(s); iv) media ecology and communication networks; v) mediating the transnational from the local to the global, and vi) the global public sphere and global citizenship.

The arguments in play draw on different disciplines and theoretical outlooks from across the humanities and social sciences, and their authors variously position themselves in respect of differing conceptions of the "transnational" and the "global" as well as closely correlated ideas of "global citizenship," "global civil society" and, of course, the "global public sphere." What they share, however, is a general recognition of the *constitutive* nature of communications and media representation in the conduct and enactment of contemporary transnational protests and a preparedness to engage conceptually, theoretically and empirically with this fast-changing field. But first a few words on the historical evolution of contentious politics and established views on media and protests that form a necessary backdrop to these new theoretical departures and critical debates.

Contentious politics and the communication of dissent

Protests and demonstrations have historically performed an integral part in struggles for democracy and contentious politics more generally (Thompson, 1991, 1993; McAdam, Tarrow, & Tilly, 2001; Tilly, 2005), and they continue to do so (Etzioni, 1970; Norris, 2002; Milne, 2005; Tarrow, 2006). Some now command attention worldwide. As I write this, "red shirt" protesters in Bangkok, Thailand, are risking their lives, and many are losing them, in anti-government mass protests demanding free and fair elections. Symbolic images of protesters splashing their own blood under the gates of Government House had earlier beamed around the world via television news services and online videos. In June 2009 images of Neda Agha-Solten, a young Iranian woman shot dead by security forces when protesting against an unfair presidential election, were captured on a videophone and circulated almost immediately on YouTube and then TV news around the globe. Protests against Chinese repression in Tibet on the occasion of China's hosting of the 2008 Olympic games and the "Saffron Revolution" led by Burmese monks in Burma in 2007 also secured extensive and generally sympathetic media attention. And two years before that, media images of the so-called "Coloured Revolutions" in Ukraine, Serbia, Georgia and Kyrgyzstan also underlined the powerful part sometimes played by mass demonstrations in ongoing struggles for democracy. (See: Afterword)

It would be easy perhaps to assume that political struggles and protests always assume the form of mass demonstrations. But it is worth remembering that "repertoires of contention" (McAdam, Tarrow, & Tilly, 2001) have evolved historically and can assume widely different forms whether, for example, strikes and marches, petitions and delegations, boycotts and mass rallies, sit-ins and occupations, acts of civil-disobedience and diverse forms of direct action including spectacular stunts, so-called "image events" (DeLuca, 1999) or "dissent events" (Scalmer, 2002), as well as culture jamming and new forms of online activism including *hactivism* and consumer campaigns. These and other forms of protest have been creatively fashioned in response to changing circumstances and opportunities—and they are destined to continue to do so.

Charles Tilly has recovered historically how many protest forms that we now take for granted in fact evolved in a key period of social and political transformation in Britain from 1790 to 1830, a period when war, urbanization and increasing state centralisation and state power changed the conditions of popular contention (Tilly, 2005; see also Thompson, 1991, 1993). In the changing conditions of the 19th century, argues Tilly, the forms of political contention discernibly shifted from the "relatively *parochial, particular* and *bifurcated* eighteenth-century forms of action," often involving patronage and brokerage at the local level, to new "*cosmopolitan, modular* and *autonomous*" forms that became increasingly national in scale, directed at national power holders and easily transferable (Tilly, 2005: 62, italics added). In this historical juncture, he suggests, a new repertoire of contention was crystallizing.

It would be too easy and possibly premature to simply extrapolate from this that what we are now witnessing is an equally momentous shift in the historical scaling up of contentious politics, this time from the national to the transnational and global, just as previously it had been from the local and community-based level to the national. Even so, the development of transnational activism and protests increasingly focused on substantive global issues in recent times suggests that an emergent shift in the scale and forms of protests may indeed now be underway (della Porta & Tarrow, 2005b) and that these increasingly register an increasingly globally interdependent and crisis-prone world–even when some "transnational" protests either target or become mediated through national or regional institutions and structures (Tarrow, 2006).

The analysis of the mainsprings and dynamics of contentious politics by Doug McAdam, Sidney Tarrow and Charles Tilly (McAdam, Tarrow, & Tilly, 2001; Tarrow, 2006) proves of relevance for study of the new transnational activism and protests (Tarrow, 2006) and is distinguished from the "social movement paradigm."

The latter is criticized for its: 1) "single-minded focus on single-actor movements and indifference to the broader field of contentious politics"; 2) "largely static framing of its major constituent variables–*opportunities, resources, framing*, and *repertoires of contention*," and 3) the "overwhelming tendency of its practitioners to study movements at the domestic level" (Tarrow, 2006: 23–24; McAdam, Tarrow, & Tilly, 2001). These are all telling criticisms. But we can also develop a further one: 4) the relatively under-developed recognition of how media and communications are now deeply implicated within the structures and opportunities of both social movements and the play of contentious politics more generally (Cottle, 2003, 2006).

In today's heavily mediated societies (Thompson, 1995), media and communications now arguably constitute *both* a political opportunity structure and a resource for mobilization in their own right. They have become, understandably, the focus of 'democratic media activism' (Carroll & Hackett, 2006). As with the field of mediated politics more widely, contentious politics and the politics of protests and demonstrations are now principally conducted and contested on the terrain of media and communications. Here old and new technologies of communication become mobilized; oppositional claims as well as passionate appeals and cultural symbols are circulated; and protests and contentious politics enter into everyday life, normatively if not institutionally reconfiguring the wider "political environment" as they do so. And further, today's media ecology and communication networks have become no less indispensable in the "scaling up" (Tarrow & McAdam, 2005) of protests and dissent to the transnational level.

The chapters that follow variously demonstrate how the contemporary communications environment is now: 1) pervasively infused in the wider field of demonstrations and protests, whether in respect of struggles of identity and the "politics of recognition" or struggles over resources and the "politics of redistribution" (Frazer & Honneth, 2003)–or indeed in struggles that involve both expressive and instrumental goals; 2) inextricably involved in providing and/or shaping *opportunities, resources, framing*, and *repertoires of contention*; and 3) pivotally positioned in the coordination and transnationalization of protests and the communication of "the political" beyond national horizons. The contributors to this volume expertly pursue how media and communications enter into the forms, practices, and contested politics of transnational protests, granting them their theoretical due and empirically mapping complexities and dynamics involved.

Evidently there are more complexities and, possibly, more political opportunities involved in the world of transnational protests and the media than earlier studies of demonstration and protest reporting have generally recognized or theorized. Much has changed since earlier studies concluded on the basis of analysis of mainstream national news media that the latter invariably report protests and demonstrations through a dominant law and (dis)order frame that labels protesters as deviant and delegitimizes their aims and politics by emphasizing drama, spectacle and violence (Halloran, Elliott, & Murdock, 1970; Gitlin, 1980; Murdock, 1981). The seminal study, *Demonstration and Communication: A Case Study* by James Halloran, Philip Elliott and Graham Murdock (1970), for example, deployed the concept of "inferential framework" to help account for how the news media collectively came to anticipate, interpret and then depict a major anti-Vietnam war demonstration in 1968 through a media frame of violence. This "definition of the event," this expectation of violence, argued Graham Murdock, "served to concentrate attention on the form of actions to the neglect of underlying causes" and in this way the march "was emptied of its radical political content" (Murdock, 1981: 210). Todd Gitlin's study, *The Whole World Is Watching: Mass Media in the Making and Unmaking of the New Left*, also a classic in the field of mass communications research, arrived at remarkably similar conclusions. Based on an in-depth study of "Students for a Democratic Society" (SDS) in the US, this analyzed how the movement became subject to media framing that increasingly *trivialized, polarized, marginalized* and *disparaged* the protesters and their aims and *emphasized the violence* of demonstrations (Gitlin, 1980: 27).

Similar findings have been replicated across the years, generally becoming the accepted wisdom in the field of critical media studies (for reviews see Waddington, 1992: 160–178; Cottle, 2006). But how secure are they in today's changing communications environment and in respect of transnational activism? In the context of an increasingly complex and expansive media ecology and its inter-linkage with new social media and interpenetrating communication flows, do mainstream media always, necessarily, impose "definitions of the situation" on protests and dissent that delegitimize the protesters' aims, label the protesters as deviant, and emphasize violence and drama at the expense of the issues and politics involved? How do these earlier findings and theoretical expectations stand up in the context of contemporary transnational protests and across different transnational protest issues? The following points to six new departures and surrounding debates that together help to open up a more nuanced, contingent and dynamic view of the politically powered ways in which media and communications now enter into transnational protests.

Politically mediated control and transnational communication flows

Earlier studies of protests and demonstrations, then, have generally pointed to how the news media define and frame protests and demonstrations through an interpretive and delegitimizing framework of law and (dis)order, focusing on violence, drama and spectacle. Developed within the critical paradigm of media and communication studies, such findings have often been theorized through a combination of political economy, Gramscian views on popular culture and hegemony and, occasionally, ethnographic insights into professional journalist practices including source dependencies and the operationalization of news values. Together these can sometimes make for a rather deterministic expectation of how protests become publicly framed and narrativized in the news and one that positions news media as invariably and ideologically supportive of dominant interests.

This remains a generally persuasive framework to this day and indeed a number of the contributors to this volume find continuing empirical support for at least some of its claims (see also Rosie & Gorringe, 2009). Whether the media's reporting predilections towards violence, spectacle and drama (see Juris, chapter 8; Archibald, chapter 9; Gavin and Marshall, chapter 15), or its structural orientation to powerful elites and their definitions of protest events (see Murray et al., chapter 4; Bowers, chapter 8). However, even those most persuaded by the continuing cultural predilections and structural orientation of the news media to elites also suggest that this is less than a foregone determinism and recognize at least some opportunity for different voices and definitions of events, whether through time, across different media, in respect of different protest issues, or based on a more open theorization of the power of spectacle and protest performance.

Craig Murray and his colleagues (see chapter 4) provide a particularly clear and theoretically engaged statement on such issues. Though generally finding ample evidence in support of the traditional protest paradigm, as summarized above, they nonetheless document at least two stories in the British press coverage of the anti-war movement in the Iraq Crisis 2002–2009. In the run-up period to the military invasion of Iraq, for example, news coverage of protest activity "was fairly extensive and played more positively than negatively for the anti-war movement," and there was "ample evidence of generous and sympathetic reporting of the million-strong rally of 15 February 2003" (Murray et al., chapter 4). At this political juncture, then, the UK anti-war movement operated within a sphere of "legitimated controversy" (Hallin, 1986), and sections of the UK press even functioned as an "advocate of the underdog" (Wolfsfeld, 1997). However, once the war got underway, their research also documents how press coverage came to conform more to the expectations of the traditional research literature, privileging elite voices in terms of "elite-indexing" (Bennett, 1990) and demonstrating how national newspapers tend to patriotically rally behind the flag. Though sceptical of recent arguments about the transformative impacts of new communication technologies and other explanations for possibly more sympathetic media when reporting protests, their analysis grounds a more nuanced and dynamic theorization of protest reporting even when concluding that the national press moved to a deferential stance generally supportive of national elites and their war aims (see also Verhulst & Walgrave, 2010).

Models of media-state interactions help to highlight how changing political dynamics inform media interactions with political elites and the representation of major issues—including protests. This changing interaction is explained as we have just heard, for example, with reference to the news media "indexing" their stance to the degree of elite consensus or dissensus (Bennett, 1990), as well as the existence of policy certainty or policy uncertainty (Robinson, 2001), the success or failure of "cascading activation" strategies deployed by governments (Entman, 2004), and the success of strategic and symbolic power played out on the ground of political opposition (Wolfsfeld, 1997). In other words, the news media's stance towards government policies can shift through time and political circumstance, and this can also impact on the editorial salience and inflection granted to reporting protests and demonstrations, as we have just heard. Findings that complement more in-depth analysis of social movements and media approached as interacting systems (Gamson & Wolfsfeld, 1993) and the contingencies of the symbiotic relationship between protest groups and news media (Deacon & Golding, 1994; Manning, 2001; Koopmans, 2004; Rucht, 2004; Hutchins & Lester, 2006).

Confronted by today's expanding and interpenetrating communication flows that infuse the "global news arena" (see Reese, chapter 5), some scholars have deliberately sought to move beyond the known national outlooks and political partisanship of the national press to explore the possible impacts of this more complex communications environment. In a world where transnational movements, NGOs and global media and their communication flows can all play to wider audiences beyond particular national borders and imagined national audiences, this, says Stephen Reese, opens up the possibility of a changing relationship of protests, media and political structures of power.

> Here it is still a matter of speculation, but there is evidence that the global news arena made for a more hospitable climate for globally coordinated anti-war protests. The centripetal tendencies of journalism professionalism and the promotion of events by interlocking NGO interests made it more likely that these protests would be received as they were intended, as a pro-peace, anti-militarism message–transcending any one national policy context where it could be easily marginalized as a less-than-patriotic discourse. (Reese, chapter 5)

In the context of war and globalizing media flows, states find it increasingly difficult to control and contain the incoming (and outgoing) communication of images and dissenting voices into the national communications environment (see Hayes & Gardino, 2010), and this means that transnational public opinion increasingly has to be factored into elite decision-making (Shaw, 2005; Tumber & Webster, 2006). As Martin Shaw observes, "governments must always recognize how integrated global media, institutions and public opinion have become" (Shaw, 2005: 75). This is not to suggest that national news organizations no longer continue to "bring back home" news from afar and "domesticate" it in terms of perceived audience interests and national cultural outlooks (Clausen, 2003; Cohen et al., 1996; Leung, 2009) or that they no longer rely predominantly on Western news agencies (Boyd-Barrett & Rantanen, 1998). But it is to say that global flows of images and ideas can now sometimes penetrate journalist practices and puncture the idea of bordered national news (Volkmer, 1999; Hannerz, 2004; Hamilton & Jenner, 2004; Rai & Cottle, 2007; Robertson, 2010). Some global issues are also inherently deterritorializing and globalizing in their origins, impacts and/or responses (see Berglez, 2008; Cottle, 2009), and this too potentially encourages a more global news outlook.

Issues such as climate change, food security and humanitarian catastrophes and the political crises they produce may even, according to some, hold the potential to generate "enforced enlightenment" and "mediated cosmopolitanism" (Beck, 2009; Robertson, 2010), prompting a transnationalizing ethics of care and based on growing recognition of the world's growing interdependency, its shared threats and "overlapping communities of fate" (Held, 2004). When protests and demonstrations are framed and narrativized in this global context (Cottle, 2009: 102–108), it is conceivable that they may yet register something of the global interdependencies that shape them and, sometimes, our ethical responsibilities to respond (Chouliaraki, 2006). "Understanding the role of transnational protests in this kind of media environment," suggests Stephen Reese, "requires an understanding of the global news sphere and its changing relationships to political structures" (chapter 5).

Delegitimizing framing and political dramaturgy

The influence of earlier studies of the news media's representations of protest and demonstrations continues to this day. This seemingly feeds into a generalized expectation about how protesters, their aims and politics can all become publicly delegitimized through processes of news framing that representationally denigrate if not demonize, disparage and dissimulate each in turn. Content analysis, semiotics and forms of critical linguistics as well as varieties of discourse analysis have all been methodologically put to work and recovered some of the systematic patterns and de-legitimizing social constructions at play. When explored in international and transnational context, however, these findings may be far from universal.

Demonstrations and protests in apartheid South Africa, glasnost Russia, Tiananmen Square in Communist China, as we know, were not predestined to be portrayed by the Western press within a delegitimizing law and (dis)order frame, and neither were those associated with the "Velvet Revolution" in Czechoslovakia and other "Autumn of Nations" demonstrations in 1989, the so-called "Coloured Revolutions" in Ukraine, Serbia, Georgia and Kyrgyzstan in 2004–2005 or, more recently, those in Burma in 2007, Iran in 2009 or Thailand 2010. (See: Afterword) Much depends, evidently, on the perceived legitimacy and democratic credentials of the state and oppositional movements involved as well as journalistic judgements about geo-political interests and cultural outlooks (see Fang, 1994).

Different or even sympathetic editorial stances towards some protests and demonstrations do not only surface when reporting international protests. A detailed analysis of the US media's coverage of the Seattle demonstrations in 1999 by Andrew Rojecki, for example, documented how, again departing from critical expectations, an "initial focus on surface features–costumes and stunts–quickly deepened to the underlying issues they symbolized" (Rojecki, 2002: 159). Mainstream media did not, he concludes, "mount an assault on the credibility or knowledgeability of its participants when their costumes, methods for gaining attention, or civil disobedience and mass arrests could easily have become the focus of coverage" (2002: 162–163). His explanation for this surprising departure from earlier research findings is based on three principal factors. First, elite dissensus at both national and international levels brought about by the differential impacts of globalization on different economic sectors, militated against the imposition of one dominant economic view. Second, the end of the Cold War produced new rhetorical advantages for the anti-globalization movement in that "the elimination of the Soviet Union as a long-standing symbol of repression and the economic system it championed" deprived "conservative opponents of a dependable ideologically-based platform for launching their attacks on dissident movements" (Rojecki, 2002: 156). And third, argues Rojecki, the Internet also offered "under-resourced interest groups tools that provide extraordinary leverage for mobilization and organization" (Rojecki, 2002: 157; see Rojecki, chapter 6)

Recent sociological work on the cultural power of dramaturgy also allows for the possibility that drama, contrary to earlier expectations (Murdock, 1981), can become progressively aligned to movement aims and ideals (McAdam, 2000; Alexander et al., 2006; Alexander, 2006: 658–659). The American civil rights movement headed by Martin Luther King in the 1960s, for example, won public support and exerted pressure on the US government to concede to civil rights demands on the basis of a skilful political strategy that made use of "dramaturgical framing" deliberately provoking racist attack and violence from the authorities in front of press and TV cameras: "The stark highly dramatic nature of this ritualized confrontation between good and evil proved irresistible to the media and, in turn, to the American public" (McAdam, 2000: 127–128).

Ideas of political dramaturgy are no less relevant when extrapolated to the "global commons" in transnational direct actions that are deliberately staged, recorded and disseminated around the globe by the activists themselves. As David Crouch and Katarina Damjanov observe in their insightful study of the *Sea Shepherd* and the drama of its anti-whaling campaign in the Southern Ocean.

> In one such encounter, protesters nailed plates to the drain outlets that spill the blood from the flensing deck of the whaling ship into the sea and hurled smoke bombs and bottles of butyric acid onto the vessel (Sea Shepherd, 2007) and almost instantaneously images are spread across the globe via satellite up-links, webcams, and around-the-clock internet blogging. Sea Shepherd takes their environmental protest in this remote and unforgiving location, impossibly beyond everyday reach, and broadcasts it back to the world, disseminating it through the Internet and blogosphere; they constantly send out fresh broadcast-quality images and a barrage of news releases, twitters, and updates of events . . . Furthermore, it is not only the tools and tactics derived from contemporary communications technologies that they use to garner support for their cause; by staging their anti-whaling protest as spectacular "pirate" attacks, they also exploit elements of popular culture, tapping into the social imagination of a potentially transnational public sphere. (Crouch & Damjanov, chapter 13)

Concerns about the undue emphases afforded by media to the "drama" of protests and seen as a framing device that delegitimizes the protesters and their political aims can, it seems, sometimes have the unintended consequence of underestimating and under-theorizing the dramaturgical power of demonstrations and protests and how, on occasions, as demonstrated above, this can work to the advantage of the protesters and their cause (see also Rojecki, chapter 6; Juris, chapter 8; Hutchins & Lester, chapter 11; and Crouch & Damjanov, chapter 13). How contemporary protests and demonstrations variously enact or benefit from the dramaturgy embedded within their actions as well as cultural resonances based in popular culture and media templates (Kitzinger, 2000; Wolfsfeld, 1997) requires a methodological approach that is sensitive to the culturally symbolic and performative nature of protests and demonstrations (Craig, 2002; DeLuca & Peeples, 2002; Kellner, 2003; Lester, 2007), to its "cultural pragmatics" (Alexander et al., 2006), as well as the more progressive possibilities of mediated "spectacle"–considered next.

Public sphere and public screen(s)

In traditional liberal democratic theory, public demonstrations as well as periodic elections are posited as a vital component of democracy, alerting publics and power-holders to grievances in civil society and establishing claims for parliamentary recognition and response. In variants of more recent social theory, protests and demonstrations can also assume the role of enacting new "cultural codes" (Melluci, 1996) and embodying forms of "prefigurative politics" that exemplify through lived practice ethical norms and desired social relations. The liberal presumption that demonstrations and protests are principally or even solely about alerting power-holders to wider grievances or claims for change can therefore underestimate their more radical nature as well as potential for crystallizing collective awareness and embodying forms of affective solidarity. The latter can often be based on a more positive appraisal of the power of protest spectacle, and this takes us to the heart of vying Enlightenment and post-Enlightenment tenets on the "public sphere." These contenting views are represented across a number of contributions in this volume. Two in particular help to exemplify the differences in play.

Nazanin Ghanavizi in her analysis of the 2009 Iranian election and the rise of the Persian blogosphere deliberately sets out to explore the role of new media in improving public reasoning and opinion formation. Her analysis and argument are made on the basis of Iran's state controlled media and a media and communications environment in which people have limited opportunities for publicly sharing and publishing their socio-political views (Ghanavizi, chapter 18). In this context Ghanavizi finds Habermas's original conceptualisation of the public sphere (1974, 1989) to have continuing political charge and radical potential.

> The Habermasian public sphere, which is based on the dialogic articulation of ideas and interests, establishes the ground for the formation of public opinion. Shared ideas form as interacting private individuals search for recognition. . . . I suggest that cyberspace provides its participants with more or less fair conditions for this kind of interaction. It moreover provides participants with the information they need to evaluate the validity of claims made in the course of this interaction. And it gives them the opportunity to participate anonymously, with limited fear of social or political threat. In fundamentalist societies in particular, as in the example of Iran, cyberspace provides its users

with more reliable and significant means of participation in the formation of public opinion. (Ghanavizi, chapter 18)

In the context of a fundamentalist state regime, argues Ghanavizi, the deliberative processes and consensus formation that can result from such online participation and exchange represent an invaluable political tool which individuals can utilize to resist fundamentalist values, recognize their collective identity and struggle for their political rights. This is a persuasive reminder, then, of how processes of public speech and deliberation can perform a vital and indispensable part in struggles for democratic inclusion and responsive, representative government. And, as we have heard, it is advanced on the basis of an appreciative view of Habermas's rationally conceived, deliberatively communicated and consensually oriented model of the "public sphere."

Writing in a very different political context and drawing upon different intellectual currents, Kevin DeLuca, Ye Sun and Jennifer Peeples (chapter 10), in contrast, question the rationalist emphases and analytical sufficiency of the Habermasian "public sphere" as a guiding framework for the interrogation of mediated protests today. In their earlier study of the World Trade Organization protests in Seattle in 1999 two of the authors had sought to reconceptualize how mediated scenes of protest communicate and coined the influential idea of the "public screen" in deliberate contrast to Habermas's "public sphere."

> In comparison to the rationality, embodied conversations, consensus, and civility of the public sphere, the public screen highlights dissemination, images, hypermediacy, spectacular publicity, cacophony, distraction, and dissent. We have focused on the image event as one practice of the public screen because it highlights the public screen as an alternative venue for participatory politics and public opinion formation that offers a striking contrast to the public sphere. (DeLuca & Peeples, 2002: 145)

Their contribution to this volume on "wild public screens" updates and expands on these arguments (DeLuca, Sun, & Peeples, chapter 10) and offers an eloquent challenge to those who continue to hold out the hope for a mediated public sphere that can embody rational public conversation and its universalization around the globe under the name of (Western) Democracy. Unlike Habermas and his lament for the bourgeois public sphere that he came to see as dangerously corroded by the onslaught of public relations and its "refeudalization" by spectacle (Habermas, 1989, 1996), DeLuca, Sun and Peeples champion a decidedly more upbeat view on the density of contemporary screen images and their capacity to serve as "mind bombs" and "philosophical-rhetorical fragments." In the context of the 1999 Seattle protests, for example, images of "anarchists shattering the glass facades of brand empires," they suggest, are "dense image events" that "opened visions of other possible worlds."

This is a provocative and philosophically conceived challenge to "public sphere" politics more rationally and deliberatively conceived and is likely to be debated for some time to come given the competing Enlightenment and post-Enlightenment views on reason, rationality and democracy at play. Whatever one's stance on such issues, it productively opens up a new vista on mediated protests in terms of spectacle and one that implicitly questions earlier studies as unduly pessimistic about the role of spectacle and drama in contemporary public life and political processes.

Perhaps in this context it is also useful to note that media images of demonstrations and protests are often found to be semiotically aligned and linguistically anchored to editorial outlooks and the partisan "views" of different media producers and outlets (Cottle, 1998: 205–213; Perlmutter & Wagner, 2004; Memou, 2010), and so too can they be strategically promoted by vested interests and authorities. The mobilization of meanings in the pursuit of public legitimacy in mediated protests often involves both an on-screen semiotic and behind-the-screens strategic battle over images (Lester, 2007). And some images can prove to be extraordinarily powerful in symbolizing and summoning sympathy worldwide, whether the image of school boy Hector Pieterson (aged 13), one of the first students to be killed during the 1976 Student Uprising in Soweto; the image of a lone student protester stopping a row of Chinese tanks in Tiananmen Square in 1989; or the image of Neda shot in the 2009 Iranian presidential election and which caused the Iranian authorities a year later to try and jam satellite broadcasts from the Voice of America Persian TV Network as it broadcast a film about her death. There can also be no doubting the profusion of images that now circulate "wildly" through the Internet and other communication channels, transforming the politics and power of media visibility (Thompson, 1995), sometimes destabilizing dominant frames and discourses and which now bombard us from a variety of ever-present public (and private) screens (see Archibald, chapter 9; Hutchins & Lester, chapter 11; Crouch & Damjanov, chapter 13; Stanyer & Davidson, chapter 19)

Media ecology and communication networks

Throughout this discussion as well as across Chapter One I have referred to both media ecology *and* communication networks. This is deliberate if a little ungainly, and reflects the current state of media and communications as both complex communications environment and seemingly bifurcated theoretical object. The term media ecology is here used to signal the complex of overlapping and relational forms of media formations and communication flows from the local to the global and now including traditional means of mass communications as well as its interpenetrations by and attempted colonizations of the Net. Today's media ecology, then, comprises traditional corporate media delivering top-down mass entertainment and civic instruction that remain, notwithstanding red button "interactions" on TV remotes, time-shifting capabilities and different viewing platforms, generally passively consumed. Surrounding traditional media of consumption and increasingly overlapping and interpenetrating them are the new communication networks of "mass self communication" (Castells, 2009) facilitated mainly by the Internet and populated by relatively purposive communication seekers and sometimes communication producers and senders accessing discrete networks.

Whereas the study of traditional mass communications has encouraged a general orientation to the "politics of representation" broadly conceived and theorized in terms of ideology-critique (or variants of discourse and framing analysis), the study of new media invites a theoretical orientation more attuned to the participatory "politics of connectivity," radical democracy and real-virtuality (Deuze, 2003; Castells, 1996, 2009; Dahlberg & Siapera, 2007). In the context of mediated protests, whether transnational or local, therefore, these broad orientations are inclined, respectively, to either forefront the politics of protest representation and political mobilization via the mainstream media or cede growing importance to online-protests and the new virtual world of protest coordination, communication and actions facilitated in and through the Internet and associated new technologies.

It seems to me that while both these general orientations are necessary for the interrogation of contemporary transnational protests and their communicative strategies and impacts, neither on its own—for the time being at least—can adequately encapsulate all that needs to be said and asked about contemporary protest communications. To what extent and in what sense these differences rooted in the wider structures of corporate power as well as communication power dispersed more widely can be equally subsumed under the overarching theorization of the "network society" and its "space of flows," as conceived by Manuel Castells, remains a moot theoretical point. Whether the master explanatory trope best suited to today's society is "the network society" (Castells, 1996, 2009) or "liquid modernity" (Bauman, 2007), "world risk society" (Beck, 1999, 2009) or the "condition of postmodernity" (Harvey, 1989), or perhaps "global complexity" (Urry, 2003) begs, of course, deeper questions about social ontology and its theorization—and these inevitably remain essentially contested matters.

What is less disputable, perhaps, is that the Internet, as many have now commented, exhibits a synergy that is particularly well suited to the new wave of transnational protests and global activism (Wall, 2003; Bennett, 2003; Castells, 1997, 2001; della Porta & Tarrow, 2005b; Donk et al., 2004; Chesters & Welsh, 2006; Dahlberg & Siapera, 2007; Dahlgren, 2009; Padovani, 2010). Cyber-protest researchers have suggested, "the fluid, non-hierarchical structure of the Internet and that of the international protest coalition prove to be a good match," and "it is no coincidence that both can be labelled as a 'network of networks'" (Van Aelst & Walgrave, 2004: 121). The Internet, while certainly no panacea for the continuing inequalities of strategic and symbolic power mobilized in and through the mass media, evidently contains a socially activated potential to unsettle and on occasion even disrupt the vertical flows of institutionally controlled "top-down" communications and does so by inserting bottom-up, interactive and horizontal communicative networks into the wider communications environment. How the different flows and networks of the contemporary media sphere interpenetrate and reciprocally influence each other will, inevitably, become a key area for future research (as well as a methodological challenge).

Today's media ecology comprising traditional media formations and new communication flows around the world, arguably contains more political opportunities for dissenting views and voices than in the past, and these are increasingly in evidence through *interpenetrating* alternative networks and mainstream news media (see Rojecki, chapter 6; DeLuca, Sun, & Peeples, chapter 10; Crouch & Damjanov, chapter 13; Gavin and Marshall, chapter 14; Adi & Miah, chapter 15; and Yüksel & Yüksel, chapter 17). Indeed such is their overlap and interpenetration that rigid conceptual distinctions of "alternative" and "mainstream" have become increasingly problematic. As Lance Bennett observes:

> ... impressive numbers of activists have followed the trail of world power into the relatively uncharted international arenas and found creative ways to communicate their concerns and to contest the power of corporations and transnational economic arrangements. In the process, many specific messages about corporate abuses, sweatshop labour, genetically modified organisms, rainforest destruction, and the rise of small resistance movements, from East Timor to southern Mexico, have made it into the mass media on their own terms. (Bennett, 2003: 18–19)

New media technologies add new communicative ingredients into the media ecology mix as well as possibilities for new forms of politics and protests. Though unlikely to displace repertoires of protest conducted in other venues or the necessity for coverage in more mainstream media, the capacity of new technologies to support and sustain dispersed coalitions of protesters and new forms of political organization has now been widely established. Post-Seattle, summit sieges whether in Prague, Melbourne, Genoa, London, Gleneagles or L'Aquila as well as countless demonstrations coordinated in major capitals around the world on a variety of global concerns, have demonstrated the power of the Internet as well as the performative power of *carnivalesque* tactics deliberately designed for the known predilections of mainstream news media (Opel & Pompper, 2003; Chesters & Welsh, 2006; Juris, 2008, chapter 8).

Mediating the transnational from the local to the global

As suggested in the introduction to this volume, the "transnational" in the contemporary politics of protest is not only characterized in terms of its political reach, motivating ethics or geographical scale but also inheres, necessarily, within its media and communication enactment. This throws the conceptual net a little wider than, say, Tarrow's definition of transnational contention as "conflicts that link transnational activists to one another; to states, and to international institutions" (Tarrow, 2006: 25). Though the latter usefully encourages analytical attention on the group-based and institutional dynamics of transnational contention, it is also necessary to recognize the increasing centrality of media and communication *within* the cultural and normative construction of the "transnational" as an ethico-political imaginary place and how this can become invoked through mediated protest actions conducted at local-to-global levels.

In a context of globalization, influential ideas of "time-space compression" (Harvey, 1989) that accelerate and shrink the world, and "time-space distanciation" (Giddens, 1990) that stretch social relations and enable "action at a distance," speak to the increasing interconnectedness of people around the world and how this new politics of space and place is being played out from the global to the local. As Roland Robertson remarked early on in the globalization debate, "the distinction between the global and the local is becoming very complex and problematic–to such an extent that we should now speak in such terms as the global institutionalization of the life-world and the localization of globality" (Robertson, 1990: 19). Today cultural flows of communication as much as institutional processes of group engagement can help to centre the "transnational" within the public eye of the media and variously place it within society's normative horizons. The following discerns some of the different scales of the "transnational" in mediated protests.

First, Chen Li and Lucy Montgomery usefully remind us that: "Awareness of the power of the mass media to communicate images of protest to global audiences and, in so doing, to capture space in global media discourses is a central feature of the transnational protest movement" (Li & Montgomery, chapter 16). Transnational recognition and wider endorsement or legitimation of political claims in the wider media sphere have become a prize worth struggling for, even though some struggles may be geographically confined and/or politically rooted in particular national contexts.

A number of protest movements have formed around opposition to concepts and practices that operate beyond national borders, such as neoliberal globalization or threats to the environment. However, transnational protests also involve more geographically discrete issues such as claims to national independence or greater religious or political freedom by groups within specific national contexts. Appealing to the international community for support is a familiar strategy for communities who feel that they are being discriminated against or ignored by a national government. (Li & Montgomery, chapter 16)

Second, sometimes relatively small-scale protest actions, conducted in local milieux and targeting national or even local institutions can also resonate with wider transnational concerns and, via today's media ecology, reverberate transnationally. As Brett Hutchins and Libby Lester convincingly argue:

> . . . the mediated environmental protests we analyse in this chapter are campaigns conducted within a particular geographical region of a nation, but whose broad environmentalist objectives are jointly shared with and understood by a transnational constellation of activists and NGOs. While these campaigns are physically located in a region, they are visible evidence of the determination to contest the instrumental logic of capital and party politics globally in the service of environmental sustainability and/or conservation. These protests also reveal the ongoing resonance of the local and regional in an age of transnational media and politics, as well as the fact that the Internet and web have opened up new possibilities for mediated politics and demonstration. (Hutchins & Lester, chapter 11)

Third, Ilke Yüksel and Murat Yüksel also observe how "even as they make transnational claims, transnational activists draw on the resources, networks, opportunities, and issues of the societies in which they are embedded" (chapter 17). In their study of *Resistanbul*, a transnational anti-capitalist action network based in Turkey, they further analyse how the local and national often mediate the "transnational" not only as expressive of a wider transnationalism based on a shared progressive global outlook but as a deliberate and localized tactic to attract mainstream media coverage and win over those potential supporters who remain firmly rooted in the national. They conclude, for example, that:

> Despite the various advantages that the new media provided, *Resistanbul* still needed to combine online mobilization with face-to-face mass activism in order to be effective in achieving its goals. For that purpose it needed the mass media to get public support and visibility, without which it cannot create the commitment necessary to sustain itself and increase its political capacity. (Yüksel & Yüksel, chapter 17)

As these and other contributors to this volume argue, then, the "transnational" cannot always be assumed to reside exclusively above and beyond nation states but can also be expressed and engaged in actions that are very much rooted in and directed at targets inside national borders—though they are no less transnationally informed and, potentially, transnationally constituted in the media. As Jenny Pickerill, Kevin Gillan and Frank Webster argue, to simply "focus on how activism becomes transnational, or jumps-scales from the local up, ignores the messy realities that local protest is always, and will always be, part of international connections, and that local resistance or place-based projects are solid building blocks for activism" (Pickerill, Gillan, & Webster, chapter 3). Transnational activists, in these contexts, can sometimes best be described, following Sydney Tarrow, as "rooted cosmopolitans" (Tarrow, 2006). But there is also a fourth scale to transnational protests discerned and discussed by some of our contributors, a scale that Crouch and Damjanov, for example, describe as "truly transnational" in terms of its global focus, processes of mediation and also national de-coupling when situated in the cultural space of the "global commons." To the extent that mediated transnational protests can help to institute a "global public sphere" and sustain an emergent and more widespread "cosmopolitan outlook" (Beck, 2006) beyond local parameters and national roots, let us move to our last theoretical departure and critical debate.

Toward the global public sphere and global citizenship?

Though today's globalising world generates new threats and opportunities for the emergence of what social theorist Ulrich Beck terms a "cosmopolitan outlook" (Beck, 2006), major difficulties inevitably hinder the development of such global awareness and the shared recognition of the necessity to engage in coordinated transnational actions in concert with others—including transnational protests. These difficulties inhere, as we have already heard, in the obdurate hold of national interests and the imagined nation and how both continue to "domesticate" global issues and events in ways that undermine their potential as "cosmopolitan moments." They also reside within the dispersed nature of transnational coalitions and their often-episodic actions, the increasingly complex and fragmented global communications environment, and the under-developed structures of transnational governance and global citizenship. Let me state each briefly.

Jenny Pickerill and her co-authors (Pickerill, Gillan, & Webster, chapter 3) observe how despite the use of new information communication technologies, efforts by transnational coalitions to sustain continuous cooperation across national borders face considerable practical and organizational difficulties. These include accommodating divergent cultural contexts and political outlooks and the compromises that therefore must be struck in terms of political aims as well as the difficulties of coalition building and maintaining relations of trust over long distances. Notwithstanding the relative ease of Internet and telephony communications, they suggest face-to-face meetings seem to provide for more meaningful, more trusting, political relationships. Some social movements they also observe are firmly rooted in national histories and national contexts and tend therefore to focus their activities at the national level. This too can dilute the "transnational" nature of protest issues and seemingly "nationalize" transnational political goals.

Dispersal and fragmentation as much as bounded and shared communications now characterize today's media ecology and communication flows, and this also undermines easy notions of "imagined community," whether presumed at local, national or transnational levels. If the "national public sphere" has become increasingly porous and fragmented through forces of commercialism and cultural diversity, so too do asynchronous media use and different platform delivery render the former "family hearth" of domestic public service media consumption something of a past ritual. If the notion of a bounded national public sphere becomes increasingly difficult to sustain in today's digital and permeable communications environment, this becomes even more improbable if simply scaled-up to global level and conceptualized as a universal "global public sphere."

And finally, as Nancy Frazer (2007) acutely reminds us, the concept of the public sphere in any case itself remains indebted to a national-based (Westphalian) view of public deliberation. Here processes of public opinion formation and citizenship are conceived within a political jurisdiction that formally recognizes them as such and which can, to some degree at least, respond through corresponding structures of governance. Transnational manifestations of public opinion and political will, in contrast, as yet have no formal citizenship status or comparable means of influencing corresponding levels of governance. "Can we still meaningfully interrogate the legitimacy of public opinion," she asks, "when the interlocutors do not constitute a demos or political citizenry?" And "can we still meaningfully interrogate the efficacy of public opinion when it is not addressed to a sovereign state that is capable in principle of regulating its territory and solving its citizens' problems in the public interest?" (Frazer, 2007: 15; see also Cammaerts & Van Audenhove, 2005)

Clearly as these real-world and theoretically discerned obstacles suggest, mediated transnational protests cannot be taken as a straightforward expression of global society or global citizenship even though many now seek to engage with the enduring inequalities and endemic threats thrown up by globalizing late modernity. And yet transnational activism and coordinated protests around the globe demonstrably *do* express something that is both historically emergent and even globally momentous, and this, however imperfectly and falteringly, begins to approach something that is akin to global civil society (Keane, 2003; Kaldor, 2003, 2007; Scholte, 2006). Across recent years transnational protests *have* periodically managed to focus much of the world's attention on diverse global issues and crises and they have done so for the most part by protest actions conducted and conveyed through extensive and intensive forms of media and communications. Often in creative, spectacular and attention-grabbing ways transnational protests have effectively installed themselves on the media landscape and within wider public imagination, positioning themselves symbolically as a bulwark that both calls attention to and resists the dominant logics and injustices of the global age. When successful, their potent images and political claims circulate in the media and beyond and reverberate in the corridors of power.

When a flotilla of ships carrying hundreds of international peace activists and humanitarian aid sought to peacefully break the Israeli blockade of Gaza in late May 2010, an assault by Israeli commandos killed nine unarmed activists and injured many more. A communications blackout was immediately imposed by the Israeli authorities on those aboard the flotilla but not before pictures of the assault taken by activists had been circulated internationally via the Internet and TV news programmes. This was followed by the release of Israel's own video footage that sought to demonstrate that their deadly actions had been precipitated and justified by the violence of the protesters—claims vociferously denied by those aboard. Protests around the world marked the Israeli actions and its continuing blockade of Gaza and denial of humanitarian supplies. The world's media helped galvanize the ensuing political storm. As a British newspaper declared on its front page: "Israel was engulfed by a wave of global condemnation last night after a botched assault on a flotilla carrying aid and supplies to the Gaza Strip ended in carnage and a diplomatic crisis involving the UN Security Council." (*The Guardian*, 1.6.10, p. 1). World attention via the mainstream news media though focused initially on the violence now also gave vent to the political furore that followed *and* the enduring humanitarian crisis caused by the Israeli blockade.

Transnational protests can and do sometimes capture the media spotlight, invigorating communication networks and placing issues of global concern on the wider political map—issues that otherwise fall off mainstream news agendas. They can also serve to contribute to collective awareness or even felt transnational solidarity and, in such moments, can contribute to a climate for political change. When conceived in these ways, transnational communication flows, though far from the "ideal" of Habermas's original conception of a "public sphere" in terms of a relatively inclusive and shared national media environment, may nonetheless provide the media space and grant the issue salience needed for wider global recognition and processes of transnational opinion formation. The "global public sphere" and even "global citizenship," in this sense, can become constituted normatively and culturally if not always institutionally and administratively. If the "cosmopolitan outlook," as Beck suggests, is "enforced enlightenment" born in part from the interdependency crises of reflexive modernization, major parts of the world may already be on the move toward a less culturally parochial, politically nationalistic and globally myopic outlook—cosmopolitan dispositions that are not confined to transnational activism and protests though they may well feed into them.

The establishment of what Scott Davidson and James Stanyer, for example, discern as the relatively recent "global human rights regime," provides institutional and normative support for such a view (Davidson & Stanyer, chapter 19). The proliferation of International NGOs, intergovernmental organizations such as the Office of the UN Commissioner for Human Rights as well as indigenous NGOs, social movements, churches, trades unions and sometimes Western governmental actors who are all now closely involved in the monitoring and exposing of human rights abuses around the world, grounds this universalising "global human rights regime" both normatively and institutionally as do international tribunals, frameworks of law and criminal prosecutions. And nor should we underestimate the increasing surveillance and exposé role performed by at least some sections of the news media in reporting or even, on occasion, championing selected human rights causes and issues around the world (Shaw, 1996; Serra, 2000; Allan, Sonwalkar, & Carter, 2007; Cottle, 2009).

> This pressure is direct but also emerges from a general outrage amongst publics in western democracies when confronted with the evidence of transgressions. With the disclosure of human rights abuses, elite and mass audiences not only learn that something has happened or is happening but they also learn about something happening which they disapprove, which transgresses laws and norms which they hold as important. Revelations exist, therefore, in tandem with an opprobrious discourse in which a range of actors report, publicise and criticise human rights abuses. (Davidson & Stanyer, chapter 19)

Notions of the "global public sphere" necessarily must be correlated and discussed in relation to ideas of "global citizenship" and "global civil society," and this, in turn, suggests that media and communications have become increasingly constitutive of all three in rapidly globalizing and heavily mediated societies. When performed and enacted in and through media and communications, as transnational protests must if they are to register in the global public sphere and invite citizen engagement in the serious life of increasingly interdependent societies, transnational protests can assume richly differentiated, often creative forms, but always with a reflexive eye on the media.

To end, I can do no better than to refer to one final contribution to this collection and its (fourth) theorization of transnational protests and creative crafting of available media and communications networks. Though we have previously heard how transnational protests often embed national agendas and localized forms of protest engagement, some protests speak unequivocally to the "transnational" as an imagined ethico-political outlook and are clearly pitched at the global level. This potentiality for "un-rooted" cosmopolitanism arguably inheres differently within and across different fields of transnational protests, with war and political conflicts and economy and trade, for example, more likely to succumb to default positions of imagined nation and national interest than say the universalising thrust of human rights and climate change, though even these of course are not beyond national discursive appropriation and political contestation. Nonetheless, some transnational protests seemingly demonstrate the capacity to clearly invoke an imagined global citizenry more than others. The case of environmental activists physically and symbolically engaging whalers in the dangerous waters of the Southern Ocean is a powerful case in point.

> Rather than suggesting transnational protest relies on an exchange between the nexus of the local and global, protests such as that of the *Sea Shepherd* are truly transnational. . . . The global commons can be seen as the physical manifestation of a cultural space for a newly imagined global citizenry. The *Sea Shepherd* uses popular culture and media to suggest that environments which belong to no one are the concern of everyone; their protest thus indicates the central place that global common spaces could occupy in the future of environmental activism. (Crouch & Damjanov, chapter 13)

To what extent transnational protests can serve, via their media and communications enactments, to create a cultural space for a newly imagined global citizenry in the years ahead, and how this can secure enhanced traction politically and institutionally as well as culturally and normatively, will demand sustained research. The new challenges and theoretical debates signalled here and advanced by the contributors to this volume provide important signposts that can help direct the way.

PART TWO

Protesting War and Peace

CHAPTER THREE

Scales of Activism

New Media and Transnational Connections in Anti-War Movements

JENNY PICKERILL, KEVIN GILLAN AND FRANK WEBSTER

Introduction[1]

Reinvigorated by the 9/11 attacks in the USA, large-scale anti-war movements emerged in many countries. By February 2003 an American-dominated "coalition of the willing" was poised to launch a military assault on Iraq. In response coordinated demonstrations against the war took place around the world on 15 February in over 600 cities. So striking was this protest that Tyler (2003) of the *New York Times* was moved to describe what he saw as "two superpowers" set against one another, the United States of America and "world public opinion" as represented by the marchers.

The anti-war movement in Britain was broad and heterogeneous. Its defining feature was that it incorporated and encompassed so many seemingly different issues and groups who had not previously worked together. As an activist in Britain herself noted, "the anti-war movement has forced some bizarre coalitions" (Yvonne Ridley interview, Respect, London). Participant groups included those committed to ideological pacifism (Society of Friends), feminism (Code Pink), anti-globalization (Wombles), political parties (Respect), artistic performance (Rhythms of Resistance), and faith (Muslim Association of Britain) (Figure 1). These anti-war groups and organizations have adopted and adapted Information and Communication Technologies (ICTs) in very different ways. Email, Internet, and mobile technologies are now integral to current campaigning (Atton, 2003; Pickerill, 2003; Gillan, 2008).

Figure 1: London anti-war rally, March 2006 (Jenny Pickerill)

This chapter is concerned with exploring how use of multiple media by this diverse anti-war movement helps us understand the processes and meanings of transnational protest. It maps the different ways in which transnational protest has been constituted—as both material and practical connections (through co-ordinated protest and meetings) and symbolic expressions of solidarity (through visual symbols and the sharing of news). These different forms use ICTs in contrasting, but complementary, ways to make anti-war activists feel global and interconnected into a transnational anti-war movement. The limitations of these different transnational forms (identified as practical problems, dominant concerns with national priorities and the importance of local connections) are not necessarily overcome by the use of ICTs, and as such while new media facilitates transnational protest, it is no panacea for the problems of operating at this scale. Moreover, we argue that in exploring transnational protest we need to rethink scale as not simply linear (and thus scaled-up from the local to global) but as relational and mutually constituted. This involves understanding the organizational forms and values of activists in their construction of scale. It requires valuing the ways in which transnational protest has been constituted over time, across difference, and in sometimes subtle and symbolic ways.

This analysis is based on five case studies of British anti-war and peace organizations; Stop the War Coalition (StWC), Faslane 365, the Society of Friends (Quakers), Justice Not Vengeance, and Campaign for Nuclear Disarmament (CND). In addition a number of explicitly Muslim anti-war organizations and networks were examined, including The Muslim Association of Britain (MAB), The Muslim Public Affairs Committee (MPACUK), and Cage Prisoner. In total 60 interviews were conducted with a range of activists, anti-war demonstrations and vigils were observed, and literature from the movement was analyzed.

Material connections

Transnational activism is likely to include material or ideological linkages made between groups at national and local levels as well as informal ties between grassroots groups. Tarrow claims that transnational collective action is formed by "rooted cosmopolitans," "who grow out of local settings and draw on domestic resources"; they engage in transnational activism through "intertwined networks of a complex international society...accelerated by increasing connections across borders" (2005b: 1). This description highlights the importance of communications such as ICTs, but it also demonstrates the key connection with international institutions and the focus on globalization that appears central to the development of recent transnational contention.

Groups and activities implicated in this process are diverse. On the one hand, we see the development of truly transnational organizations targeting the international policy-making context. Both Greenpeace and Friends of the Earth have garnered enough respect in policy circles to serve as representatives on various countries' delegations to important UN summits such as the "Earth Summits" in Rio in 1992 and Johannesburg a decade later (Willetts, 1996). The number of movement organizations with such competencies has increased dramatically, along with the increasing opportunities for influencing policy at the international level (Smith & Bandy, 2004).

On the other hand, the summit-hopping demonstrations of the late 1990s included a wide range of groups involved in the "global days of action," often called by the international network People's Global Action (PGA) (Wood, 2004; Routledge & Cumbers, 2009). These have involved protesters travelling internationally to bring pressure to bear at the location of major international policy meetings. These examples demonstrate the possibility for taking advantage of a political opportunity structure that has been created at the international level. They also offer a point of comparison, against which we may evaluate the transnational nature of contemporary anti-war movements.

Coordinated transnational protest

National governments may be considered "international actors" inasmuch as they are clearly acting on the world stage. With worldwide media attention, the mass internationally coordinated demonstrations occurring regularly between October 2002 and March 2003 demonstrate the movement's ability to act internationally. These demonstrations did echo the "global days of action" against economic globalization. PGA's calls for global days of action aimed to "make resistance as transnational as capital" (PGA, 1998). While some participants in such demonstrations had travelled internationally, there were additional, simultaneous protests elsewhere. These allowed those who could not travel to participate, which ensured that the "global" action was brought to a large number of local contexts and encouraged wider media coverage.

The mass anti-war demonstrations of early 2003 were "global days of action" in this latter sense. While international travel was not the norm, and there was no equivalent network to PGA to act as a central decision-making space, participants and the media were well aware that individual demonstrations were part of a much larger protest. Without a unifying international anti-war organization, the coordination of these international demonstrations required networking among a large number of organizations with national bases. The date for the biggest protest of all–15 February 2003–was set in meetings at the first European Social Forum, in Florence in November 2002 (Waterman, 2004: 58). With hundreds of protests organized on every continent this was the most global protest in history.

Of course such political participation is enhanced by ICTs through, for example: faster interaction, sharing of strategies and tactics across large distances, low cost dissemination of information, and interactive creation of news and commentary (Bennett, 2003b; Bimber, 2003; Chadwick, 2006). The Internet is by no means a panacea for the problems activists face. Activists have shown concern about uneven accessibility, surveillance, unknowable and diffuse audiences, a lack of personal engagement and difficulties in building trust online (Pickerill, 2003).

There is evidence that participation in the latest anti-war movements has been boosted by activists' Internet practices (Nah, Veenstra, & Shah, 2006). Internet technologies have become central to protesters' daily activity. The more central the Internet has come to political activism, the more it has become the route through which individuals first experience key collective actors. At least in the US, those most central to the anti-war movement are "disproportionately likely to rely on digital communications media," and those with close movement affiliations "overwhelmingly received their information about the Iraq crisis through e-media" (Bennett & Givens, 2006: 1, 17). The Internet has also helped the anti-war movement cross borders:

> The US and British lefts are historically quite separated . . . [they] don't communicate much, two lefts separated by a common language. With the Internet, all that's changed. (Mike Marqusee interview, writer and activist, London)

From the UK perspective, both CND and StWC have been actively involved in international coordination. For instance, Kate Hudson, Chair of CND, described working with the French *Mouvement de la Paix* to organize events at some of the social forums. She added that "we've participated in the last three World Social Forums, although we're not going this year because . . . there's a chance to concentrate our efforts on Trident replacement, so it doesn't seem an appropriate use of our resources at the moment to go there" (Kate Hudson interview). The second half of that quotation refers to the domestic political context, where a debate on the renewal of the British nuclear weapons system was going through Parliament. So, even while Kate Hudson considers international links to be "extremely important" for CND's goals, it is clear that domestic priorities may override such considerations.

International meetings

Attempts have been made to extend the impact of international coordination beyond the setting of dates for demonstrations. A typical activity of international meetings is the production of declarations. CND was represented at a conference in Hiroshima in 2003, organized by the Japanese peace group Gensuikyo (Japan Council Against Atomic and Hydrogen Bombs). Recognition of these "new" movements is captured in the declaration's expression of "solidarity with diverse campaigns against growing military spending, to eradicate hunger, poverty, evils of globalization led by big powers, destruction of the environment, discrimination against women and social injustice" (Gensuikyo, 2003).

Similarly, StWC has been involved in a series of three meetings of anti-war organizations. The meetings took place in Cairo in December 2002, Tokyo in May 2003, and Cairo in December 2003. The second Cairo declaration expressed the need for anti-war movements to "continue solidarity with the Iraqi people and its resistance against the occupation forces with all legitimate means including military struggle and helping the Iraqi people in sabotaging the American plan" (StWC, 2003). However, while international discussions may have given a transnational character to anti-war activism, this is hardly generalizable across the UK movements as a whole. Indeed, the only UK signatories to the Tokyo declaration of 2003 are StWC and Just Peace. Even while attempting to present a united front in the domestic sphere, these organizations appeared to be carrying out distinct (and potentially divisive) activities at the transnational level.

The lived experience of the vast majority of activists seems markedly disconnected from such meetings. In national-level organizations, international coordination is one task of typically overworked officers with limited resources and is easily dropped as domestic pressures and opportunities occur. In local groups the drives for action rarely come from the kinds of meetings that the movement's elite may attend.

Weak transnational ties

Two sets of constraints reduce potential for transnational anti-war activism. First, despite use of ICTs, attempts at continuous cooperation across borders face considerable practical and organizational difficulties. Second, the (perceived) domestic political context, in combination with movement organizations' defined roles and histories, tends to focus their activities at the national level.

Practical difficulties

Any ongoing coalition work between movement organizations that goes beyond the sharing of information must cope with political and strategic differences and must successfully build trust among participants. Activists recognize that incorporating political differences can serve to diffuse and complicate a campaign: "whenever movements grow. . .their composition becomes more diverse and more politically uneven, people come with a variety of political consciousnesses, assumptions and experiences, and confusions" (Mike Marqusee interview). Notably, Tarrow argues that "all shifting and reticular movements reduce ideological cohesion, but the internet may be extreme in its centrifugal effects" (2005a: 138).

Typically, in those countries that have seen stable, national-level anti-war coalitions, there is evidence that member organizations share resources and have some regular, structured interaction through which conflict may be resolved (Levi & Murphy, 2006). While it is conceivable that Internet communications could offer the possibility of having detailed, regular meetings across borders without long-distance travel, this is not something currently utilized to any great extent within anti-war activism.

There is no necessary reason why international coordination must involve the kinds of resource sharing seen within stable, national coalitions. But such resource sharing would provide evidence of strong common ground and would probably encourage further participation in coalition activities. Bandy and Smith express ambivalence about the power of the Internet to provide the basis for coalition building, arguing that face-to-face meetings are more conducive to the creation of trusting relationships (2004: 234). Without regular meetings it seems impossible to build coalitions that share resources beyond those that are effectively free to exchange—i.e., informational resources. Indeed initial responses to questions regarding the value of the Internet in campaigning frequently referred to the easy availability of informational resources. Some groups, such as Justice Not Vengeance, define their primary purpose as exactly to provide such resources for other campaigners (Milan Rai interview, Hastings).

The differences between groups were more divisive than the potential unity of sharing common goals. Thus, for example, formal alliances with the British StWC and the US were not possible because of political differences: "[StWC] wouldn't have done what some parts of the anti-war movement in America have recently done which is. . .they met representatives from what we regard as a puppet government in Iraq" (StWC informant interview, London). Such divisions were evident between many groups but were more acute transnationally where the possibility of personal networks and face-to-face meetings through which to build trust were dramatically reduced.

National priorities

The actions of the "coalition of the willing" in invading Afghanistan and Iraq can be understood as a reassertion of power by particular nations, notably the United States of America. Those who subsequently opposed the protagonists of the "War on Terror" have, to some extent, shifted their focus back from the global level to the national. The strength of national boundaries is further highlighted by a consideration of the interaction of movement organizations' relationships with domestic political structures. When asked about whether CND's work should be focused on international activities, Richard Johnson explained:

> There's always a discussion about which to prioritize, and there'll always be people who stand up and say "but our aim is to get rid of Trident—it's a British issue—if our government moves that will affect the international situation, but that's what we should be focusing on." And that's right of course at the moment. . .at the centre there's a very clear sense of priorities (interview, CND Leicester)

Indeed, for most groups with their organizational roots in the UK, it can be difficult to overcome the barriers created by organizational demands. For instance, David Gee noted that "the idea of working internationally together, all the Quaker agencies doing international campaigns is a good one, but the opportunities for that aren't very big, because of the way that decisions are made at a national level. . .so

it actually makes more sense to have a national campaign" (interview, Quakers).
Other groups included within the broad anti-war and peace movements are nationally focused by definition, with Faslane 365 set up purely to mobilize in relation to
one particular British policy decision.

Since the leadership of the StWC saw the "War on Terror" as a consequence
of the imperialist policies of particular nation states, and given that the StWC was
the primary source of strategic planning for the anti-war movement in the UK, the
anti-war movement was bound to be oriented to changing the behaviour of individual nation states. Locating the power to make war at this level, the movement
sought to stop war at this level, despite understanding war as part of broader capitalist processes (Figure 2).

Figure 2: London anti-war rally, August 2007 (Kevin Gillan)

Using a large dataset drawn from interviews with participants of demonstrations on 15 February 2003 in six countries Walgrave and Verhulst (2003) demonstrate the importance of the national government's stance on the war to the mobilization processes in those countries. Superficially, this was the preeminent example of transnational opposition to the "War on Terror." The identical timing of protests in all countries and joint coordination among mobilizing groups even meant that very similar slogans and images were being used in the mobilization effort: "Triggering event, protest timing, issues, claims and goals were the same in all protest countries" (2003: 7). The level of mobilization, measured as a percentage of the population participating, varied with averages of 1.3 per cent for initiating countries (US, UK), 2.6 per cent for supporting countries (Italy, Spain) and 0.7 per cent for countries opposed to the war (France, Germany). These findings establish the importance of domestic context in the mobilization of the most apparently transnational of demonstrations. It is clear that in those countries that initiated the war, participation against it took root far beyond the "usual suspects" of the far left. Participants in these contexts did not necessarily march because of a pacifist ideology or to oppose one further instantiation of unjust globalization but to oppose the particular actions of their particular governments.

Local connections

Additionally, the context may be even more local. From our qualitative dataset, it is clear that many activists see the power of anti-war movements located in grounded, locally contextualized activities and networks, such as meetings (Figure 3). This is typically related to the potential for mobilizing action at the local level. For instance, in describing a meeting with a Pakistani government minister, Yvonne Ridley (of Respect and StWC) described the UK anti-war movement in such terms. She explained,

> He was wanting to know, "so this anti-war movement, how is it funded, which businessmen are promoting it?" And I said, "oh it's funded through buckets and pennies. Yes, village halls, church halls, community centres, you know, the buckets passed round, you might get twenty-three pounds and fifty pence. Just out of people's pockets." And he said . . ."so the two million people who came to London, who told them to go to London?" And I said "well, what we do is we go round all these little halls and towns and gather the movement," and I said, "it really is people power."

When Yvonne Ridley describes "gathering the movement," practicalities mean that it is local organizers who bring local people together. When it came to the massed national demonstrations, these were essential in making arrangements to transport thousands of protesters to the capital: "Usually our local mosques just organize coaches to go down, so we went down a couple of times with them, or once I remember me and my uncle went with Peterborough CND branch" (Arif Sayeed interview, University of Leicester Islamic Society).

Figure 3: Anti-war meeting, Highfields, Leicester, July 2006 (Jenny Pickerill)

Symbolic solidarities

Although there are limitations in the material and practical connections made in transnational activism, we need to consider how transnational protest was expressed and experienced in other ways (Pickerill, 2009). Many respondents referred to morale-boosting benefits of connecting to other anti-war groups online and the desire to find and express solidarity. Following Bayat (2005), we might term this "imagined solidarity." Bayat draws on Anderson's work defining the nation as an imagined community "because the members of even the smallest nation will never know most of their fellow-members. . .yet in the minds of each lives the image of their communion" (Anderson, 1991: 5).

Online anti-war networks are particularly suited to sharing symbolic expressions of solidarity. Visual symbols and simple slogans translate easily into different contexts, and the Internet certainly provides a plausible avenue for the sharing of symbols (O'Neill, 2004) (Figure 4). Imagined solidarity may be achieved through projecting locally grounded actions into the global arena, thereby increasing the significance of a campaign for participants. Interviewees highlighted their ability to communicate their participation in protest:

> A lot of the big demonstrations have coincided with demonstrations internationally. . . if nothing else—if we don't stop the wars—at least you can hope that word about our actions gets out around the world. (Chris Goodwin interview, Leicester Campaign to Stop the War)

Figure 4: The ubiquitous disarmament and CND symbol in New York and on a London anti-war demonstration (source: Jenny Pickerill)

This need to show solidarity was felt most keenly amongst activists who closely identified with those being persecuted in the Iraq war. In the UK this was most obviously represented by Muslim communities and reflects the Islamic concept of one *umma*: "the unity, the brotherhood, the sisterhood, of all Muslims, wherever you are, whatever colour your skin is, wherever you live" (Arif Sayeed interview, Islamic Students Society [ISS], Leicester). For some, this extended to a concern for justice for all: "You stand up for an injustice wherever it is—it doesn't matter whether they're Muslim or not" (Naazish Azaim interview, ISS, Leicester) (see also Phillips, 2009) (Figure 5).

Figure 5: London anti-war rally, March 2006 (Jenny Pickerill)

In other instances ICTs were crucial in solidifying activists' experience of acting at the transnational scale. A key interchange of expressions of solidarity is in the sharing of news. Interviewees utilized a broad range of alternative media sources to locate local struggles in the transnational context. Sites such as Indymedia have become a core medium for interchange between anti-war groups. Again, we see the possibility of imagining solidarity online since the structure of Indymedia is designed to prioritize place-rooted action while offering communication at a transnational scale (Pickerill, 2007).

Thus for activists "being global" is less about building formal connections between international groups and far more about re-scaling the meaning of local actions to a global audience. This is achieved primarily by articulating a form of imagined solidarity, while simultaneously maintaining the importance of domestic issues. An StWC informant explained that while he used the Internet to scour global sites for information to put on the StWC website–itself examined by Internet users around the world–he considered that "it's what you do at home that counts" (interview, London).

This importance of being grounded in place, despite the possibilities the Internet offers, reflects the notion of "rooted cosmopolitanism" (Tarrow, 2005a, 2005b). So, while concrete action remains predominantly affixed to place and to the political context of the nation, ICTs help activists locate their action within much broader movements. The value of informational linkages does not, therefore, lie in their potential for enabling more formal alliances between organizations (*pace* Diani, 2001). Rather, because the sharing of information across borders allows activists to gain a sense of solidarity, Internet networks help the rooted cosmopolitan to *feel* global.

Rethinking transnational relations

The transnational should not be thought of as in binary opposition to the local (McFarlane, 2009). Instead we need to take a relational approach to place and networks which identifies the international geographies of political activism as being constituted in historical connections, co-production, and multiple spatialities (Featherstone, 2008). As different networks of protest overlap during particular campaigns, changes occur in the political identities and political imaginaries that they express. Thus political identities are not established before they interact on the international scale, and international activism is not simply local activism "scaled-up."

Featherstone is able to illustrate that transnational linkages and activism have long existed and the contemporary anti-capitalist networks are built upon historical international spatial practices—even if these were partial, situated and contested. This approach critiques the notion that protest used to be bounded and local, and that ICTs have facilitated a transnationalism unlike ever before. Featherstone argues that we need to understand the historical tenets of activism before we can fully comprehend its contemporary transnational character. This requires us to critically rethink how we understand transnational activism in two key ways.

First, it is often assumed that international solidarities are based on commonalities between activists. Featherstone has illustrated, however, that a productive transnational network need not be based on a shared common understanding of an issue but simply an agreement on practices and tactics. This opens up possibilities for unlike actors to work together across difference more easily, and this is supported by the ways in which the diverse and heterogeneous anti-war movement operated in the UK.

Second, is the need to understand place and scale in more complex and nuanced ways. All too often scale is perceived in a linear and hierarchical fashion; with the local opposed to the larger more powerful transnational scale. Using this approach the transnational becomes the more important—the scale at which activists aspire to act and influence. This misunderstands much about how scale and place are constructed; place is relational and mutually constituted. Thus we cannot define, or understand, the local without seeing its construction in relation to national and transnational acts. These are not separate scales, they are intimately interwoven. No place is simply bounded and local–it is formed in its *relation* to all other places (Castree, 2004). Thus a focus on how activism becomes transnational, or jumps-scales from the local up, ignores the messy realities that local protest is always, and will always be, part of international connections, and that local resistance or place-based projects are solid building blocks for activism.

Moreover, the idea that transnational activism is superior to local ignores the very real tensions in organizational forms. For those who value horizontal prefigurative politics, local (or micro) political actions can have transnational effects. Others are committed to hierarchical organizing around a centre and bureaucracy which results in very different spatial formations. Thus we can distinguish these different kinds of relationships by their tendencies to use *vertical* linkages, on the one hand, and *horizontal* on the other.

Vertical linkages between levels imply a flow of information or resources from local, to national, to (potentially) transnational levels. This is the image Yvonne Ridley conjures in her description of bucket collections in town halls. For some affiliated local Stop the War groups this was the primary mode of operation. National events gave local groups a reason to mobilize, and they took their lead, politically, from StWC.

By following plans made at the national level, a local group can hope to have a broader impact. This makes sense particularly for those who see the national government as the relevant point of decision-making:

> The main target is the Government, because obviously . . . they're the ones who want to go to war every single week. So that's why we've always pushed for national demonstrations. We think local demonstrations are important, but national demonstrations–when you get everybody together marching past the Houses of Parliament–that's when you're going to make a big impact. (Sadia Jabeen interview, District Organizer for Socialist Workers Party, based in Leicester)

For those who see the national level as being crucial to political contestation, it is important for them to have a platform that reaches out to the nation. For instance, Anas Altikriti, of British Muslim Initiative and formerly MAB, said of arguments concerning Muslim public engagement, that "before MAB [voices] expressing those particular views were quite faint. They weren't as powerful and as forceful as, I think, the context needed" (interview). Hence the mass mobilization strategy may ultimately depend on the effectiveness of the high profile organizations at the centre (and their presence was obvious on demonstrations, Figure 6). Essentially, what we see is the channelling of broad-based opposition to war through to a single point of pressure targeted at the national government. Under this strategy, transnational contention would require an international organization to achieve the kind of stability that some authors see as essential to developing individual protests into a coherent movement (Tarrow, 1998: 176–96). In its vertical linkages, therefore, contemporary anti-war activism seems better understood as a number of national movements with occasional and temporary connections in the transnational realm.

Figure 6: London anti-war rally, March 2006 (Jenny Pickerill)

In addition to these vertical linkages we see horizontal connections on, and across, a number of levels. Activists endeavour to reach out across borders to provide mutual support. Perhaps the most obvious of horizontal linkages occur through ICTs. Informational connection can create a belief in being "part of something bigger." This may give some individuals the confidence to become participants. Tom Shelton, of CND, described the potential power in "the way you can connect with someone on the other side of the world who has the same views as you" (interview).

Online interaction goes beyond the simple sharing of information to concrete planning of protest. David Webb, of Yorkshire CND, for instance, describes his connection with the Global Network Against Weapons and Nuclear Power in Space.

> We've got contacts now through networks in Europe, in the States and in Australia, around the world really, and it's helped I think an incredible amount in terms of awareness and feeling that you're not on your own . . . You don't read about them in the newspapers. You wouldn't know they were there unless you actually had those contacts.

Other horizontal connections appear less systematic. An example here is the Faslane Academics Blockade (FAB) including, in addition to around 30 academics from UK universities, international participants and the organizational driving force of an academic in Sweden. This was enabled, on the one hand, by the ready accessibility of modern ICTs to all academics and, on the other, by the existence of an efficient and experienced coordinating committee in Scotland.

The Faslane 365 campaign has grown out of what we might call the grassroots peace movement. This helps to explain why F365 has, across a range of blockades, shown a propensity to utilizing horizontal cross-border linkages. The grassroots peace movement may be understood as a long-standing, developing network of those for whom peace is always the pre-eminent political cause, no matter what the current political context. Characteristic of this action is the attempt to connect with and support those facing a war situation. Groups have made efforts to share resources with Iraq with Voices in the Wilderness UK, breaking the sanctions imposed on the country by delivering medical equipment and supplies during the 1990s. As the build up to the recent war progressed, "human shields" peace caravans set out, driving from London to Baghdad in a mission of solidarity and practical aid.

Among the largest networks that rest on this philosophy is Women in Black. Women in Black represents ways in which a particular political perspective influences a decision to use horizontal, rather than vertical, linkages. They offer an analysis of militarism that links it squarely with patriarchy (Cockburn, 2003). Since patriarchy highlights the domination of institutionalized structures of power by men, appropriate action circumvents those structures.

There is, therefore, evidence of orientations to two kinds of linkages between levels of anti-war movement activity. On the one hand, organizations seek to move information and resources vertically, as seems to have been particularly effective in mobilizing large, national demonstrations. However, the lack of a single organizational centre, and abundance of political difference, at the international level makes it hard for such organizations to operate transnationally. On the other hand, over a longer time frame grassroots peace groups, and particularly women's peace groups, have developed substantial cross-border connections. Information and resources flow with little respect for territorial boundaries but a great respect for human well-being. Some links were made internationally between disparate grassroots groups, and some activists sought to build a decentralized transnationalism, but such links remained reliant upon personal ties and rarely crossed ideological differences.

Thus an attendance to the complexity of scale helps us understand that transnational protest is not simply a matter of acting, or interacting via ICTs, at a particular scale. It is not simply about material connections across national borders. Rather it concerns an articulation, narratives and inspirations, which assertively link local conditions and acts to transnational perspectives. Thus, as Katz (2001) argues, we need to build counter-topographies:

> I want to imagine a politics that maintains the distinctness of a place while recognizing that it is connected analytically to other places along contour lines that represent not elevation but particular relations to a process (e.g., globalizing capitalist relations of production).

These narratives of connection are often woven by particular activists. For example, during the early anti-capitalist protests of the 1990s there was a heavy presence of such transnational narrators who grounded an active internationalist imaginary within local activism. They were able to make relational connections between the injustices of one locality and broader institutional factors. Making these relational connections should have been relatively easy for an anti-war movement objecting to an invasion on foreign soil, but perhaps because of the predominance of vertical linkages, a lack of transnational narrators, or the national political context, few chose to articulate the links between local activism and transnational spaces in this way.

Conclusions

The anti-war movement may be understood as symbolically oriented to the transnational level, while simultaneously being politically and organizationally focused at the national level. There were internationally coordinated demonstrations and concrete examples of attempts at international agreement-making at a few meetings, at all of which ICTs were invaluable.

We have highlighted the importance of mobilization within more local contexts as vital to the possibility for significant action. Indeed, we find it impossible to consider transnational, national and local anti-war activity in isolation. A series of high-profile international, national and regional events drawing many thousands of participants punctuated the local efforts to state the case against war. They offered a reason to mobilize and a timetable for action. The national demonstrations also offered activists the knowledge that their locality was not alone. Comparing "scores" ("how many coaches from Birmingham?", "how many from Manchester?") positioned the local organizers within a national movement. Online activities create the appearance of diversity of anti-war movements and therefore affect the experience of the movement for those who encounter it on the Internet. However, our interviewees noted the lack of face-to-face interaction necessary to enhance trust and offered only limited evidence of the sharing of non-informational resources. Consequently, activists' ability to build transnational ties for action was limited. There was no international decision-making centre for anti-war activists and overall a lack of a transnational imaginary. We also need to rethink how we consider scale and the mutual constitution of scales in relation to each other.

We hope that we have illustrated in this chapter that transnational protest can mean anything from symbolic expressions of solidarity to very grounded entwined collaborations. The anti-war movement is both internally differentiated and operating at multiple levels of power. These distinctions interact such that the relationship between the local and the global is influenced by the structures of meaning by which actors make sense of their context and their behaviour, and ICTs facilitate such processes but are no panacea for the broader difficulties of transnational activism.

Note

1. Sections of this chapter have previously appeared in Gillan, K. Pickerill, J. and Webster, F. 2008. *Anti-War Activism: New Media and Protest in the Information Age*. Palgrave MacMillan, and Gillan, K. and Pickerill, J. 2008. Transnational anti-war activism: solidarity, diversity and the internet in Australia, Britain and the United States after 9/11. *Australian Journal of Political Science*, 43, 1, 59–78. We would like to thank the publishers for permission to reprint some elements of these works.

CHAPTER FOUR

"Not in Our Name"

British Press, the Anti-war Movement and the Iraq Crisis 2002–2009[1]

CRAIG MURRAY, PIERS ROBINSON, PETER GODDARD
AND KATY PARRY

Introduction

On 20 March 2003, Britain joined the United States in leading a military invasion of Iraq. This decision came in spite of a remarkable period of debate and controversy, both in the UK and internationally. Iraq's supposed non-compliance with United Nations resolutions aimed at eliminating Iraqi weapons of mass destruction (WMDs) provided the immediate justification for war. In addition, the US used claims of Iraqi involvement with terrorism (specifically Al Qaeda) to justify the invasion and, in the UK, the Iraqi regime's human rights record enabled the government to claim a humanitarian purpose. However, the US and Britain were unable to gain UN support for military action. In the UK, even after intensive media relations efforts, the Blair government also failed to convince the majority of the British public of the necessity of war in Iraq. Nevertheless, Britain was a key member of the US government's "coalition of the willing," committing 45,000 troops to the invasion.

The Iraq leadership was quickly overthrown, but a long-term "low-intensity conflict" followed, characterized by armed opposition to coalition forces and inter-ethnic strife. No credible evidence of WMD or related activity was found. Between 2003 and 2009, violence against coalition forces and between Iraqi groups led to deaths numbering well in excess of 100,000. Meanwhile, controversy over the invasion continued to dominate debate in Britain and worldwide, sparked by the failure to find evidence of WMDs, US forces' treatment of Iraqi prisoners at Abu Ghraib and Iraq's continuing instability, among other issues. Only in 2009, six years after the invasion, did the British government announce the ending of "combat operations" and the withdrawal of forces from Iraq while, at the time of writing, US policy remains committed to a staged withdrawal from Iraq.

The coalition's failure to secure UN endorsement reflected the great unpopularity of the conflict internationally. In the UK, opinion polls taken in the lead-up to the invasion consistently showed a majority of Britons opposed an Iraq invasion without UN backing. This opposition peaked in January 2003, when Ipsos-MORI polling showed that 77 percent of Britons were anti-war. Even as late as 14–16 March, Ipsos-MORI found 63 percent still opposed war without UN approval. Majority public opinion did eventually fall in behind the war policy but not until the decision to invade was final and British troops were about to enter the battlefield. Respective *Guardian* ICM polls indicated a sharp rise in support from 38 percent to 54 percent and a fall in opposition from 44 percent to 30 percent between 14 and 21 March.[2] Yet even with British troops in action, ongoing polling by YouGov showed that 30–40 percent continued to believe that the invasion was wrong, with one poll two weeks into the war revealing that 26 percent thought British troops should be withdrawn.[3] Lewis et al. (2005: 52) have suggested that these figures may even underestimate the extent of anti-war feeling, arguing that: "Many people who expressed support during the war may *still* have opposed the decision to go to war, but felt obliged to show support for British troops once war began" (original emphasis).

The considerable grassroots resistance to war found expression in a large domestic anti-war movement which staged various large demonstrations across the UK before, during and after the invasion. In turn, this domestic movement formed part of what was perhaps history's largest-ever global anti-war movement, whose transnational nature was most forcibly displayed on the weekend of 15–16 February 2003, when 6–10 million people (BBC estimate) joined coordinated protest demonstrations in major cities across the world. Among these, the largest took place in Rome, London, Barcelona and Baghdad.[4] In addition to the London protest, large British demonstrations were held in Glasgow and Belfast.

Although perceived as a major global occurrence, the transnational anti-Iraq War movement remained "emphatically oriented towards the national" (Gillan, Pickerill, & Webster, 2008: 37) and found expression primarily in "local" events. It is appropriate, therefore, that we should examine how the transnational protest movement against war in Iraq was represented in Britain's national press.[5] Consistent with traditional news values, most of the UK's news coverage focused on British individuals, groups and events. In this chapter, we assess the tone of the coverage that the anti-war movement received in the period immediately prior to the outbreak of the war, when the Commons voted on military action, and during the invasion itself, drawing upon a detailed analysis of seven national newspapers. In addition, we also provide an overview of press coverage of anti-war activity beyond this invasion phase–during the run up to the invasion (July 2002–March 2003) and from the fall of Baghdad (April 2003) until the withdrawal of British troops in April 2009. The findings of our analysis are instructive not only for our understanding of press treatment of the anti-war movement in the case of the 2003 Iraq War, but also for the role of media and public protest in wartime generally.

Media, war and protest

Existing studies suggest that, on the whole, media have served the military well during times of war (e.g., Bennett, 1990; Carruthers, 2000; Hallin, 1986). Several factors help explain this pattern of media deference to government war objectives. These include dependence upon official sources, ideological factors such as anticommunism during the Cold War (Robinson et al., 2010), patriotism, fear of flak (if reporting is seen as undermining the war effort) and news values rooted in dramatic episodic coverage. Overall, in times of war, media are often characterized as behaving like a "faithful servant," "publicizing official frames of [a] conflict and either ignoring or discrediting challengers" (Wolfsfeld, 1997: 69; see also Robinson et al., 2010, 2009).

Consistent with such deference to official policy in wartime, anti-war movements tend to fare poorly in the media. Hallin (1986) found that during the Vietnam War, anti-war dissenters, including "elite" sources, were "granted much less time to speak when they appeared on the evening news" and "had nothing comparable to the day-to-day ability of the administration, through its position as the primary provider of authoritative information about world events, to affect news coverage." He concluded that "[t]he anti-war movement stood at the bottom of the media's hierarchy of legitimate political actors, and its access to the news and influence over it were still more limited" (1986: 198). In short, the anti-war movement fell into a "sphere of deviance" (Hallin, 1986). Other studies indicate that protest movements, and dissent in general, are marginalized in times of war.

Trends towards marginalization and de-legitimization have also been a consistent finding in research into other, non-war-related protest movements. The research literature on media and protest points to the existence of a "protest paradigm," through which media framing of protest activity commonly undermines dissenting groups (Gitlin, 1980; Hackett & Zhao, 1994; Luther & Miller, 2005; McLeod & Detenber, 1999; Smith et al., 2001). Among the most commonly cited "de-legitimisation cues" (Gitlin, 1980) in protest coverage are a focus on radicalism, "extremism," strange appearance or behaviours, violence and disruption. For several of these cues, protest groups are undermined by coverage concentrating on elements that appear "deviant" in relation to normal or "mainstream" society. Accordingly, as McLeod and Detenber (1999: 6) argue, "the more a protest group challenges the status quo, the more closely the media will adhere to the characteristics of the protest paradigm." Another problem for protesters is a tendency towards what Iyengar (1991) and others call "episodic" reporting. Here acts of protest are reported as "spectacles" in their own right, with little attention given to the reasons behind the demonstrations or the message protesters wish to convey (Hallin, 1986; Iyengar, 1991; Luther & Miller, 2005; Smith et al., 2001).

While most of the studies cited above are American, analyses of British media have reached broadly similar conclusions (Hall, 1973a; Murdock, 1973; Glasgow University Media Group, 1985). However, recently a number of scholars have begun to challenge the key assumptions of the "protest paradigm." According to Cottle (2008: 855):

> Much has changed since earlier studies documented how the mainstream news media invariably report protests and demonstrations through a dominant law and (dis)order frame, labelling protesters as deviant and de-legitimising their aims and politics by emphasizing drama, spectacle and violence.

Cottle argues that protest demonstrations themselves have become more socially acceptable and that it is no longer so common for media to ignore or dismiss them. In addition, Gillan, Pickerill and Webster (2008; see also Bennett et al., 2008) have effectively documented the ways in which the Iraq anti-war movements mobilized via the use of new and emerging communication technologies such as the Internet. Indeed, especially with respect to the anti-Iraq War protest movement, there are good logical grounds for questioning whether coverage would conform to the expectations of the "protest paradigm." The anti-Iraq War movement was far more popular than most other protest movements, even reflecting the views of a clear majority of Britons in the run-up to the invasion. In this case, a combination of high levels of political and public opposition and a well-organized anti-war movement, the Stop the War Coalition (StWC), raises the possibility of a significant, perhaps unprecedented, degree of sympathetic media coverage.

Methodology

We examined coverage of anti-war dissent in seven national newspapers, seeking to assess the extent to which they presented the anti-war movement as belonging to a "sphere of deviance" (Hallin, 1986)–a position which favoured the British government and its case for war–or, alternatively, functioned as an "advocate of the underdog" (Wolfsfeld, 1997: 69) in helping to reinforce those opposing the war. Our analysis was drawn from a broader study assessing media performance during this conflict.[6] Previous work by the same authors (Robinson et al., 2010; Goddard, Robinson, & Parry, 2008; Murray et al., 2008) offers a detailed overview of our approach and method, so what follows is merely a brief summary.

Our survey period ran from 17 March to 18 April 2003, beginning four days before the invasion and ending four days after the fall of Tikrit. This period enabled examination of a short pre-war stage, in which the controversial House of Commons vote on military action took place, as well as the whole of the "major combat" phase of the invasion (beginning with newspapers published on 21 March), thus allowing comparison between the two periods. In this 33-day period, we coded all leader articles and all major news articles (n = 4449) appearing on the "Iraq War" news pages of seven national newspapers–*Sun*, *Daily Mirror*, *Daily Mail*, *Independent*, *Guardian*, *Times* and *Daily Telegraph*, together with their Sunday equivalents.[7] For convenience, we have coupled daily and Sunday newspapers together in reporting our findings. One indicator of the controversy surrounding the policy of war in Britain was that three newspapers in our survey (*Mirror*, *Independent*, *Guardian*) chose to oppose it (see Goddard, Robinson, & Parry, 2008; Robinson et al., 2010) and continued to do so even while the invasion was in progress. The other four newspapers showed support for the war to varying degrees—the *Sun* most of all.

We created a refined approach to analysing media content and tone, enabling us to document key indicators relating to media autonomy—from the variety of sources used through to the prevalence of pro- and anti-coalition frames. Specifically, each news report was coded in relation to three main areas:

- *story subjects*–identifying the subject matter of news reports: We coded each subject that featured significantly in a story.
- *story sources*–identifying the source for all quotes used in a story.
- *subject tone*–we assigned a tone code (positive, negative, straight, i.e. non-evaluative–in relation to the main protagonist) to each occurrence of a story subject. Where both positive and negative elements were present, subject tone was coded as "mixed."[8]

To complement our detailed analysis of the invasion period, we have used the research database LexisNexis to compile data for press coverage of anti-Iraq War activity from mid-2002 through to the end of British combat operations in April 2009. Here our data are based on the occurrence of the search terms "Iraq" and "anti-war," as well as variations thereon. In addition to providing a statistical overview of anti-Iraq War protest coverage in the periods before and after the invasion phase, we examine qualitatively the clearest trends that could be identified in press coverage of a selection of key protest events. This more qualitative analysis does not rely upon the same detailed methodology as was used in the original analysis of the invasion period, and as such the two approaches are not directly comparable. Nevertheless, as discussed below, we find some evidence that several trends that we identify during the invasion period are also present before and after the invasion.

Results from our main survey period

Despite the strength of opposition to war in Iraq and the notion that protest generally has received a kinder media profile of late, our analysis found that despite an early positive start, anti-war actors had a difficult time in gaining access to the British media and winning sympathetic coverage once the invasion got underway.

Most protest stories appeared in the first week of our five-week sample period, in connection with the Commons debate and vote on the war (17 and 18 March), in which numerous Labour MPs rebelled against their party, and the street demonstrations held between 19 and 22 March. Between 17 and 23 March (allowing for the time-lag in press reporting), anti-war dissent was a main subject in 15.8 percent of newspaper stories (n=161). The great majority of stories that played positively for the anti-war lobby also occurred during this early period: Between 17 and 23 March, "pro-antiwar" subjects outnumbered "anti-antiwar" subjects dramatically (40.0 percent compared to 9.2 percent, with 50.8 percent coded as "mixed" or "straight"). The Commons debate and the Labour rebellion were responsible for 47 percent of all positive protest subjects in the five-week sample. Anti-war MPs were quoted extensively in many of these stories, and often the size of the rebellion was framed as a problem for the Blair government. Coverage of the street demonstrations organized by StWC between 19 and 22 March also produced more positive than negative coverage, although mixed or straight coverage was most common. Many of these stories quoted anti-war activists, and the size of the demonstrations, when reported, also tended to play positively for the anti-war lobby.

While there was a significant amount of positive coverage during this early period, it is also important to note two distinctive features of it. The first relates to a differentiation between elite and non-elite dissent; the second concerns the variation between newspapers. We will deal with each in turn. It was "elite" dissenters such as politicians, religious leaders and other prominent individuals, who fared best in the media. Elite protest actions in the UK were a subject in nearly twice as many newspaper stories (n=127) as "non-elite" actions (n=74) such as street demonstrations, conscientious objectors or voluntary human shields. Similarly, elite anti-war actors received three times as many lines of quotations as non-elites (3134 to 913).[9] Furthermore, coverage of "elite" protesters more often contained reference to substantive anti-war arguments than did reporting of grassroots activism. Pro- or anti-war rationales were present in 38 percent of newspaper stories about elite protesters, compared to only 14 percent of stories about grassroots campaigners. There was, for instance, detailed reporting of pro- and anti-war arguments in coverage of the pre-war parliamentary debates.

Second, and regarding variation across newspapers, the press did not adopt a uniform approach in its tone towards anti-war protest (see Table 1). Overall, the *Mirror*, *Independent* and *Guardian*, which opposed the war, were much more likely to report anti-war activity positively than the remaining newspapers. The *Sun's* reporting never favoured anti-war protest at all. Similar patterns to those found in Table 1 were apparent in our data for the sources of quotes. Anti-war voices were the source for 8.3 percent of all quotations in the *Mirror*, 7.0 percent in the *Guardian* and 5.7 percent in the *Independent*. In contrast, 4.2 percent of quotations in the *Times*, 4.0 percent in the *Mail*, 3.7 percent in the *Telegraph* and only 2.3 percent in the *Sun* came from anti-war actors. The variations in press coverage could clearly be seen in their treatment of the anti-war demonstrations. For example, the pro-war press often employed "de-legitimisation cues" (Gitlin, 1980) including head-

Newspaper	Pro-AW	Mixed/ Straight AW	Anti-AW	Other
Mirror	70.3 %	24.3 %	2.7 %	2.7 %
Independent	40.7 %	53.7 %	5.6 %	0.0 %
Guardian/ Observer	39.3 %	54.1 %	3.3 %	3.3 %
Mail	17.9 %	50.0 %	32.1 %	0.0 %
Telegraph	16.7 %	43.8 %	33.3 %	6.3 %
Times	16.0 %	50.0 %	34.0 %	0.0 %
Sun/ News of the World	0.0 %	19.4 %	77.4 %	3.2 %

Table 1: Tone for protest subjects in each newspaper

lines and photographs with negative connotations and deflating or implicitly patronizing reporter commentary. Among such negative cues were an emphasis on disruption ("Schoolchildren bring city to a halt," *Times*, 20 March 2003), on decline in turnout ("Poor show on marches," *News of the World*, 23 March 2003), as well as other de-legitimizing themes ("Hard left agitators behind school demos," *Daily Mail*, 23 March 2003: 18; "Council pays its workers to attend demos," *Daily Telegraph*, 21 March 2003: 11; "Terror fears as marchers jam the capital again," *Mail on Sunday*, 23 March 2003: 18). By contrast, anti-war newspapers (*Guardian*, *Independent* and *Mirror*) were more likely to emphasize positive aspects of these protests, such as the large turnout ("100,000 expected at London peace march," *Guardian*, 22 March 2003: 9; "200,000 marchers join 'very British demonstration,'" *Independent*, 23 March 2003: 8).

Despite an early positive start for the anti-war movement, even in the face of a relatively hostile pro-war press, for the remainder of our main survey period (beginning on 24 March) positive media attention declined rapidly, appearing as a main subject in only 3.2 percent (n=110) of stories. The same trend can be detected in our findings for the presence of anti-war actors. Between 17 and 23 March, anti-war actors were the source for 26.5 percent of all lines of text quoted in newspaper stories, compared to 3.9 percent for the period from 24 March to 18 April. Importantly, the tone of reporting towards the anti-war movement also changed from 24 March onwards, with only 17.0 percent of reports coded "pro-antiwar" and 46.4 percent "anti-antiwar" (36.6 percent were mixed/straight). In part, this decline is simply a reflection of declining protest activity in Britain. With British troops in the field and majority public opinion having swung behind them, anti-war politicians and other public figures became less vocal during the invasion. Public participation in anti-war rallies also declined during the war. Yet decreased protest activity was not the only factor involved. Once the war got underway, the press itself became less accommodating to dissent. For instance, although protest activity declined in scale, it never ceased, continuing even during the main combat phase of the conflict. In the UK, this included demonstrations involving thousands on 27 March in Manchester and 28 March in Edinburgh. There were also large demonstrations internationally.[10] None of these events received much press coverage in the UK. Another notable feature of the protest coverage after the war started was an increase in the proportion of stories that appeared in the pro-war press. Between 17 and 23 March the three anti-war newspapers had published 51.6 percent of all protest stories (83 of 161). From 24 March onwards, the four pro-war newspapers were responsible for 58.2 percent of stories (64 of 110). Hence, while protest coverage declined across all newspapers, this trend was most pronounced among anti-war publications. This suggests that the anti-war newspapers began to distance themselves somewhat from dissent as the war got underway. Indeed, on 20 March the *Independent* argued in a leader article that "The debate about the rights and wrongs of this war is over."

> Politicians across the political spectrum are united in the conviction that the time has come "to support our troops." This newspaper agrees and fervently hopes for a swift conclusion with as few casualties on both sides as is possible in war ("When democracies do battle with a despot, they must hold on to their moral superiority," 20 March 2003: 18).

The decline in the press's openness to dissent was perhaps most clearly shown in the treatment of anti-war MPs Robin Cook and George Galloway. Cook became a prominent figure among elite anti-war actors largely because of his high-profile status within the Blair Government, serving as Foreign Secretary from 1997 to 2001 and then as Leader of the House until his resignation on the eve of the war. His eloquent resignation speech received broadly sympathetic treatment in the press, with deflating treatment restricted only to the avidly pro-war *Sun*, which derided him as a "war wobbler" and "gnome-like" ("War wobbler Cook resigns," 18 March: 1; "Cook: I quit: Gnome won't back PM," 18 March: 8). Media treatment of Cook changed markedly almost two weeks into hostilities, however, when he restated his opposition to war in a *Sunday Mirror* opinion piece and seemingly called for British troops to be withdrawn. This time, press reaction was overwhelmingly negative. Editorials in six of the seven newspapers in our survey criticized Cook's stand, with only the *Mirror* defending the statement. Besides these editorial criticisms, most newspapers granted generous access to key government ministers who lined up to attack Cook's comments. In contrast to Cook, fellow Labour MP George Galloway was almost invisible in our news sample until the *Sun* propelled him onto its front-page under the headline "TRAITOR" on 1 April. The *Sun*'s story related to comments Galloway had made on Abu Dhabi TV, where he asserted that George Bush and Tony Blair had attacked Iraq "like wolves" and said that "the best thing British troops can do is to refuse to obey illegal orders." After 1 April, Galloway was much more prominent in the media but received explicitly negative reporter treatment in 54 percent of his press appearances.

Pre- and post-invasion protest coverage

Broadly similar trends were also evident in coverage of the Iraq crisis as a whole. Figure 1 gives the number of stories relating to anti-war activity in our seven national newspapers month by month from July 2002 to April 2009. Anti-war activity received most coverage in early 2003 in connection with the build-up to war and the invasion itself. Outside this period, we also notice significant levels of attention in September 2002 and November 2003, corresponding respectively to a 150,000 to 400,000-strong anti-war rally in London and a series of demonstrations to coincide with an official visit to London by US President George W. Bush.

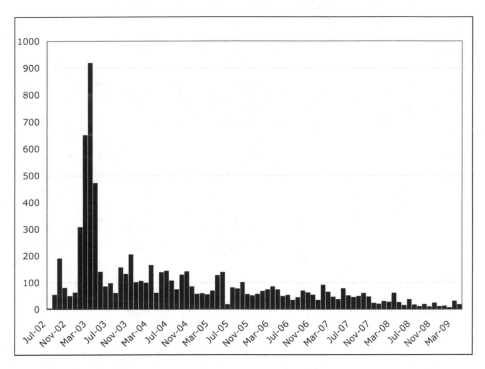

Figure 1: Reporting of anti-war activity among our sample newspapers by month, July 2002–April 2009

Looking first at the pre-war period, we found high levels of coverage across all newspapers sampled. Taking just the 15 February 2003 demonstration, 184 articles between 10 and 17 February mentioned the protests, and most of these focused on the demonstrations in considerable detail. Among individual newspapers we found most articles in the *Mirror* (37), *Independent* (34), *Times* (33) and *Guardian* (30). Coverage in the *Telegraph* (23), *Mail* (17) and *Sun* (10) was less detailed by comparison, yet every newspaper gave quite extensive coverage on the days closest to the demonstration (i.e., 15–17 February). Although we have not conducted detailed analysis of tone, we observed evidence of sympathetic coverage across nearly all newspapers. It was common to focus on the size of the demonstrations ("1,500,000 say no to war on Iraq," *Mail on Sunday*, 16 February 2003; "Biggest protest in UK history likely to pack Hyde Park," *Independent*, 14 February 2003) and the presence of "ordinary people" or "Middle Britain" ("The People's Protest: The day Middle England marched with the militants," *Independent on Sunday*, 16 February 2003; "The usual suspects were joined by thousands of ordinary people who strongly believe Britain is about to make the most terrible mistake," *Mail on Sunday*, 17 February 2003). Both themes could be interpreted as "legitimising cues" for anti-war dissent. There was also more directly supportive commentary in opinion pieces and, to a lesser extent, editorials in some newspapers. Most papers included at least one supportive comment piece, including those whose leader articles supported a military solution to the crisis. However, we observed direct editorial support only in the *Mirror*, *Independent* and, rather surprisingly, the *Mail*. It is possible that the *Mail*, a traditionally Conservative paper, viewed the demonstrations as a chance to humiliate Prime Minister Blair and his Labour government. Here, the protests were characterized in leader articles from 17 February 2003 as "a howl of rage over lies and spin" and "a massive demonstration of distrust of no confidence [sic] in Tony Blair and his New Labour Government." For the remaining newspapers we either did not find direct editorial commentary (for example in the *Guardian*) or found arguments against the anti-war objective of the demonstrations. In the latter case, it is notable that papers felt compelled to address the substance of the movement's anti-war message, and most did so quite respectfully. Examining the coverage as a whole, it was only in the *Sun* and, to a lesser extent, the *News of the World* that sympathetic treatment was more difficult to find. We should also note, however, that clearly negative comment pieces were present in most newspapers, including the *Independent* and *Guardian*.

Moving to the post-invasion phase, we found a significantly reduced focus on anti-war activity. Initially this decline is consistent with weakening anti-war sentiment in Britain. Polling by YouGov indicates that most Britons continued to support the war throughout most of the 12 months following the major combat phase. From May 2004 onwards, however, a growing majority would characterize the invasion as "wrong."[11] But this trend was not mirrored by a corresponding increase in newspaper coverage of dissent. Indeed, there was a decline in press attention paid to key demonstrations in the post-war period.

There was, however, one key exception to this trend: the demonstrations held to coincide with George W. Bush's visit to the UK in November 2003. Stories referring to planned mass protests against Bush's visit were evident months in advance of the president's arrival, and the actual demonstrations received substantial media coverage during the visit. Iraq was one of several issues the protesters wanted to address, and reporting of this event focused primarily on security concerns or the importance of US-UK relations. Nonetheless, Bush's visit stands out among post-war protest activity, as reflected by the largest peak in post-war protest coverage in Figure 1 above. Beyond this event, the dominant trend is towards more limited coverage of anti-war activity, especially in comparison to the extensive reporting of pre-war demonstrations.

This trend is evident in coverage of street demonstrations that were staged in March of 2004, 2005 and 2006 to mark the anniversary of the 2003 invasion. By the time of the 2005 demonstration, the rallying cry had shifted from "Stop the War" to "Troops Out." The first two of these involved perhaps 50,000 protesters each, but the 2006 demonstration was somewhat smaller (the police estimate was 15,000).[12] The decline in turnout seems to relate to the fact that, although an increasing percentage of Britons disagreed with the decision to go to war, the number of people calling for "immediate withdrawal" represented a distinct minority.[13] In contrast to the extensive reporting of the million-strong 15 February 2003 demonstration, for which we found 184 stories, we observed respectively 27, 16 and 10 stories that mentioned these anniversary protests. The higher number of protest stories in 2004 relates in part to a stunt by Greenpeace protesters who climbed Big Ben, sparking a debate over security capabilities which raised the spectre of an Al-Qaeda terrorist attack ("These two climbed Big Ben for a stunt. But they could have been Al-Qaeda killers," *News of the World*, 21 March 2003). Looking at the tone of coverage, we found very little editorial reinforcement for these anniversary demonstrations. In the *Mirror*, *Guardian* and *Independent*, there were a small number of supportive, by-lined commentary pieces, and coverage in these titles was usually a little more detailed. With these exceptions, however, and the more thorough coverage of the 2004 Big Ben stunt, the dominant trend across the press as a whole was towards brief articles or passing references.

Discussion and conclusions

Overall then, the case of British news coverage of the anti-war movement tells two stories. Our main analysis found that, in the days prior to military action and for a brief period after the start of the war, coverage of protest activity was fairly extensive and played more positively than negatively for the anti-war movement. We observed a similar pattern in pre-war coverage generally, finding high levels of protest coverage in January, February and March 2003. We also found ample evidence of generous and sympathetic reporting of the million-strong rally of 15 February 2003. So, the data here suggest that, prior to military action, the UK anti-war movement operated within a sphere of "legitimated controversy" (Hallin, 1986) and that sections of the UK press functioned as an "advocate of the underdog" (Wolfsfeld, 1997), producing largely mixed or positive coverage. Although coverage was to become more negative over time, this finding reflects an unusual and probably unprecedented degree of reporting favourable to a wartime protest movement. It also provides some support to recent notions that media framing of protest has become less negative (Cottle, 2008) and implies a measure of increased power amongst protest movements due to new communications technology (Bennett et al., 2008; Gillan, Pickerill, & Webster, 2008). In addition, the variation between newspapers that we found is indicative of at least a measure of plurality within the UK media system. As we argue in *Pockets of Resistance* (Robinson et al., 2010; see also Goddard, Robinson, & Parry, 2008), classic models of media deference (e.g., Bennett, 1990; Hallin, 1986), which tend to predict a homogenous and deferential media, require modification in the UK context.

Crucially though, after this initial period, coverage came to conform more to the expectations of the traditional research literature. With the war in progress, even the interjections of prominent politicians were deemed unacceptable by most media outlets, as reflected in the treatment of Robin Cook and George Galloway. Cook's treatment in particular seems to illustrate the limits of "legitimate controversy" during wartime. When he voiced opposition to war before the invasion and then resigned when his Government proceeded with it, he received favourable coverage. However, when, nearly two weeks into the war, he reasserted his opposition and appeared to call for an immediate withdrawal of British troops, he was broadly criticized. Before the invasion, then, anti-war dissent was apparently part of the "sphere of legitimate controversy" (Hallin, 1986), but by the time of Cook's second intervention and Galloway's remarks this sphere had narrowed sufficiently to push such sentiment into a "sphere of deviance" (Hallin, 1986). Coverage of anti-war activity remained at relatively low levels also throughout most of the post-invasion period. In the case of anniversary protests held in March of 2004, 2005 and 2006, we identified both diminished (and declining) coverage and fewer signs of clearly favourable media treatment. Moreover, "elite" dissenters received most favourable coverage overall among anti-war actors. Our findings vis-à-vis "elite" versus "non-elite" dissent are consistent with other research into "elite" voices and access to media, such as Bennett's "indexing hypothesis" (1990) and Entman and Page's (1994: 84) observation in an analysis of the 1991 Gulf War that attention to critics and supporters of the war was calibrated according to their power to influence war policy. The large-scale absence of reference to substantive anti-war rationales in coverage of non-elite protest also conforms to the expectation of the "protest paradigm" that coverage will concentrate on the "spectacle" of protest demonstrations rather than the message the protesters are trying to convey (McLeod & Detenber, 1999: 3).

In terms of understanding war, media and protest at a broader level, what lessons should we draw from this study? First, despite claims about the increased capacity of protest groups to mobilize support due to the emergence of new forms of communication technology (Bennett, Breunig, & Givens, 2008; Gillan, Pickerill, & Webster, 2008; Cottle, 2006), the evidence here indicates that there exists a relatively brief window of opportunity during which substantial and positive access to mainstream media has the potential to influence political outcomes. This occurred during the run-up to war, when opinions were divided and public opposition to military conflict was strong. After this, the implicit patriotic norm of "support our boys" operating across political, public and media spectrums worked against the potency of an anti-war movement. In addition, the fact that the major parties avoided making subsequent calls to withdraw from Iraq generated an elite consensus to maintain British forces in the country. Whatever success the anti-war movement might have had in terms of maintaining a presence and organizing demonstrations, its influence on mainstream media and debate waned. In short, developments in communication technology (ease of communication, alternative media, the Internet and so on), however empowering in the run-up to war, become secondary to broader structural imperatives such as patriotism and the tendency of mainstream media to index (Bennett, 1990) news to elite political opinion.

Second, there are obvious parallels between our findings in the case of UK-based protest during and after the 2003 Iraq invasion and previous studies (Gitlin, 1980; Hallin,1986) of protest during the Vietnam war. Despite the passing of 40 years, the "protest paradigm" is clearly not moribund. And yet, whatever the reality, Vietnam has been remembered by many, perhaps most, as a war in which domestic dissent and an oppositional media undermined the ability of the US government to "win." It will be interesting to see to what extent a similar set of claims arise vis-à-vis the 2003–2009 Iraq conflict as well as the continuing war in Afghanistan. Indeed, some commentators have already started to promote the idea of there being a new era of chaos in which political control has been lost to the imperatives of a new and chaotic information environment (for an unrestrained account along these lines, see Gowing, 2009). At the same time, on the eve of his departure from office, Tony Blair described the British news media as a "feral beast" during a lecture at the University of Oxford Reuters Institute (Blair, 2007). As the history of the Iraq conflict starts to be written, and events in Afghanistan continue to unfurl, it will be important to keep in check this side of political and scholarly debate. As with the Vietnam war, the sources of discontent and failure surrounding Iraq policy are more likely to be found in the course of events themselves, the casualty counts flowing from the conflict and the material failures of policy makers rather than in some notions of an influential protest movement and a cantankerous and oppositional media.

Notes

1. This research was funded by the Economic and Social Research Council (ESRC): RES-000–23–0551; "Media Wars: News Media Performance and Media Management During

the 2003 Iraq War", Award holders: Piers Robinson, Peter Goddard, Robin Brown and Phil Taylor. Some material here has appeared in the *European Journal of Communication* (Murray et al., 2008). All correspondence should be sent to Piers Robinson, piers.robinson@ manchester.ac.uk.

2. See "Support for war surges," *Guardian*, 25 March 2003: 1.
3. YouGov, "Part 6 of War Tracker," 31 March 2003, and "Iraq War Right or Wrong," 15 June 2007, www.yougov.co.uk/corporate/archives/press-archives-pol-Main.asp?iID=1 (accessed 12 February 2009).
4. BBC News (online), "Millions join global anti-war protests," 17 February 2003 (accessed 29 March 2010).
5. Several factors guided our decision to restrict our analysis of anti-Iraq War dissent to press coverage: newspaper material was more readily accessible (via LexisNexis) and significantly more detailed and diverse than television coverage. Our comparison of different time periods also made it necessary to narrow the focus of the analysis. Additionally, in 2003 online newspapers lacked the significance and authority that they have since gained. However, for an overview of television reporting on anti-war dissent during the 2003 invasion, see Robinson et al., 2010).
6. See note 1.
7. Due to the large number of news articles, coders selected the three major news stories from each page of the "Iraq War" section. This ensured that all significant articles were analysed and only brief articles excluded from analysis. Articles written by experts, "news in brief" and political sketches were omitted. The occurrence and subject description of excluded stories (n = 444) were noted in the database. The coding handbook, containing instructions on which articles to exclude, is available from the authors.
8. In reporting our findings below, we have aggregated anti-coalition and pro-antiwar codes for subject tone, as well as pro-coalition and anti-antiwar.
9. These figures for quotations cover all anti-war actors in our sample, not just British dissenters.
10. For a list of demonstrations between the invasion and the fall of Baghdad, including estimates for turnout, see Wikipedia: http://en.wikipedia.org/wiki/Protests_against_the_ Iraq_War#Invasion_to_the_fall_of_Baghdad–accessed 12 February 2009.
11. YouGov, www.yougov.co.uk/corporate/archives/press-archives-pol-Main.asp?iID=1 (accessed 11 January 2009).
12. Organizers' estimates and police estimates vary for every demonstration. With respect to the post-war demonstrations mentioned above, organizers claimed up to 100,000 protesters at every rally, while police estimates were 25,000 for 2004, 45,000 for 2005 and 15,000 for 2006.
13. YouGov, www.yougov.co.uk/corporate/archives/press-archives-pol-Main.asp?iID=1 (accessed 11 January 2009).

CHAPTER FIVE

On Anti-Iraq War Protests and the Global News Sphere

STEPHEN D. REESE

As social protests have become transnationalized, so too have the media platforms on which they play out. They have become mediatized: designed with media in mind and dependent on media for their success—none more so perhaps than the anti-war protest movement. One could say that globalized anti-war expression came of age with the world protests of post-9/11 US military action in Afghanistan and Iraq, particularly the globally coordinated and boundary-spanning protests by millions of people on 15 February 2003, which anticipated the unilateral decision of the Bush Administration to invade Iraq in March. Called the largest mass protest in history, the rally in Rome was considered at the time as the largest single anti-war rally. One participant in New York was quoted as saying "I came to go to the rally and be a part of a *global voice* against going to war against Iraq again" (McFadden, 2003). A combination of faith groups, non-governmental organizations (NGOs), trade unions and peace groups have mobilized since 2002 to become perhaps the largest anti-war movement in history. A global-scale movement like this one engages a similarly globally scaled media, but we are only just beginning to understand that dynamic relationship. In this chapter, I consider how to approach this transnational phenomenon in light of the global journalism supporting it.

As a social phenomenon, protests are the visible and concrete face of public opinion, and no longer merely a local expression but one that is globally directed. Whether with war or other issues, we need to ask what happens when both protests and media become global—and how the relationship changes between them and with policy makers? What are the prospects for social protest in this new media environment, especially protest against state actors with their own agenda and framing power? Certainly, these transnational links help invigorate the global public sphere, where the military policy of superpowers is more subject to critique than ever before. The world watches as the media cover globally staged and coordinated public events.

When considering transnational protests, anti-war movements can easily be grouped with other global issues, whether humanitarian, ecological, or anti-authoritarian. These movements and their various public actions are often inter-connected ideologically, with anti-(economic) globalization protesters, for example, finding common cause with anti-nuclear and environmental groups. The terrain of political struggle in the world has become "global" in the sense proposed by Hardt and Negri (2000) that these struggles have become economic, political, and cultural, all at once. Struggles in Tiananmen Square, the Los Angeles riots, Chiapas, and the Intifada, are all particular to their specific situation; they aren't commensurable in the sense of worker revolutions that find a common internationalist language but have in common the fact that they do speak to global forces with which each grapples. In Hardt and Negri's conception of "Empire," these movements take on meaning as a group only as they pass through the level of global citizenship more generally. Thus, they jump to the supranational, global level, without linking up horizontally with corresponding local movements.

Taken as a whole or separately, the transnational coordination of these issue-movements and emerging transnational media platforms give these groups a larger voice than would have been the case otherwise. The issue of war, however, raises its own particular concerns. International conflict has always been with us, but when carried out by super-powers like the US, wars have been rapid-onset issues that have provoked the strongest and most concentrated public opposition. Anti-authoritarian regime protests may bring international pressure to bear and hasten political change, and pro-environmental or human rights demonstrations may put issues on the table that hadn't been there before. In the case of anti-war protests, however, they face national policies that have already been set in motion. Wars by superpowers are energetically promoted by their instigators and sold with their own narrative support, a discourse that must be confronted by opponents if they are to be successful. Anti-war protests, then, take place within a more explicit framing context with which they must contend.

The globalized anti-war movement demonstrates an important development in the flow of political influence through transnational networks—and in recent years shows evidence of having significant political consequences. National elites must increasingly take world opinion into account, since their own citizens are part of those networks and have easy access to coverage of major events. This extends beyond the old conception of the "CNN-effect," where the media spotlight causes actions by raising awareness of a particular humanitarian concern in the world. The anti-war movement represents a specific political struggle, changing the balance of power between state actors and citizens. Although dissent seemed easily marginalized two decades ago in the days of Desert Storm, the 1991 US-led conflict with Iraq, the more diffused current media environment does not permit such easy dismissal of the public voice. The protest of the more recent Iraq invasion of 2003 revealed a widespread opposition to American military policy and had serious political fallout. Certainly, in Spain and the UK, national policy was at odds with public opinion—contributing in the case of the Spanish election of 2004 to the rejection of the prime minister in favor of an anti-war candidate.

The levels through which this political influence flows have been redistributed, through a combination of changing media platforms and transnational organizing. Social protest has traditionally been understood within the political context of the host culture, and in earlier days the idea of anti-war protest was relatively straightforward. Public expressions of social protest would be staged in hopes of influencing local and national officials. Whether public demonstrations were intended for local or distant policy makers, it was possible to trace the lines of influence more easily. During the anti-Vietnam War protests, US university campuses were the sites of regular demonstrations, which were designed to affect local institutions but also play to a national audience. In 1967, for example, students at the University of Wisconsin sought to prevent Dow Chemical company, the maker of napalm, from recruiting on campus, a position that nested within a larger national political movement. Of course, the North Vietnamese leadership was well aware of US protests against the war and regarded them as an important political asset in their own strategic planning. The primary audience for such demonstrations, however, was the university, the corporate programs it hosted, and the national administration. The anti-war message had a very specific political objective within the host culture. Now these expressions are staged for a more wide-spread audience.

Protests and national frames

Anti-war protests must contend with the political issue culture that was exploited to launch military action in the first place. As Smith (2005) argues from a cultural sociology perspective, cultural codes are invoked to legitimize military action. War is not just something that elites decide to do, with the help of public relations techniques. They make use of pre-existing cultural resources and genres of interpretation to mobilize support. The most extreme genre, "apocalyptic," pushes the good and bad guys to their most divergent and, according to Smith, is the only narrative capable of mobilizing mass support for warfare by making it culturally acceptable. But it is also most susceptible to being deflated when factual discrepancies are discovered. As an expression of power, wars happen when policy actors successfully align their goals with favorable cultural codes. Thus, the anti-war movements have had to assert a counter-narrative if they are to successfully derail decisions to move toward military action. These counter-frames are developed as movements interact with media routines and systems, with the transnational dimension helping to destabilize the "good guys/bad guys" distinction and highlight issues of factual discrepancy.

The US conflicts with Iraq since 1990 show the changing role of media coverage from the CNN video-war period of Desert Storm to the much more globalized news environment of the Bush administration's invasion of Iraq in 2003. Social protest against these conflicts has confronted greatly different news cultures in the period spanning the two conflicts. The Persian Gulf War of 1991 provided the most dramatic example until then of war as spectacle, with the media strongly implicated in its construction (Kellner, 1992). The merits of the decision to use military force to push Saddam Hussein out of Kuwait took a back seat to the dramatic emphasis on the showdown between the first President Bush and Hussein, the setting of a 15 January deadline for withdrawal, and the use of high-tech weapons once war was launched. The media seemed disturbingly pro-war in the logic of coverage, relying on military officials and former military figures to help frame the conflict to the exclusion of opposition and peace groups. In spite of seeking UN approval, this seemed more like a rubber stamp, with the international community taking a back seat to White House decision-making. Ultimately, the introduction of foreign troops into Saudi Arabia sowed the seeds of Islamic extremists' resentment toward the US role in the Middle East, but this and other issues of historical context figured little in media coverage.

Within that context, the Desert Storm period featured a predictable marginalization of protest to the war. Research on news coverage of anti-war protest within a specific geographical community revealed frames that managed the protest within comfortable ideological boundaries, particularly in making it difficult to disentangle criticism of the policy from the support for American troops. Anti-war protests had a difficult time combating the narrative of the administration (Reese, 2004; Reese & Buckalew, 1995). Since Desert Storm, however, new more global communities have become crucial venues for protest.

The attacks by Al-Qaeda in 2001 against targets in New York and Washington, D.C., dramatically demonstrated the globalization of war itself and the importance of non-state actors. When the administration of George W. Bush framed the post-9/11 military strategy as the Global War on Terror, the narrative became irresistible to the US press. The frame located the conflicts within a war between good and evil, a Manichaean struggle between the forces of freedom and enslavement. Depicting the enemy as the Axis of Evil connected the policy to the "Good War" of World War II and the Axis powers of Japan and Nazi Germany. By depicting the enemy as an undifferentiated threat, the War on Terror provided the discursive foundation for linking the attacks on September 11th to Iraq, rendering it what Bush would term a "vital front" in the larger conflict.

This frame was widely adopted through the US press, in spite of its flaws as a guide for policy (Lewis & Reese, 2008; Reese & Lewis, 2009). Even within the national security community, Record (2003) argued that the Global War on Terror's insistence on moral clarity lacked strategic focus, that its open-ended quest for absolute security is not politically sustainable and risks involving the military in conflicts it is not designed to fight, much less win. Former National Security Adviser Zbigniew Brzezinski (2004) argued similarly. Critics on the left regarded it as a front for an imperialistic project (Chomsky, 2002), feared its threat to a greater sense of "world community" or more generally rejected what they saw as an unconditional and uncritical celebration of American life (e.g., Falk, 2002). Framing terrorism as the global equivalent of a hijacking brackets off criticism of state actors as they reassert their authority in dealing with threats to security, and state-sponsored terrorism is excluded from consideration (see also Reese, 2010a).

In the post-9/11 launching of the "Global War on Terror" by the Bush administration, selling the policy met with success domestically, marshaling the support of the US public and leading a majority of them to believe that Saddam Hussein was behind the 9/11 attacks. Although, the decisions to go to war must be sold at home, they also quickly become important centerpieces of global discourse as well. Within the global community issue frames will always be more multi-lateral, with non-US journalists more likely to challenge the administration discourse with less parochial perspectives. Compared to previous periods, the emerging global news arena made it more difficult for the US to monopolize the coverage, and the wide dissemination of global protest activities made this much more clear.

The narratives of the various sides in conflicts are now more available. Certainly, the presence of news outlets like the Qatar-based satellite network, Al-Jazeera, makes it less likely that the "enemy" would remain faceless, and the sanitization of battle that characterized Desert Storm was not as easy in the second Gulf War, the US-led Iraq invasion. Scenes of civilian casualties and property damage made information-management more difficult for administration officials seeking to maintain public support at home and beyond.

In the case of Bush policies and military interventions, these decisions have not been well received outside the country, as indicated by international polling trends. At the same time the War on Terror was being effectively sold at home, the rest of the world was rapidly losing confidence in the US and its policies. Poll results from the Pew Center Global Attitudes Project show that world opinion toward the US slipped considerably during the Bush years. The US brand in general and the perception that American influence was a positive force in the world slipped during that decade but has shown signs of revival with the election of President Obama, a much more popular figure in Europe and most of the rest of the world. It's a logical inference to attribute those differences to the kinds of policies promoted in the Bush years, particularly the tendency to go it alone in environmental and military decisions, with relatively little regard for multi-lateral global cooperation. Perhaps it wasn't surprising that in claiming for itself a unique role in the right to launch unilaterally preemptive military action, the US image suffered in a more globally distributed court of public opinion. The precipitous decline in poll numbers further suggests that the global media played a part in amplifying the disquiet, allowing the resentments and suspicions toward the US to quickly find a broader audience. That, of course, leads to asking what is the nature of that global platform now?

We don't yet clearly know how issues aired through global news discourses circulate back into national spheres. If it was up to the rest of the world, President Obama would be reelected handily judging from the broad support he received in the global "electoral college" (an analysis provided by *The Economist* magazine on 4 November 2008). But in the increasingly polarized political climate in the US, the right-wing eagerly pounces on any suggestions of lack of patriotism. When 2004 candidate John Kerry, for example, proposed that policies be mindful of international legitimacy and meet the "global test," he was roundly rebuked for surrendering national prerogatives. The world doesn't have veto power over US decisions, but in a globalized public sphere those decisions and their legitimacy will be more closely scrutinized than ever. Indeed, that 2004 election pointed to an important fault line between US and world opinion. In order to be politically successful, American leaders may need to take nationalistic positions that don't resonate well with the rest of the world. But the American public is also able to receive news from the rest of the world and may become more aware of world opinion as a political consideration. This notion is part of a larger hope for "media globalization," that it may support a more cosmopolitan "global village" public sphere, which will mitigate against conflicts based on nationalistic urges.

Media globalization

Understanding the new context for anti-war protests requires understanding the media environment in which they take place. Because their intended audience is global, they play an important role in the transnational flow of information through new systems of global journalism. The crucial aspect of a globalized journalism is not some vast scale, but the news source, producer, and audience no longer necessarily share the same national frame of reference. If that is the case, then by what logic is this journalism guided? Understanding the role of transnational protests in this kind of media environment requires an understanding of the global news sphere and its changing relationships to political structures.

The great interest from communication scholars in "media globalization" suggests the tight relationship between media and the globalization process, each reinforcing the other. This has led to high expectations for international journalism in producing a global public sphere, where world issues can be clearly understood and responded to with a strengthened sense of global consciousness. A few clearly transnational news forms have emerged, particularly in the form of satellite news networks like CNN. Among print media, business-oriented media such as the *International Herald Tribune, Wall St. Journal Europe* and the *Financial Times* have been particularly effective in claiming this role given the global appeal and portability of commerce. Otherwise, media globalization skeptics argue that no truly transnational news platforms have emerged, permitting the kind of cross-boundary dialogs associated with a public sphere (e.g., Sparks, 2007). Indeed, critics like Kai Hafez suggest that regional enclaves, linguistic divides, and parochial zones of ethnocentric discourse have become even more sharply defined (Hafez, 2007). Such skeptics point to the continued weaknesses of international reporting: elite-focused, conflict-based, and focused on scandal and the sensational. World events are processed through the same national filters as before, leading them to conclude that the "global village" has been blocked by domestication (reviewed in Reese, 2010b).

Emerging global news platforms have tempted others to regard them as a new and separate "space." Volkmer (1999) theorized that global political communication (into which she groups CNN, Al-Jazeera, and extra-territorial Chinese websites) feeds a correspondingly global public sphere, which in turn yields global civil society, where communication is made possible in ways not otherwise available at the national level. I'm more inclined to agree with Hjarvard (2001), who argues that there is no new autonomous zone that we may call the global public sphere, operating in parallel with existing national spheres. The globalization of the public sphere is a process, in which national zones have become deterritorialized and connected in new ways. The media role in all of this should not be narrowly regarded as the specific message, medium, or audience—the "CNN version" of media globalization. In the case of journalism, I go so far as to picture a "global news arena" as the visible face of these systemic changes in global interconnectivity (Reese, 2008).

The entire world need not be tuned into the same news broadcast, or news products need not become completely homogenized, for us to say that the media system has become more in tune with itself. One perceives the "world as a single place"—the central image of globalization—in the sense that there is an increasingly well-defined agenda of news and issues circulating around the globe. Shifts in the attention of the world press now take place at a rapid pace, with various national, regional, and local media reacting to and expanding on what is available in a new capacity for mutual awareness and reflexivity. This reconfigured and expanded world news grid has become dramatically apparent in recent years, especially when powered to the highest levels with major events such as September 11, terrorist actions designed as the ultimate global media event.

Globalizing impulses

The media globalization debates have centered on whether a truly global news sphere is emerging, permitting undistorted opportunities for cross-boundary dialogs. By focusing on the media system and its audiences, skeptics argue that no such sphere has or likely will emerge in the new term. People prefer their own national fare, and linguistic divides prevent much cross-culture platforms, other than for the privileged elite who travel easily and consume the global news content intended for them. But there are other globalizing impulses that work to support a more supranational expression, including the anti-war movement and related protests. "Global" in this context refers to the cross-border and deterritorialized aspect rather than a particularly huge scale. Global protests, as coordinated expression, serve as a centripetal force for the world news agenda, operating against the domestication of the issues into the various national spheres.

Journalists themselves are globalizing, beyond the traditional "foreign correspondents," even if we cannot easily classify a special group of "global journalists" [although the phrase can make for a compelling label (Reese, 2001; Weaver, 1998)]. Even when away from home journalists continue for the most part to work on behalf of a specific national audience and domesticate their coverage accordingly. Coverage, for example, of such international events as world political summits led Hallin and Mancini (1992) to observe how rooted journalists still are in country and professional culture. They go on to suggest, however, that greater global-level cohesion among journalists will emerge when more international institutions develop for journalists to congregate around, such as now is the case with financial reporting, centered as it is around commonly understood world economic structures (Corcoran & Fahy, 2009). Beyond these new formal structures, they suggest that major events of global interest may propel newsgathering toward a more globally coordinated journalism.

Much has happened since they made those observations, and the number of such global events has increased steadily. The scale of world anti-war protests certainly fit this criterion. Hallin and Mancini suggest that international political summits, by drawing together world journalists, generate a dialogue that may be considered a quasi-international public sphere and that the institutionalization of the world press corps plays a highly visible—if symbolic—role in such events. Globally organized anti-war protests don't have the same official underpinnings but may have the same result, especially when organized in tandem with such events as G8 summits of major political leaders or the World Economic Forum. From the standpoint of the anti-war movement, coordinators hope that journalists covering such protests would approach the issue with a broader professional and cosmopolitan mindset than just reflecting their respective national news cultures.

The extent to which these global anti-war events are translated into a respectful hearing in the world press will ultimately be indicated by the kind of news coverage that results. Indeed, research has begun to consider the extent to which news contains certain intrinsically global issues and perspectives (Berglez, 2008). Others have looked more specifically at the content of explicitly "global" satellite news media like CNN International and BBC World, finding that these programs contained frames with the potential to move beyond "dominance" to cultural recognition—acknowledging and affirming cultural differences (Cottle & Rai, 2008). To the extent that national media and others in the global media hierarchy take their cues from such organizations, and their relatively more cosmopolitan outlook, perhaps the globalized anti-war message will find a more supportive platform than in any one country itself. Of course, others emphasize that global news agencies and satellite networks are prey to the same superficial and sensationalistic tendencies as any national media (Paterson, 2001; Thussu & Freedman, 2003), but this is something to sort out further in future studies.

The anti-war movement connects to other organized movements for economic justice, human rights, and environmental protection. As the array of issues with global dimensions grows, so does the importance of the layer of civil society represented by NGOs. These organizations play an important coordinating function in promoting a vigorous transnational message, but this important zone of interstitial influence between government and corporate structures has received scarcely any scholarly attention. As Cottle and Nolan (2007) point out, the NGOs have adapted to the same media logic that affects other competers for the media spotlight, especially in the increasingly crowded humanitarian aid field. The use of celebrities and compelling visuals makes it more likely that an NGO's brand will be established effectively. In the case of the anti-war movement, organized protests are usually formed by a coalition of such groups finding common cause.

Conclusion

In this chapter I have tried to combine two concerns, one grounded in research and the other more speculative. In the first case, I have observed how easy it is for anti-war dissent to be marginalized by the mainstream media, rooted as they are in con-flict-oriented, sensationalistic coverage, which relies heavily on officials and the military establishment for framing issues of war. These are long-standing con-cerns, but the question now is whether the new transnational media environment will disrupt these tendencies and pave the way for new ones. Although the Iraq War launched in 2003 took place within a broader, more vigorous global media environ-ment, US journalists still absorbed the national frame of reference promoted by the Bush administration and embodied in the phrase: "Global War on Terror." Even serious national-level print journalists seemed all too willing to view the conflict as "us vs. them," and "good vs. evil," a perspective that helped provide the rationale for the invasion of Iraq as a continuing response to 9/11.

The US media may have bought into the official rationale for the Iraq invasion, but the rest of the world, guided in part by new media voices such as Al-Jazeera, was less likely to go along. A casual reading of the world press following 9/11 sug-gests that a number of national regimes found the War on Terror a strategically valu-able frame for their own needs. The Russians claimed they were in a War on Terror against Chechnyan separatists, the Israelis said the same about the Palestinians, and various Asian governments could find their own targets of "terrorists" in political opponents. But citizens in general appeared less likely to accept the organizing prin-ciple of the War on Terror, as suggested by the steadily slipping image for the US and enthusiasm for the candidacy of Barack Obama, who avoided the phrase and favored greater engagement, even with pariah states like Iran.

Here it is still a matter of speculation, but there is evidence that the global news arena made for a more hospitable climate for globally coordinated anti-war protests. The centripetal tendencies of journalism professionalism and the promotion of events by inter-locking NGO interests made it more likely that these protests would be received as they were intended, as a pro-peace, anti-militarism mes-sage—transcending any one national policy context where it could be easily mar-ginalized as a less-than-patriotic discourse. More research is needed to determine what kind of environment the globalized media will ultimately provide for this kind of public expression, especially concerning such momentous issues as war and peace.

PART THREE

Protesting Economy and Trade

CHAPTER SIX

Leaderless Crowds, Self-Organizing Publics, and Virtual Masses

The New Media Politics of Dissent

ANDREW ROJECKI

Political protest is an indicator of disenchantment with institutional politics, but assessing its meaning and significance requires study of specific issue domains, historical context, the permeability of political institutions to external dissent, and the means of information transmission between political movements and the wider public. Prior to the 1990s political movements calibrated their strategies in part to anticipate the reaction of the mass media, principal carriers of movement messages to a potentially responsive public, a hopeful application of Schattschneider's proposition (1960) that "the outcome of all conflict is determined by the scope of its contagion." Until the collapse of the Soviet bloc and the proliferation of information technologies, the scope of conflict could be contained by the discursive limits imposed by political and media elites (Gitlin, 1980).

The 1999 meetings of the WTO in Seattle marked a significant inflection point in the study of the symbiosis between political movements and the mass media. The collapse of the Soviet Union had opened a widened space for market capitalism that, in turn, disturbed the equilibrium of the world political economy. Capital markets expanded beyond state borders, which further weakened the political leverage of labor by the global dispersion of corporate functions, notably manufacturing. Yet, the disappearance of the signature exemplar of opposition to capitalism deprived elites of an ideological demon for vitiating political dissent, and the rapid growth and development of a digital communication infrastructure offered the promise of reducing the power of corporate media and thereby the hegemony of state control over responses to challenges to its preferred issue frames. To be sure, elite dissensus would remain a key resource for political movements (Bennett, 2003c), but those lower in the cascade of power (Entman, 2004) seemed especially advantaged by the changed environment.

From a scholarly perspective movement politics had moved into uncharted waters because its targets were no longer exclusively the nation state but corporations and especially international governmental organizations (IGOs) that regulated economic transactions and capital flows that were indifferent to state borders. Nation states still had the power to negotiate agreements with these institutions, but negotiations were conducted in secret and seemed insulated from democratic influence. While proponents of economic globalization rationalized the process by the long-term benefits of greater economic interdependence (e.g., Wolf, 2004; Friedman, 2005), opponents objected to despoilment of local environments, exploitation of unorganized labor, and increased income inequality (Rapley, 2004). Meanwhile, the same communication infrastructure that had facilitated the global dispersion of capital and labor had also led to innovative forms of political dissent. Web-driven tools and techniques such as e-mail campaigns, meet-ups, social media, flash mobs, and tweets entered the lexicon of protest. These technically driven developments were taking place at the same time that mass media channels were proliferating across an expanded digital bandwidth, thereby fragmenting a once near-unitary mass audience across a range of socio-demographic market-driven categories. In this chapter I examine whether the fragmentation of media audiences and the proliferation of web-based communication in the years since the Seattle events have disturbed the equilibrium between political movements, political elites, and public opinion.

The Battle of Seattle

A mass demonstration in 1999 that successfully disrupted the WTO meetings in Seattle signaled a change in the focus of protest politics and in the dynamics of the protest itself. Protesters mounted a politically effective coalition with (among other key Democratic constituencies) labor unions that put Bill Clinton into the untenable position of defending the expansion of trade that would permit US corporations to shift their manufacturing operations to the cheapest labor pools in nations with no unions or environmental regulation. While Clinton was conceding the movement had a point on the exploitation of labor, protesters evaded the best efforts of the Seattle police department to prevent the shutdown of the meetings by using a variety of web-based functions to mobilize members, coordinate strategy, and provide expertise. A flat, network-based model of organization enabled protesters to use a flexible strategy of confrontation that eluded containment (Rojecki, 2002). The event also marked the birth of what came to be known as Indymedia—Independent Media Center (IMC)—a group of independent journalists who used the web to provide an alternative source of reporting freed of what they regarded as the constraints imposed by mainstream commercial media. Perhaps taking their cue from national and local political elites who could not defend WTO immunity from democratic governance, mainstream media treated the protest with much more nuance and deference than one would have expected from earlier studies of political protest during the Cold War (Rojecki, 2002; Bennett, 2003b).

The event marked the first widely reported example of transnational protest, a "coordinated international campaign on the part of networks of activists against international actors, other states, or international institutions" (della Porta & Tarrow, 2005a: 2–3). The Battle of Seattle represented a signal example of post-Cold War protest in a new media environment that called for a reassessment of the concepts and theory on the media politics of dissent (Cottle, 2008).

Transnational protest

The interaction of a new communication environment with political dissent changes our perceptions of the nature and significance of demonstration and protest, a crucial point when one considers what Simon Cottle points out is the degree to which protesters are "reflexively conditioned by their pursuit of media attention" (2008: 853). This is a necessary consideration given the goal of movements for spreading the level of contagion. Several examples illustrate the analytical challenges of understanding the contemporary nature of contentious politics. In the spring of 2010, for example, 18,000 high school students walked out of their suburban New Jersey classrooms in response to an appeal posted on Facebook to protest voter rejection of school board budgets (Hu, 2010: 19). In the words of its author, "All I did was make a Facebook page. . . . Anyone who has an opinion could do that and have their opinion heard."

Similarly, a Facebook page critical of high fructose corn syrup (HFCS) and, by extension, of the subsidized agribusiness that manufactured it, drew the approval of 120,000 "fans." An equally impressively sized audience viewed YouTube videos that mocked industry's subsequent defense of its product, an indication of mainstream opposition that by 2009 had reduced its consumption of HCFS by nine percent. So effective was this consumer-driven boycott that in 2010 ConAgra announced it would eliminate the syrup from their Hunt's ketchup line (Warner, 2010). Meanwhile, a wave of protests under the umbrella of what came to be known as the Tea (taxed enough already) Party movement used the same Web 2.0 technology to disseminate its arguments and appeals for reducing the scope of US government intervention in the capital and health markets. Some politicians who subscribed to the movement's goals (or at least incorporated its issue frames into their campaign rhetoric) had by 2010 won primaries and even been elected to office.

For the New Jersey high school students, health-minded opponents of corn syrup, and tea-partiers, social media afforded a low-cost means of reaching, informing, and persuading individuals that by-passed a traditional media strategy for spreading the scope of conflict. Do alternative information media alter the dynamics of political protest? Have the tactics of contemporary movements changed because of their increased independence from mainstream media? What role do traditional media play in the new politics of dissent? Research, largely on transnational protest and much of that on the so-called anti-globalization movement, offers some answers.

New movement politics

Over the last decade scholars of the politics of dissent have focused on the strategies and tactics of a movement known variously as the movement for global justice, against neoliberal globalization, or more popularly (though inaccurately) as the anti-globalization movement (hereafter I will refer to it as the global social justice movement, the name used often by its participants). The movement is not opposed to the integration of the world economy but to the absence of transparency in and democratic control of its governing institutions, corporate evasion of labor laws and environmental protection, and issues related to sustainable development and human rights (James, 2000). Though the movement has multiple targets in its sights, local and global (Klein, 2001), much of its most visible action is directed at IGOs. Its importance to scholars is its status as a transnational movement, one that responds to the unique historical situation that enabled its birth (della Porta & Tarrow, 2005a).

Scholars who sought to map the multiple changes in this movement's strategies and tactics opened new theoretical grounds for explaining such things as the resurgence of once quiescent political structures (e.g., NGOs) and seemingly spontaneous outbursts of collective dissent. McAdam, Tarrow, and Tilly (2001) formulated the concept of scale shift to define the broadening of protest beyond state borders and della Porta and Tarrow (2005a) coined the concepts of diffusion, domestication, and externalization to map the dynamics of protest that hopscotched national borders. Skeptics, meanwhile, doubted the staying power of these new political actors or the promise of an energized public sphere. Capitalism had retained and even enhanced its ideological power, and states continued to rely on nationalism to shore up their political power, especially in times of crisis. The fall of the World Trade Center on 11 September 2001 may have brought down the symbols of US economic prowess, but it reinvigorated the power of the national security state as it sought to eradicate the network of young Muslim radicals who used the same new communication infrastructure to coordinate their asymmetrical campaign of terror against the US and its allies. One of the principal diagnoses of al-Qaeda terrorism was economic inequality and the political unrest this provoked, remedies for which included the strengthening of the state and the promotion of neoliberal economic policy (Rojecki, 2004). In this sense, the elite dissensus on free trade policy that existed at the time of the Seattle WTO meetings had nearly disappeared after 9/11. That thus far the reaction against the global economic downturn of the late 2000s has focused less on neoliberalism than on government application of Keynesian economic policy lends further support for this conclusion. The fate of movement success hinges on the interaction of its specific tactics with the openness of domestic and international institutions to the politics of dissent.

Political opportunity and movement structure

Because the targets of the global social justice movement include IGOs, the state, and individual corporations, it is difficult to assess its effectiveness in broad strokes. One way to begin is to map the susceptibility of these targets to specific movement tactics but also to assess the structure of political opportunity at the domestic and international levels. Although the dynamics of globalization by definition transcend conventional political boundaries, the global social justice movement nonetheless operates in a political arena demarcated by national borders (Tarrow, 2001) and governed by international institutions. Sikkink (2005) proposes a model of multilevel governance that specifies the openness of domestic and international institutions to dissent as important causal variables. In the model, the Battle of Seattle represents an instance of international institutions resistant to external influence (e.g., the WTO) and domestic politics open to dissent. By contrast the incipient Iranian Green Revolution is an instance of domestic repression amid a sympathetic (though as yet ineffectual) set of international actors and institutions. As with the "Great Fire Wall" of China, the latter case reveals the utopian optimism of theories that elevate the primacy of modern communication technology for leading to democratic reform, at least in the short run.

Superimposed on these national boundaries and fields of international institutional power are networks of activists whose organizational structure reflects their immersion in the dispersed communication technology of the Internet and the world-wide web. Scholars have adopted the network metaphor for developing a conceptual and theoretical vocabulary for their analysis of transnational movements, and what one notices immediately is the fruitful heuristic nature of that metaphor. For example, unlike the Civil Rights and New Left movements that preceded it, what is most striking about the global social justice movement is its facelessness, fluidity, and organizational anonymity (note this is also true for the US tea partiers). A large number of networked individuals of indeterminate identity (nodes) linked to each other and to organizations that come and go (hubs) have replaced the charisma of readily identifiable leaders. The consequences of this low-cost membership are resilience that avoids the pitfalls of coalition building, compromise on a single issue, and cooptation but also lack of ideological clarity and coherence (Bennett, 2005). But there are other factors in play as well.

What Bennett defines as the ideological thinness of the movement is an overdetermined effect that largely results from the numerous interests involved in the coalition. Thus a campaign against Microsoft included competing businesses such as Sun and Oracle, consumer protection organizations, "hacktivists" (individuals who engage in civil cyber disobedience, e.g., flooding a web-site with numerous requests and thereby effectively shutting it down), and even a Republican Senator (Bennett, 2003b). From this broad spectrum conflicting interests inevitably arise, making it difficult to sustain a coherent and powerful "collective action frame" (Snow & Benford, 1992; see, e.g., Van Aelst & Walgrave, 2004 and le Grignou & Patou, 2004, for case studies that draw conflicting conclusions). It is also possible that the low costs of involvement explain corresponding low commitment and weakness of self-identification (see Finke & Stark, 2005 for an application of this proposition in the religious domain). It is one thing to sign a petition on a Facebook page and quite another to give time to a political campaign for a candidate committed to a movement goal.

But perhaps the most important reason for the movement's ideological thinness is its inherently reformist nature. It is not opposed to global market capitalism per se, merely its operation and governance. It is unclear further whether a hard-edged critique can be launched from what theorists have noted are the consumption-driven lifestyle and identity politics of postmodern society (e.g., Jameson, 1984; Giddens, 1991; Castells, 1997). Bennett (2003b) argues that individual narratives linked to networks of other such lifestyle narratives have displaced hierarchical institutions as sources of identification and social recognition. Some theorists (Castells, 1996; Arquilla & Ronfeldt, 2001) declare this seeming weakness a strength: robust and adaptable, networks of activists are led more by a reliable common political agenda than a potentially vulnerable centralized leadership. Harcourt and Escobar's (2002) concept of "meshworks" addresses the "self-organizing" dynamics of a movement embedded (and constituted) in a communication network:

> [M]eshworks tend to be nonhierarchical and self-organizing. They are created out of the interlocking of heterogeneous and diverse elements brought together because of complementarity or common experiences. They grow in unplanned directions. Anti-globalization social movements, in their heterogeneity and self-organizing character, might be seen as incipient meshworks of this kind. Meshworks involve two parallel dynamics: strategies of localization and of interweaving. Localization strategies contribute to the internal consistency of each particular point in the network, as well as making it more distinct from the rest. Interweaving, on the other hand, links sites together, making use of and emphasizing their similarities. The resulting meshworks of the antiglobalization movement, for example, could be in the position of holding the big financial and development institutions more accountable for the hierarchies they continue to support. (Harcourt & Escobar, 2002: 12–13)

In an analysis of the participants in the European Social Forum (ESF), della Porta (2005) coined the concept of "tolerant identity" to characterize the diversity and overlapping identities of the participants in the Florence counter-demonstration to the G8 Genoa summit. People from diverse backgrounds could agree on short-term concrete goals, on "immediately gratifying action" rather than "old style militancy." Echoing longstanding trends in the US, the left-leaning participants in the ESF had become wary and distrustful of institutionalized politics. Politically emergent and diffuse in structure, the movement is also polymorphous in its tactical repertoire.

New movement tactics and effectiveness

Despite its remove from precursors such as the Civil Rights and Anti-War movements of the Cold War era, the global social justice movement has relied nevertheless on familiar confrontational activities such as sit-ins, demonstrations, and blockades and also more conventional political tactics. Patterns of research findings indicate that the use of new communication technologies has reduced the costs of mobilization but not necessarily participation across the categories of protest repertoire (Diani, 2005). The movement uses whatever mode of collective action seems effective for a specific goal, including the same tactics used by opponents, such as institutional lobbying (Fisher et al., 2005).

Though mass demonstrations and other confrontational modes of action remain part of the standard repertoire of dissent (an estimated seven million people worldwide protested the US invasion of Iraq in 2003), research points to their higher costs and risks and diminished effectiveness. For example, the movement sometimes attracts disruptive elements such as the Black Bloc, a group of anarchists who (are logically compelled to) deny they have an organization but who do otherwise agree on a set of tactics designed to provoke confrontation with the police (infoshop.org/page/Blackbloc-Faq). The ensuing vandalism and disruption guarantee mainstream media coverage and thereby a focus for elite marginalization of the movement's progressive goals. These predictable disruptions may have inadvertently led to reactive strategies, even on the part of movement organizers themselves. Anticipating disruptions, state organizers of meetings of the WTO, G8, IMF, and other IGOs have opted for remote (e.g., Doha, Qatar) or easily secured venues for their meetings. Web-based sites for mobilization and training of movement activists have also been useful for efficient design of counter-measures by political elites who have learned not to be surprised as were local Seattle authorities. Moreover, the Seattle events have led to increased cooperation, cross-training, and border control among states for crowd control, and even to negotiations between local police forces and demonstrators themselves (O'Neill, 2004).

Whether the increased costs of confrontation have put off movement organizers is uncertain, but it is the case that the movement has turned to more traditional pressure activities such as lobbying efforts and consumer awareness campaigns. Here is where the movement has had its most conspicuous success. Nike, Nestle, Monsanto, and the aforementioned HCFS are now tainted as brands because of movement projects intended to raise consumer awareness of unfair labor practices and potential dangers to health and the environment. One could argue that a movement defined by lifestyle and consumption has had its greatest success by adopting the practices and techniques of its lifestyle-creating opponents. Indeed, some movement organizations have marketing strategies that can scarcely be distinguished from their establishment foes. For example, Global Exchange, one of the pioneering organizations at the Seattle WTO protests, now offers reality tours, a gift registry, and stores where one can purchase fair trade goods and gift baskets, the latter available for corporate clients who wish to project an image of concern for social justice (globalexchange.org).

From the standpoint of broader political effects, the evidence is mixed. Bimber (2001) finds that despite the increase in information generated by movement activists and other Internet information providers, survey evidence shows little evidence of increased political activity among the general public. Nevertheless, Garrett (2006) points out that the Internet provides an astonishing potential for aggregating small monetary contributions and on-line coordination of canvassing and phone banks, thus lowering coordination costs. The most prominent example is Moveon.org—essentially a web address—that since 2004 has raised nearly US$60 million from visitors to its website.

Relevance of mainstream media

Given its success using new media, mainstream media would seem to matter less for the movement, but they remain an important albeit transformed resource. Perhaps it exaggerates the point to say that "a movement that doesn't make it into the media is non-existent" (quoted in Bennett, 2003b: 17), but issues of selective exposure, credibility, self-interest, and sheer audience reach continue to make the mainstream media a relevant factor in the new politics of dissent. The mass media may no longer be as relevant for mobilizing participation (Fisher et al., 2005; cf., Kolb, 2005), but they still matter for lending legitimacy to certain movement activities.

Is is clear that the peer-to-peer structure of Internet-based communication invites selective exposure among participants, a pattern echoed in the audience fragmentation evident in traditional media (Bennett & Iyengar, 2008; cf., Holbert et al., 2010). Still, the passive audience base for the mass media remains a valuable resource for political movements, in particular for certifying their legitimacy. Studies show that protesters still adapt to the needs and interests of journalists and regard mainstream media attention as certification of legitimacy (Kolb, 2005; Lester & Hutchins, 2009). Meanwhile, journalists themselves are skeptical of media content created by self-interested protesters (Jha, 2008) and of stage-managed media events (Lester & Hutchins, 2009). And while the most prominent studies of the relation between political movements and mainstream media draw pessimistic conclusions about media bias, there is growing evidence that this is far from consistent (Oliver & Maney, 2000; Boyle et al., 2005). Moreover, journalists are beginning to adopt a global perspective on reporting (Berglez, 2008) that may have an independent influence on their coverage of politics and issues that transcend national borders. In sum, the evidence remains suggestive but as yet inconclusive for the relatively short time period that marks the emergence of transnational protest.

Questions and directions

Assessing the influence of a transnational movement in a new media environment answers some questions, raises numerous others, and offers some paths for follow-up research. The politics of dissent in a networked, economically interdependent world derives from the disturbance of interests driven by comparative advantage and the velocity and scope of "complex interdependence" (Keohane & Nye, 2000). The primary issue remains whether one can speak of a single transnational movement for global social justice. The category itself subsumes a number of issues that hold different priorities depending on the interests of specific groups in specific locations.

It is true that members of a transnational movement that remains geographically bound have the capacity to think beyond parochial interests; Tarrow's (2005a) concept of "rooted cosmopolitanism" squares the circle of the apparent paradox.

Nevertheless, it is very unlikely that the welter of groups and individuals who have an interest at stake in the new political economy make up a unitary movement. Interests may be specific, local, and disconnected from a conscious membership in a broader global movement. The research cited here does not always specify whether the various groups under study subscribe to a single collective action frame that subsumes a single movement. Members of labor unions in the industrial regions of the US Midwest may be opposed to free trade agreements for entirely different reasons than members of the Sierra Club, with whom they may differ on the order of priority for environmental regulation. Scholars such as Bennett and della Porta have coined concepts that relax standards of membership in networked movements, and Harcourt and Escobar's concept of "meshworks" posit as yet an unproven hypothesis regarding the self-organizing dynamics of a new form of political organization; yet it is still unclear whether this nascent form of organization or the identities of lifestyle politics are sufficient for dislodging entrenched interests, effectively countering the power of professional lobbyists, or for reaching a public of sufficient size to elect representatives that respond to movement goals.

It is of course possible to measure progress by reference to a statement of purpose similar to that developed by the Students for a Democratic Society in 1962. The Port Huron Statement outlined a comprehensive analysis of specific issues that troubled its authors: the reform of an unresponsive political system, reform of an economic system that promoted inequality, dependence of the economy on military expenditure, elimination of nuclear weapons, elimination of discrimination, etc. The document specified a set of findings and propositions that could be translated into a specific targeted political agenda. Incremental progress toward specific goals would constitute a fair measure of movement success. Thus the Freedom Summer campaign of 1964 brought thousands of white college students (some, members of SDS) from the north into Mississippi to register Blacks who were kept from exercising their right to vote. The deaths of three volunteers in Philadelphia, Mississippi were nationally publicized and, combined with similarly highly publicized acts of violence by local officials in Selma, Alabama, created a wave of public anger that Lyndon Johnson used to lobby Congress to pass the 1965 Voting Rights Act. The success of the Freedom Summer campaign inspired other students to pressure the government to withdraw US troops from Vietnam. That campaign would not achieve the same level of policy success, but it created a wave of demonstrations that had a major impact on public discourse and, eventually, on public opinion.

Although the global justice movement has a published a number of books (e.g., James, 2000) and websites that outline specific goals, they remain relatively unknown to the public, while the movement's principal targets, the IGOs that formulate policy, retain their immunity from dissent. Thus, against strong currents of Greek public opinion, in 2010 the European Community and the IMF succeeded in pressuring Greece to raise the age of retirement, raise taxes, and reduce public expenditures in return for loans that would keep the government from defaulting on its debt and threatening the value of the euro. And a move to regulate US financial speculation in derivatives and other financial instruments, a key goal of the movement, did not occur until the stock market crash of 2007–8. By contrast, the movement did succeed in making fair trade a widely known concept (i.e., a meme) that had the capacity to raise consciousness and influence consumers to buy products from growers who pay a fair wage or use methods of sustainable development.

The movement's key political objectives remain (1) transparency in and democratic influence of IGOs, and especially the WTO, IMF, and World Bank; (2) corporate responsibility, including providing fair wages and adhering to labor and environmental regulations; (3) regulating global financial transactions; (4) forgiving the debt of developing nations, ending structural adjustment, and promoting economic sovereignty, unlike that, for example, imposed on the governments of Argentina and Greece; (5) raising the priority of human rights in trade agreements; (6) promoting sustainable development, especially protection for workers and the environment; (7) elevating women's participation in the development of economic policy; (8) promoting internationally enforced labor standards and building strong labor unions; (9) elevating local economic control versus that exerted by IGOs; and (10) promoting fair trade practices, including labeling of fair-trade, sustainable, and organic goods (James, 2000).

A research agenda that gauges the influence and success of the first transnational movement of the Internet era should include studies that measure the relative success of progress across these issue groupings and the institutions that have the power to effect change or influence public discourse and opinion. Which tactics are most successful for achieving success as measured by issue salience and issue frames? Which information medium is most effective (or resistant) for a specific issue category? Which issues have the capacity to rise through the information media hierarchy—from, e.g., the blogosphere to mainstream media? How does the permeability of domestic and international institutions to political dissent interact with the issues and their capacity to penetrate to the highest levels of the information hierarchy? Which combination of issues and movement tactics can bypass the mainstream media entirely for influencing public discourse and opinion?

A systematic program of research that addresses these questions will provide a clarifying set of concepts and theory for mapping the unique and potentially transformative dynamics of transnational protest.

CHAPTER SEVEN

Mediating and Embodying Transnational Protest

Internal and External Effects of Mass Global Justice Actions

JEFFREY S. JURIS

In order to achieve their goals, whether concrete policy change or longer-term cultural transformation, social movements have to make their struggles visible, while communicating their demands and aspirations.* On the hand, movements have to reach out to activists who are already mobilized, which they often do through their own alternative media sources (cf. Juris, 2005a). On the other hand, movements have to speak to a broader public of potential supporters and sympathizers, for which they rely on the mass media. One important mechanism for eliciting coverage in the mainstream press is to organize spectacular mass direct actions. Ever since the protest against the World Trade Organization (WTO) in Seattle, the anti-corporate globalization or global justice movement has made particularly high profile use of this strategy, engaging in mass counter-summit actions against the major institutional symbols of neoliberal capitalism: the World Bank, International Monetary Fund, WTO, and G8 (now the G20). Beyond their external media impact, however, mass direct actions also produce an important internal effect: generating the emotions needed to facilitate lasting commitments among activists, particularly within more diffuse, informal networks and collectives. Scholars have explored the media-related aspects of social movements (Gamson & Modigliani, 1989; Gitlin, 1980; Juris, 2005b), and have recently begun to examine the emotional side of activism (Goodwin et al., 2001), but there has been scant attention to the way these domains interact (but see Routledge, 1997). This chapter considers the relation between the mediated and affective dimensions of social movement practice through an analysis of protest performance.

Counter-summit actions are critical networking tools that allow activists to communicate political messages to an audience, while eliciting deeply felt emotions and identities. Given their highly unpredictable, confrontational nature, mass direct actions produce powerful images and affective ties. However, their effects may be contradictory. On the one hand, counter-summits generate high levels of affective solidarity, but their emotional and media impact diminish over time. On the other hand, the most unpredictable, free-form actions, which may be emotionally satisfying for core activists, often result in media frames that stigmatize or trivialize protesters. In contrast, traditional protests may be ignored, but when they *are* covered they tend to receive sympathetic treatment. Based on ethnographic accounts of global justice protests in Prague and Barcelona as a participant in the Barcelona-based Movement for Global Resistance, as well as analysis of subsequent media representations in the Spanish and Catalan press,[1] I argue that mass counter-summit actions reflect a tension between the emotional and media dimensions of protest, involving a contradiction between what Jennifer Earl (2000) calls "intra-" and "extra-movement" outcomes.[2] Given the recent global justice actions against the G20 in Pittsburgh and the Climate Summit in Copenhagen, this analysis remains relevant to both academic and activist concerns.

Protest, media, and performance

Counter-summit protests are complex ritual performances that generate a dual effect. Externally, they are powerful "image events" (DeLuca, 1999), where diverse activist networks communicate their messages to an audience by "hijacking" the global media space afforded by multilateral summits (Peterson, 2001). Internally, they produce terrains where identities are expressed through distinct bodily techniques, and emotions are generated through ritual conflict and the lived experience of prefigured utopias. Mass counter-summits thus involve what Paul Routledge (1997) calls "imagineered resistance": struggles that are mediated *and* embodied.

In terms of image, counter-summits are performative "terrains of resistance" (Routledge, 1994) where social movements struggle for visibility. Spectacular protests conform to prevailing media logics, a way of seeing and interpreting the world through the production formats and modes of transmission of mass media as entertainment (Altheide & Snow, 1991). The growing influence of "infotainment" means unusual, spontaneous, dramatic, or emotionally satisfying events often garner significant media attention, while less visually and emotionally compelling incidents go unnoticed (Altheide & Snow, 1991: 17; Castells, 1996). By staging spectacular image events, global justice activists thus attempt to make power visible and challenge dominant symbolic codes.

Image is linked to emotion through embodied performance. Performances communicate verbal and non-verbal messages to an audience (Bauman, 1977), while allowing participants to experience symbolic meanings through ritual interaction (Schieffelin, 1985). Performances are constitutive, as Debra Kapchan suggests, "To perform is to carry something into effect" (1995: 479). Counter-summit protests provide multiple theatrical spaces where oppositional politics are communicated and new subjectivities are forged (Hetherington, 1998). Tactics such as militant confrontation, symbolic conflict, and carnivalesque revelry involve distinct activist "techniques of the body" (Mauss, 1973), which generate alternative meanings and identities.

As performative rituals, mass direct actions operate by transforming affect: amplifying an initiating emotion, such as anger or rage, and transferring it into feelings of solidarity (Collins, 2001). Randall Collins (2001) has called such Durkheimian collective effervescence "emotional energy," which I refer to in less mystical terms as "affective solidarity." Organizers use emotion strategically to generate the commitment necessary to maintain participation (Gould, 2001). In this sense, protests provide arenas not only for eliciting images and identities but also for living moments of freedom, liberation, and joy (Gould, 2001; Calhoun, 2001). At the same time, distinct kinds of protest produce contrasting emotional effects. Compared to institutionalized marches and rallies, for example, free-form actions are more emotively potent, in part, because they introduce elements of danger, uncertainty, and play. The intense feelings, egalitarian sentiments, and oppositional identities associated with mass protests provide a store of emotional resources activists can draw upon to facilitate ongoing movement building. As Collins (2001) suggests, however, peak emotional mobilizations are time-bound, while the ebbs and flows of protest are tied to emotional shifts. In this sense, core activists eventually tire while public interest may wane, particularly as protests become routine. In terms of extra-movement outcomes the most unpredictable confrontational actions often elicit significant media attention, but protesters are more likely to be stigmatized or trivialized. Traditional protests are thus less exhilarating and less newsworthy, but, as we shall see, when they *are* covered they generate more positive images.

Anti-world bank/IMF protest in Prague

Nearly 50,000 people took to the streets to protest corporate globalization at the World Trade Organization (WTO) meetings in Seattle on 30 November 1999. A diverse coalition of environmental, labor, and economic justice activists succeeded in disrupting the meetings and helping to prevent another round of trade liberalization talks. Media images of giant puppets, tear gas, and street clashes between protesters and police were broadcast worldwide, bringing the WTO and a novel form of collective action into view. The "Battle of Seattle" was a prime-time image event, cascading through global mediascapes (Appadurai, 1996) and capturing the imagination of long-time activists and would-be postmodern revolutionaries alike. Although Seattle was a key moment of visibility, social movements had been organizing against corporate globalization for years (cf. Juris, 2008b). However, Seattle sparked a proliferation of global justice organizing and mass counter-summit protests around the world, including the protests against the World Bank and IMF in Prague in September 2000.

My own experience in Prague began with a bus caravan from Barcelona along with my new affinity group, the Open Veins.[3] On the evening of the day of our arrival, we went down to the convergence center, a teeming beehive of activity on the edge of town where activists were preparing for the action. We got there just in time for a coordinating meeting with 350 activists from dozens of countries. Organizers went over the battle plan, explaining that the march would begin at the *Náměstí Míru Square* before splitting into three blocs: Blue for militant action, Pink for non-violent protest, Yellow for an intermediate level of conflict. This "swarming" (Arquilla & Ronfeldt, 2001) strategy would involve blockading the primary access road to the Congress Center and then entirely surrounding the Summit. Two additional blocs were formed later: a Pink & Silver march led by a UK-based samba band and autonomous blockades in the South. My affinity group decided to join the Pink March, which desperately needed more bodies.

On the morning of September 26, the main day of the action, *Náměstí Míru Square* was bustling with thousands of activists holding colorful puppets, signs, and props. We lined up in the street along with the Pink March early that afternoon, and, after sending out a scout to make sure the route was clear, we moved out, chanting "Hey hey, ho, ho, the World Bank has got to go!" Dozens of Czech and international journalists began snapping pictures and recording video footage. Sandra, Miguel, and I exchanged glances, as our moral outrage was transformed into a feeling of collective power. As Nuria recalled, "There are times when something surges up from inside, as if your body were saying, 'now you are living something truly important.'"

Yellow March

After a few minutes people began shouting at us to slow down. Most of the Pink March had followed the Ya Basta! sound system toward the bridge. The Blue March navigated their way along the western side of the congress center, but the

Pink Bloc was in disarray. Rather than continue with depleted numbers, we decided to turn around and walk back toward the bridge, where thousands of activists from the Pink and Yellow Blocs were standing around a grassy plaza. I made my way through the crowd to get a closer look, and sure enough, two tanks were blocking the bridge flanked by an impressive battalion of soldiers and riot cops. Several hundred Italian, Spanish, and Finnish activists dressed from head to toe in white overalls and protective padding were pushing up against police lines with huge plastic shields and inner tubes.

The white overalls tactic was designed to create evocative images of resistance while generating powerful feelings of affective solidarity. As I looked on from a safe distance, row after row of similarly outfitted, yet uniquely adorned bodies, with elbows linked, were pushing up against multiple lines of riot police protecting the entrance to the bridge. Behind them were the two armored vehicles, as the coercive power of the Czech state was on display. Across the battle line, the multitude of bodies was at once a collective yet individualized force. In addition to white overalls, activists wore multiply-colored head gear, including black, silver, white, yellow, blue, and orange helmets. Some also carried shields made from black inner tubes, clear plastic panels, and detached seat cushions. The mass of assembled bodies continued to push against the police barricade for several hours, communicating resistance, while creating an emotionally and visually compelling conflict. Indeed, the action had practical *and* performative dimensions. The bizarre, padded outfits, inner tubes, helmets, and foam padding protected activists from baton blows, but they also provided ready-made images for the mass media, while expressing messages about the importance of frivolity, laughter, and unity through difference.

Pink March

After observing the *Tute Bianche* for several minutes, I rejoined my affinity group, and together with several others from Britain, Sweden, and Norway, we began to reorganize the Pink March using our giant flags to lead people down the narrow streets along the eastern flank of the congress center. As we guided hundreds of protesters around the corner, Jorge looked up at me and observed, "This is great; I've never felt so alive!" Indeed, using our bodies to direct such a large and determined crowd generated powerful feelings of agency and solidarity. Eager to begin the blockade, we became more purposeful and serious. By the time we approached the access highway, our ranks numbered several thousand. A contingent of Swedes and Norwegians marched directly up the ramp, while the rest of us wound our way around the side streets, where we took up blockades, using our bodies to occupy the space in front of the police lines.

The other Pink Bloc group soon joined us. Men in business suits would occasionally try to break through, at which point we would stand up and lock arms to prevent them from passing. The police stood by, some looking fearful, others mildly amused. Beyond the practical impact of the action, protesters were communicating messages of determined, yet non-violent opposition, reproducing archetypical scenes of civil disobedience. Non-violent performances symbolically contrasted the vulnerable, morally righteous bodies of the protesters with the menacing bodies of the police, while creating an emotional tone of serene, determined resistance.

After maintaining the blockade for several hours, rumors began circulating that most of the delegates had been whisked away through an escape route before the Summit had concluded. Our initial euphoria had given way to malaise, but our spirits picked up when we realized we were having an impact. With stories of violent clashes circulating, we began to sense the nervous excitement preceding a "discharging" crowd (Canetti, 1962). Shortly after dinner, dozens of masked and hooded anarchists appeared, hurling stones and empty bottles at the police lines surrounding us. When the melee ended, I went around the corner to join my affinity group, which had initiated another blockade. An armored police vehicle approached, and we maintained our position. After a brief, but intense standoff, the vehicle backed away, as a small group of hooded Czech anarchists banged on the windows. The police soon reinforced their lines, and we feared another attack. Our fear transformed into elation, however, when the riot cops backed off again. "They're retreating!" exclaimed Gerard. We had successfully held the space. Miguel, Gerard, and I cheered and hugged, and then the entire group began celebrating our momentary victory through playful mockery and dancing in front of the stoic, heavily armed riot cops. We had entered a riveting space of carnivalesque revelry, inducing feelings of power and solidarity.

Many of us had experienced shifting emotions throughout the day, as Gerard recalled, "There was a pre-Prague and a post-Prague in my life. I met so many people there and had such an incredible experience. There were moments of happiness, then times when your morale sunk through the floor. There was fear, panic, but also festivity; it was incredible!" It was precisely the flexible, constantly changing, spontaneous, and open-ended nature of the Pink March, and the overall Prague action that generated such high levels of affective solidarity.

Pink & Silver March

As we patiently held our Pink March blockades, the Pink & Silver Bloc danced in and out behind the UK-based samba band. Several dozen dancers wearing pink skirts, tights, pants, and leotards, and the occasional silver jump suit, frolicked to the beat of the drums along with their brightly colored masks and flags. Drumming, dance, and music help create what Elias Canetti (1962) calls the "rhythmic" crowd. Activist bands, including samba troupes or the Infernal Noise Brigade from Seattle, provide focal points during mass actions and elicit widespread feelings of embodied agency. In Prague, samba dancers not only helped generate affective solidarity, their festive and playful performances also represented a stark contrast to both militant protesters and the Czech police. Meanwhile, Radical Cheerleaders and Pink Fairies occasionally broke away from the group, performing ironic cheers and taunting the police. As we held our intersection, a Pink Fairy approached a nearby police vehicle and began "cleaning" it with her feather duster, much to the delight of the crowd. When the police failed to respond, she was emboldened, and started to approach individual officers, brushing their shoes as they nervously looked on. Such playful provocation represents a form of ritual opposition, a symbolic overturning of hierarchy much like a medieval carnival (Bakhtin, 1984).

Pink & Silver used burlesque activist bodies to symbolically contrast a world of utopian creativity, color, and play to the dark, oppressive forces of law and order. Such performances are "emergent" in that they make social structure visible and amenable to change (Bauman, 1977). Play, in particular, reveals the possibility of radically reorganizing current social arrangements. It exists in the subjunctive mood: "the domain of the 'as-if' (Turner, 1986: 169)." Pink & Silver thus involved the strategic appropriation of carnivalesque performance and aesthetics, including playful mockery, ritualized inversion, gender bending, drumming, dance, outlandish costumes, and wild masks. Unlike the other blocs, Pink & Silver succeeded in penetrating the congress center, using their creative, mobile blend of tactics to confound the police. Pink & Silver, like the larger action, created a performative terrain that was oppositional *and* subjunctive, a platform for critiquing prevailing social, political, and economic orders, enacting new forms of sociality, and generating affective solidarity through mobile and free form virtuoso performance.

Blue March

Meanwhile, as we held our blockades, the Blue March battle raged in the west. Raul and Paco, from MRG-Zaragoza, had offered to navigate; assuming the march would be non violent. When they attempted to direct the crowd away from a battalion of riot cops, militants screamed, "police!" and charged at them up a hill pushing a huge plastic blue ball from *Náměstí Míru*. Activists were repelled but regrouped at the bottom of the hill and continued to charge again and again. They were able to move police lines back until riot cops responded with tear gas and water cannons. Militants then began to dig up cobblestones, hurling them along with Molotov cocktails. The street battle raged for hours, as Paco, from MRG-Zaragoza, later recalled, "I had never seen such a violent confrontation, before or after. Genoa was a battlefield, but there wasn't as much body-to-body contact. There was fire everywhere; cops were burning."

Militant tactics involve the ritual enactment of violent performances via distinct bodily techniques, political symbols, and protest styles, including black pants and jumpers, combat boots, and bandanas to cover the face, which serve to express solidarity while simultaneously portraying archetypical images of rebellion. As Peterson (2001: 55) suggests, militant activists generate identities through emotionally powerful embodied ritual performances that construct the militant body as the ground of agency and produce an "embattled" activist subjectivity. The typical image of the Black Bloc activist reflects a masculine ideal of aggressive confrontation. Violent performances constitute militant networks by physically expressing a radical rejection of the dominant order, including the major symbols of capitalism and the state. They also allow activists to express powerful feelings of anger and rage. However, mass mediated images of violence are often used to stigmatize protesters (Juris, 2005b). Militant violence thus constitutes a clear expression of the tension between the emotional and external impact of direct action protest with respect to a wider public.

The next morning I attended a press conference at the media center for the mobilization. Despite the focus on violence, the action had elicited significant press coverage. Correspondents from Spanish, Catalan, and other international news and television outlets covered the protests, creating an anti-corporate globalization media boom in the Spanish State. Indeed, Prague was an emotionally and visibly compelling free-form action. Activists generated affective solidarity and oppositional identities through diverse bodily movements and techniques, each involving distinct emotional tones and intensities. At the same time, Prague was a potent image event, as diverse networks communicated alternative political messages, rendering conflicts visible.

Mobilization against the EU in Barcelona

The spring 2002 mobilization against the EU in Barcelona provides a clear contrast with Prague, illustrating how different forms of protest generate distinct emotional and visual effects. Rather than free-form direct action, a highly scripted "unity march" took center stage, in part, because organizers were concerned about police repression due to the increasing violence at recent global justice protests. There *were* highly charged moments during the protest, but many core activists experienced the unity march as less emotionally intense than previous actions.

In the early evening of March 16, I arrived at the *Plaça de Catalunya* to meet up with my affinity group before the march began. We waited anxiously for the masses to appear, and after what felt like an eternity, thousands of people started pouring in, seemingly from nowhere. Suddenly, the large banners and floats separating the blocks moved into place, and before we could figure out who was supposed to go where, a huge crowd swept us along. As the march began, we danced alongside a samba band, chanting "Another World Is Possible, Another World Is Possible." Other protesters carried colorful banners denouncing the Europe of Capital, depicting greedy businessman clenching euros and dollar bills, or portraying Presidents Aznar and Bush as war criminals. Meanwhile, packs of Euro-Fighters began darting in and out, while further along, we passed a drumming troupe dressed as red devils and giants. As we neared the port, I glanced back and saw hundreds of thousands of protesters. Ecstatic organizers claimed that this was the largest demonstration they had seen, more than a half million people. The next morning's headline in *La Vanguardia*, a popular pro-business daily, exclaimed: "Victory in the Streets!" The press hailed protesters as paragons of "civic virtue."

Although the unity march mobilized masses of people it was far less confrontational than past actions and failed to communicate a message of radical dissent. Many activists expressed a sense of frustration, even defeat, suggesting the movement had been contained and neutralized. Rather than an open-ended, confrontational event of representation, the march felt overly formal and routine. Compared to past actions, many radicals felt the protest lacked risk and excitement and was thus less emotionally empowering as Paula pointed out, "We were afraid to organize confrontational actions, which really make conflicts visible. The actions were great in terms of content—extremely transparent and public. But making sure people weren't afraid to bring their young kids to the actions was excessive." Despite occasional moments of community, there were few outbursts of freedom, excitement and uncertainty, as Joan pointed out:

> The mobilization was a success, but not an epic experience. There were epic moments, but not like in Prague, Genoa, or last year in Barcelona. . . . The demonstration was a numerical success, and it produced an image that makes our critiques acceptable, but it wasn't a life-changing experience where you radically confront the system and live through dangerous situations full of adrenaline, at least not for me.

Given Joan's thirst for "epic" moments of transformation, a traditional protest was bound to disappoint. The unity march failed to generate the same degree of affective solidarity as past counter-summit actions. For many radicals, the anti-EU mobilization felt controlled, staged, and predictable, as if the open crowd had been caged. Mass direct actions were beginning to lose their confrontational edge. Their emotional impact was waning, they were becoming routine. Nonetheless, the large number of participants, traditional format, and peaceful tone of the march generated sympathetic media images, facilitating wider movement building and recruitment.

Contrasting media coverage of prague and barcelona

Confrontational, free-form actions such as the anti-World Bank/IMF protest in Prague generate high levels of affective solidarity, but they may be difficult to reproduce over time. In contrast, traditional protests, including the anti-EU march in Barcelona, are more sustainable but are often experienced as less emotionally transformative. The media impact of protest tends to work in the opposite direction. Spectacular actions draw more media attention, but the coverage is likely to be disparaging. For their part, traditional marches and rallies are less likely to elicit media interest, but when they do, they generally receive more sympathetic treatment.

One way to assess the latter is to examine the impact of protest on political discourse and public opinion through the mass media. Protesters stage spectacular image events, in part, to gain visibility. At the same time, however, reporters tend to focus on violence and intrigue rather than underlying political issues. By employing widespread "media frames" (Gitlin, 1980), journalists select, exclude, emphasize, and interpret verbal and visual cues in particular ways. As Gamson and Modigliani (1989) suggest, individual frames composed of metaphors, images, catchphrases, and other devices are grouped together as "media packages," which continually incorporate new events into their interpretive schemes.

With respect to protest, the mass media are more sympathetic to discourses and practices that reflect dominant values, such as the sanctity of private property and the state, and can be easily incorporated into hegemonic frameworks. On the other hand, dominant media packages employ various techniques such as trivialization, marginalization, disparagement, and a focus on violence and internal division, to deflect and contain radical dissent (Gitlin, 1980). Consequently, global justice movements receive more favorable press coverage to the extent they engage in peaceful protest, emphasize reforms, and include institutional actors. Ironically, perhaps, these conditions produce less emotionally compelling events. In order to demonstrate the contradiction between internal and external impacts of mass actions, this section contrasts the mass media coverage of protests in Prague and Barcelona in the Spanish and Catalan press.[4]

Prague—September 2000

Large numbers of Spanish and Catalan activists took part in the September 2000 anti-World Bank and IMF protests in Prague, eliciting significant media interest back home. Among the dominant media packages was the division between "good" and "bad" protesters. Radical youths were disparaged and criminalized, while more moderate non-governmental organizations received favorable treatment, including coverage of their political demands. The headlines on 25 September portrayed massive street battles from the day before with photos depicting the Black Bloc and white overall militants hurling stones, breaking windows, and confronting police lines. A story in *El País* characterized the action in this way, "Protesters numbered 9,000 by morning, with nighttime reinforcements from Italy, Greece, and Spain. They ripped up cobblestones, made Molotov cocktails, gathered sharp objects, and set off for the Convention Center singing fight songs" (27 September: 74). When protesters closed delegates inside, reporters attributed to them a victory, "Thousands of demonstrators scored a success in their battle against globalization after surrounding the international capitalist elite in Prague" (*El País*, 27 September: 74).

There was a significant discrepancy, however, between media representations of radicals and moderates. A story in *El País* thus characterized militants as, "rioters with colored hair and gas masks, radicals for the sake of being radical, with no more ideological foundation than trashing windows and luxury cars, and punks with *pierced penises* urinating all over the streets" (28 September: 70). Other reports echoed specious assertions that Spanish detainees were "associated with radical Basque movements" (*El País*, 29 September: 102). Militants were specifically contrasted to Reformists, as an *El País* article explained, "Wolfensohn met with 350 moderate NGOs requesting dialogue...but radicals are not interested in building bridges and will play revolution in the streets" (23 September: 73). Another article asserted that, "Various NGOs, who have struggled for years to force the IMF and World Bank to forgive the debt of the world's poorest countries, separated themselves from the rioters" (*El País*, 28 September: 70).

The anti-World Bank and IMF protests in Prague elicited significant media attention in the Spanish and Catalan press. However, much of the coverage portrayed protesters in a negative light, stigmatizing them as violent criminals or trivializing them as marginal squatters and punks committed more to their subcultural lifestyles than political change. In contrast, moderates were depicted as legitimate political actors engaging in peaceful protest and offering a reasonable challenge to World Bank and IMF policies. Overall, the media impact was mixed. On one level, radicals and moderates worked well together, the former stimulating media interest through militant protest, the latter providing legitimacy and a focused message. On another level, the dominant frames stigmatized and trivialized radicals, making it more difficult for organizers to reach beyond a committed core of activists. In this sense, the same factors that generate affective solidarity among militants may complicate efforts to recruit more broadly.

Barcelona—March 2002

By the time of the March 2002 protests against the EU in Barcelona, institutional actors, including the Spanish Communist Party (PCE) and the Catalan Socialist Party (PSC) had aligned themselves with moderates inside the Barcelona Social Forum (BSF). Before the mobilization, protesters and officials from the conservative Popular Party (PP), which controlled the central government, promoted contrasting media packages. In particular, the PP stepped up its attempts to link protesters with Basque street fighters. As an *El País* headline exclaimed, "Barcelona arms itself for protests against globalization, Aznar [the Spanish President from the PP party] warns demonstrators of the risk of joining Batasuna" (10 March). A story in *El Mundo* called, "More than a thousand Basque radicals will go to Barcelona," portrayed a city poised for an epic battle between militants and police (14 March: 3). Another headline in *La Vanguardia* read, "Spain impedes entrance of 118 anti-globalization activists," and was accompanied by an image of sequestered bats, sticks, and guns (15 March: 23), setting the stage for police repression.

Activists and leftist parties promoted an alternative media package stressing non-violence and blaming the tension on the central government. A story in *El Periodico* thus reported that the Campaign "accuses police of 'provocation,'" and asks officials to "'let us demonstrate in peace'" (12 March: 17). *El Mundo* ran headlines declaring that the, "PSC criticizes 'obsession' with security" (12 March: 17), and that the "Barcelona Social Forum advocates massive, 'peaceful' demonstration" (12 March: 19). At the same time, beyond violence and tension, several stories focused on political content, as an article in *El Periodico* explained, activists denounced the Spanish EU Presidency for being "guided by . . . deregulation, flexibilization, and privatization," and thus, "imposing the 'law of the market above all else'" (12 March: 16).

Following the massive non-violent demonstration on 16 March, the "peaceful protester" package won out. A headline in *El País* thus exclaimed, "300,000 people peacefully demand another globalization" (17 March: 1). A *La Vanguardia* headline similarly announced, "Huge anti-globalization march, hundreds of thousands march peacefully in Barcelona." For its part, a headline in *El Periodico* triumphantly declared "300,000 people demonstrate peacefully in the largest anti-globalization march in Europe" (17 March: 1). A story in *El País* praised the new "Barcelona model" (17 March: 4), while its editorial page lauded the "maturity" of protesters and the city's "civic display." The prevailing sentiment was perhaps best summarized in this way: "Anti-globalization forces are seen as more legitimate" (*La Vanguardia*, 18 March: 6).

The press coverage during the anti-EU mobilization in Barcelona began by emphasizing familiar media packages, including protest as a battle, the threat of militant violence, and internal divisions. For their part, activists and leftist parties promoted an alternative "peaceful protester" package, which carried the day following the massive unity march. However, for radicals, the media impact, once again, was mixed. On the one hand, the dominant media frames emphasized reformist critiques while extolling the virtue of cooperation. On the other hand, the sympathetic coverage made it more likely that potential adherents would be willing to take part in future protests. Whereas the action in Prague was emotionally potent but resulted in media packages that stigmatized and trivialized radicals, the march in Barcelona was experienced as routine by many core activists but led to triumphant headlines that helped legitimize the wider movement.

Conclusion

Counter-summit protests are important mobilizing tools that allow activists to perform their networks and make their struggles visible while generating affective solidarity through ritual catharsis. On the one hand, mass direct actions, in particular, constitute high-profile image events where activist networks represent themselves through diverse embodied spatial practices. Spectacular actions involving Pink Bloc, white overall, and Black Bloc tactics are thus meant, in part, to capture media attention, while communicating political messages to an audience. In this sense, the action in Prague and the anti-EU march in Barcelona made headlines in Spain and Catalonia and throughout Europe. However, as the novelty of counter-summits wears off, more and more spectacular actions may be needed to break into busy media cycles (Routledge, 1997).

Mass counter-summit protests also generate affective solidarity. Activists perform their networks through diverse bodily movements, techniques, and styles, generating distinct identities and emotions. This was evident in Prague, where organizers divided the urban terrain into color-coded zones, each reserved for specific forms of embodied action. At the same time, different kinds of protest generate varying degrees of emotional intensity. Prague was a classic free-form action, producing powerful emotions through heated conflict between protesters and police and the lived experience of prefigured utopias. The march against the EU in Barcelona, on the other hand, created a significant impact through sheer numbers, but for many activists, it felt scripted and routine. In this sense, counter-summit protests are key networking tools, but they generate diminishing returns with respect to visibility and affective solidarity.

Moreover, as I have argued, mass counter-summit actions are often contradictory with respect to intra- and extra-movement outcomes. The most spectacular, confrontational free form actions, which are particularly potent in emotional terms, tend to elicit media frames that stigmatize or belittle protesters. As we have seen, many activists experienced the anti-World Bank and IMF action in Prague as emotionally transformative, but the press coverage portrayed radicals in a disparaging light. Conversely, although peaceful protests are often ignored, when they are covered, because of large numbers, the participation of institutional forces, or *threat* of violence, they are more likely to elicit sympathetic treatment. For many core activists, however, they tend to generate lower levels of affective solidarity, as we saw with the anti-EU protest in Barcelona. Organizers thus have to balance affective solidarity with sustainability, while also managing the tension between the emotional and mass media impacts of political protest.

Global justice activists have devised multiple strategies for dealing with these dilemmas, including a long-term shift toward more local, everyday struggles and the turn toward regional and world social forums as periodic moments for broader movement convergence. At the same time, mass counter-summit actions continue to have a role in generating emotions and visibility, even if less central and more intermittent. In this sense, global justice activists have organized mass direct actions every two or three years, particularly against the G8/G20, but also targeting Democratic and Republican National Conventions in the U.S., the European Union in Europe, and most recently the Global Climate Summit in Copenhagen. Organizers still have to confront the strategic tension between the affective and media dimensions of mass actions. This was made particularly evident during the summer 2007 action against the G8 in Heiligendamm, Germany, when a militant Black Bloc set police cars ablaze during a march in the town of Rostock prior to the Summit, and this past September at the anti-G20 protest in Pittsburgh, when masked protesters took to the streets and confronted police. These emotively and visually compelling actions elicited significant press coverage, but they led to stories and images that stigmatized activists as senseless and violent. Ultimately, the success of the global justice and other movements depends on the ability of organizers to creatively negotiate such strategic tensions.

Notes

*(Portions of this chapter have previously appeared in modified form in *Ethnography* 9(1): 61–97)

1. Barcelona-based research was supported by a Dissertation Field Research Grant from the Wenner-Gren Foundation for Anthropological Research, Inc., and a Dissertation Field Research Fellowship from the Social Science Research Council (with Andrew W. Mellon Foundation funding).

2. Intra-movement outcomes include factors such as emotion, biographical impact, and collective identity. Extra-movement outcomes include institutional/policy change, cultural

transformation, and media impact, which mediates between cultural and institutional/policy spheres.

3. An "affinity group" is a collection of ten to fifteen activists that coordinates with other groups to form larger clusters and blocs, constituting the basic building bloc of direct action protests. The name "Open Veins" was taken from a book of the same name by Eduardo Galeano about the destructive effects of foreign intervention in Latin America.

4. My sources include two of the top-selling national dailies in Spain—*El País* and *El Mundo*, and the two most popular Catalan regional papers—*El Periodico de Catalunya* and *La Vanguardia*. *El País* is center-left, *El Mundo* is center-right, while *El Periodico* is left leaning and provides the most sympathetic coverage of protesters. For its part, *La Vanguardia* promotes a pro-business, Catalanist line. It is important to recognize such differences, but a finely-tuned analysis of the contrasting coverage within these sources is beyond the scope of this article.

CHAPTER EIGHT

Protest
and Public Relations

A new era
for non-institutional sources?

ADAM BOWERS

Introduction

The increasingly sophisticated communication strategies of non-governmental organizations (NGOs), pressure groups and protest movements have led to some success in securing coverage for non-institutional[1] views in the news media. Davis suggests that the "1990s might be seen as a period in which alternative interest group PR began to break into the established elite discourse networks and use the media to bring policy debates into the public sphere" (Davis, 2003: 41). Schudson observed that by 1999 "some of the Blair government's most difficult communication struggles were with consumer groups, the environmental lobby, the countryside alliance and the campaign for freedom of information" (Schudson, 2005: 107). By the end of the first decade of the 21st century, NGO tactics had moved to reflect the increasingly transnational nature of political decision-making. The international composition and focus of anti-globalization protest events in the late 1990s in Genoa, Seattle, Davos and London increasingly became the norm for protests targeting international meetings on global issues, including the environment, human rights, trade and the economy. Della Porta and Tarrow describe the emergence of "transnational collective action" at the turn of the century, "coordinated international campaigns on the part of networks of activists against international actors, other states, or international institutions" (della Porta & Tarrow, 2005: 3).

Cottle (2008), DeLuca and Peeples (2002) and Rojecki (2002) amongst others report with some optimism that the emergence of transnational protest has coincided with a shift to more positive reporting of protest events in the media. Through an analysis of news coverage of the London G20 protests in April 2009 and interviews with press officers at leading UK-based international NGOs, this chapter will consider just how much news reporting of protest has changed in the transnational era and whether news media savvy NGOs have been able to challenge institutional source dominance in media reporting on global issues. The investigation has implications for broader arguments regarding the role of the news media in democracies and the ability of certain sources to gain access to journalists over others. Hall et al. (1978), Schlesinger and Tumber (1994), Herman and Chomsky (2008), Bennett (1990) and others differ in their reasoning but are consistent in their assertion that powerful, institutional sources generally dominate news reporting, whether by serving as "primary definers," through competitive and unequally weighted "source fields," or by news processes of "elite indexing" (see Cottle, 2000, 2003). If a democracy's health can be measured by the diversity of voices and opinions mediated by journalists to the public sphere, then it is important to monitor who gains access and who doesn't and why. An increase in coverage of non-institutional voices over time would provide grounds for optimism and a reassessment of earlier studies.

This chapter begins therefore with a review of recent research on media coverage of protest movements, assessing the extent to which reporting has changed. This is followed by a presentation of the study on news coverage of the 2009 London G20 Summit, the results of which lead the author to conclude that non-institutional sources remain heavily disadvantaged in their ongoing struggle to get their voices heard, whether through PR or protest.

Protest movement studies

Rojecki's 2002 study of media coverage of the World Trade Organization (WTO) meetings in Seattle in 1999 suggests that the anti-globalization movement gained more favourable media coverage than previous studies would lead us to expect (Rojecki, 2002). Citing Gitlin's 1980 analysis of the media's interaction with the Students for a Democratic Society, Rojecki identifies that such studies highlight the inclination of the media to attend to "the actions of the most reckless in the movement" (cited in Rojecki, 2002: 155). Cottle also argues that "much has changed since earlier studies documented how the mainstream news media invariably report protests and demonstrations through a dominant law and (dis)order frame, labelling protesters as deviant and delegitimizing their aims and politics by emphasizing drama, spectacle and violence" (Cottle, 2008: 4).

Rojecki concludes with optimism that, "the range of views in the news and commentaries was as wide as that expressed by the protesters themselves, creating a critical field that encompassed a heretofore unimaginable combination of conservative elites, traditional reformers and neo-Marxist protesters (Rojecki, 2002: 166). Whether this represents a general shift in reporting of protest movements is debatable however. Other interventions at the WTO meeting in Seattle may have proved decisive in altering the pattern of news reporting on this occasion. As Rojecki observes, the mayor of the city, for example, told journalists that he had an excellent relationship with many of the demonstration's planners and said that "there is no battle in Seattle. What there is is a wonderful expression of free speech." President Clinton also expressed sympathy with some of the protesters' views and suggested he would "steer a course between the WTO and protesters" (Rojecki, 2002: 162). Therefore, one might suggest that the news reporting of the meetings reflect Bennett's 1990 indexing hypothesis, in that the views expressed by elites in Seattle allowed space for other viewpoints to be heard in the media. Rojecki alludes to this himself in his conclusion but maintains that the study points to a "reenergized pluralism in which the mass media play a constructive role in building democratically responsive institutions" (Rojecki, 2002: 167).

DeLuca and Peeples take a different approach in their study of the 1999 WTO protests in Seattle. They suggest that the attention to the conflict outside the conference increased coverage of the WTO in general (DeLuca & Peeples, 2002: 141). They argue that the spectacle of violence in TV images and press photos served to draw further media attention and in fact that, "symbolic protest violence is often a necessary prerequisite to highlight the non-violent elements of a movement that might otherwise be marginalized in the daily struggle for media coverage" (DeLuca & Peeples, 2002: 144). In other words, a non-violent protest may not get covered and initial focus on the "actions of the most reckless in the movement" can have some benefits in terms of coverage of wider views. The authors use their findings to articulate their concept of a public screen as an alternative to the public sphere. They suggest that in an age where the image dominates news coverage, spectacle and drama can work to bring diverse viewpoints to the attention of the many via the public screen.

Other studies, however, point back to the endurance of traditional frames of protest reporting identified by Gitlin. For example, a three-year study of *New York Times* coverage of the World Economic Forum and World Social Forum by W. Lance Bennett and his colleagues found that news coverage "actively constructed the grassroots globalization critics as marginal, largely nameless scruffians who threatened civil order" (Bennett et al., 2004: 452). The study argues that, "instead of taking the claims of each side to the other for reaction, the press framed the protesters in ways that limited their legitimacy, marginalized their status, and ultimately gave ownership of their issues to the higher status actors on the terms those actors chose" (Bennett et al., 2004: 452).

Therefore, while it can be observed, as Cottle does, that "social movements need the news for wider mobilization" (Cottle, 2008: 1), the success of non-institutional organizations and groups' strategies, including employment of media-relations specialists, protests and events, in displacing the dominance of institutional voices in the media is less clear. This study sets out to examine whether a theory of dominance should persist with regard to source media relations and what difference the tactics of non-institutional sources and protest movements can make.

Researching G20 April 2009

Taking UK national newspaper coverage of the April 2009 G20 meetings as its starting point a content analysis was undertaken of the Daily and Sunday versions of four leading UK national newspapers (*Daily Mail, Daily Telegraph, Financial Times, The Guardian* and *The Observer*) printed from 30 March to 12 April 2009. This period covered the days before and the week after the G20 meetings in London, which took place on 2 and 3 April 2009, therefore covering the window of opportunity for institutional and non-institutional sources to voice their opinions and attempt to secure coverage. In all, 247 articles were counted across the newspapers and coded.[2] Alongside the content analysis, 15 UK-based NGOs were also consulted[3] and their media officers interviewed in order to gain an understanding of the communication strategies of some of the non-institutional sources vying for press coverage during the period of the G20. By understanding their objectives, methods and expectations, it is possible to gain an improved insight into the relationship dynamic between non-institutional sources and journalists and how this can influence the nature of contemporary protest reporting.

The aim of the content analysis was to discover what issues were covered and whose arguments were given space. The variables in the coding schedule were designed to measure if a source was quoted in an article, if so the number of sources quoted, who they were, how they were quoted, the part of the article they were quoted in, the space given over to the source quote and how they were referred to by the journalist. Where possible the original source of the article was recorded. This was not always straightforward as almost all the articles analyzed were credited to the newspaper journalist. As Lewis and colleagues pointed out in their study of the origins of news articles, "news, especially in print, is routinely recycled from elsewhere, and yet the widespread use of other material is rarely attributed to its source (e.g., 'according to PA . . .' or 'a press release from X suggests that . . .'). Such practices would, elsewhere, be regarded as straightforward plagiarism" (Lewis, Williams, &

Franklin, 2008: 18). There were some cases, however, where the original source was clearly evident, as discussed below.

The themes covered by the newspapers in their G20 reporting were also important to measure, to gain an understanding of how the Summit and surrounding protests were being presented to the public. Activist issues were coded as a separate theme to identify those articles that particularly focused on the issues that NGOs and protest groups wanted to raise. While it might be argued that the G20 Summit agenda itself dealt with global issues, the purpose of this coding was to distinguish those articles that presented issues that activists are concerned about. Through consideration of NGO press releases ahead of the G20 and the coverage, a selection of issues were settled upon. These included globalization/capitalism; global trade; climate change; financial system/banking reform; international institution reform; international development and poverty.

Results and analysis

Whose voice?

It was important first of all to gain an understanding of whose voices were represented in the coverage. This would provide the first basic indicator of whether institutional sources dominated.

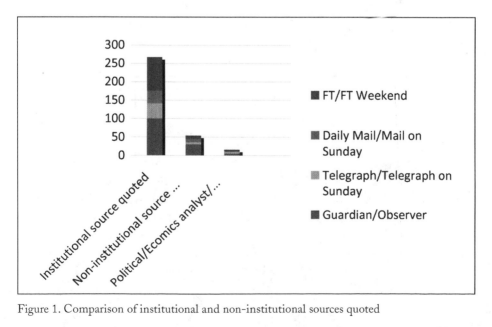

Figure 1. Comparison of institutional and non-institutional sources quoted

Taking the figures displayed in figure 1 at face value, one can see that 267 or 79 percent of all quotes across the newspaper articles analyzed were institutional. Non-institutional sources (including NGOs and protesters) counted for only 54 or 16 percent of those quoted, while political/economic analyst (where it was not clear if they were institutional or non-institutional sources) and "Other" made up the remaining 5 per cent. By considering the extent to which the 54 non-institutional sources were quoted—that is, the space given over to the quote in the article—an even starker picture emerges of how they were reported.

Figure 2 below shows that of the 55 non-institutional sources quoted across the 247 articles, 28 of them or 51 percent, received only a brief mention.

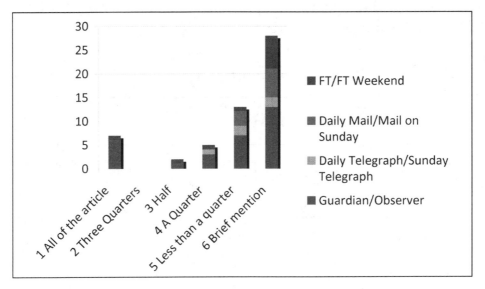

Figure 2. Proportion of article devoted to non-institutional source

It should also be noted that of the six articles printed in *The Guardian*, which quoted non-institutional sources throughout, four were letters to the editor from NGOs, one followed an International Trade Union Congress (ITUC) press release and the final article was an interview with the member of the public who captured video of Ian Tomlinson being pushed from behind by police. However it is also quite evident that had *The Guardian* and *The Observer* not been included in the content analysis, there would be considerably less coverage of non-institutional sources to report (*The Guardian* printed 56 percent of all non-institutional source quotes counted).

While institutional sources also received a significant number of brief mentions (75–see figure 3 below), this represented only 28 percent of all institutional quotes across the 247 articles. However, 44 percent of the institutional source quotes took up a quarter or more of the text in the articles they appeared in.

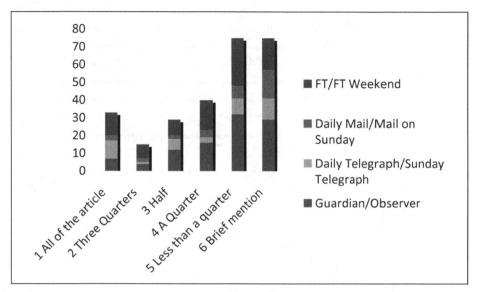

Figure 3. Proportion of article devoted to institutional source

Therefore, as well as significantly outnumbering non-institutional sources in the coverage, the voices and opinions of institutional sources were also given more article space, when they were quoted. In fact 12 percent of institutional sources had their views appear throughout the article in which they featured. This was particularly true in the *FT*, where, for example, full page interviews with G20 leaders, including US President Barack Obama and Indian Prime Minster Manmohan Singh, appeared in the run up to the Summit. Both *The Telegraph* and *FT* also carried comment pieces, penned, for example, by international organization heads or ministers, such as UK Business Secretary Lord Mandelson. This is not reason for criticism in itself. Journalists would not be doing their job if they did not capture and report the voices of the leaders of the day. The problem lies in the fact that, in the presented sample at least, this sort of coverage is just not reciprocated for non-institutional voices. The opinions of the chief executive of Care International or the executive director of Friends of the Earth, for example, found their expression in the letters pages, on page 35 and 45 of *The Guardian,* respectively (*The Guardian*, 2 April and 4 April 2009).

Whose story?

Where possible the original source of a news article was identified and counted. In some cases identification was straightforward, such as the Brown-Obama press conference or the release of the G20 communiqué. Other examples included a statement by Lord Mandelson on the eve of the Summit, which was covered on the front page of *The Telegraph* on 30 March with the headline "Give banks a break says Mandelson" (*The Telegraph*, 30 March 2009: 1). *The Daily Mail* ran with "Mandy: Give bankers a break" (*Daily Mail*, 30 March 2009: 10), *The Guardian*, however, ran a quote from the Mandelson statement in an article titled "New blow to Brown on eve of G20 summit" (*The Guardian*, 30 March 2009: 2). The generation of new economic figures by international organizations such as the International Monetary Fund (IMF) and the Organization for Economic Co-operation and Development (OECD) ahead of the summit also generated coverage. The aforementioned *Guardian* article on the ITUC–"Unions press G20 leaders to end casino capitalism"–was the result of a press release sent by the ITUC (*The Guardian*, 1 April 2009: 29). *The Guardian* was the only newspaper in the analysis to cover it, however, and it was one of only two news stories in the study that could have been argued to originate from a non-institutional source (the rest were letters). While press releases were sent by campaigning organizations ahead of and during the summit, including 12 from the NGOs in this study, none received coverage in the newspapers analyzed. As Lewis and colleagues found in their 2008 study of public relations and news sources, "releases from NGOs and charities are occasionally used as the basis for a story, but more often a quotation from one of these groups will be used to provide a contextual or opposing viewpoint to the main focus of an item" (Lewis, Williams, & Franklin, 2008: 13). An example of this practice appeared in *The Guardian* on 4 April in a page 9 article regarding the G20 leaders' decision to increase funding to the IMF, entitled "Concern grows on powerful role for fund." The second to last paragraph read:

> "This is an institution that has effectively just been given the world's cheque book," said Clare Melamed, head of policy at Action Aid. "Reform is now more urgent than ever." Or as a spokeswoman for Oxfam put it, "the IMF is big, it's bad and it's back" (*The Guardian*, 4 April 2009: 9)

Even this however was the exception to the rule in this study, where very few comments appeared to have been sought from non-institutional sources during the period of the G20.

As for the original source of news articles, figure 4 below clearly shows the disparity between institutional sources and non-institutional sources.

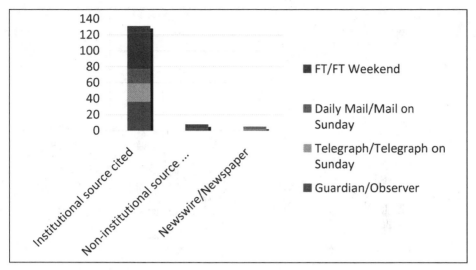

Figure 4. Comparison of institutional and non-institutional sources cited

While these figures come with the qualification that it was not possible to identify with confidence the original source of all articles, complete identification would be likely to have extended the institutional source count rather than non-institutional.

Themes covered

Further evidence of institutional source dominance or rather lack of non-institutional source presence was found in the count of themes covered by the newspapers studied (figure 5 provides the full breakdown). It was fully expected that reporting of the discussions between G20 country leaders and their outcomes would dominate, and it might be argued that this is as it should be. However, out of the 247 articles analyzed, only 14 percent or 25 articles included coverage of those issues considered of concern to activists.

Perhaps unsurprisingly, it was *The Guardian* that carried the majority of articles featuring activist issues (14 pieces in all covering global institutional reform, climate change, banking reform, poverty, development and globalization). Four of these, however, were letters to the editor from the Jubilee Debt campaign, the Put People First campaign, Friends of the Earth and Care International. In terms of news articles, the ITUC article and the piece on IMF funding quoted earlier were included in the count along with a news piece on climate change, which did not appear elsewhere. The article, "Climate change experts call on G20 members to commit action," appeared on page 2 of *The Guardian* on 31 March and detailed a

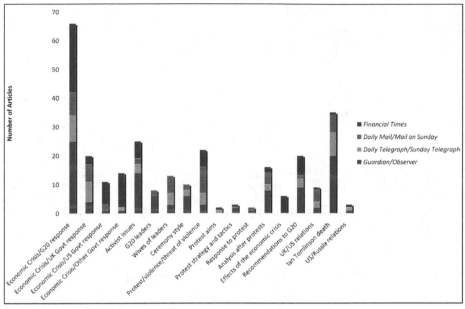

Figure 5 Frequency of theme in all papers

"last ditch effort to insert clearer green commitments into the global economic recovery package." However, the sources it quoted—a NASA climatologist, chief scientific adviser to the Department for Environment, Food and Rural Affairs and former government adviser, Lord Stern—were hardly non-institutional. Perhaps this reflects source selection on the basis of a "hierarchy of credibility" (Becker, 1967) but it is hard to say for certain. What was shown, however, was that six of the 14 articles considered to cover activist issues in *The Guardian* did not actually quote a non-institutional source.

The minimal coverage of non-institutional sources and activist issues, within these newspapers at least, was despite the public relations efforts of NGOs and campaigning organizations during the course of the two weeks. The next section will look at these efforts in more detail.

Non-governmental organization tactics

All of the fifteen NGOs interviewed engaged in proactive media relations' efforts associated with the summit, including dissemination of press releases. None of the releases received coverage in the newspapers analyzed, but some had successes elsewhere, including in other newspapers, online and via broadcast media. Others used different strategies to ensure coverage; for example, ONE Campaign initiated a special report with the *Financial Times*, entitled "The G20: Africa and the World." The partnership secured coverage in the *FT* and on broadcast outlets such as CNN and BBC who wanted to interview the ONE campaign group's spokesperson, Bob Geldof. The combination of the agreement with the *FT* and a high-profile campaigning celebrity was key to success, which was achieved despite the fact that the ONE campaign group has only one media-relations director and an assistant. Support may be found here for Davis's (2000) argument that an understanding of news values and sophisticated media strategies is helping non-institutional sources gain more media coverage. While agreeing that strategy makes a difference, however, the ONE campaign group's media relations director also suggested that issue coverage is declining. When asked, "Do you consider that the media covers the issues you want to raise?," she answered:

> Yes but increasingly less so over time. It's always necessary to be extremely focused and targeted on the story at play, find ways to make sure our message feeds very directly into that story, and having celebrity spokespeople such as Bob Geldof is a great advantage.

The press officer responsible for G20 coverage at Action Aid went further:

> I think coverage of issues really peaked in 2005 with the Make Poverty History campaign. Post 2005 it has been harder for NGOs to fight for space.

And Care International's senior press officer explained:

> I think it is generally getting harder for NGOs to get into the news, as journalists seem to be shying away from using NGOs to comment in news stories.

Equally Oxfam's press officer said:

> coverage for aid issues has become harder to secure than it was at the time of Make Poverty History. There is a lot of coverage for something when it is being discussed at the political level.

This would tend to support Bennett's (1990) indexing hypothesis, and other NGOs explained how this could sometimes work to their advantage in securing coverage. For example, Friends of the Earth's press officer was more positive in response to the question of whether the media give enough coverage to activist issues. He said that:

> We are one of the leading NGOs in the UK dealing with climate change, which has become a high profile issue in recent years.

World Development Movement also pointed out that:

> More recently *The Times* has taken a more enlightened line on climate change and have become more receptive to us.

Other NGOs described how they have worked to become perceived by journalists as experts in a particular field. For example, Care International's senior press officer explained that:

> We now tend to put all our focus on two issues to concentrate resources and efforts. For example sexual violence in conflict situations is an area not dealt with by many organizations and Care is focusing on it.

Therefore, one begins to observe a hierarchy of credibility amongst NGOs within which each works to establish themselves as the expert on a particular issue and therefore the primary source for journalists. Christian Aid's spokeswoman said:

> I worked as a journalist for 14 years before joining Christian Aid and had a sense of there being an unwritten hierarchy on particular issues. However within a multifaceted subject such as climate change there are opportunities for NGOs to find a niche in which they have credibility as experts. Christian Aid for example has worked hard over the last few years to increase understanding that climate change is a development issue as well as an environmental issue. Our campaign–and those of other development NGOs–has contributed to a better understanding in the media that climate change is a major problem for people in poor countries and we now receive more journalist inquiries on the subject than previously.

However, expertise in itself does not guarantee coverage. The press officer at World Development Movement found that:

> As the (financial) crisis unfolded, we produced a research report on banking and the fact that people in the Global south lack access to banking services and that this exacerbates their poverty. . . . I spoke to several economics editors who said they were interested but that they were focusing on the UK. It was something topical and newsworthy but because the banking crisis was hitting the UK, this is what gained coverage.

A decline in interest in development issues as the economic crisis unfolded was an experience shared across all the NGOs interviewed because journalists were more interested in covering its domestic impact. Despite resources and strategy, the success of non-institutional sources can seemingly shift over time. For example, in 2005 during a time of relative prosperity in the UK, many NGOs saw a peak in their access to the media through campaigns such as Make Poverty History. In times of economic crisis, however, the news media were seen to become more inward looking. This can mean success for other sources, for example the TUC saw:

> An increase in the number of journalist calls in the past year due to the big unemployment increases. When a new set of figures are released by the government, we tend to be asked for comment.

In this situation, campaigning organizations look to different strategies to make their case. This was true in the run up to the G20 when 150 NGOs, including the majority of those interviewed, joined forces with the TUC, to make their voices heard as part of the "Put People First" campaign and took to the streets. The campaign organized a mass rally on the weekend before the G20, which attracted an estimated 35,000 marchers, along with media interest. The campaign also took part in protests in central London during the Summit. Here it is valuable to return to the content analysis, to see to what extent their voices and actions were represented in the news reports.

Coverage of the protests

In the days immediately before and during the Summit, 22 articles were coded as reporting protest/violence/threat of violence and 16 were coded as analysis after the protests.[4] Only two articles were considered to have captured the protest aims and arguments. In this respect, the findings have less in common with Rojecki's study of the 1999 Seattle protests (Rojecki, 2002: 166). The coverage analyzed points to results more in common with Bennett's study of protests at the World Economic Forum and earlier studies which described the media's tendency to report "the actions of the most reckless in the movement" (cited in Rojecki, 2002: 155).

The *Daily Mail* for example labeled its entire coverage of the first day of the G20 with the headline "Love and Hate"—"Love" between the Obamas and the Browns, "hate" on the streets outside. A photo taking up half the front page of the issue captured a protester remonstrating with police. The caption read "Confrontation: Snarling and bloodied, a protester challenges police near the Bank of England" (*Daily Mail*, 2 April 2009: 1). The *Daily Mail* made extensive use of photos, and the following day, two inside pages were taken up by colour photos under the headline "Intimacy at No 10, mayhem outside" and one caption read "Under siege: Officers hold their ground as stick-wielding protesters go on the attack" (*Daily Mail*, 2 April 2009: 2). Such examples may support Cottle's assertion that "media visuals of demonstrations and protests are often semiotically aligned to editorial outlooks" (Cottle, 2008: 866). The same might be argued of some of the *Mail's* news articles, which also focused on the violent elements of the protest. Their report on the vandalism at the Royal Bank of Scotland included the line:

> The targets were clear: the police and anything resembling a bank. This was not an assault on capitalism, just another assault on authority. And authority won. (*Daily Mail*, 2 April 2009: 7)

The Telegraph also reported the protests through a frame of violence and law and order and an extensive use of images, although with more moderate headlines. *The Telegraph,* however, allowed criticism of policing methods and quoted protesters, for example:

> Many blamed the police for the 'kettle' containment tactics which forced the large numbers of demonstrators within the cordons. (*The Daily Telegraph,* 3 April 2009: 6)

The *Financial Times,* however, took a more balanced view of the protests and quoted protesters and eyewitnesses more extensively. For example, Imogen Carter, 20, a photography student, said, "a lot of people got hurt. I don't think the police acted well." This was balanced in the same article with, "but others wanted trouble. 'I'd have liked to have seen more smashed windows', said a 33-year-old artist" (*Financial Times,* 2 April 2009: 4).

Perhaps most tellingly, on the same page, however, was an article by *FT* columnist Matthew Engel, who attended the protests and described a carnival atmosphere marred by the actions of a small group. He wrote:

> The attack on the RBS building which apparently involved about 20 people, or about 0.1 percent of those there. . . . The codename for their [police] operation was "Glencoe" after the brutal Highland massacre (1692, about 80 dead). Not a good start. (*Financial Times,* 2 April 2009: 4)

One can see similarities with Rojecki's study, in terms of the criticism, with the exception of the *Daily Mail,* of policing methods at the G20. In the context of source media relations, however, the messages of protesters and the movements they represented, in this case, got lost in the reporting of spectacle and violence. As the press officer for the CND commented in our interview, "A lot of the media covered the protest as an event and took comments regarding accessibility to the protests route, who could get in or out of the area and the protest experience rather than the issues."

Conclusion

This study can only claim to be a very small contribution to the much larger collection of more in-depth studies in the field of source/media relations. It has focused on one international event and one element of the coverage within the UK national newspapers analyzed and does not seek to add to the already high volume of evidence regarding news production. The findings presented, however, do provide evidence which points towards an ongoing trend in news journalism to report the views of institutional sources over non-institutional sources. The content analysis along with the conversations with NGO press officers help to shed further light on source/media relations and do not provide evidence of an emerging pluralism in media coverage, or indeed that newspaper coverage of protest has entered a new era. Furthermore, in this study at least, the actions and coverage of the most reckless had no significant benefits in terms of drawing broader attention to the protest movement and their messages, as DeLuca and Peeples (2002) suggested it might.

Studies focused more on news production suggest that time, resource and editorial pressures on journalists make some more susceptible to political communication methods and reliant on PR material. However these pressures don't appear to have significantly increased the use of material from non-institutional sources. It is not that NGO PR practitioners lack the skills; many of those interviewed employ ex-journalists as their media officers. It has also been seen through the interviews undertaken, that NGOs invest in developing expertise in particular areas and fund and produce reports on the issues. While this may have led to a hierarchy of credibility amongst NGOs, it does not seem to have had a significant impact in terms of redressing the balance with institutional sources. The role of many NGOs remains as a source of comment on somebody else's story

The content analysis and interviews perhaps provide support for a combination of Schlesinger and Tumber's (1994) arguments and Bennett's (1990) indexing hypothesis. Thus while dominance persists, one can see that some opportunities do open up for other voices over time, as the political debate evolves or crisis forces issues on to the agenda. The interviews, in particular, showed recognition on the part of NGOs that these opportunities arise more often than not when their issues, for example, climate change, are part of the broader political discussion. Therefore this does not suggest that non-institutional sources can become "primary definers" (Hall et al., 1978), but their voices can be part of the debate as it is carried into the public sphere by the media. An imbalance in this scenario in favour of government compared to NGO voices in the newspapers may be argued to be expected and indeed perhaps not deeply problematic. While the news media should present a range of views it should not become simply a conduit for the views, issues and arguments that un-elected campaigning groups wish to put forward. What is of more concern is the broader lack of serious issues coverage within which these non-institutional arguments can be presented. Equally, with a growing plethora of web-based alternatives available for groups to convey their opinions, founded on research or otherwise, the need for the news media to be a trusted source of issue information and mediation in the public sphere is more vital than ever.

Notes

1. Non-institutional in this study refers to non-governmental organizations (NGOs), including campaigning organizations, charities and pressure groups, along with trade unions. Institutional refers to the institutions of State—government, parliament, the police, and judiciary, along with officials in intergovernmental institutions, corporations, financial institutions and business federations.

2. Reporting of the death of Ian Tomlinson was given a separate coding. This was because coverage of the incident escalated a week after the G20 summit when it became clear that his death could have been linked to police action and it became a separate story in itself.

3. War on Want, Action Aid, Greenpeace, Save the Children, World Development Movement, Christian Aid, Oxfam, Climate Camp, Friends of the Earth, Drop the Debt Campaign, Stop the War Coalition, CND, Amnesty International, Cafod, Care International, the TUC and the ONE Campaign were contacted. All interviews were undertaken during July and August 2009.

4. These did not include coverage of Ian Tomlinson's death, which was to dominate reporting later in the second week.

CHAPTER NINE

Photography, the Police and Protest Images of the G20, London 2009

DAVID ARCHIBALD

As has become the norm since its inaugural meeting in Berlin in 1999, when representatives of the Group of Twenty (G20) gathered in London on 2 April 2009, this transnational summit of the world's leading financiers attracted significant levels of protest. As the G20 leaders (The London Summit, 2009) reiterated their view that, despite the shadow cast by the international banking crisis, sustainable globalization was dependent on, as they put it, "an open world economy based on market principles, effective regulation, and strong global institutions," tens of thousands of demonstrators, from both Britain and abroad, including anti-capitalist activists, climate change campaigners and trade unionists, converged on the UK capital in a diverse series of events which sought to challenge the G20's neoliberal agenda. In common with similar transnational events, most notably the 2001 G8 summit in Genoa, violence marked a number of the protests.[1] One bystander, Ian Tomlinson, died on the eve of the summit after coming into contact with police officers as he passed by the demonstration on the way to his home. A vigil marking his death was organized on 2 April, and this involved further violence, although there were no further fatalities. Initial media reports of the protests followed a pattern consistent with previous reporting of protests both in the UK and beyond; the media constructed a narrative which was consistent with that offered by the police and one which tended to focus on violence perpetrated by protesters. In subsequent days, however, the emergence of footage shot by photographers, protesters and members of the public on the 1st and 2nd of April protests, most importantly, footage of the events surrounding Tomlinson's death, challenged the dominant narrative and forced a shift in the media's focus, at least in part, to police tactics on the demonstrations and to acts of violence perpetrated by police officers. The London G20 protests took place against a background of growing unease on the part of both the police and the government over their inability to control the capturing and dissemination of images in the public sphere. This chapter outlines the nature of the state's unease over new technology, offers an analysis of the coverage of the London G20 protests, and argues that when certain images, and their ordering, or distribution, move out with state control, problems for the state, and individuals working for the state, are likely to arise. The chapter also argues that the G20 coverage is significant for the study of transnational protests because it provides an illuminating example of the way that images of protest taken by photographers, protesters and members of the public can lead to significant changes in the way that protests are reported in the mainstream media.

Police and photography

The reproductive capabilities of photographic technology—both still and moving images—have long proved useful to the state. Tom Gunning (1999: 50-1) notes that the first mobile hand cameras were originally known as "detective cameras," and he cites an article in an early French amateur photographic journal which highlights their potential benefits to "police officers and amateur spies." As it transpired, police officers more than amateur spies appeared to benefit most from the new technology as photographic technology was incorporated into the criminal justice system. John Tagg (2009: 25) problematizes the progressive tradition of social documentary photography and filmmaking by noting that in the nineteenth century "panoptic machines constituted one of the technologies of power and one of the arenas of tactics through which the social field was to be reconstituted within a new microphysics of power as the object of a new regime of truth and knowledge." Tagg (2009: 13) notes, however, that the state's appropriation of the means of representation could only be effective if it was placed alongside an efficient ordering system of knowledge, which depended on "the development of a composite machine—a computer—in which the camera. . .was hooked up to that other great nineteenth-century machine, the upright filing cabinet, which, when combined with the classificatory structure of the catalog, constituted a new information technology that would radically redirect the public and legislative function of the archive." For Tagg, the image, coupled with the ordering, or fixing in place of the image, both within and beyond the frame, became central to the needs of the nineteenth-century state. This continues to be the case, therefore individuals or organizations who disrupt this process are liable to come into conflict with the state as is evidenced by recent events in the UK involving the state and photographers.

There is footage available on the *Guardian* website, which was shot by two police photographers at a Climate Camp demonstration in Kingsnorth, Kent, on 8 August 2008. The officers are members of one of the many Forward Intelligence Teams which are tasked with the taking of images of protesters at demonstrations. What is significant about the footage is the officers' concern with the activities of the photographers who are present, not just the protesters. At one moment, as the camera focuses on three members of an *ITN Meridian Tonight* camera crew emerging from a field, the following exchange takes place between the two officers:

> Officer A: "A lot of press officers aren't there? They just think they can wander in and out of the field."
> Officer B: "It's wrong I think."
> Officer A: "I agree."
> Officer B: "I trust them less than the protesters."[2]

What might lie behind this lack of trust on the part of individual police officers? Moreover, is it illustrative of a wider lack of trust at the governmental level? There are two strands here. Firstly, in relation to government, since the turn of the century, but particularly after 11 September 2001, there has been a marked increase in attempts to utilize anti-terrorist legislation to impose restrictions on the right to take photographs in public places. For instance, Section 76 of the Counter-Terrorism Act 2008 (OPSI, 2008) makes it illegal to "publish or communicate any information about a member of the armed forces or a police officer which is of a kind likely to be useful to a person committing or preparing an act of terrorism." This legislation replaced Section 58 of the Terrorism Act 2000 (OPSI, 2000), which criminalized the collecting, making or possession of a record, including a photographic record and was—note the identical wording—"of a kind likely to be useful to a person committing or preparing an act of terrorism." Breaching the law carries a jail sentence of up to 10 years. Secondly, there has been a marked increase in the incidences of individual police officers preventing photographers from taking photographs in public places. A number of such events are catalogued in the response of the National Union of Journalists' (NUJ) General Secretary, Jeremy Dear (Dear, 2008), to a Home Office committee; the examples range from the seemingly ludicrous—an amateur photographer being prevented by police from photographing the switching on of Christmas lights in Ipswich—to demands that photographs of police officers that have been taken, legally, by professional photographers, be deleted from their digital cameras. Dear also notes that there have been accusations of violence being perpetrated by police officers on photographers whilst they have been capturing images of police officers on demonstrations.[3] Dear's position appears to concur with accusations levelled by campaigners who regularly take photographs of members of Forward Intelligence Teams and who claim that they are systematically arrested then released without charge when they attempt to carry out this activity.[4] Della Porta, Andretta, Mosca and Reiter (2006:150) suggest that "(t)he public order strategies employed by the police reflect the respect the state shows for the rights and freedoms of citizens." The authors write in connection with the rights and freedoms of protesters; however, these words could be applied equally to photographers. The fear of photography on the part of the government and the police provides some of the context in which the G20 protests took place; from the perspective of the police, however, the restrictions placed on the right to take photographs in public places, regardless of their lawfulness, appeared to make some kind of sense.

Reporting the London G20 protests

Speaking in Parliament on the first day of the protests, the Parliamentary Under-Secretary of State for the Home Department, Shahid Malik (Hansard, 1 April 2009), in a debate unconnected to the G20 entitled Photography (Public Places) stated, "(l)et me start by saying that our counter-terrorism laws are not designed or intended to stop people taking photographs. That is simply not their aim. People have the right to take photographs in public places for legitimate reasons and we will do everything we can to uphold that right." Yet, the following day, on 2 April 2009, at a memorial to mark Tomlinson's death, a Metropolitan Police Inspector addressed a group of photographers and camera crews (including a Sky News crew) in the following terms:

> Ladies and gentlemen of the press, I have been asked to ask you to leave the area for the time being under section 14 of the Public Order Act that can be imposed by the senior officer on the scene. What this means is that I want you to go away for half an hour. . .You have got a choice, you either go away now or you spend the rest of the afternoon in the cell.[5]

It is not clear what action the police did not want recorded; what is clear is that this request was a contravention of the Public Order Act, which should only be invoked if there is "a threat to serious public disorder, serious damage to property or serious disruption to the life of the community."[6] Yet the serious threat to life at the G20 protests did not come from photographers. On the contrary, mobile phone footage shot by an anonymous US businessman who witnessed the 1 April protest emerged six days later, which appears to show a police officer striking Ian Tomlinson with a baton and then pushing him in the back, resulting in Tomlinson falling to the ground.[7] Tomlinson walked away from the incident, but died shortly after. Further footage of Tomlinson later emerged from a combination of protesters and passers-by, which was often shot on mobile phones, and from television camera crews; CCTV footage is also available, although, so far at least, this has been withheld from the public. The officer who struck Tomlinson has been questioned under caution, and over one year after the event the case remains in the hands of the Crown Prosecution Service. The emergence of the footage of Tomlinson's death was a significant factor in shaping the evolving media narrative of the protests.

The initial media reporting of the G20 was consistent with what has been presented in earlier research of media representations of protest; as Simon Cottle (2008: 855) notes, such studies found "the mainstream news media invariably report protests and demonstrations through a dominant law and (dis)order frame, labelling protestors as deviant and de-legitimizing their aims and politics by emphasizing drama, spectacle and violence." This is exemplified by an analysis of the BBC News 24 (1 April 2009) coverage of the initial protest, which began with two pieces of footage edited together; the first–of a lone masked protester, surrounded by a group of on-lookers, smashing a Royal Bank of Scotland window–was followed by a cut to a small group of police officers surrounded and under pressure from by a considerably larger group of hostile protesters. The favored reading–that of besieged police officers struggling to cope with large groups of potentially violent protesters–coincided with the narrative that was put forward by the police and was reported, unproblematically, by the BBC. Moreover, the BBC reporting of Tomlinson's death, in common, with the majority of mainstream media outlets, was based primarily on information provided from the police. Thus BBC News (1 April 2009) stated simply that "a man died after collapsing, *police said*." The initial police response contained no comment on the contact that Tomlinson had come under from a police officer, on the contrary, a Scotland Yard spokesperson, quoted in *The Telegraph* (Edwards et al., 2 April 2009), attempted to create a picture of police officers attempting to save the man's life as protesters hampered their efforts, claiming that "officers took the decision to move him as during this time a number of missiles–believed to be bottles–were being thrown at them. LAS [London Ambulance Service] took the man to hospital where he was pronounced dead." In a statement exemplifying the manner in which the mainstream press accepted what is now known to be a fabricated account, *The Telegraph* (Edwards et al., 2 April 2009) reported that "(p)olice medics managed to get the man to a safe area where they tried to resuscitate him before an ambulance arrived and rushed him to hospital, where he died at around 8pm."[8]

Of course, it would be naive to view the media as a monolithic mass automatically churning out an identical, if misleading, narrative. Indeed *Guardian* writer, Paul

Lewis, was named as reporter of the year at the 2010 British Press Awards for his work in attempting to uncover the details of Tomlinson's death. Significantly, Lewis (Luft, 24 March 2010), who is critical of journalists who take at face value the narrative spun by the police press spokespersons, claims that in the six days between Tomlinson's death and the appearance of the footage of his death, he utilized social networking sites such as Twitter to appeal to protesters and the public to come forward with information which could illuminate the events of the day. Other journalists, writing mainly in the broadsheets, also questioned the police version of events: writing in *The Times*, Whipple (Whipple, 3 April 2009), comments, "Wednesday's police operation against G20 protesters was, by most accounts, a success. Minimal violence, stoical police, and London back up and running a few hours later. But there is another story. . . . Most of all, it is the story of how the police willfully criminalised and alienated 4,000 innocent people." Whipple's on-the-ground report is particularly critical of the police tactic of placing a cordon around demonstrators which prevents anyone entering or leaving the protest, often for hours at a time, a practice known as kettling: "The police tactics were simple. At the first hint of trouble, they enacted a long-planned strategy—trapping and detaining all the protesters, violent or not. . . . Once established, the cordon slowly squeezed—each police charge rolling past any protesters who refused to move, battering them. No one was released." However, although alternative but marginal voices were reported in the press, it was only after the footage of Tomlinson being pushed to the ground appeared on the *Guardian* website that the BBC amended their narrative and on 7 April, a BBC (BBC News, 7 April 2009) news item opened with the words "(a) man who died during the G20 protest was pushed to the ground by a police officer, video footage has shown." Rosie and Gorringe (2009: 1.6) suggest that the initial reporting, at least until 2 or 3 April, "offered a mirror image of previous international summits." They also identify the media *volte face* after Tomlinson's death (2009: 3.1). This also appears to be the position of Her Majesty's Inspector of Constabulary, which produced a report in July 2009 "Adapting to Protest: Inspecting Police in the Public Interest" (2009: 24), in which the authors note that "(d)uring the 1st April protests, the live news broadcasts by BBC News 24 and Sky were predominately positive." The authors appear to be more concerned with whether the reports were "positive" in their reporting of police actions than an accurate report of the events of the day, but they also note (2009: 9) that "by the 5th April this was becoming more critical. This intensified following the emergence of images relating to the death of Ian Tomlinson." Guy Aitchison (2009b) notes, moreover, that "(i)t was only after the overwhelming evidence of police brutality coming from citizen journalists that the media narrative changed." It is important to add that it was the overwhelming evidence provided in the form of moving images and their appearance on the Internet which forced this change. Indeed it is likely that without the appearance of moving images challenging the dominant narrative then the voices of journalists like Lewis and Whipple would have remained marginal.

Arguably, it was the appearance of footage from three events, which taken together challenged the police account of events and the dominant media narrative. The first is the footage of Ian Tomlinson's death. Secondly, despite the attempted restrictions on the right to photograph protests on 2 April outlined above, it later emerged that mobile phone footage was taken by a protester of a member of the Metropolitan Police Territorial Support Group, Sergeant Delroy Smellie, striking Nicola Fisher, a 36-year-old female animal-rights protester, across the face with the back of his hand and then hitting her twice on the legs with an extended metal baton. The footage was placed subsequently on YouTube and reported widely subsequently.[9] Thirdly, footage of police tactics in clearing a peaceful Climate Camp demonstration at Bishopsgate in the City of London on 1 April, which shows environmental protesters being forcibly cleared from the streets. As the campaigners stand with their hands held aloft, chanting, in unison, "shame on you" and "this is not a riot," members of the Metropolitan Police repeatedly strike the protesters with shields and batons in an attempt to disperse the peaceful crowd.[10] Thus, footage taken by protesters and photographers, which appear to show orchestrated harassment and violence against protesters *and* photographers, coalesced to create a public image of police officers either out of control, or, at least, acting disproportionately.

The impact of the images: The story so far

As stated above, no charges were brought against the officer involved in Tomlinson's death,[11] although the various pieces of footage that emerged were a key factor in out-of-court settlements between the police and protesters who had been unlawfully arrested during the protests (BBC News, 22 March 2010a, b). One officer, Sergeant Smellie, was charged with common assault for striking the aforementioned female protester and a trial took place in March 2010. Smellie claimed in his defence that in hitting the woman he was making a pre-emptive strike because he feared that he would be assaulted by one of two weapons that she was carrying—a carton of orange juice, and, perhaps unaware of the irony, a camera. Indeed in the footage, a number of protesters can be seen attempting to capture photographic images of police violence, thereby utilizing their cameras as "weapons" against police violence. Defence witnesses (BBC News, 23 March 2010) claimed, that the woman was behaving like a "lunatic" and that she was "out of control," in contrast to Smellie, who, they argued, exercised restraint. In his defence Smellie (Lewis, 25 March 2010) claimed that he used "a flick of the hand" when he could have "broken her jaw." Noticeably, Smellie (Lewis, 25 March 2010) called into question the referential qualities of the images themselves when he stated, "(n)ot one photograph or piece of footage comes close to reflecting the fear as I turned around to see this crowd and its proximity, both to myself and my officers." Although for many this was a clear example of police violence, in finding the officer not guilty, the magistrate who presided over the case stated (BBC News, 13 March 2010), "I am satisfied he honestly believed it was necessary to use force to defend himself."

The Smellie trial underlines the notion that images do not simply speak for themselves and indicates that moving image footage alone is far from sufficient to anchor, or fix in place, the interpretation of images. In the wake of the G20 protests *Journalist,* the National Union of Journalists magazine, carried a four-page article which included a series of photographs of conflict between police and photographers, claiming (2009: 14) that "the pictures tell the story." But, as Bill Nichols (1994: 33) suggests, "(n)o image, can show intent or motivation. Images, whether in real time, slow motion, or freeze frame, can, however, help corroborate a narrative account of what happened." Nichols was referring to the footage surrounding the arrest of Rodney King, whose case can be useful in helping to illuminate the discourse surrounding moving images in courtroom situations. On 3 March 1991, officers of the Los Angeles Police Department (LAPD) stopped, restrained, beat repeatedly and then arrested Rodney King. King suffered severe injuries, including a fractured skull, during the assault. A local resident, George Holliday, recorded some of this action using a video camera.[12] When sections of this raw footage were screened on televisions across the US, many viewers regarded it as incontrovertible evidence of LAPD violence being inflicted on a black man: for many observers, the video spoke for itself, it told its own story. Nichols (1994: 22) points out that, in the subsequent trial of four of the officers, this was the approach taken by the prosecution whose argument, as he puts it "hinged heavily on the positivist fallacy: the videotape offered the proverbial smoking gun. The prosecution could treat its images as raw evidence. . . . The prosecution neglected to consider the image as symptom in need of diagnosis. The prosecution chose to treat the tape as evidence, exposing itself to compelling counter-arguments that it was no such thing (in and of itself)." On the contrary, the defence constructed "an interpretive frame in which the videotape itself would serve as confirmation. Confirmation of what? Of the rough and brutal nature of police work. Of the risk and uncertainty that confront officers in the street. Of the dire necessity of controlled force to safeguard the men in blue and preserve the lives of suspects who might otherwise be killed." Moreover, they slowed the tape down and conducted a close textual analysis of each still image to attempt to prove that every police action, every blow, was intended to prevent a potentially life-threatening act being carried out by King. The defence, as Frank P. Tomasulo (1996: 75) notes, "were able to provide sophisticated 'spin control' of the beating by repeatedly showing the infamous home video recording (in slow motion) and by telling the jury that Rodney King was behaving irrationally and was resolutely disobeying the officers' commands to stop moving—a classic instance of the 'reading against the grain,' 'structuring absence' methodology valorized by many film and video scholars." As is well known, four officers were cleared in the first trial, but two of the four were sentenced to 30 months in a subsequent federal trial. The King case is significant for the study of visual culture because it raises important questions about the referential nature of the image in a manner that goes beyond the normal arena of academic discourse. It also finds an echo in the discourse surrounding the Smellie assault trial and is likely to be of interest in the study of any further legal action arising from the G20 protests.

The impact on future images

The controversy provoked by the images of the G20 protests provided an impetus to those campaigners who were questioning the policing of photographers and appears to have had a significant impact. In July 2009, the Metropolitan Police (2009) responded to the controversy when they released a document entitled "photography advice" which states that "(i)t should ordinarily be considered inappropriate to use Section 58a to arrest people photographing police officers in the course of normal policing activities, including protests, as without more, there is no link to terrorism." It remains to be seen what, in practice, "ordinarily" might involve here. The statement added, ominously, that "(t)here is however nothing preventing officers asking questions of an individual who appears to be taking photographs of someone who is or has been a member of Her Majesty's Forces (HMF), Intelligence Services or a constable." Under pressure to clarify the position of the government, the Home Office (Circular 012/2009) issued a statement outlining that sections 43 and 44 of the Terrorism Act 2000 do not "prohibit the taking of photographs, film or digital images in a public place and members of the public and the press should not be prevented from doing so." In addition, in relation to section 58A, it states that "(l)egitimate journalistic activity (such as covering a demonstration for a newspaper) is likely to constitute such an excuse." A recent House of Commons Home Affairs Committee report (2009: 4) states, moreover, that "(t)he police must be aware that, as a matter of course, their actions will be filmed whether or not journalists are present. They must amend their attitudes and tactics accordingly." Thus police officers may, at least legally, be required to allow themselves to be photographed, nevertheless, there remains an unresolved tension here, which is likely to lead to further controversy in this area.

It is not, however, the images alone that forced a re-examination of the G20 reporting. As outlined above, the images were inserted into a field of discourse, the

Internet, which operates, relatively free of state control, at least in Britain. Cottle (2008: 859) notes that the Internet "contains a socially activated potential to unsettle and on occasion even disrupt the vertical flows of institutionally controlled 'top-down' communications and does so by inserting a horizontal communicative network into the wider communications environment." The regime of truth and knowledge which was facilitated by the development of photography and the filing cabinet in the nineteenth century, as outlined by Tagg, is struggling to come to terms with developments in new technology. The Internet functions as the twenty-first century equivalent of the filing cabinet; it is within the reach of the long arm of the law but beyond its control and can, therefore, be a useful tool to those who wish to counter the narratives of the mainstream media and of the state.

Rosie and Gorringe (2009: 6–7) argue that "(w)hile it is tempting to view the G20 as a landmark event that has changed the contours of protest policing and reportage, the media attention cycle is notoriously short. Once interest in the G20 fades, there is no guarantee against a return to earlier practices." Of course, there are no guarantees here, but without the ubiquity of machines that can capture moving images which can then be placed so readily onto a horizontal communication network relatively free from state control, it is unlikely that the media narratives would have changed so dramatically, there would have been no trial of Sergeant Smellie, and the initial police account of Tomlinson's death would have remained unchallenged. Of course, it is important not to be too euphoric about the democratization of image-making technology and note that access to screen images, for instance, CCTV footage, often lies in the hands of the police and the state, and is treated far from democratically. Nevertheless, the controversy surrounding the G20 footage is useful in highlighting the tension that exists between the state, individual officers, and those who seek to capture images of police officers or protest, whether they be professional photographers or twenty-first century "amateur spies" equipped with digital cameras and mobile phones. The reporting of the 2009 G20 London summit does indeed represent a landmark in the reporting of protests in that it reveals the positive impact that citizen journalism can have on shaping mainstream media reporting of transnational protests. The continued unease with which the state, the police as an institution, and individual police officers display towards the capturing and dissemination of images of both police and protest, however, is far from resolved and is likely to resurface in future transnational protests, both in the UK and elsewhere.

Notes

1. The Genoa summit was marred by the death of anti-capitalist protestor, Carlo Giuliani, who was shot in the face by a police officer. Initial charges against the officer were dropped after

a judge ruled that the officer had acted in self-defence. The case is currently at the European Court of Human Rights. For background see della Porta, Andretta, Mosca and Reiter, 2006, chapter six: Transnational Protest and Public Order.

2. The video is available at http://www.guardian.co.uk/uk/video/2009/mar/06/police-surveillance-climate-camp-journalists, accessed on 10 May 2009.

3. The increased incidence of photographers being questioned under anti-terrorist legislation is the impetus behind the campaign "I am a Photographer not a Terrorist": see http://www.photographernotaterrorist.org

4. See http://fitwatch.blogspot.com/ for more information on this campaign. Footage of pro-testers being arrested after asking a police officer to identify himself is available here: http://www.youtube.com/watch?v=iyR6UKnA3mo

5. A video of this incident is available at http://www.guardian.co.uk/uk/video/2009/apr/15/g20-protests-police-press, viewed on 20 May 2009.

6. The Metropolitan Police Authority's Civil Rights Panel acknowledged subsequently that the Public Order Act was used inappropriately and that the "use of this power prevented jour-nalists from carrying out their duties." (2010: 30)

7. Available at http://www.guardian.co.uk/uk/2009/apr/07/ian-tomlinson-g20-death-video, viewed on 10 May 2009. Tomlinson's death sparked renewed discussion of another fatality on a demonstration, that of Blair Peach, who died whilst attending an anti-fascist demon-stration in London on March 1979. One consequence of the Tomlinson controversy was the release of the initial report into Peach's death (Metropolitan Police, 2010) which states, "it can reasonably be concluded that a police officer struck the fatal blow" although the report also concluded that there was insufficient evidence to justify criminal proceedings. Notably the report states that there was no photographic evidence of the incident. More informa-tion on the Blair Peach case is available at http://inquest.gn.apc.org/

8. Fears of a cover-up deepened when Nick Hardwick, from the Independent Police Complaints Commission, the body charged with investigating police complaints, stated (C4 News, 9 April 2009) of the Tomlinson case "there is no CCTV footage, there were no cameras in the location where he was assaulted." A statement which tuned out to be wholly inaccurate.

9. http://www.guardian.co.uk/uk/video/2009/apr/14/g20-police-action-tomlinson-memori-al, viewed 20 May 2009.

10. Footage of this incident is available at http://www.youtube.com/watch?v=t244-zEENSs, viewed on 20 May 2009. A short documentary prepared by the Climate Camp legal team is available at http://www.youtube.com/watch?v=DnaaaEnO3k8, viewed on 28 March 2010.

11. This is against a backdrop of data released under the Freedom of Information Act which shows that in recent years the Territorial Support Group had received over 5000 complaints in a four-year period, yet only nine (0.18%) were substantiated after internal investigations, leading to accusations from Jenny Jones (Lewis and Taylor, 6 November 2009), a member of the Metropolitan Police Authority that there was, as she puts it, "a culture of impunity within the organisation."

12. An example of the footage is available at http://www.youtube.com/watch?v=ROn_9302UHg &feature=PlayList&p=54B4333565D77058&playnext=1&playnext_from=PL&index=3, Accessed 20 May 2009.

PART FOUR

Protesting Ecology and Climate

CHAPTER TEN

Wild Public Screens and Image Events from Seattle to China

Using Social Media to Broadcast Activism

KEVIN MICHAEL DELUCA, YE SUN AND JENNIFER PEEPLES

Strolling down Nanjing Lu in Shanghai, among the neon signs one is inundated by a multiplicity of public screens. They range from giant public screens draped over the sides of buildings to billboards to TVs to smartphones. In Beijing, a skyscraper overlooking the Olympic Bird's Nest is crowned with four giant public screens, broadcasting nature scenes between commercials and sometimes nature scenes as commercials. It seems every corner of Beijing flashes us with giant illuminated public screens, markers of capitalism and echoes of the archaic Mao image surveying Tiananmen Square. The ubiquitousness of public screens is evident around the world, from Tokyo's Shibuya District to London's Piccadilly Circus. In the United States, the most famous site of public screens is Times Square, transformed from a seedy sex district into a visual mecca of commercial porn. Although we can single out the shrines of public screens ringing the globe, really, these public screens are everywhere, from our televisions to our computers to our pockets in the forms of iPods, iPhones, and BlackBerries. And although they communicate everything, from words to music, images are their *lingua franca*. And although there is a certain commercial bias, public screens mark a reality and a metaphor that has transformed all forms of discourse, from the commercial to the political to the athletic to the educational to the environmental to the activist.

The point of this chapter will be to explore the constraints and opportunities of this literal and metaphorical transformation of society from the public sphere to public screens.[1] It is incumbent upon activists, academics, indeed, all citizens of the world, to understand the new topography of being and becoming, thinking and acting. In comparison to the rationality, detachment, embodied conversations, and compulsory civility of the public sphere, public screens highlight dissemination, images, hypermediacy, spectacular publicity, cacophony, immersion, distraction, and dissent. Exploring how images eclipse words, image events displace books/newspapers, glances replace gazes, speed shatters contemplation, immersion erases objectivity, broadcasting drowns out dialogue, panmediation trumps mediation, and distraction erodes focus as a mode of perception highlights public screens as contemporary venues for participatory politics and public opinion formation that offer striking contrasts to the public sphere.

The dominant discourses of our time, advertising and public relations, are expertly adapted for public screens. This statement rings truer when one considers how the structure and content of news media in the United States are built around advertising and public relations. The enormous expenditures of corporations on advertising and public relations are evidence of the importance corporations attribute to public screens. McDonald's and Coke, owners of two of the most recognizable icons in the world today (rivaling the Christian cross), annually spend over US\$1.97 billion and \$2.26 billion, respectively, on advertising alone (http://adage.com/ globalmarketers09/). Advertising and public relations become dominant discourses with the advent of 20th century mass media. Besides being the favored form of communication for corporations, public relations and advertising have become the templates for all other areas on public screens. This includes politicians whose discourse is molded more by the requirements of public screens than by the rationality of the public sphere, recently witnessed in the Kabuki theatre of the US 2010 Health Care Summit. It includes the staged campaigns of electoral politics, managed by contemporary wizards of Oz such as Karl Rove, David Axelrod, and David Plouffe. It includes sitcoms and other entertainment TV, where national "discussions" on social issues take place on *Southpark*, *Grey's Anatomy*, and *Lost*. It includes films that deliver the definitive verdict for public memory on such key moments as the Holocaust (*Schindler's List*), World War II (*Saving Private Ryan*), the Kennedy assassination (*JFK*), and the '60s (*Forrest Gump*). Of particular interest to us, it includes activism, such as the case of MoveOn.org morphing from mass protests to mass advertising. This is also true with respect to environmentalism—witness Greenpeace's reliance on dramatic image events and slogans, the Sea Shepherd Conservation Society's "Whale Wars," and the celebrityhood of penguins and polar bears.

This chapter is an exploration of the conditions of possibility for activism in the techno-industrial corporate-controlled culture that bestrides the planet. In the glare of public screens, being mesmerized into moral misgivings is not a sufficient response. Thinking about activism and culture through the prism of public screens, however, enables another seeing of the world. Anti-corporate globalization protests, TV sitcoms, Hollywood films, advertising, and public relations do not represent lack, multiple signs of the decline of civilization. Instead, thought through the metaphor of the public screen, such practices are productive of new modes of intelligence, activism, politics, rhetoric, in short, new modes of being in the world. The concept of the public screen is neither working within a moral economy nor positing a normative ideal, but is opening a space for retheorizing the places of the political. The public screen images a complex world of opportunities and dangers. The complexity of public screens warrants neither nostalgia nor utopianism. The task of thinking is to chart the topography of these new worlds. This charting will focus on how public screens transform activism, especially environmental activism. To that end, we will offer an exploration of the concept of the public screen and contrast it to the public sphere before focusing on image events, broadcasting, and activism beyond the confines of Democracy.[2] These concepts will be explored through examples of the Seattle WTO protests, Julia "Butterfly" Hill's tree-sit, Tim DeChristopher's Peaceful Uprising, 350.org's climate chaos campaign, and Chinese environmental non-government organizations (ENGOs).

Remediation, hypermediacy, panmediation and the public/people

The public screen. Such a concept takes technology seriously. It recognizes that most, and the most important, public discussions take place via "screens"—televisions, computers, smartphones, iPods, cinemas, the front page of newspapers. Further, it suggests that we cannot simply adopt the term "public sphere" and all it entails, a term indebted to print and orality, for the current screen age. Our starting premise, then, is that television, digital cameras, the computer, the Internet, Web 2.0, and smartphones in concert have fundamentally transformed the media matrix that constitutes our social milieu, producing new forms of social organization and new modes of perception. As Internet and virtual reality pioneer Jaron Lanier explains,

> Technologists don't use persuasion to influence you. . . . We make up extensions to your being, like remote eyes and ears (web-cams and mobile phones) and expanded memory (the world of details you can search for online). These become the structures by which you connect to the world and other people. These structures in turn can change how you conceive of yourself and the world. We tinker with your philosophy by direct manipulation of your cognitive experience, not indirectly, through argument. It takes only a tiny group of engineers to create technology that can shape the entire future of experience with incredible speed (2010: 5–6).

The communication technologies that emerged in the 1800s, especially photography, cinema, and the telegraph, intensified the speed of communication and obliterated space as a barrier to communication (Carey, 1989; Solnit, 2003). The avalanche of media in the 1900s and now 2000s have accelerated and amplified time and space—"We are the World" living in McLuhan's global village. They physically shrink the world while simultaneously mentally expanding it, producing a vast expansion of consciousness. Thoreau's caustic comments about the telegraph have come true. Texas may not have much to say to Maine, but it is transmitted nevertheless. Twitter has exacerbated to excess the broadcasting of trivial movements, bowel included. In this expansion, segregated space is breached, flattening multiple forms of hierarchy (Meyrowitz, 1985). As media scholar Ian Angus sums up, "Media of communication constitute primal scenes, a complex of which defines the culture of a given place and time, an Epoch of Being" (2000: 190). It is the scenes of public screens that we will be exploring.

Media are rarely in isolation, but rather at any historical moment a plurality of media coexist and interact. This point, suggested by McLuhan's observation that "the 'content' of any medium is always another medium" (1964: 23), is usefully extended by Bolter and Grusin's discussions of remediation and hypermediacy. Remediation is "the representation of one medium in another" (1999: 45) and examples include web sites such as Hulu that air television shows. Remediation is not a linear process and "older media can also remediate newer ones" (1999: 55). Remediation is closely linked to the logic of hypermediacy: "contemporary hypermediacy offers a heterogeneous space, in which representation is conceived of not as a window on to the world, but rather as 'windowed' itself–with windows that open on to other representations or other media" (Bolter & Grusin, 1999: 34).

Public screens are scenes of remediation and hypermediacy. Remediation and hypermediacy culminate in the concept of "panmediation," which suggests that with the emergence of smartphones we live in mobile spaces of multiple media, immersed in the cloud of wi-fi. Space and time have ceased to be barriers to living in a mediated world all the time. We need no longer go to a medium or find an Internet connection, for they are in our pocket, a part of us. When thinking of how a medium transforms and creates an environment, a basic criterion is ubiquity. On a small scale, a medium is just a tool within an environment created by other media. So, for example, that was the case for cell phones in the early 1990s. If diffusion accelerates enough, however, the medium reaches a tipping point, what McLuhan terms a break boundary (1964: 49) and moves from being a tool within an environment to helping create the environment within which we operate. Cell phones have crossed that break boundary. As Castells et al. argue, "Wireless communication has diffused faster than any other communication technology in history" (2007: 7). Cell phones are the crucial locus of panmediation. Castells et al. compare their growth in relation to landline phones. In 1991 the ratio was 1:34, in 1995 1:8, and by 2004 cell phones exceeded landline phones (2007: 7). Cell phones originally intended for car emergencies now cause car emergencies and prompt laws as they saturate society and create new senses of time and space and promote distraction as a mode of perception.

To understand media as constitutive is to argue that in techno-industrial societies media become the ground of Being. Media are not mere means of communicating in a public sphere or on public screens; media produce the public sphere and public screens as primal scenes of Being. Particular configurations of media institute the scenes or open the spaces from which epistemologies and ontologies emerge. Today's scene is predominantly a visual one. For example, TV's imagistic discourse has become so dominant that even newspapers can do no better than imitate TV, moving to shorter stories and color images. Even the grey lady (*The New York Times*) is now draped in color. To state the obvious, words remain and remain important, but the power dynamics between words and images have changed. As Burnett describes this new world, "Images combine all media forms and are a synthesis of language, discourse, and viewing. . . . Images are both the outcome and progenitors of vast and interconnected image-worlds" (2005: 2–3).

Even critics of our image culture recognize this new world, however bitterly. Sontag's disparaging observations on photography are also illuminating with respect to images on public screens: "Industrial societies turn their citizens into image-junkies. . .turn experience itself into a way of seeing. . .an event has come to mean, precisely, something worth photographing," something that has appeared on a public screen (1977: 24, 18–19). In our public discourse of images, images are important not because they represent reality but create it: "They are the place where collective social action, individual identity and symbolic imagination meet— the nexus between culture and politics" (Hartley, 1992: 3). Hartley suggests that there is no real public, but, rather that the public is the product of publicity, of pictures. The arc of the movement here from Sontag to Hartley is significant. Sontag is suggesting that images corrupt pre-existing individuals who then can only see through the lens of the camera. Hartley extends and transforms the point, so that the public does not pre-exist as an entity of rational subjects that is then corrupted by images, but instead comes into being through images on public screens. McGee (1975) theorizes this process, arguing that although the People/public are often omnipotent in political discourse, they are not an objective phenomenon, literal extensions of individuals, but a discursive phenomenon. Social theorists need "to conceive 'people' as an essential rhetorical fiction with both a 'social' and 'objective' reality. . .they are conjured into objective reality, remain so long as the rhetoric which defined them has rhetorical force" (1975: 240, 242). An essentialized public is not corrupted by the images of public screens but is called into being by the multiple imagistic discourses of public screens.[3]

The afterlife of the public sphere

Despite the rise of images, the public sphere remains ubiquitous in contemporary social theory, continuously savaged by critics but then resuscitated again and again so that we are left with a social theory landscape scarred by the tracks of a multitude of Frankenstein public spheres. Despite this bewildering array of mutilated permutations, the initial conceptualization of the public sphere had a certain focused coherence. Inaugurated by Habermas's *Structural Transformation of the Public Sphere*, ideally the public sphere denotes a social space wherein private citizens gather as a public body with the rights of assembly, association, and expression in order to form public opinion. The public sphere mediates between civil society and the state, with the expression of public opinion working to both legitimate and check the power of the state. This public opinion is decidedly rational: "the critical judgment of a public making use of its reason" (Habermas, 1989: 24). The public sphere assumes open access, the bracketing of social inequalities, rational discussion, focus on common issues, face-to-face conversation as the privileged medium, and the ability to achieve consensus. It is important to remember that Habermas's book was an historical study of the rise of the bourgeois public sphere and its decline in late capitalist society. Habermas laments the passing of the bourgeoisie public sphere and the rise of mass media spectacles, a turn of events he sees as the disintegration or refeudalization of the public sphere—a return to the spectacle of the Middle Ages.

When academics imagine the ideal public sphere as the seat of civic life, the soul of Democracy, they imagine a place of embodied voices, of people talking to each other, of conversation. Dewey imagined the primordial act of communication as two people sitting on a log, face-to-face, talking. As Habermas puts it, "A portion of the public sphere comes into being in every conversation in which private individuals assemble to form a public body" (1974: 49). Although the public sphere includes written forms of communication, embodied conversation functions as the ideal baseline. Yet the dream of the public sphere as the engagement of embodied voices, democracy via dialogue, cloisters us, for perforce its vision compels us to see the contemporary landscape of public screens as a nightmare. Plus, it is a dream based on a lie. The conversations that Habermas and Dewey champion are based on print. The salons of Paris and the "penny universities" of London (coffee houses) are scenes of celebrated conversations premised on the literacy of their interlocutors. The printing press and its newspapers produce the literate citizenry that makes possible the conversations of the public sphere that Habermas and others read as the key to Democracy.[4]

If fantasizing about a public sphere of embodied voices makes sense within the Western imaginary, Jacques Derrida and John Peters give us a clearer vision of our situation. Much of Derrida's work traces and deconstructs the privileging of face-to-face speech in the history of Western thought, what he terms a "logocentrism which is also a phonocentrism: absolute proximity of voice and being, of voice and the meaning of being, of voice and the ideality of meaning" (1976: 11–12). Peters, in his history of communication as "a registry of modern longings" (1999: 2), traces and critiques a similar history of the privileging of presence, wherein "dialogue has attained something of a holy status. It is held up as the summit of human encounter, the essence of liberal education, and the medium of participatory democracy" (1999: 33). Both Derrida and Peters offer dissemination as the primordial form of communication, the first turn before dialogue. For all forms of communication it is broadcasting, dissemination not dialogue, that is the fundamental form. This structure is highlighted in an age of public screens. Clearly, the giant public screens of Beijing are broadcasting, but so are forms of media consolidated in our pockets, purses, and backpacks. A smartphone or laptop turns all of us into broadcasters, mobile media outlets broadcasting messages, photographs, and video via Twitter, Facebook, and YouTube.

Taking dissemination rather than dialogue as characteristic of contemporary communication practices, then, necessarily alters the trajectory of our thinking about politics and society. The public screen is an accounting that starts from the premise of dissemination, of broadcasting. Broadcasting amplifies voices, enabling one person or small groups to broadcast to many via public screens. This understanding of media and public screens has translated into a practice of staging image events for dissemination. The star of Whale Wars, Sea Shepherd Conservation Society founder, and former Greenpeace member, Captain Paul Watson, has long acted upon the understanding that "The more dramatic you can make it, the more controversial it is, the more publicity you will get. . . . Then you tie the message into that exposure and fire it into the brains of millions of people in the process" (quoted in Scarce, 1990: 104). If broadcasting was once dominated by one-to-many forms (TV, radio), social media have popularized many-to-many forms of broadcasting.

Although today's public screens are not the liberal public sphere of which Habermas dreams, neither are they the medieval public sphere of representative publicity that Habermas fears, a site where rulers stage their status in the form of spectacles before the ruled. Rather, on today's public screens corporations and nation-states stage spectacles (advertising and photo ops) certifying their status before the people/public *and* activists participate through the performance of image events, employing the consequent publicity as a social medium for forming public opinion and holding corporations and states accountable. The publicity activists generate via public screens is just as often directed toward corporations as toward governments, since even powerful corporations are vulnerable to imagefare on public screens. A compelling recent example has been the campaign against sweatshop labor. Activists, many of them college students, have used public screens to generate public opinion against the use of sweatshop labor by global corporations, including Nike, Wal-Mart, and the GAP (Gourevitch, 2001; the major groups in this effort are United Students Against Sweatshops, the National Labor Committee, the Fair Labor Association, and the Worker Rights Consortium). Anarchic public screens enable activists to perform and broadcast image events that call into being the people/publics that challenge corporations and nations. Critique through spectacle, not critique versus spectacle. This optimistic understanding of activism on public screens warrants elaboration.

The dense surfaces of image events

Our use of the term image event is a declaration that images are ontological. There are two aspects to this claim. The first is a response to the alarmingly widespread belief that images are not real and that we live in the real, which is too often corrupted by illusions, the virtual. Sontag famously condemned the unreality of images as "mere images of Truth. . . . Photos can only give a semblance of knowledge, a semblance of wisdom" (1977: 3, 23–24). If it ever once made sense, the distinction between image and reality is impossible to delineate, never mind justify, in our image-centric media matrix. As Burnett argues, "To varying degrees, therefore, images have always been an ecological phenomenon. They have formed an environment. As images have become increasingly prevalent through mass production, they have redefined human action, interaction, and subjectivity" (2005: 89–90). In the landscape of public screens the feel of images constitutes the real.

The second reason for our insistence on the term image event, for the image as event, is that we too often reduce images to representations of the real, confining images to the regime of representation, yoking images to words, anchoring images in logocentrism. Barthes and Baudrillard articulate the need for the resistance to meaning and a rejection of representation. Barthes writes, "The essence of the image is to be altogether outside, without signification. . . . It is precisely in this arrest of interpretation that the photograph's certainty resides" (1981: 106–7). Baudrillard suggests that photos "resist the moral imperative of meaning" and "the violence of interpretation" (2000: 138). The excess of images always transgresses the bonds of representation and interpretation.

The capacity to transgress points to the event quality of images. Images are not subsumable to language because the two are fundamentally distinct. As Derrida notes, "A sign is never an event, if by event we mean an irreplaceable and irreversible empirical particular" (1973: 50). An image is exactly an event—irreplaceable and irreversible. As Derrida explains, "An event that remains an event is an arrival, an absolute arrival: it surprises and resists analysis after the fact. . . . another origin of

the world." (2002: 20). From a different orientation, Badiou's more committed theorizing of the event concurs, "something that cannot be reduced to its ordinary
inscription in 'what there is.' Let us call this *supplement* an *event* . . . which compels
us to decide a *new* way of being" (2001: 41).

The 1999 Seattle WTO protests provide a rich example of the force of image
events, in part because Seattle was a contested image event wherein several groups
competed over its meaning: the Clinton Administration, corporate sponsors, peaceful protesters, uncivil disobedience activists, and anarchists; and in part because a
key component of Seattle was violence, a type of "communication" *a priori* ruled out
of the public sphere. Anarchists shattering the glass facades of brand empires were
dense image events, gliffs, that opened visions of other possible worlds.

The symbolic violence and the uncivil disobedience fulfilled the function of
gaining the attention of the distracted media. Counter to charges by peaceful protesters, then, such image events did not drown out their message, but enabled it to
be played more extensively. Media coverage of this issue was not a zero-sum game.
Uncivil disobedience and the anarchists' actions expanded the totality of coverage.
If we take image events seriously as ontological, however, we cannot simply reduce
them to the function of gaining attention for the "real" rhetoric of words. We must
consider image events, then, as visual philosophical-rhetorical fragments, mind
bombs that expand the universe of thinkable thoughts. Image events are dense sur-
faces meant to provoke in an instant the shock of the familiar made strange. In this
sense, some image events are gliffs. A gliff is "a moment; a transient glance; an unexpected view of something that startles one" (www.websters-online-dictionary.org/
Gl/Gliff.html). The word gliff gets at the unpredictable, contingent, startling, not
making sense in the situation as it is, ephemeral qualities of the event.[5] Image events
suggest a Benjaminian sense of time, where any moment can open up on eternity,
any moment can be the moment that changes everything, the moment that redeems
the past and the future. And it is all there on the surface. In a familiar city, Seattle,
home of the Mariners, Microsoft, airplanes, rain, and coffee, a familiar place,
Starbucks, the national neighborhood coffee shop, is shattered by a hammer, everyday object and sign of national industriousness. The familiar made strange, the shock
of recognition that the familiar is not necessarily innocuous, the hint of the "banal-
ity of evil." The chain of targets reinforces the message: Nike Town, Old Navy,
McDonald's, Banana Republic, Planet Hollywood. The hopes of an anarchist display an acute appreciation of public screens and image events: "You stare at a television and you see logos and you're in a daze and these symbols pop up everywhere
in your life. When that is shattered, it breaks a spell and we're trying to get people
to wake up before it's too late." The anarchists' image event of shattering windows
enacts the praxis of public screens. It both participates in and punctures the habit
of distraction characteristic of the contemporary mode of perception. It participates

in order to be aired—it is brief, visual, dramatic, and emotional. It punctures to punctuate, to interrupt the flow, to give pause. It punctures by making the mundane malevolent, the familiar fantastic.

Broadcasting distractions

Public screens are a constant current of images and words, a ceaseless circulation of jarring juxtapositions that constitutes the mediascape we inhabit. Public screens promote a mode of perception that could best be characterized as "distraction." The public sphere, in privileging rational argument, assumed a mode of perception characterized by attention and focus. Many social theorists contemplating the effects of media recognize the emergence of distraction as a new mode of perception (or, negatively, as a loss of focus).[6] The focused gaze has been displaced by the distracted look, the glance of habit while immersed in a sea of imagery. Distraction is not simply a lack of attention but a necessary form of perception when immersed in the torrent of images and information that constitutes public screens. If speed and images annihilate contemplation, the question for activists becomes how to engage distracted publics amidst a landscape of public screens. Butterfly's public screen performances provide one answer.

In December 1997, Julia "Butterfly" Hill, an ex-waitress, climbed Luna, a 1000-year-old redwood and potential victim of a chainsaw massacre. So began the longest tree-sit in United States environmental protest history. Butterfly had to perform on a world stage structured by corporate globalization. As such, she provides a vision for activism and broadcasting in a landscape of public screens. During her two years in the tree, Butterfly managed to become the public face of Earth First! through the broadcasting of her rhetoric and image. Butterfly's use of her body and the redwood Luna suggests her awareness of the image landscape she is operating in. A former model, Butterfly realizes that a pretty face and a striking image are irresistible to the media, the daily staple of public screens. In multiple media, two types of images predominate. First, there are close-ups of Butterfly, barefoot and hugging Luna, her traditionally pretty white face framed by her windswept long, black hair. It is a face that is both pleasing and comforting, a cliché of small-town America. Second, there are long-range shots that give more of a sense of the grandeur of Luna. Among the most spectacular are those of Butterfly standing on the very pinnacle of the ancient redwood, hundreds of feet in the air, arms outstretched toward the sky, hair flowing in the wind, tenuously tethered to the tree by her feet. In thus deploying her body, Butterfly turns her protest into an image event worthy of the public screen.

The longer Butterfly dwelled in Luna, the more of an international image event she became. A steady pilgrimage of journalists traveled to Luna, many ascending the tree, to interview Butterfly. As Butterfly joked, "I'm an introvert by nature, which is part of the reason I climbed a tree. But when you climb a tree, you don't expect the world to arrive at your platform" (Berton, 2009). In addition, Butterfly's solar-powered radiophone was her broadcasting platform to the media worlds of radio and the Internet. In the end, Butterfly forced Pacific Lumber to capitulate, saving Luna and her neighbors and propelling herself into environmental stardom (including a forthcoming Hollywood movie).[7]

Two snapshots of climate chaos[8] activism update the possibilities of public screen activism after the advent of Web 2.0 and social media. On a bitterly cold December morning University of Utah student DeChristopher went to downtown Salt Lake City to protest the dying Bush Administration's firesale of oil and gas leases in southern Utah's wild canyon country. Perhaps sensing the futility of walking in circles in front of the building (or perhaps just cold), DeChristopher walked into the building and was asked to sign up for the auction. Accepting the offer, DeChristopher then bid on numerous leases, wreaking such havoc on the total process that all the sales were annulled. Since then, the Obama Administration has deemed many of the proposed leases inappropriate. Nonetheless, since DeChristopher had neither the intention nor the money nor the heart to desecrate Utah's beautiful canyon country, he is facing felony charges and awaiting trial. Since the event that transformed him from a student to a climate chaos crusader, DeChristopher has deployed the political opportunities of public screens and Web 2.0 to found the group Peaceful Uprising (http://www.peacefuluprising.org) to agitate on behalf of climate chaos issues.

No climate chaos activists have been more adept at exploiting public screens and social media than writer Bill McKibben, who founded 350.org to draw attention to the science of climate chaos and the need for action. As an incarnation of public screens and Web 2.0 activism, they are more of a social media network than an activist group:

> In order to unite the public, media, and our political leaders behind the 350 goal, we've harnessed the power of the internet to coordinate a planetary day of action on October 24, 2009. There were actions at thousands of iconic places around the world—5281 to be exact. People assembled all over the world—from the Himalayan peaks to the Great Barrier Reef to your community—to send a clear message to world leaders. (www.350.org)

For the day of international action, 350.org used Web 2.0 for awareness and organizational coordination in order to stage image events for myriad public screens. Schoolchildren, skiers, surfers, scuba divers, elephants, turtles, kayaks, candles, sailboats, and multiple others were organized into the number 350 at iconic locations around the globe, both natural and made, from Angkor Wat to the Alps to the Great

Pyramids to Mount Everest to Mumbai to the Maldives to Shanghai to the Great Barrier Reef to Hollywood to Mount Kilimanjaro to the Sydney Opera House to Yosemite to the Tour de Eiffel. The images remain archived and organized by region and topic and action and audience at Flickr (http://www.flickr.com/photos/350org/sets/).

Activism beyond the confines of democracy: Wild public screens

Thinking in the West about activism has revolved around concepts of the public and the public sphere. Such thinking has been built upon and limited by axiomatic tendencies with respect to Democracy and freedom. This is clear in Habermas's theorizing: "Citizens act as a public when they deal with matters of general interest without being subject to coercion; thus with the guarantee that they may assemble and unite freely, and express and publicize their opinions freely" (1989: 231). We want to hesitate on the word "freely," suggesting that such a word, that the concept of freedom itself, is deeply parochial and suspect, a flag used to cover-up and distract us from the myriad ways in which nothing is ever done freely. Though we cannot expand on this point here, we will leave you with a proper name: Foucault. Indeed, Habermas's point becomes suspect in his own writing, for in the same paragraph he writes of "Public discussions that are institutionally protected. . . ." Institutional protection suggests not so much freedom as taming, a domestication. The link of Democracy, the public sphere and activism becomes even more dubious when trying to internationalize the concept. It is time to decouple Democracy and activism. Though people write of transnational public spheres, if such imaginings require Democracy they are impossible, since many nations are not Democracies and since there is not a global Democracy mechanism. In addition, America's imperialism has rendered Democracy a dubious and violent export, as the hundreds of thousands of Iraqi corpses can testify.[9] In opposition, we want to embrace here a proliferation of *wild public screens*, public screens full of risk, without protection, without guarantees. We see hints of wildness in Habermas's discussion of the origins of the public sphere. Today, we see it in China, wherein there are no guarantees of domesticating protection, where the ritualized performances of the public sphere are absent, but there are risky and powerful conversations and protests and activism. We are suggesting, then, displacing the ossified architectural metaphor of the public sphere, cluttered by essentialized detritus, with the excessive proliferation of wild public screens characterized by *arrangiasti* (making do in the civic spaces of the world). The importance of these everyday engagements in multiple media about the issues of the day, of these risky practices, of these wild public screens, is clear in the Chinese expression *"shui neng zai zhou, yi neng fu zhou"*—the water carries the boat but can also capsize it. Public screens and their publics constitute the water that sustains corporations and nations.

The heart of democracy is activism, not institutionalism. Dead architectural metaphors, fenced-in pre-approved "free" speech zones, and dusty laws guarantee nothing but moribund public spaces and an apathetic public. Through activist communication acts, publics come into being and democracy lives. Focusing on practices moves us beyond "*a priori* conceptual restrictions of citizenship to certain people, places, and topics" (Asen, 2004: 207). Instead of neglecting environmental activist practices in China because China is not a Democracy, such a perspective pushes us to explore how environmental activism *is* practiced in China, how citizen practices form publics that hold the government accountable and foment social change. ENGOs on the ground in China through their activism on wild public screens are constituting publics and transforming environmental practices in China.

Too much of the thinking in the US about China is tethered to Cold War nightmares, as the *LA Times* recently exemplified: "China's gray, staid Communist chiefs" (11 April 2009). A case study of contemporary coverage of China in *The New York Times*, the *Washington Post*, and *USA Today* bears out this ossified stereotypical thinking (Sun & DeLuca: 2009). As Greenpeace China activist Ailun Yang observes, "It's a very simplistic way of thinking of China as just one singular thing. It is a place where you have 1.3 billion people and there are huge differences from region to region, and economic structures are different, education levels are different. So it's actually a country with huge diversity" (personal interview, March 2008). While this diversity may be largely absent from America's public screens, another look from a different vantage reveals both the proliferation of wild public screens and social media and the flowering of activism, especially environmental activism.

Although the West periodically bemoans the censoring of Google or the closing of Facebook or YouTube in China, such closures mainly affect the technologically obtuse and the linguistically impaired. China is awash in the public screens of Web 2.0. The counterpart to YouTube is Youku (http://www.youku.com/), to Google is Baidu (http://www.baidu.com/), to Facebook is Renren (http://www.renren.com/), to Twitter is Taotao (http://www.taotao.com/). The plethora of social media activity both echoes and inspires social activism at large. Far from gray staidness, in 2004 China experienced at least 74,000 protests, riots and mass petitions, compared to a mere 10,000 such cases a decade earlier (*South China Morning Post*, 8 February 2004).

This dramatic rise in activism is especially evident in environmentalism. Friends of Nature, established in 1994, was the first ENGO in China. In 15 years, the number of ENGOs in China has risen to 3539 ("Report of Chinese Environmental

NGO Development" by ACEF, 2008).[10] This number does not include numerous active ENGOs that are not registered due to various issues with official registration. Among these 3539 ENGOs, there are 508 grassroots organizations, 1309 government-organized ENGOs, 90 international ENGOs, and 1382 school-based groups including students organizations and university research centers.[11]

The examples of Chinese ENGOs deploying social media and image events on public screens are endless. The Friends of Nature, the Green River, the Wild Yak Brigade and the Greener Beijing Institute in concert acted to help save the Tibetan Antelope, endangered by poaching for its fine wool—one shawl can command $15,000. The Greener Beijing Institute has distinguished itself as the first and most active Internet-based ENGO in China, with more than 2000 volunteers spread all over China (http://www.grchina.com/gb/greenerbeijing.htm). Green Web Alliance helps other ENGOs to develop a web presence and, through its own site, promotes "online action with real-world results." By way of example, it cites a 2004 online campaign to protect the Beijing Zoo. Wang Yongchen, president of Green Earth Volunteers, observed, "The very existence of NGOs is supposed to provide a way for the voice of people on the local level to be heard. I'd like to take as an example the issue of the relocation of the Beijing Zoo. The government wanted to relocate the zoo, but the people did not. As a result, the relocation was cancelled. This is the power of public participation."[12]

On significantly more controversial issues, ENGOs have successfully challenged the Chinese government and corporations. In 2003, the State Development and Reform Commission approved of a proposal by Huadian Corporation and the local government to build 13 dams along the Nu River in southwest China. The Nu River, 1,750 miles long, is home to 7,000 species of plants, more than half of China's animal species, and 22 ethnic groups. ENGOs in Yunnan and Beijing, including Green Watershed, Green Earth Volunteers, Friends of Nature and a few others, launched a high-profile campaign that garnered extensive publicity and international support. Under pressure from the public, Premier Wen Jiaobao announced his decision in April 2004 to suspend the construction. In 2006, citizens of Xiamen (pop. 1.5 million) used a text messaging campaign to stop construction of a $1.6 billion chemical plant. The texting reached over one million phones and led to effective protests.

The Internet in its traditional forms and Web 2.0 are being used to coordinate ENGOs across the vast spaces and disparate issues in China. NGOCN Development and Exchange Network (http://www.ngocn.org/) is one of the most popular communication platforms for NGOs in China, witnessing a total of 4,623,645 page views from 2007 to 2009.[13] Via a variety of announcements, it facilitates networking among NGOs in China. NGO 2.0 Project, developed by Jing Wang and launched in May 2009 by MIT, Ogilvy in Beijing, Friends of Nature, and others, is designed to teach NGOs in China "how to collaborate with each other via Web 2.0 tools on a new social networking platform" (http://web.mit.edu/fll/www/people/images/JingWangAmChamArticle.pdf).

The Wild Yak Brigade and other utopian tales

Social theorizing is as risky as life. Who knows what will happen? The Wild Yak Brigade (*Yemaoniu Dui*) was disbanded, though they live on on the Internet and in the movie *Mountain Patrol* and in bodies and memories and myths. The Tibetan Antelope lives on, though the living is a struggle on the lonely yet dangerous Kekexili Plateau, and the tale seems destined to end in extinction in the face of insatiable human wants. The proliferation of public screens and social media has transformed our environment in myriad ways on multiple levels. Amidst such a cataclysm, the future remains obscure. Even trying to understand the possibilities and dangers of just activism on the transformed terrain is a risky undertaking. It is clear, however, that nostalgia and retreat are ineffective means of confronting and engaging the new landscape of public screens and social media. That said, we are not advocating a technological utopianism. Under the rule of the techno-industrial corporate juggernaut we euphemistically call civilization, bad outcomes are neither uncommon nor surprising. Still . . . cataclysms are always unruly and provide unexpected opportunities beyond calculation. Activists deploying social media to broadcast image events on countless public screens that call into being publics that transgress the boundaries of nations and the fences of corporations will produce changes that exceed all hopes. Activism lives.

Notes

1. We introduced the concept of the public screen in the essay "From Public Sphere to Public Screen: Democracy, Activism, and the 'Violence' of Seattle," DeLuca and Peeples, 2002. This chapter starts from that essay but develops and transforms the thinking in light of the rapid proliferation of both public screens and social media.
2. "Democracy" will be contrasted with "democracy" throughout the essay, with Democracy in the United States criticized as a catatonic myth invoked to provoke flag-waving and jingoistic war-mongering but having little impact on how the US corporate plutocracy functions.
3. Following Laclau and Mouffe (1985), we understand discourse to be material and to include both the linguistic and the non-linguistic (pp. 107–112).
4. In the end, the public sphere is still another example of the West's enchantment with logo-centrism that Derrida was at such pains to deconstruct.
5. For example, with respect to the U.S. 20th century civil rights movement, for many Americans the moment of glimpsing the abject in the monstrous image of Emmett Till's lynched face

was an event, a gliff, an unexpected view that startles. Although some did not respond to this event and kept living in the white supremacist world as it was, for many others Till's monstrous face ripped the fabric of the world of Jim Crow and opened other possible worlds (Harold and DeLuca, 2005).

6. The new media of the early 20th century caused German social theorists such as Simmel, Horkheimer, Adorno, Benjamin, and Kracauer to consider how distraction was displacing focus and thinking. Today, new media, especially cell phones, have spawned another bout of anxiety over distraction—see *Distracted: The Erosion of Attention and the Coming Dark Age* by Maggie Jackson (2008).

7. For a fuller analysis of Butterfly's tree-sit, see DeLuca, 2003. Some information about Butterfly's tree-sit is archived at: http://www.circleoflife.org/

8. We prefer the term "climate chaos" to climate change or global warming because it more accurately reflects the scientific understanding of what is likely to happen as the planet's average temperature warms.

9. Though purposefully uncounted, the best scientific estimate by The Johns Hopkins University and *Lancet* study estimated between 400,000–900,000 Iraqis died as a result of the United States' invasion by 2006 http://www.guardian.co.uk/world/2008/mar/19/iraq

10. "Report of Chinese Environmental NGO Development" by All-China Environmental Federation, 2008. Last retrieved from http://www.greenlaw.org.cn/enblog/?p=258 on Feb 10th, 2010.

11. For more information about Chinese ENGOs, see to Xie, L. (2009). Environmental Activism in China. London: Routledge; Chinese Development Brief: http://www.chinadevelopmentbrief.com/;

China's Environment: http://newton.uor.edu/Departments&Programs/AsianStudiesDept/china-environ.html; China Environmental Forum: http://wilsoncenter.org/index.cfm?topic_id=1421&categoryid=EE5586BC-9247-863E-B7C96B9489272423&fuseaction=topics.publications_topics

12. On August 13, 2004, People's Daily Online invited Ms. Wang to an Internet chat at www.people.com.cn. (see http://www.fon.org.cn/content.php?aid=8801).

13. Statistics are cited from "NGO 2.0: An Experiment with Web 2.0 and CSR" by Jing Wang and Mikko Lan, http://web.mit.edu/fll/www/people/images/JingWangAmChamArticle.pdf.

CHAPTER ELEVEN

Politics, Power and Online Protest in an Age of Environmental Conflict

BRETT HUTCHINS AND LIBBY LESTER[1]

The environmental movement is a locally rooted, globally connected network which aims to change the public mind as a means of influencing policy decisions to save the planet or one's own neighborhood . . .

. . . The conflicts of our time are fought by networked social actors aiming to reach their constituencies and target audiences through the decisive switch to multimedia communication networks.

MANUEL CASTELLS, 2009: 49

Many environmental protests are identifiable by the physically rooted character of their objectives–stopping logging in a forest, holding back unsustainable development on a coastline, protecting a natural waterway–which masks their significance as transnational media endeavors. As indicated by the opening quotations, often highly localized and regional protests are increasingly projected nationally and globally to audiences and users via networked digital media in the service of specific campaign and policy goals. The pressure applied by activists to locally and regionally based politicians and businesses by this "outside attention" is maximized by information, opinions and strategies distributed through major networks of news production and distribution, and more loosely organized networks of environmentalist websites, social networking profiles and mobile media. Significantly, the global connectivity of local experience in the service of overarching environmental goals situates protests and campaigns as unique "transnational media projects" (Artz, 2007: 148), albeit with very different goals to the transnational corporate media conglomerates like News Corporation and Time Warner with which this term is usually associated. In substantially modifying this concept, the mediated environmental protests we analyze in this chapter are campaigns conducted within a particular geographical region of a nation, but whose broad environmental objectives are jointly shared with and understood by a transnational constellation of activists and NGOs. While these campaigns are identified by and physically located in a region, they are visible evidence of a determination to contest the instrumental logic of capital and party politics globally in the service of environmental sustainability and/or conservation. These protests also reveal the ongoing resonance of the local and regional in an age of transnational media and politics as well as the fact that the internet and web have opened up new possibilities for mediated politics and demonstration (Cottle, 2008).

This definition suggests an acute and ongoing need to investigate the actual operation and effectiveness of environmental protests. If protests and campaigns are as important symbolically and politically as has been suggested, it is essential to continue moving beyond the banal observation that protests are evidence of "political resistance" to capital and the state. This move requires the application of theoretical tools that reveal how power, in its manifold forms, actually operates in the network society (Castells, 2000), and, by extension, enables a finely tuned assessment of environmental protests that employ a suite of tactics organized around networked digital communications and news media strategies. Building upon earlier research published in *Media, Culture & Society* (Hutchins & Lester, 2006; Lester & Hutchins, 2009), we apply and adapt selected elements of Manuel Castells's sociological scholarship on environmental politics, social movements and the network society (2004a, 2004b), with a particular emphasis on his most recent work (2008, 2009; Arsenault & Castells, 2008). The case presented in this chapter is based upon analysis of three major internet-based protest campaigns undertaken in Tasmania over a 10-year period. This task involved monitoring and content analysis of activist websites and web-based archives, and 25 semi-structured interviews with journalists and environmental activists. Data are contextualized within a longitudinal study of mediated environmental conflict in this island state of Australia (Lester, 2007). Tasmania is an apposite site to examine internet-based protest given its international significance as a physical and symbolic site for environmental politics and green values; it is the home of the world's first green political party and possesses 1.38 million hectares of World Heritage-listed wilderness, one of only three such areas remaining in the Southern Hemisphere. Tasmania also hosted the Franklin blockade of 1982–83, described as the first environmental campaign to attain global stature (Hay, 1991–1992: 64; also see Lester, 2006; Hutchins & Lester, 2006;

Harper, 2009). The argument presented here is that protest groups are experiencing successful *moments* that draw attention to the destruction and degradation of the natural environment, but the limits of their impact must also be acknowledged and properly understood. In the final section of the chapter, these limitations are explained in terms of how media and communication power function, as media networks constitute the arena in which power struggles between competing political, social and media actors are conducted.

Castells's latest book, *Communication Power* (2009), details how power is accumulated, maintained, exercised and articulated in the "global public sphere" (Volkmer, 2003). Reservoirs of power and resources are contained within business, media, political and social networks, but it is the capacity to control and/or influence how these networks connect and interact that determines which actors possess most power. Media mogul Rupert Murdoch, head of News Corporation, is an emblematic figure in this respect, possessing the ability to connect these different networks to his company's benefit, and using different parts of his global media and business empire to affect political and public opinion (Arsenault & Castells, 2008; Castells, 2009: 416–32). This ability is conceptualized as "switching power"–"the ability to control connection points between different networks (e.g. business, media and economic networks)" (Arsenault & Castells, 2008: 488; Castells, 2004c: 33–34)–with Murdoch an experienced and skilled "switcher." This chapter reveals that the environmental movement desires, but conspicuously lacks, switching power. Activists instead relying on spectacular, but often short-lived protest action to garner media coverage and sustain public pressure upon political decision-makers. In rudimentary terms, the difference between Murdoch and environmental groups is that the former can attract and keep the attention of regional and national politicians, other news media, international business figures, and global publics through editorial and news coverage, investment decisions, hired professional lobbyists and even a personal phone call. The latter, by contrast, need to attract considerable news media coverage, usually via protests and campaigning, to maintain the attention of these disparate groups for a relatively short period of time.

Environmental activists are not switchers. They cannot *control* connection points between business (e.g., the forestry and fossil fuel industries), political networks (governments at various levels), and news media (established broadcast, print and online outlets). Rather, through the use of mobile and social networking media, actions by protest groups such as Greenpeace, The Wilderness Society and "Still Wild, Still Threatened" (discussed below) aim to temporarily *destabilize* or, optimally, *disrupt* the smooth functioning of capital and government. These groups shine a spotlight on activities such as the logging of old-growth forest in order to provoke a political response and public reaction. This is no small achievement given the limited resources of many environmental activist groups, particularly when compared to the wealth of, and listed logging operators such as the Tasmanian-based Gunns Limited, the largest hardwood woodchip exporter in the world with a reported revenue of AUD$427 million for the first half of 2009. Public relations victories by environmentalists may also be derided by critics as largely symbolic, doing little to stop the advance of bulldozers and chainsaws, but symbols matter politically in media-based symbolic struggles competing for the hearts and minds of readers, viewers, listeners and users. Indeed, symbolic power is the source of any destabilization and/or disruption of dominant power flows achieved by activists in a convergent media culture (Jenkins, 2006). Attention now turns to Internet-based protest actions that provide insight into the issues that have been outlined so far.

Protest actions, online media and news

Environmental campaigns, often accompanied by protests acting as "flashpoints" to focus public, media and political attention, have acted intermittently as fertile sites for the innovative use of online communications since the late 1980s (Goggin, 2003, 2004; Lester & Hutchins, 2009). In reporting these innovations, news media have played a central role in environmental politics: negotiating access, shaping meanings and circulating symbols. It is this situation that highlights a problem in contemporary politics. Formal political agendas around the world are substantially framed "by the inherent logic of the media system," which means proposals and causes that do not appear in the news media are thought to have no hope of attracting broad, widespread support (Castells, 2004b). For this reason, the Internet and web have been a tantalizing source of hope and experimentation for environmental campaigners over the past decade or more, offering the promise—if not always the reality—of independent information distribution and political communication devoid of the mediating effect of news journalists and the established news media industries (Rucht, 2004; Downey, 2007). Investigation of protest actions enables evaluation of this promise, allowing scrutiny of the interaction between networked digital media, news and politics.

The first noteworthy use of the Internet as a protest tool in Tasmania occurred in March 1998, in the eucalyptus forests on the slopes of Mother Cummings Peak, in Tasmania's north. An electrical engineer, Neil Smith, with help from local residents but no formal support from environmental groups, constructed a platform 25 metres above ground in a tree in the direct path of a proposed logging road. As loggers moved into the coupe on 3 March, Smith established a tree-sit on the platform, with a mobile phone, computer and Internet connection as his means of communication. Materials, excluding the computer, cost AUD$600. The computer ran off a car-sized 12-volt battery that was charged by a solar panel with a pedal-powered generator as backup. Over the next 10 days, Smith–dubbed Hector the Forest Protector–emailed politicians and media repeatedly, describing events in the forest and providing political and forests policy commentary. Smith later described his motivation for establishing the tree-sit:

> I thought this was the way to get publicity, sit up a tree on a well prepared platform with an Internet connection, bombard the politicians and hope the media get interested. They did. . . . It might have been a first in the world. The Americans didn't indicate anyone else had ever done it quite this way. (Julia Hill, nicknamed "Butterfly," was tree-sitting "Luna" a giant Californian redwood at the time but did not personally use a computer on her tree-sit.) (Smith, 2001: 108)

Smith was removed from the platform and arrested by police on 12 March. The following day, his tree was felled and logging of the coupe continued. Despite this failure, it was, nonetheless, argued that Smith's campaign was successful in drawing attention via news media to forestry activities in the area. News stories reporting this protest focused primarily on the novelty of Smith's Internet connection, as in this page one example from Hobart's *The Mercury* (the state capital's daily newspaper), headlined, "Alone up a tree, linked to the world."

> For the past five days Hector has kept a lone vigil 25m up a tree in one of Tasmania's remotest spots–to send his protest around the world. From the top of his stringy-bark he has set up a communications centre to draw attention to his mission to stop logging in a hotly disputed Western Tiers coupe. (Maguire, 1998: 1)

The telling feature of the headline that accompanied this story is the words, "linked to the world." This phrase is an early indication–occurring prior to the advent of Facebook, Twitter, YouTube and even Google–of a growing and widespread awareness that the transborder communications flows available through the web and mobile media made it possible for protests to reach a national and international audience. It is the perception and reality of this broader audience that helps to apply pressure to Tasmanian-based logging companies and State politicians.

Smith's later reflections indicate that the overall success of the action was measured in terms of the news media coverage generated:

> I could have been so much better prepared if I'd had another couple of days. In retrospect there were one or two things I got wrong, like the padlock on the trapdoor. But on the other hand I had so much good luck: I got it all in there before the boom gate was put in, and the support team brought the missing part; the computer worked; the phone worked; I *did* get stuff out to the media, and they *did* put me on the front page twice. (Smith, 2001: 112)

The compression of time and space afforded by the Internet in transmitting messages made it possible for Smith to overcome the geographical isolation of both the forest and northern Tasmania, allowing his protest to be recognized by journalists, be reported on by the news media and read about by citizens located in Tasmania, on mainland Australia and, at least potentially, overseas. The novelty of this type of action in 1998 contributed to its success, which opened up new possibilities for action by environmental activists and NGOs.

During the southern summer of 2003–04, the strategy of "going online up a tree in a forest" received a capital injection and expanded significantly under the control of two of Australia's largest environmental organizations, Greenpeace and the Wilderness Society. For five months and at a total cost of almost AUD$200,000, the two organizations combined to establish a "Global Rescue Station" in the Styx Valley, 100 kilometres west of the state capital, Hobart. Employment of the term "global rescue" demonstrates that the appeal to overseas users, activist communities, audiences and journalists was now being used explicitly in the planning, presentation and conduct of protest action. Specifically regional issues and threats facing the Styx Valley and Tasmanian forests were now framed in terms of a globally felt need to protect the natural environment. The transnational architecture of the Internet is the material foundation of this global frame, helping to "spread the word"–in real-time–beyond the shores of the state and mainland Australia in the ongoing constitution and affirmation of a global community of environmentalists sharing a common project.

The station comprised a base camp and platform in a giant *Eucalyptus regnans*, 65 metres above ground, on which activists from countries including Japan, Germany, Canada and Australia maintained a vigil and maintained blogs in their own languages. There were also with regular visits from well-known Australian celebrities, including singers John Butler, Jimmy Barnes and Olivia Newton-John, and popular novelist Bryce Courtenay. These celebrities were recorded "performing" at the camp, with recordings then made available on the campaign website (http://weblog.greenpeace.org/tasmania/). The visits also attracted news coverage from large news media outlets. Another feature differentiating this action from Smith's was the fact that the area was not under immediate threat, allowing the action to continue for a longer period.

It is clear from the environmental groups' website, produced during the action, and subsequent interviews with organizers that news media access was the primary aim of the action. On the motivation behind the decision by the two organizations to join forces and mount a joint operation, Wilderness Society campaigner, Vica Bayley, explained that they were able to produce a "much better and much bigger story and much bigger and better spotlight on the forest" (interview, 6 June 2006). According to Greenpeace Australia Pacific's Communications Team Leader, Dan Cass:

It's really just about giving the media access to the story ultimately. It's very much with that, although we did also engage cyber activists who were our online supporters and tens of thousands of them e-mailed Japanese companies. New media is increasingly important, but the mainstream media is still very much the main game of the environmental campaigns. You do the groundwork; you build the community of opposition. That's the foundation, but then the icing on the cake is still mainstream media opinion. That's just how it is and that's okay. I mean that's where democracy looks at itself and judges its own values and priorities. (interview, 16 June 2006)

News coverage in the establishment phase of the Global Rescue Station applied common industry/government-preferred frames on protest action: "cheap publicity stunt," "juvenile and meaningless," "useless stunt," and "a desperate bid to attract media attention." But stories using environmental movement-sponsored frames did appear alongside the criticisms, albeit less frequently. Here the angle was the role of online communications, with the protest presented both as an action to save the forest and a highly sophisticated direct communications strategy premised on the potency of making the protest visible to web users:

> The protesters say they will make the tree their home until the area is exempt from logging operations, and will share their experience with the world via the Internet. "We're going to take a stand here until the Government intervenes and does the right thing," said Greenpeace Australia/Pacific campaigns manager Danny Kennedy. "We have satellite communications that enable web broadcasts and weblogs will be uploaded daily on to the Wilderness Society's site for people around Australia and the world to look at." (Martain, 2003: 2)

This is a strategy underpinned by what John Thompson (2005) terms a new "mediated visibility," or making the otherwise unnoticed or unseen visible via the Internet and networked media, bringing into public view what was previously hidden due to spatial-temporal limitations:

> The industry thought they could fix it by locking the gate at the end of the coupe. This is what was so beautiful about it. It was specifically to maintain communication with the media. They could have the biggest padlock on the biggest gate they could find and it wouldn't have made a flying bit of difference. It was genuinely novel. (Alastair Graham, campaigner, Tasmanian Conservation Trust, interview, 29 November 2004)

Online visibility overcame the isolation of the Styx Valley and Tasmania, and the role and innovation of using the Internet in this way became a feature of news stories covering the protest. Readers were also encouraged by journalists—intentionally or unintentionally—to log on and see for themselves, amplifying the protest action's immediacy by allowing web users to see with their own eyes and "bear witness" to events in the valley.

Interestingly, international news media coverage was less concerned about the Internet's role in the protest action, focusing to a greater degree on the height of the tree-sit, the nationality of the protesters involved and/or the threat to the forests themselves:

> Environmentalists yesterday began a treetop protest to highlight the threat to the world's tallest hardwood trees, endangered by logging in Australia's island state of Tasmania. Greenpeace launched the "tree-sit" protest in conjunction with the Wilderness Society, pointing out that without action the Styx forest, located near the state capital Hobart, would be gone within months. (*Irish Examiner*, 2003)

Despite the infrequency of direct reference to activists' use of the Internet by overseas journalists, its utility in generating international media coverage is apparent as comments by The Wilderness Society's Vica Bayley show:

> I guess the benefit of having a Belgian up a tree in Tasmania is that, sure, there may only be diehard rusted on Greenpeace people that actually log on first up, but if they tell someone else. . .it starts to spread, especially if it starts to get in the mainstream media over there. We did see a bit of that second-round media coverage, especially in Japan, of people who saw the website, maybe saw it on the Greenpeace website as well, and then it started to bite within the media. The Japanese photographers and journalists that I took through the Styx over that campaign I can't count, but it was definitely in the double figures, which is significant. (interview, 6 June 2006)

Here the Internet was a tool targeted at harvesting news media attention for activists, although built within this objective were two discrete functions. In Australian and local coverage, it was a representational novelty or "point of difference" that journalists could write about, thereby attracting the attention of the news media and public to the campaign. Internationally, the Internet became a mechanism valued more for its functionality, allowing overseas users and journalists to observe the protest.

In relation to international attention, what emerges from our investigation is the clear priority and value accorded to receiving coverage from news media outlets. The amount of website activity generated and the matter of whether logging had been stopped were significant issues, with over 19,000 visits to the Global Rescue Station website in the first month of the action (Greenpeace Australia Pacific, 2003). But, in terms of understanding the strategic and tactical logic of environmental protest, the following Greenpeace media releases indicate that it was the cultural and political legitimacy that accompanied coverage in a news publication like the *Guardian* or *LA Times* that afforded particular satisfaction for protest organizers:

The campaign to save the Styx has received international attention since the launch. Media coverage in countries such as Mexico, Japan, Italy and South Africa has put the issue of Tasmania's forests on the world stage. (Greenpeace Australia Pacific, 2004a)

The tree sit has been inhabited by environmentalists from Australia, Japan, Canada and Germany for four months now, attracting the national and international media attention and launching the issue into the international spotlight. (Greenpeace Australia Pacific, 2004b)

"Reports in UK Newspaper *The Guardian*, the *LA Times* and on BBC TV have brought this issue to a global audience–Tasmania's threatened forests are already on the international agenda," she said. Major international media outlets have visited the Styx, airing the story in countries such as Japan, Germany, the US, The Netherlands, Denmark, Belgium and the UK, and Opposition Leader Mark Latham's visit to the Styx last month further builds on the campaign's momentum. (Greenpeace Australia Pacific, 2004c)

These comments again highlight the notion that without print or television news coverage, environmental action and values–at least in the minds and strategies of their proponents–lose both legitimacy and effect and fail to appear on influential political and cultural agendas (Castells, 2004b).

The final protest discussed here occurred on 21 October 2008, in the nearby Upper Florentine Valley (Lester, 2010). Two environmentalists from the unaligned and modestly resourced group, "Still Wild, Still Threatened," blockaded a logging road with a car body in which they lay with their arms embedded in a pipe concreted into the ground. Logging contractors allegedly responded by attacking the car with sledgehammers. No journalists or police were present, although a representative of Forestry Tasmania–the government agency in charge of forestry activity on the island–was on-site. Hiding in the bush, a third protester filmed the encounter and posted it on the group's MySpace profile. The footage was available for viewing around the world within hours, and media releases from a variety of sources, including the activists themselves, other environmental NGOs and formal political representatives, quickly alerted news media to its presence. Journalists in Tasmania and interstate soon began to cover the story. Over the next fortnight, the event and the broader environmental issue of logging in Tasmania continued to feature in the news media. This prominence forced–among others–the new Premier of Tasmania, David Bartlett, to defend not only his views on the violence, but to reveal his environmental policies and support for forestry practices in news forums. Meanwhile, the environmental campaign gathered momentum as the publicity and debate triggered by the incident in broadcast, print and online news media travelled throughout an international network of activist and news websites.

It is this incident that ably demonstrates the potency of mediated visibility achieved via online and mobile communications technologies in the conduct of protest actions. Digitised audio-visual footage posted on MySpace (and YouTube the day after) revealed the violence and physicality of an incident that would have otherwise remained hidden from view, and without which may have limited the public impact of the alleged attack to verbal accusation and counter-accusation communicated through official spokespeople in the local news media. The transnational significance of mediated visibility is made clear by this extract from an opinion column that appeared in *The Mercury*, authored by chief reporter Sue Neales:

> Small wonder that Mr Bartlett—in a perfect world—would like to govern a Tasmania that is renowned worldwide as a clean, green and clever island, famed for its beauty, wilderness, tourism and niche hi-tech and high-value industries.
>
> Not one that is reliant on an old-school chop-it-down-as-fast-as-you-can mentality; where an extreme distrust of change, new ideas and new approaches still dominates popular debate.
>
> The continuing clash—or at best friction—between these visions of the state should worry all Tasmanians.
>
> Then there is the importance of Tasmania's image and reputation to think of.
>
> Why spend millions of dollars of taxpayers' dollars portraying our little island as a haven of tranquility when YouTube and TV news programs around the world are filled with horrific images of sledgehammers viciously attacking greenies' cars in the deep forests? (Neales, 2008: 30)

This situation reveals Thompson's (2005) point that, given the ubiquity of networked computing and mobile communications, visibility is a crucial weapon in political power struggles, particularly when governments and corporations lose control over the dissemination of photographs or footage of disturbing events. The desired public image of the forestry industry and Tasmanian State Government was, at least for a moment, punctured and destabilized, forcing both to defend their records and activities. Certainly, the fact that the premier was compelled to respond in a detailed fashion under sustained interrogation from journalists suggests that Still Wild, Still Threatened managed to temporarily disrupt the smooth interaction between government and industry. As with the previous two protests under discussion, however, it is worth noting that these outcomes did not stop logging of old-growth or high conservation-value native forests.

Audience numbers are a useful measure when considering the interconnections and relative strengths of the various strategies and platforms relating to this protest, although we concede they are an ineffective indicator of how audiences interpret the political and cultural symbols and meanings generated by protest events. Six months after the loggers' alleged assault on the protesters, the MySpace video had been downloaded more than 11,000 times, while a second version of the video on YouTube, captioned as "featured on Channel 9 news," had been played 6603 times. Still Wild, Still Threatened's MySpace site listed 384 friends and its "Causes on Facebook" listing had 7595 members. A rough comparison between these sites and broadcast and print news media outlets is appropriate here, particularly in trying to avoid an unwarranted celebration of Internet and social networking sites as a "revolutionary" mode of political activism for challenger groups. While its popularity has fallen in recent times, the Channel 9 network in Australia still manages to attract approximately one million viewers to its main nightly television bulletin, while its online presence is channelled through *ninemsn* (http://ninemsn.com.au/), which claims 8.2 million visits a month to its website. Large metropolitan daily newspapers, Melbourne's *The Age* and the *Sydney Morning Herald*, which both ran prominent stories on the Tasmanian forest violence, have a combined Monday-Friday circulation of more than 400,000, and Hobart's *The Mercury* has a circulation of just under 50,000. The point here is not to deny that the Internet and web are transforming the activities of environmental activists and other political challengers. Rather, via comparison, it is to emphasize the need to exercise caution when making claims about the *amount* of media power possessed and exercised by environmental activists through new technologies.

It should also be remembered that the ability to deploy digital communications for political ends is possessed by both challenger groups and government and industry. For example, six months after the sledgehammer incident, police and forestry contractors moved in to dismantle the protesters' longstanding camp in the Upper Florentine. The group quickly mobilized supporters using a variety of social networking platforms, including MySpace and Twitter. Countering this activity, Forestry Tasmania then used the Internet to justify its actions by posting a series of photographs of the camp on its website—suggesting uncleanness and a decrepit, unsafe state.

Conclusion: The capacity and limitations of environmental protest

The picture that emerges from these protest case studies is obviously complex and many-layered. Online media are an important new means of reaching supporters for protest groups, but it is major news stories that still serve to apply most pressure to industry and politicians by attracting the attention of wider audiences and voters. This differentiation speaks to a reality that environmental protests and campaigns are presently characterized by *multi*-media strategies (Castells, 2009: 327). Online digital media channels, mobile media and social networking tools are used to connect and share information with a transnational community of like-minded activists, supporters and interested observers. Local, national and international news media coverage remains the primary driver for pressuring politicians and industry by reaching as many citizens as possible. And, as our case studies indicate, news coverage, accompanied by compelling images and footage, remains the key objective in attaining and maintaining widespread political and cultural legitimacy for environmental protest, even 15 years after the arrival and development of the world wide web.

The intricate pattern of continuity and discontinuity outlined here suggests that the promise held by networked digital communications for independent online media production and distribution by activists has been only partly realized. The efficiency and speed of Internet and web-based communication have undeniable advantages in terms of organization, advocacy and inter- and intra-group interaction across vast expanses of space. But it also cannot be denied that environmentalists are yet to enjoy the early and largely theoretical promise held forth by the Internet and web for "self-representation" (Couldry, 2003) to large national and global populations, thereby allowing journalists to be bypassed. As the figures presented above show, professional news media networks and programs still possess considerable agenda-setting power by their attraction of comparatively enormous audiences for news content; a point borne out even online, with long established brands and mastheads such as the *Sydney Morning Herald* and *ninemsn* amongst Australia's top 20 websites across all categories.

We have noted elsewhere (Lester & Hutchins, 2009) that environmental activists would be well advised to place as much emphasis on online self-representation as news coverage in the longer term. However, even this course of action would not alter the underlying power dynamics that limit the impact of environmental protests and campaigns to destabilizing or, at best, disrupting dominant flows of corporate and government networks of power. As stated at the outset, the power of environmental activism falls well short of "switching power," which entails an ability to alter how these different economic and political networks interact. The fact that elected Green politicians now sit in many state and national parliaments around the world has perhaps changed this situation slightly, although, given their minority status in terms of seats in lower and upper houses, their governmental influence and media profile are often minimized unless they hold the balance of power. News media networks are also willing to enter into ongoing exchange with environmentalists, but even this usually requires that protest groups adhere to preferred frames of presentation for news formats before stories are posted, aired or printed (Hutchins & Lester, 2006). The consolation here is that when coverage is received, the results are occasionally impressive, with industry and government brought to public account for their actions.

If environmental activists are devoid of "switching power," what then is the function of environmental protest and why does it continue to be a prominent feature of social movement politics? It remains a useful symbolic intervention into the operation of networks of power via media in order to affect, however marginally and indirectly, the "ideas, visions, projects and frames" (Castells, 2009: 46) that form the cultural materials from which the network society continues to built. This is not the direct, harder power of switchers but a softer, more diffuse and incremental influence that slowly permeates the collective mindset of civil society, albeit unevenly. When a politician or a company director is forced to respond to a protest or the violent actions of their workers in a faraway forest, they are conceding that environmental issues are *deserving* of a response in the public domain, irrespective of their personal feelings. These minor local and regional victories by protesters are then shared and learnt from by a transnational community of environmentalists via online media. It is important not to overstate the effect and power of protest, but it is also erroneous to believe that it plays little or no role in the creation and perpetuation of resonant cultural discourses that influence public debate about the environment.

Notes

1. Small sections of this chapter have appeared in the following journal article: Lester, L. & Hutchins, B. (2009) "Power Games: Environmental Protest, News Media and the Internet," *Media, Culture & Society* 31(4): 579–96. The presentation of new materials was assisted by an Australian Research Council funded project (DP1095173), "Changing Landscapes: Online Media and Politics in an Age of Environmental Conflict."

CHAPTER TWELVE

Amazon Struggles in the Global Media Age

Framing and Discourses in Environmental Conflict

CONNY DAVIDSEN

Introduction

Latin America has a tremendous history of social movements and local struggles over resource rights, promoting a new depth in political debate around environmental justice, indigenous land rights, national economic strategies, and conflicting ideas of "development." Peru's culture of local political resistance is slowly entering a new phase of transregional protests, marked by a stronger influence of media in a time when information and communication technologies (ICTs) are profoundly impacting news reporting and politics worldwide. Discourses reflect growing stakeholder participation, plurality of voices and NGO involvement that have shifted the portrayal of issues across media. At the same time, they continue to be influenced by a wide range of media imagery between "modern" realities and old colonial myths, making media representations of environmental conflict more complex. Indigenous rights movements are increasingly using local and global media to strengthen their voice in public debate, strategically forming key coalitions with environmental groups for stronger representation in environmental conflict. This linkage between environmental and indigenous issues is not new and reflects their inherent connection through livelihood, resource distribution and justice issues. What is new, however, is the way media shape the conflict across globalized scales, often creating shortcuts between the local and the "global" or transregional and becoming new channels of representation or even empowerment. Also new are the pace and magnitude of issue framing within media on both sides of the conflict. These dynamics raise important questions about potential political impacts on local indigenous and environmental resistance. In 2008–2009, the Peruvian Amazon saw massive indigenous protests in response to a neoliberal reform that announced the commercialization of public rainforest lands in favor of resource extraction. This chapter is interested in how the discourses that flowed in and around media over multiple levels helped create unprecedented political momentum and stronger attention to indigenous land rights, sustainable rainforest futures, and ultimately a new level of neoliberal resistance across the country.

Historically as well as today, the Amazon rainforest has come to represent one of the foremost frontiers of clashing economic and environmental interests on all scales from local to global. As transnational protests and environmental conflict have now been accelerating worldwide, the Amazon has–after an already tumultuous colonial history–once again become the site of a globalized protest, problem and conflict. It is at the centre of a volatile environmental debate between global climate change and "megadiversity" concerns, neoliberal state interests in natural resource exploitation, unresolved indigenous territorial claims and local environmental rights. The Peruvian part of the Amazon covers an area of about 63 million hectares. In 2008–2009, a legal reform in Peru introduced laws that enabled companies to buy rainforest lands off public lands for natural resource exploitation, which could have triggered tremendous land use change, deforestation and ecological impact on the region. This was only the most recent measure among a larger neoliberal strategy that used privatization to attract foreign investment and promote capital-intense strategies of economic "growth" through large-scale natural resource exploitation.

The most controversial parts of the reform package were soon coined the "Law of the Jungle," which referred both to the rainforest as the geographic issue of concern as well as to frontier attitudes with a certain lawlessness and competitive ruthlessness. Local and national groups generated a wave of resistance against the reform, supported by wide public attention and media coverage. In particular, Amazon indigenous groups protested against the potential sell-out of rainforest lands that represented their livelihood base. International, national and regional news channels added political pressure by directing public attention to long-standing and unresolved issues around Amazon exploitation, indigenous resource access and local rights in general. Supported by this local to global media coverage, the indigenous protests ultimately sparked political resistance across the country with such a force that it successfully halted parts of the reform.

In times of globalization, the divides of information access, knowledge, and ultimately power, often grow between those that benefit from resource exploitation and those that are marginalized (Peet & Watts, 2004). The new diversity of media may mitigate or somehow change this trend. While large parts of the indigenous population do not have access to global or digital media themselves, indigenous leaders increasingly seek the opportunities of transregional media in collaboration with policy actors on the national or global level or see their interests being publicized by the latter. These interpreted representations of indigenous interests create a more powerful but also more selective picture for the public. Where increasingly globalized and digitalized media allow for more local voices "from the ground," they can selectively access more formalized discourses and change their momentum. As a result, indigenous issues may gain greater attention but could again be misrepresented in these new power spheres. Global and digital media need to be carefully understood as a two-sided coin between representation and misrepresentation and between empowerment and suppression.

These new forms and flows of media represent one of the most urgent and unknown frontiers in society's construction and (de-)colonization of discourses and knowledge. For protest movements, the potential impacts of these media tools range from a facilitation of more transparent information access through participatory online tools, coordinating communication during protests and actions (Juris, 2005) and new senses of engagement and citizenship through participatory web-based tools (Altman, 2002) to even deeper structural changes associated with digital democracy that may boost or overcome an otherwise systemic lack of infrastructure in remote rural areas. As a previously unknown plethora of equal-access sources, they may also create new shortcuts between the local and the global, thus circumventing the often-limiting power base of regional or national media outlets and boosting the ability of less powerful policy actors towards a stronger political representation (Altman, 2002). At the same time, globalized media structures and digital communication technologies may open the possibility of widening gaps of knowledge and representation even further between those that have access and those whose access is impeded. Postcolonial knowledge and power divides between the Global North and the Global South, as well as between different demographic and ethnic groups, are a growing concern.

The challenges of the global media age for indigenous representation in socio-environmental conflicts are only starting to be addressed. We need to ask to what extent, and particularly how, potentially negative dynamics are impacting on the power, representation and political framing of socio-environmental issues from the local to the global level (Bryant & Bailey, 1997; Peet & Watts, 2004; Yashar, 1998). The historical suppression of non-Eurocentric local histories and forms of knowledge may continue and even be reinforced by new media channels. This may ring particularly true where indigenous peoples are facing political and socio-environmental underrepresentation, in the past referred to as "nations within" (Fleras & Elliott, 1999: 191) and even a "Fourth World" (Manuel & Posluns, 1974) inside a First or Third World state. Natural resource use, ecological integrity and environmental well-being continue to be the focus of power struggles given their far-reaching implications for today's national resource economies, global environmental concerns, and local means of survival. Media portrayals of the clashing parties' interests add another layer to this complex power struggle that needs to be carefully understood. The global media age thus poses new challenges for the expression of indigenous interests and their political representation, where discourses can be either potentially de-colonized or indeed further colonized.

Framing Amazon rainforest struggles

The 2008–2009 Amazon protests are deeply embedded in underlying conflicts that have continued since early colonial times. Part of the problem is that the region has been struggling against misinformation, false imagery and myths that still influence the debate. Seven of these myths have been identified by Karp Toledo (2006). One image that remains particularly compelling is that the Amazon is a solution to global environmental problems, seen in the reference to it as the "lungs of the world." This modern idea of global salvation in times of climate change seems to repeat old colonial themes. The region has a long history as a perceived "reserve" or "buffer," as expandable and abandonable "hinterland" at free disposal for consumption elsewhere, readily serving external populations while suffering through resource booms and busts. Ever since climate change directed the modern focus of environmentalism on the Amazon, this "reserve" imagery has become even more powerful and ubiquitous, which made it sometimes more difficult for local indigenous interests to get through the layers of imagery and gain public attention for their local concerns. Similarly, problems emerge from modern environmentalist imagery that portrays the Amazon as a nurturing, deeply spiritual place based on somewhat romanticized notions of an archaic wilderness, more on aesthetic than ecological values. These notions have influenced evolving forms of colonialisms from early Amazon adventurers to modern environmentalism today. The region's ecological richness and "abundance" also often go hand in hand with an iconic imagery of traditional lifestyles and indigeneity that sometimes recall the "noble savage" (MacLean Stearman, 1994). This further influences another myth around historical and modern indigenous development; some in the debate continue to assume that the indigenous population would indiscriminately oppose and slow down economic development, thus pushing indigenous interests into a preconceived cliché that frames indigenous views as a "problem" itself. Some even suggest that this is what indigenous people ought to do, thus maintaining a static idea of indigenous interests embedded in traditionality and romanticist environmentalism (Hames, 2007). Both views create powerful preconceptions that may act as a trap, denying indigenous interests their own actual voice in debate.

Another historical misconception is that the Amazon is a vast and "empty" space, unpopulated and unclaimed. This is a remnant from a colonial frontier idea in which natural resources were unclaimed and free for exploration. The population of the entire larger region is around 22 million people, with 17 million of them in Brazil and 2.4 million in Peru. The local indigenous population is estimated at 936,000 across the Amazon, occupying a territory of roughly 110 million hectares, with 3.82 million hectares recognized as indigenous territories in Peru (BID, 1992). The region is sometimes perceived as "under-" or "de-populated" with a population density of only 2.17 inhabitants per square kilometer, compared to a Peruvian average of 16 inhabitants per square kilometer (Yánez, 1998). However, the lower population density is a result of the limited carrying capacity of rainforest soils and the seasonal demands of flooded forest ecosystems (Vandermeer & Perfecto, 2005). The image of fertile abundance is trapped in a further irony. While the Amazon is considered a very rich environment with a sheer endless supply of natural resources and undiscovered wealth for the future, it is also presented as a poverty-stricken, underdeveloped and neglected region–depicted by a figurative "beggar on a golden bench" (phrase used by Antonio Raimondi, cited by Schuldt, 2005: 31). The Amazon has been the setting of several dramatic boom-and-bust industries that fed into both extremes, ranging from silver mining (Assadourian et al., 1980) to guano (Levin, 1960; Gootenberg, 1993), the rubber boom (Barham & Coomes, 1994) and interim bust phases. Hardly any further processing industries were established in the Amazon, and thus the region remained dependent on primary resource extraction (Schuldt, 2005). The extraction typically occurred at exploitative levels that quickly depleted resources, repeatedly causing and increasing the region's boom and bust cycles. One of the latest resource booms is oil.

Another common misconception that is becoming more prevalent on a global media level is that "the Amazon" is a homogeneous place that can be simplified by "one size fits all" approaches in environmental management and governance. While often portrayed as a uniform ecosystem, there is actually a great diversity of climates, different geomorphologic conditions, soils, and thus flora and fauna. Moreover, there is a plethora of cultural, social, political and economic diversity that spans across eight different countries: Peru, Brazil, Ecuador, Chile, Bolivia, Colombia, Venezuela, Guyana and Suriname. There are an estimated 379 different ethnic groups across all countries, with 60 of them in Peru alone (BID, 1992). These countries have separate and distinct environmental policies, while policy coordination across the Amazon is still under construction, possibly taking governance much further in the future than the initial 1978 Treaty on Cooperation in Amazonia (TCA). Such myths continue to shape debate, however subtly. The next section explores the 2008–2009 protests as a conflict deeply embedded in colonial layers of deprivation and misrepresentation, which reemerged as a massive critique against legal reforms that threatened the livelihoods of the local Amazon population and led to an unprecedented level of resistance and the formation of a stronger indigenous movement in Peru.

Protesting the Law of the Jungle

The controversial reform package consisted of about one hundred legislative changes that were introduced around 2008. Ten of these ultimately became the critical focus of the protest, criticized by key policy actors and local indigenous groups as a sell-out of the rainforest via legal modifications that enabled privatization of forest lands that were considered public property of the state. These affected the rights of the local population and the protection of these rights through the state. In August 2008, shortly after government approval of the "Law of the Jungle," Amazon indigenous groups started to rally, calling for a withdrawal or derogation of the governmental decrees 1015 and 1043 that were threatening to affect their local land rights the most. The Amazon Indigenous Organization AIDESEP (Asociación Interétnica de Desarrollo de la Selva Peruana) announced early that it would fight the reform until the annulment of the controversial decrees. Dialogues were initiated between the two indigenous organizations, AIDESEP and CONAP, and government representatives over the summer of 2008, which continued to fuel the controversy.

After several months of growing resistance from regional and national actors, with increasing support from Peruvian and international non-governmental organizations but without a substantial change or discussion of the reform, the conflict erupted and led to widespread indigenous demonstrations and road blockades in several Amazon provinces. The mobilization led to numerous smaller protests across the country, particularly in the Amazon and supported by around 65 tribes. Thousands of people joined the protests in the streets wearing red face paint and brandishing traditional wooden spears. They seized strategically important sites such as highways, waterways and key processing facilities of the oil industry, effectively blocking normal business operations of the resource industries and their logistical infrastructure for weeks. Oil companies faced growing economic losses as their operations were interrupted. A group of Achuar Indios blocked a small airport in Trompeteros in the Northeastern province of Loreto, preventing normal oil operations of the Argentine oil company, Pluspetrol. Other local groups blocked the Amazon highway between Tarapoto and Yurimaguas, other waterways and oil facilities. Roadblocks interrupted the transport of goods in more remote regions, causing price hikes and even cutoffs of food and other items, which aggravated the situation even further. Serious criticism and protests also emerged in Lima and across the Andes, both in resistance to the legal reform and reflecting growing concern over the implications for the Amazon.

On 8 May 2009, the government declared a 60-day state of emergency in four Amazon provinces, arguing that security was at risk in the areas facing escalating protests. The government sent in military troops and banned public gatherings for 30 days. The state of emergency gave special power to the military and suspended constitutional guarantees in favor of intervention attempts to re-establish public safety. The protesting indigenous groups called for the state of emergency to be lifted as it exacerbated the political tension between the lines. Both groups claimed rights to the region and argued unlawful invasion of the other. Alberto Pizango, leader of the Peruvian Jungle Inter-Ethnic Development Association (AIDESEP), announced a resistance (or "insurgency") in response to the government's attempt to regain control of the region without any legal authority. Ancestral laws were to be recognized as obligatory on indigenous Amazon territory, and any attempt by state forces to enter the area was regarded as aggression. The political lines and framed identities of "we" and "they" between government stakeholders and indigenous groups hardened substantially, spiking the momentum of the protests over the next few weeks. By early June 2009, tens of thousands of Indians had joined the protests. Indigenous groups were increasingly mobilizing across the Peruvian Amazon, blocking roads and demonstrating at hydro-electric dams, oil and gas processing facilities across the Upper Amazon basin for weeks; these were relatively peaceful incidents but accompanied by growing media attention, dissatisfaction and further mobilization across the region.

The protests erupted into violence on 5 June 2009 when Peru's military and local police forces intervened against a protesting crowd of about 800 people in the town of Bagua, North Peru. The violent clashes left more than 60 people dead with about 40 casualties and 200 injured on the side of the indigenous protesters, as well as 24 casualties and 35 injured among the police forces. The incident was widely reported and condemned from local to national and global media, but the details of the events vary depending on the source. Military helicopters were reported to have dropped tear bombs while police violently moved in on the protesters. Armed only with wooden spears to symbolize the indigenous spirit behind their struggle, protesters reported that the police's forceful move into the crowd led to the eruption of violence, with several bullets fired, and protesters injured or killed. Some unarmed protesters wrestled with police, taking away their guns and fighting back in self-defense. Several police officers died as a result. During the violence, police were accused of sealing off the area, even to ambulances, so the injured could not get the medical attention they needed. Dead bodies were allegedly "disappeared" or burnt by government forces.

Two days after the Bagua clashes, Alberto Pizango–facing arrest on sedition charges–sought political asylum in the Nicaraguan embassy. Ten days later, he continued his political struggle from his Nicaraguan exile through occasional media statements. With their foremost leader waiting out in Nicaragua, AIDESEP was pushed to replace its leadership as soon as possible in order to secure its functioning role in the political round table. This created pressure against the leaders and on AIDESEP and was interpreted as an attack by the government on AIDESEP's popularity during the protests. The second leader, Champion Nonimgo, formally took his place in Peru and requested the Organization of American States and other international bodies to launch an impartial investigation into the violent events.

Within a week after the Bagua clashes, the local radio station that reported on the events ("La Voz" in Utcubamba) was shut down by the Ministry of Transport and Communication, withdrawing its broadcasting license (Gobierno del Perú, 2010). The Ministry later contradicted itself with different explanations as to why the radio station was shut down, and later also changed its statements to identify uncertified broadcasting equipment as the reason. The Global Association of Community Radios backed the local radio station and criticized the shutdown as unjustifiable. Nobel Peace Prize Laureate Rigoberta Menchú also supported the media profile of the petition through an open letter to President Alan García. In a protest against the shutdown of the local radio station, another 800 people returned to the streets of Bagua, and again drew national attention to Bagua as the symbolic epicenter of the political crisis. The violent events in Bagua moved discourse from the legal reform to the government's action and indigenous rights in general. The events caused a national outcry that was mirrored by international news coverage and support by numerous non-governmental organizations worldwide. The dramatic and devastating turn of events provided a powerful boost, triggering a more concentrated wave of criticism beyond the initial conflict.

Framing the conflict

Although demonstrations, road blockades and local protests are a relatively common element of politics that frequently interrupts daily life across the country, news coverage brought these particular protests to a new level. Media produced strong narratives about the underlying conflict, framing indigenous rights and goals as central to debate. Within Peru, the events triggered a highly active and dynamic day-to-day discourse with an involvement of policy-makers and the general public alike, raising questions of distributive justice between legal norms of a young system struggling with an inconsistent institutional framework, political trajectories of an ambitious growth-oriented resource economy, and underlying moral values ("ought to") of a post-colonial society that has yet to reconcile its national rifts between past and future, ethnic and national identities. Who "owns" what of Peru's natural resources (and based on what notion of ownership); as an individual, as a people, as a nation, and they are decided and controlled on what terms?

The violent turn of events in Bagua clearly redirected media focus within Peru from the underlying issue to the trigger. The aftermath discussion widely condemned government action as the country's worst since the Shining Path's insurgency during the 1980s and 1990s. Both sides, government and indigenous protesters, blamed each other for the conflict's escalation and argued over whether intervention and the use of violence were justified. The government claimed the first shots were fired against and not by the police forces, prompting a comment by President Alan García that the protesters had fallen to a criminal level. Many held the government responsible for a violent intervention against what had been a peaceful demonstration; among the strongest voices were the indigenous leaders during the protests, including Alberto Pizango, from AIDESEP. Extreme rifts between the positions developed in the mediated discourse. The emotionally charged exchange among key voices opened the rifts even further, and framing of arguments revealed irreconcilable differences in policy beliefs. For example, the government broadcasted a television spot with footage of fallen policemen and described the indigenous protesters as "extremists" (Gobierno del Perú, 2010: 65). President Alan García was reported as describing the clash as undesirable chaos, disobedience, and terror that would bring the country into a weaker position compared to its competitors. By framing the indigenous protesters as "terrorists" and the police and military intervention as an anti-terrorist effort, he sought to legitimize his argument by referring to the Shining Path's long insurgency and the resulting civil war between indigenous rebels and the military. But what Alan García stressed as "law and democratic order," Alberto Pizango referred to as "expropriation"; where the first sought to frame debate within "confusion and chaos," the latter stressed "provocation" and a responsibility of a "pacifist" people to defend territory for future generations.

Amidst the flurry of high-profile media reports following the violent turn of events, AIDESEP reiterated its original critique and explained its resistance as part of a necessary struggle against the neoliberal pressures that threatened to deplete the Amazon as a livelihood base, land base, and home. The protests not only aimed to have parts of the recent statutes repealed but also reiterated indigenous demands towards the government for a respectful treatment that would maintain certain land and resource rights as part of their future cultural and socio-economic existence.

The mediated debate revealed deep layers of disagreement over development paradigms, ranging from specific rainforest use models to a global critique of neoliberalism. While AIDESEP's immediate strategy was focused primarily on defending their immediate rights in the region and the withdrawal of the contro-versial reform, the larger national and global debate surfaced old and new themes beyond the indigenous group's direct demands. The debate that unfolded across media—and increasingly engaged the general public in Peru—contextualized this as a global concern over livelihood, conservation and biodiversity issues in rainforest exploitation, re-visited unresolved postcolonial tensions between indigenous rights and modern state, and ultimately contributed to the growing notion of neoliberal critique and resistance in the country that the indigenous protests were embedded in.

The heated debate quickly revealed key notions about roles, rights, and future prospects of the Amazon that highlighted the clash of paradigms between indige-nous groups and the government. President Alan García often defended the neolib-eral strategy as in line with the public property rights of the Amazon as a whole, arguing out that the region belonged to all Peruvians, not only to those who lived in the immediate area. He further described indigenous local interests and resistance as backward-oriented, inherent obstacles to economic growth (e.g., García Pérez, 2007). Pizango's media statements, in contrast, stressed from early on that he was not opposed to development per se, only against the exploitive measures it current-ly entailed because they were against indigenous long-term visions of development (e.g., interview with ombloguismo.com on 19 August 2008). The clash between political positions became further entrenched when Alan García in a TV interview reportedly did not outrule an involvement of Venezuelan political influence in the uprise in Bagua, and the media continued to raise questions about an agitating stim-ulus from outside the country (TeleSur, 8 June 2009, TV interview with Alan García). Alberto Pizango's media presence at this point, limited to few public state-ments from his exile in Nicaragua, seemingly tried not to feed into any speculation over political allies or economic paradigms but focused on immediate demands. Embedded within was a repeated message on the coloniality and repetition of his-tory in a timeless dichotomy of clashing corporate resource exploitation and indige-nous resistance in defense of its traditional territory (see Ubaquivel, 2009 for interview with Alberto Pizango upon his arrival in Nicaragua, 17 June 2009).

Eventually, the global media coverage of the indigenous protests grew from focused local reports to an overarching condemnation of the treatment of indige-nous people worldwide. Compelling simplified storylines and framed notions were also put forward in international media, such as "Amazon's Tiananmen" (e.g., *The Independent*, 2009). The international US-based NGO Amazon Watch criticized the military police intervention as a violent raid. Many international media initial-ly became interested in the conflict due to the violence of the events in Bagua, but the momentum transformed into a revisiting of the underlying conflict. Increasingly, media turned Bagua into a symbolic news moment in history that visualized a clash that had been around for centuries. This framing provided an effective starting point to remind the global community of the long-standing indigenous resource rights and civil participation that had remained unaddressed and unresolved in Peru since independence.

The Amazon groups used the high media interest and political momentum in the country to renew their call for demands that sounded very familiar, reminding the government that their position had been ignored for decades. They focused on: 1) Recognition and protection of indigenous territories, including ancestral lands; 2) Recognition of self-determination of indigenous peoples; fulfillment of the government's obligations to Convention 169 of the International Labour Organization and the UN Declaration of Indigenous Peoples' Rights; 3) Health care services and bilingual education; and 4) Economic development of alternative income activities, such as medical plants and local crafts. Alberto Pizango himself compared the Bagua tragedy to a "genocide" (public press conference, 6 June 2009, reported, e.g., by TeleSur on Peruvian TV). He framed the protests as part of a self-defensive struggle in the larger post-colonial picture, stating that the protests represented a mobilization for the right to life, the right to keep traditional territory, and a defense of the environment. The sheer extent of the exploration boom of oil and gas was threatening to destroy the social structures, customs and livelihood strategies that the region had developed over centuries. Pizango also continued the powerful imagery of the Amazon as the "lungs of the world," using old myths as a powerful political narrative for AIDESEP's ecological argument beyond that of indigenous livelihoods.

After the violent clash in Bagua, media coverage included concern and frustration by the general public over government protection of its own interests. Indigenous protesters demanded justice and called for an investigation into the military and police action during the violent clash to shed light on the reasons behind the escalation of violence, lack of post-injury care and the alleged cover-up of "disappeared" people. Peru's government formed a special commission on 7 September 2009 to conduct an investigation of the events in Bagua. Their final report was published on 4 January 2010 (see Gobierno del Perú, 2010) and presented a more government-based version of the events, portraying indigenous protesters as the aggressors. The descriptions of the events as told especially by national media continued to differ between the government, on-site reports of local sources and further interpretations on NGO websites.

Conclusion

Peru's indigenous protests of 2008–2009 emerged into a broad engagement of multi-scale media that helped diversify the perspectives, storylines and breadth of the initial reform-focused debate into a wider discussion of neoliberal conflict. This is particularly interesting as environmental and indigenous movements may empower each other while their themes and storylines disperse. The media discourse surrounding the Amazon movement created powerful layers of conflicting scales and goals—most accentuated between global interests and local struggles for more resource rights that created new linkages outside the realms of the state on the national level. This chapter has highlighted the conflictive interfaces of Amazon exploitation, neoliberal resistance and indigenous rights and shown how the arguments of both sides were framed by various media. The description of the events indicated a rising engagement of joint indigenous-environmental efforts towards grassroots democratization in the Peruvian Amazon, a strengthened representation of indigenous interests from political discourse to public media and emerging debates about local environmental rights that increasingly demand participation in decisions that used to be withheld by the postcolonial state.

The violence of the 2008–2009 Amazon protests was a highly media-processed storyline with a manageable direct scope, which created a media screenshot that was able to hint towards the Amazon's old and new conflicts. The story of Bagua showed a new difficult chapter in Amazon indigenous resistance that reminded the global community of the long-standing Amazon clash between corporate privatization and traditional territorial rights. The multi-scale news media coverage, along with the agitated involvement of the national media and public, triggered a powerful political momentum in which the national government rescinded substantial parts of its recent legal reform in seemingly direct response to the protests. The environmental discourse continues to be volatile as the underlying causes of conflict remain unresolved. Economic and social exclusion, scarcity of opportunities and lack of access to basic services such as drinking water, waste water, electricity, health care and formal education continue to be highly disparate privileges in Peru, and systemic issues of abandonment, marginalization, racism, prejudice and distrust still divide the country. At the same time, events surrounding the "Law of the Jungle" indicate a strengthening of indigenous representation in the long run. The conflict served as a catalyst that drew indigenous interests together towards a stronger national forum, ultimately transforming the isolated battles of indigenous groups against local resource exploration firms into a national issue with a more united political voice and growing strategic use of the media.

The chapter also suggested that the new range of local representation, diversity of voices, meanings and knowledge, however, need to be re-assessed in the context of the global media age. Struggling against the neoliberalization efforts of the national government, indigenous groups were traditionally forced to articulate their arguments in not necessarily indigenous but rather nation-based ideas of land property, territory, resource economies, and economic returns. In other words, indigenous groups were forced to frame their key socio-environmental concerns reactively; not based on their own terms, but on those of the Peruvian government and the Global North. Facing an entirely new set of mechanisms of selection and competition over the power and access to have one's voice heard, global and digital media suggest new potentials but also key challenges; the diversification can work towards a potential decolonization but also towards an even further colonization of socio-environmental discourses. Both potential impacts, however difficult to grasp in the multi-scale complexities of real-world discourses, are now accelerated.

CHAPTER THIRTEEN

Piracy Up-Linked

Sea Shepherd and the Spectacle of Protest on the High Seas

DAVID CROUCH AND KATARINA DAMJANOV

Since the austral summer of 2006, the Southern Ocean has become the setting for a battle between pirates and whalers. Sailing under the Jolly Roger, the international environmental organization Sea Shepherd conducts their anti-whaling protest against the Japanese Institute of Cetacean Research (ICR). Self-styled pirates, the Sea Shepherd crew frame themselves in a host of piratical regalia and romance, including their skull and cross-bones motif framed everywhere in black on ships, helicopters and uniforms. In their skirmishes at sea they ram vessels, board ships, hurl projectiles, and deploy propeller entanglements. However, unlike the traditional practice of piracy which has been historically conducted for private economic ends, the "pirate" attacks of Sea Shepherd are part of their mission "to end the destruction of habitat and slaughter of wildlife in the world's oceans in order to conserve and protect ecosystems and species" (Sea Shepherd, *Mission Statement*, n.d.). Founded in 1977 by influential ex-member of Greenpeace Paul Watson, Sea Shepherd gathers volunteers from all over the world, grouped around the idea of marine wildlife preservation. The aim of Sea Shepherd campaigns in the Southern Ocean is to end the activities of the ICR, who they accuse of commercially harvesting whales under the disguise of scientific research, thus breaking the 1986 International Moratorium on Whaling that banned the commercial hunting of whales. They claim to act for the common good under the authority of the United Nations World Charter for Nature, upholding international conservation regulations prohibiting the commercial slaughter of whales in the Antarctic Whale Sanctuary.

Through their anti-whaling campaign Sea Shepherd has initiated a series of direct confrontations with ICR vessels. In one such encounter, protesters nailed plates to the drain outlets that spill the blood from the flensing deck of the whaling ship into the sea and hurled smoke bombs and bottles of butyric acid onto the vessel (Sea Shepherd, 2007). Sea Shepherd crews carrying cameras record these events, and almost instantaneously images are spread across the globe via satellite up-links, webcams, and around-the-clock Internet blogging. Sea Shepherd takes their environmental protest in this remote and unforgiving location, impossibly beyond everyday reach, and broadcasts it back to the world, disseminating it through the Internet and blogosphere; they constantly send out fresh broadcast-quality images and a barrage of news releases, twitters, and updates of events. Their commentators respond almost instantly to these communications, and within a few hours of an event, fuelled by the controversial and colourful nature of their activities, there are literally hundreds of passionate viewpoints, debates, and rants spreading across blogs, news sites and online networks, and subsequently their actions are swiftly drawn into national political debates. Furthermore, it is not only the tools and tactics derived from contemporary communications technologies that they use to garner support for their cause; by staging their anti-whaling protest as spectacular "pirate" attacks, they also exploit elements of popular culture, tapping into the social imagination of a potentially transnational public sphere. Moreover, the crucial element that makes their protest truly transnational is the geographic location in which it is conducted—the international waters of the high seas, one of the world's global commons, a domain legislated to lie outside nations' territorial jurisdictions and private ownership rights.

Taken together, Sea Shepherd strategies of protest and the spaces in which they are enacted make their anti-whaling campaign in the Southern Ocean a productive case study from which to consider the emerging complex of intersections between the idea of the transnational, environmental protest, and the harnessing of a global popular culture and public sphere in a technologically mediated world. We suggest that the environmental activism of Sea Shepherd indicates the convergence of transnational protest through information and communications technologies, the international spaces of the high seas, and elements of popular culture. This is not to say that Sea Shepherd's protest is entirely novel. For decades NGOs and other protest organizations have been using shock campaigns and high levels of media visibility in order to communicate their message, applying a strategy that Kevin DeLuca (1999) calls the production of "image events" as a rhetorical tactic. Indeed, the past use of such methods by anti-whaling activists effectively resulted in a ban on commercial whaling (Epstein, 2008). As Charlotte Epstein points out in her study of the birth of anti-whaling discourse, not only did the early anti-whaling campaign rewrite whaling as "illegal" it was also able to establish the dubious legality of its own actions as "acceptable" (2008: 145). The early anti-whaling campaigns also made an influential contribution to the creation of a sense of global community, reinforcing the idea of transnational movements and affinities. Enacting their protest on the high seas and projecting it to a world-wide audience, "anti-whaling activists effectively carved out a new type of political space, beyond the traditional space of the state" (Epstein, 2008: 142). Moreover, these campaigns cast their global audience as an "imagined community" (Anderson, 1991) with a transnational social imaginary. Sea Shepherd continues to uphold the ideals of the anti-whaling movement. Yet, we argue that via an approach which exploits a saturation of media communications and a broad dissemination in elements of popular culture, Sea Shepherd moves the protest of the past into a new arena, shaping it in ways which takes advantage of contemporary technological and social phenomena.

Sea Shepherd has taken what Epstein calls the acceptable "criminal deeds" (2008: 145) of environmental protest and packaged them in terms of an international cultural fascination with the pirate imaginary. As a number of studies have made clear, there is an increasingly nuanced relationship between environmental rhetoric and popular culture (Meister & Japp, 2002). Popular culture has apparently had an ongoing influence in raising awareness of environmental issues. However, while sitcoms and movies become vehicles through which to convey an environmental message, an organization like Sea Shepherd instead influences and acts upon popular culture itself—rather than packaging their message in a fictional world they take their real protest activities and work them into the fabric of popular culture. In other words, the mode of the Sea Shepherd protest relies in part on its filtration into a cultural imaginary; the conscious evocation of a popular image of piracy fuels their protest against the ICR. Sea Shepherd plays upon an idea of a shared cultural imaginary, using pop culture and media to create a hybrid "transnational scape" (Appadurai, 1996).

A number of critical studies examining the relationship between the media and environmental movements suggest that environmental activists must be extraordinarily media savvy in order to successfully convey their message (Hansen, 1993; Anderson, 1997; Cottle, 2003; Lester & Hutchins, 2009). In the case of Sea Shepherd, we argue that this process relies upon a sophisticated interplay between popular culture, spectacle and environment, in which their protest is necessarily mediated, but remains undiluted. We suggest that rather than pitting themselves against the potential "implosion of meaning" (Baudrillard, 1994) in the contemporary mediaphere, Sea Shepherd uses new forms of communication technology in ways which enhance the idea of a global society and encourage a nascent transnational public sphere of eco-citizens.

Protest, eco-piracy, and popular culture

Eco-politics, as critics such as Sean Cubitt (2005) observe, feature prominently within in the contemporary production of law, knowledge, wealth, and the practices of everyday life. By domesticating environmental issues—within the news, cinematography, television, advertisements, books, magazines and Internet content—popular culture and mass media have, in particular, played a significant role in establishing environmental discourses as critical to all spheres of human life. As Mark Meister and Phyllis M. Japp summarize it:

> the languages and images of popular culture situate humans in relation to natural environments, create and maintain hierarchies of importance, reinforce extant values and beliefs, justify actions or inaction, suggest heroes and villains, create past contexts and future expectations. (2002: 4)

Through the activities of Sea Shepherd environmental discourse has become twinned with an idea of piracy derived from popular culture. Apparently aware of the significant influence of popular culture in the perception of environmental issues, they draw on popular representations of piracy to frame their radical approach to environmental activism. In juridical terms however, their activities do not clearly fall within the category of piracy. For example, Nagtzaam and Lentini suggest that "the Sea Shepherds constitute an example of a gray area phenomenon" and that they "may be best categorized as a vigilante group, because they claim they are seeking to enforce a legal status quo because of states' and the international community's inabilities or unwillingness to do so" (2008: 110). Moreover the activities of the Sea Shepherd are quite distinct from modern day pirates who commit theft and violence for personal gain, such as the increasing pirate attacks reported off the coast of Somalia, which have recently received significant media coverage. Nonetheless, Sea Shepherd appears to oscillate their piratical public image between that of heroic defenders of the ocean and anarchic villains involved in criminal activities. Their protest has polarized opinions, attitudes and feelings regarding the justification of their sometimes violent actions. However, this ethical and moral debate—the question of whether their direct action is a help or hindrance to their cause—is not our focus here, nor is the question of whether they should be theoretically characterized as "vigilantes," "eco-terrorists," "militants," "whale warriors" or "conservationists." We are concerned with the manner in which Sea Shepherd frames and disseminates their environmental protest and what this says about forms of transnational conceptions of culture and space.

In recent years the pirate appeal has become increasingly prevalent in popular culture. From the Hollywood blockbuster trilogy *Pirates of the Caribbean*, to street fashion and merchandise, the image of piracy is a resource much exploited by creative and fashion industries. As Melissa Campbell (2004) describes in an article for *The Age*:

> pirate chic has inspired decades of fashion designers and trend-setters. Filtered through literature and cinema, pirates are idealised as the ultimate free agents–avoiding society's rules and taking command of their own destiny. Brutal maritime gangster, romantic pin-up, savvy adventurer–the pirate has it all.

What Campbell calls "pirate chic" is drawn from a history of celebratory and romanticized pirate iconography: the provocative pirate image, with its symbolism of swashbuckling anarchy, sexy swaggering freedom, roving adventure and true-hearted vigilantes sailing in the face of the authorities. Sea Shepherd intentionally utilizes the evident popularity of the pirate image in order to make their activities more acceptable and appealing to their audience and more intriguing for the media. As Paul Watson (2008) explains in *The Guardian*:

> We decided years ago that if people were going to call us pirates, we would adopt our own version, and designed the crossed Neptune trident and shepherd's staff with the skull. As soon as we hoisted that black flag, kids from around the world began to write to us in support. Our Jolly Roger hats and shirts have become our most popular merchandise. Why? Because there is a romance associated with piracy that is separate from the reality.

Through this kind of tactic Sea Shepherds themselves are today well established in popular culture–from references to them on popular shows such as the *South Park* episode "Whale Whores" or the reality TV series *Whale Wars* on Animal Planet, to people wearing t-shirts emblazoned with their Jolly Roger logo as a fashion statement–they have developed their cultural cachet into what could perhaps be called "Sea Shepherd chic."

Labelling these activists "pirates" throws up a host of conflicting and competing ideas surrounding current understandings of the term piracy. From the perspective of films such as *Pirates of the Caribbean,* Sea Shepherd "pirates" might be seen as the true protectors of the sea, attempting to liberate the ocean from the various uncaring regimes of voracious nations and institutions; in this sense Sea Shepherd could be cast in the mould of Captain Jack Sparrow and his pirates, who attempt to preserve the ocean's emblematic openness to freedom, competing against the ICR, who would represent English Lord Cutler Beckett's troops, the self-proclaimed owners of the ocean who do not deserve the bounty of the sea. From a different perspective, a parallel can be drawn between the piracy of the Sea Shepherd and the discourse of "righteous theft" associated with electronic piracy, another controversial issue that surrounds the concept of the "global commons" and the rhetoric of unfettered global exchange; the controversial actions of the Sea Shepherd, purportedly conducted for the "common good," align their form of piracy with the so-called piracy of peer-to-peer networks such as the site "Pirate Bay," which facilitates unlawful downloads of bit torrent files that contain snatched computer software, music and films under copyright, making them available to all for free. In this sense, there is a popular cultural collision between the high seas and the Internet. Both spaces are conceived as globally shared domains, and in both cases, a popular pirate imaginary is projected as a sort of protest, a protest which is facilitated by the idea of a transnational space. Sea Shepherd piracy is an environmental protest against the killing of marine life, while Internet piracy is represented as a protest against copyright laws, in favour of an open cultural commons. Sea Shepherd's appropriation of piracy thus suggests how old forms of conceptual rebellion–aggressive assertions of freedom and disdain for the system–are reworked as global gestures of protection, preservation and shared citizenship. Integrating real and imagined practices and iconographies of piracy into their direct actions, Sea Shepherd introduces a new breed of "piracy" into the contemporary vocabulary of protest in order to engage in environmental politics through popular culture.

Mediascapes and the pirate spectacle

Like all gestures of social and political dissent, Sea Shepherd relies upon the visibility of their protest. Although Sea Shepherd conducts their protest in the remote Southern Ocean, contemporary media technologies enable them to make their actions visible to a world-wide audience. They disseminate their message through online media and social networks; they are active through a comprehensive and colourful website, they regularly upload webcam recordings of their campaigns, and have highly active international discussion forums containing news, image galleries, and research papers. The organization also has over 3000 YouTube clips online, more than 60,000 Facebook friends, a substantial MySpace presence, and sends out regular "tweets" on Twitter to over 8000 followers. In addition they also maintain a high visibility through mainstream media forms, including online and print news, and the controversial series *Whale Wars*.

As has been acknowledged, many environmental protesters such as Greenpeace have proved themselves to be highly successful in obtaining wide media coverage (DeLuca, 1999; Epstein, 2008). In the case of Sea Shepherd, their protest relies not only upon skillful manipulation of the media but also a sophisticated interaction with the vicissitudes of popular culture and societies increasingly dominated by spectacle. Rather than using the spectacle of nature under threat, as is done by other environmental protest groups (Lester & Cottle, 2009), Sea Shepherd stages their protest as the spectacle itself, clearly evoking DeLuca's concept of "tactical image events" (1999: 3). By producing breathtaking images of "pirate" attacks and delivering them to a global audience, they contribute to what could be called the "spectacularization of protest."

In these terms, Sea Shepherd participates in contemporary culture's obsession with the production and consumption of images, in what Guy Debord (1983) famously identifies as the "society of the spectacle" and what Douglas Kellner more recently calls "spectacle culture" (2003: vii). Debord emphasizes the fundamental significance of the image in contemporary society and suggests it has supplanted direct experience and human interaction, and that social relationships have become mediated by a spectacle of images. As Kellner points out, "(e)very form of culture and more and more spheres of social life are permeated by the logic of the spectacle" (2003: vii). The profusion of old and new media technologies has heightened the reaches of an image-driven culture. Rather than resisting this, Sea Shepherd exploits this condition of social and cultural mediation, gearing the form of their protest to take advantage of this logic of spectacle. Aboard each of the Society's vessels there is a dedicated photographer and separate video camera operator, whose images are posted directly to the mediasphere. They take their direct physical interaction and mediate it, a process which, perhaps paradoxically, renews a sense of community and meaningful interaction through the very, apparently atomising, logic that Debord deplores. Sea Shepherd activities exemplify and exploit a culture and society in which, as Debord describes, "reality emerges within the spectacle, and the spectacle is real" (1983: 9). The Sea Shepherd strategy suggests that spectacle can be paradoxically exploited as a galvanizing political tool, rather than it becoming, as Debord suggests, an opiate which leaves the masses stupefied.

The manufacture of celebrity is also central to this culture of media spectacle and to the Sea Shepherd anti-whaling protest. Like old forms of propaganda and politics, Sea Shepherd is still using a charismatic central figure to rally around. Paul Watson is the undeniable star of the show. His dramatic appearance, with drooping moustache and shock of white windswept hair, combined with a stern weather-beaten demeanour and captain's garb, is used in a huge number of the Sea Shepherd images. Graeme Turner describes contemporary media's sophisticated "production of celebrity," and argues that in "a highly convergent media environment," celebrity is "also a commodity: produced, traded and marketed by the media" (2004: 9). However, this interpretation appears to give complete agency to the media in the process of celebrity production. On the other hand, individuals themselves sometimes produce and manufacture their celebrity status; Paul Watson is an interesting example of this. He effectively creates his celebrity, marketing it as another element in his protest through media and popular culture. In this sense Watson and Sea Shepherd additionally exploit contemporary culture's cult of celebrity in order to enhance the reception of their protest within a society increasingly bred upon the consumption of spectacle.

The eco-imaginary of global citizens: Towards a transnational public sphere

The protest of the Sea Shepherd is based upon what Cubitt terms the "fundamentally social shape of human life" (2005: 4); they take advantage of the idea of space as socially constructed, rendering, as Cubitt puts it in another context, "space as malleable performance" (2005: 81). Sea Shepherd's oscillation between their performances conducted purportedly for the common good out on the high seas and their culturally inflected transmissions within the flows enabled by digital technologies can be seen as a set of tactics which illustrates the potential for the formation of a social space aspiring to a kind of planetary citizenship of shared environmental ideals. As Libby Lester and Brett Hutchins point out, environmental politics and issues "are increasingly and more appropriately located within the broad domain of contemporary citizenship" (2009: 591). Like many environmental movements, the Sea Shepherd assumes a concept of global citizenry, a network of cosmopolitan, eco-aware, transborder audiences, activists, and affiliates, prompting concerns about issues which are beyond the local. This global "imagined community" (Anderson, 1991) has a culture of its own and requires the same kind of myths and symbols as any national culture (Macnaghten & Urry, 1998: 152).

From this perspective it can be argued that groups such as the Sea Shepherd are potentially both instances and incubators of a putative postnational global order. They encourage and exploit a concept of shared global space and the idea of a public sphere which has been accommodated by the rise of the Internet and other media forms. This in turn implies a spatially oriented approach to conceptualizing ideas about community and a transnational social sphere, what Ingrid Volkmer refers to as "global public space" (2007). At very least it can be argued that the nature of the Sea Shepherd's approach to "eco-globalism" is further evidence that the possibility of a translocal public sphere is only possible through media. As Cubitt describes:

> The attempt to build a public sphere, even in the immanently global terms of eco-politics, will always be tainted with the history of nationalism, unless and until the dimensions of the public sphere extend to an appreciation that on global scales it cannot be other than mediated. (2005: 93)

Sea Shepherd activities are an example of how contemporary use of electronic media appears to prompt a new dominance of the image and spectacle in communicative social life and how this in turn presumes the existence of new imagined communities which reformat old imaginaries into a necessarily mediated space.

In this sense the technologically mediated activities of the Sea Shepherd can be related to ideas about an emerging global public sphere. Angela Crack points out in her recent study *Global Communication and Transnational Public Spheres* that Jürgen Habermas sees organizations like Greenpeace as "representative of an emergent cosmopolitan consciousness and nascent global citizenry," yet he also sees new media forms as promoting the "fragmentation of civil society"(2008: 41). The work of Habermas has been used to claim that the Internet both does and does not provide the medium for a global public sphere (Salter, 2003: 117). Lee Salter, for instance, argues that the Internet, as a medium of "unrestricted communications" (2003: 125), has the potential to lay the foundation for an "informal public sphere" (2003: 129). Habermas' (1989) theory of the public sphere describes the dialogical relationship which was created in eighteenth-century salons and newspapers; according to Habermas this space becomes eroded by the expansion of mass media in the twentieth century. The dialogic is replaced by a system of public displays designed to generate consent. For Habermas the new media technology is manipulative, unable to generate new forms of social and cultural exchange. However, as Featherstone and Lash observe:

> Contra Habermas, for whom technology is unavoidably tainted with instrumentality and is seen as part of the extension of system rationality which is closing off communicative interaction, it can be argued that the new forms of electronic communication could well provide a range of new quasi-public spaces, which encourage debate and active citizenship. In addition, as critics have pointed out against Habermas, the possibility of a unitary public sphere may not only be historically suspect, but also an unrealizable goal. Instead it is possible to conceive a series of separate, yet overlapping, counter-public spheres. (1999: 7)

New media, from this perspective, do not necessarily breed anomie. The old public sphere attempted to forge a common will, while the Internet appears intensely pluralistic and fragmented; yet as the Sea Shepherd approach demonstrates, this does not mean it cannot operate as a public sphere but rather that the emerging transnational social space in which they operate can be seen as one of many "overlapping counter-public spheres." As Macnaghten and Urry describe, this results in "the very category of the global fragmenting into a multiplicity of globals, with competing notions of global citizenship" (1998: 153).

More recently, Habermas has contended that the public sphere must:

> amplify the pressure of problems, that is, not only detect and identify problems but also convincingly and *influentially* thematize them, furnish them with possible solutions, and dramatize them in such a way that they are taken up with and dealt with by parliamentary complexes. (1996, p. 359)

The influence of Sea Shepherd in this potentially global public sphere suggests a simple solution to the problems they identify—namely, the end of whaling. As in Habermas's formulation, they "thematize" and "dramatize" their protest so that it has an impact on political systems. The organization thus encompasses the prerequisites Crack outlines as crucial to transnational public spheres: "transborder communicative capacity, transformations in sites of political authority, and transnational networks of mutual affinity" (2008: 68). Thus it can be argued that the Sea Shepherd reinforces the possibility of a transnational public sphere. Yet they do so by making essentially imaginary spaces somehow real and meaningful. This is an increasingly common phenomenon of environmental protest and awareness, as Lester and Cottle describe, "(g)eographically remote places become literally perceptible places of possible concern" (2009: 921). In an era in which spatially and geographically diverse locations and events have increasingly immediate effects on societies around the globe, Sea Shepherd presents the Southern Ocean as a site of global concern. For most of the world's population the icy seas far down at the bottom of the globe are spaces characterized by a certain unreality, inaccessible to most, they are nearly always mediated in the social imaginary via images. Paradoxically, Sea Shepherd takes this almost unreal space, and via the nature of their own mediated protest, renders it a pressing reality in a global public sphere, an imaginary community which is itself an abstract, mediated space.

This appears to contradict what the cultural theorist Jean Baudrillard suggests is peculiar to contemporary media images, that rather than produce meaning and representation, the modern spheres of mediated images are "sites of the *disappearance* of meaning and representation" (1987: 27). As Baudrillard puts it:

> the image has taken over and imposed its own immanent ephemeral logic; an immoral logic without depth, beyond good and evil, beyond truth and falsity; a logic of extermination of its own referent, a logic of the implosion of meaning in which the message disappears on the horizon of the medium. (1987: 21–22)

Baudrillard posits that mass media are fully capable of neutralizing dissent by converting political resistance into another set of empty signs and simulacra. However, contra Baudrillard, it seems that the Sea Shepherd uses the "ephemeral logic" of the image in order to maintain and gather support for their gestures of dissent. From one perspective their piracy can be seen, as Cubitt describes in relation to contemporary "ecomedia," as a rejoicing in the "the authenticity of artifice" (2005: 20). Sea Shepherd appears to accept the ambivalence between truth and falsity which technologically mediated spaces produce, yet their message does not disappear within its medium. Instead, in what could be called a process of "infusion," it becomes a perceptible and everyday part of global popular culture. In this way the activities of Sea Shepherd reveal a more complex way in which the imagery of protest becomes part of contemporary culture and generates public awareness and action. The success of this kind of tactic suggests that the empty messages and meanings (and their unresponsive audience) that Baudrillard imagined, can actually be used to make forms of transnational protest more effective. In the context of the televized Sea Shepherd protests on the freezing seas off Antarctica, Baudrillard's speculations about a "cold event,", reheated by the "cold medium" of television for the "masses who are themselves cold" (1987: 23), seems undermined; their global audience responds with more than "a tactile chill and a posthumous emotion, a dissuasive shiver, which sends them into oblivion with a kind of aesthetic good faith" (Baudrillard, 1987: 23). This is not to suggest that there are none who would respond in this way; undoubtedly there are those who feel their responsibility satiated by an episode of *Whale Wars*; however, as Sea Shepherd forums testify, there are many who are warmly inspired by these chilly actions conveyed through the cold medium of television and other communications technologies.

While the constraints of geography appear to recede in this new media communication environment–the audience of Sea Shepherd activities are brought instantaneously to view a stage set out in the middle of the ocean–it can also be argued that it is the physical existence or geographic reality of global commons spaces which make possible the transnational dimension of the Sea Shepherd protest. Global networks sustained by new media technologies have allowed the concept of protest to move beyond the bounded territories of nations into unfixed flows of communication, however, these transnational exchanges and identifications rely on virtual cartographies. Perhaps the only real physical spaces in which a transnational protest can be enacted are in the regions identified as the global commons, because regardless of their broader scope, all other forms of protest are held within national spaces. The global commons can effectively be seen as both physical and figurative spaces within which the virtual and actual converge into a truly transnational phenomenon. The Sea Shepherd organization suggests the increasing significance and centrality of the global commons in transnational protest and politics. Filtering their real activities on the high seas into the intangible spaces of a global mediasphere highlights the complex nexus between physical and mediated protest. The organization suggests the importance of an old form of active embodied protest which has been re-worked to take advantage of new mediating technologies.

Rather than suggesting transnational protest relies on an exchange between the nexus of the local and global, protests such as that of the Sea Shepherd are truly transnational; unlike other protests, the Sea Shepherd protests are not held in a "local" context which are then projected globally, they are always enacted in what could be termed a "global" space. Moreover, the virtual space of the Internet is also conceived as a global common; here connections between the idea of Internet commons and natural commons meld and converge into a new formation of protest.

The Sea Shepherd does not localize their imagery of protest in the Southern Ocean, rather they use the unique geographic qualities of the location to enhance the transnational dimension of their message. As Featherstone and Lash write, "to speak of the possibility of global citizenship. . .is to raise a whole range of questions about the nature of cultural spaces in which these new forms can develop" (1999: 7). The global commons can be seen as the physical manifestation of a cultural space for a newly imagined global citizenry. The Sea Shepherd uses popular culture and media to suggest that environments which belong to no one are the concern of everyone; their protest thus indicates the central place that global common spaces could occupy in the future of environmental activism. From this position the Sea Shepherd's pop-culturally inflected pirate spectacle in the Southern Ocean could very well imply the potentially significant role of environmental protest in remapping contemporary culture and its spaces through the prism of a postnational cartography.

CHAPTER FOURTEEN

Climate Change and International Protest at Copenhagen

Reflections on British Television and the Web

NEIL T. GAVIN AND TOM MARSHALL

Introduction

Climate science ("climategate" notwithstanding) suggests that global warming is real and humankind is contributing to it substantially (Risbey, 2008; Bray & von Storch, 2008). Furthermore, British governments have not made an impressive contribution to alleviating the problem (Carter, 2009). The initial phase of the EU emissions trading scheme was not an unalloyed success (Environmental Audit Committee, 2007, among others), and the recent carbon price collapse threatens its effectiveness (Environmental Audit Committee, 2009).[1] Some large emitters were never party to Kyoto, and current world CO_2 output is at the top of the range of the 2001 IPCC Report projections. Against this backdrop pressure groups and activists have become increasingly disenchanted with current political action on the issue and more prepared to mobilize and protest (Gavin, 2010). They want to raise the profile of the issue, especially in Britain where currently it is low, relative to bread-and-butter issues like health and crime (Gavin, 2009), and is, consequently, scarcely on the public's radar (Gavin, 2007a).

But climate change is the quintessential internationalized issue. Addressing it requires coordinated action by *all* countries, not just Britain. The Copenhagen negotiations in 2009 were billed as an opportunity to produce an effective successor to Kyoto, drawing in the entire global community. So it was an obvious place to coordinate, internationally, to put pressure on politicians to reach an accommodation. This sort of action should be differentiated from locally- or nationally-based actions directed at issues which have an international complexion, and in this sense they are transnational in both their coordination and their remit. Umbrella organizations like Global Campaign for Climate Action[2] were certainly active at Copenhagen in this respect and represented groups of conventional NGOs, such as Oxfam International, Greenpeace International, the World Council of Churches, and the World Wildlife Fund.

But Copenhagen also offered opportunity for comparable consolidated and internationally organized activity by direct action groups from around the globe. These were spearheaded by a loosely affiliated set of campaigning organizations, among them Global Climate Campaign, who planned a demonstration on 12 December.[3] These organizations would be bringing their grievances onto the streets of Copenhagen, and appeared intent on raising climate change's profile on a world stage, and re-expressing public exasperation with political inertia on the issue. One can only presume that this was intended to pressure politicians and delegates into making an accommodation. But such protests can be, at least in part, organized to catch the eye of world media. Although some activists are wary of them (Doherty, Plows, & Wall, 2003), others see eye-catching protest as a way of garnering coverage (Plows, Wall, & Doherty, 2004). Those involved presumably hoped their action would reverberate internationally through the media, thereby raising the profile of the talks, generating interest, and resonating positively with citizens world-wide. The web can also play an important part in this form of mobilization, in terms of organization and coordination (Owens & Palmer, 2003; Bennett, 2003b: 143), or in dissemination of information and ideas (Doherty, Plows, & Wall, 2007). Indeed, some argue that disruptive (even violent) direct action can be consciously deployed to achieve a high media profile, thereby prompting uninvolved citizens to seek information about the issues via the web (DeLuca & Peeples, 2002: 144).

In the analysis that follows we explore how television reflected and refracted internationally organized protest activities at Copenhagen, particularly for those watching the action from Britain. Citizens here—or, indeed, in any country outside Denmark—would have been at one stage removed, geographically, from the action, and few will have had any *direct* experience of it. They will, therefore, have been more dependent on the media for a sense of how things panned out, than they would have been in relation to *nationally* situated issues, like crime or health (Ball-Rokeach, 1985; Thussu, 2000). But the question is, what would they have seen of the protests? What was the nature of the coverage, and what contribution would reports have made to British public understanding of the protesters and what they were about? We were also interested in how the web contributed to public appreciation of protests, and whether it changed the contours of the mediated landscape, and if so, how.

Television coverage of Copenhagen protesters

In answering these questions, the initial focus was on British, high-audience, late evening, flagship television news bulletins, during the course of the Copenhagen negotiations–on the BBC, and on ITN, its main commercial rival. These are primarily the "Ten O'clock" items on both channels, though the times at weekends varied. This encompassed a time when the conference will almost certainly have had its highest profile–from the day it started until the end of the weekend following it (7–20 December). The television focus is justified on the grounds that it is, according to a range of surveys, one of the main sources of political information for the British public (Gavin, 2007b: 5–6; Ofcom, 2007).

The first noteworthy thing is that television coverage of Copenhagen was evident throughout (the starred items in Table 1). Within this, four bulletins on BBC and three on ITN dealt in some way with protests and protesters, a considerable number, constituting nearly a third (the stories emphasized in bold in Table 1). But the significant issue here is not the *regularity* of their appearance, but a) the context in which they appeared, b) how they were described, and c) the brevity of the commentary. On "description" and "brevity," things did not start well for the protesters. On the opening day the BBC noted there were " . . . thousands of activists descending on Copenhagen for what the host nation is describing as the last best chance to save the world from disastrous climate change." The idea of them "descending" had an ominous ring. But on 12 December–the day Global Climate Campaign had pegged for action–on ITN, the commentary was equally brief, and referring to criminality and disorder: "Hundreds of climate activists have been arrested following scuffles at the march in Copenhagen. The protest had been part of a day of global action urging world leaders to do more to combat climate change." Here, besides an unflattering connection to arrests, scuffles and disorder, the protesters evidently suffered from the fact that this bulletin was already truncated (as

Table 1: Protests and protesters in TV coverage of the Copenhagen conference, Monday 7th Dec–Sunday 20th Dec

	M	T	W	T	F	S	S	M	T	W	T	F	S	S
	7	8	9	10	11	12	13	14	15	16	17	18	19	20
BBC	*	*	*		*	*		*	*	*	*	*	*	*
ITN	*			*	*			*	*	*	*	*	*	*

Note: stories where protests or protesters figured are in bold weekend evening ones normally are), but their action also rather unfortunately coincided with the finale of the extremely popular "X Factor" talent show, which received much attention.[4]

Brevity was also a marked feature of the coverage on 11 December, when protesters figured in an item on the BBC dealing with the aid package to developing countries the EU had had difficulty brokering. But so too was the context. The visuals focused initially on a march by demonstrators—one vigorously waving a red flag—all being snapped by numerous photographers. While the protest was sedate, nevertheless, it was flanked by a heavy police presence. The footage included one activist with an illegible banner being moved on by them very forcibly. From here, the action moved indoors, to footage of activists putting banners together (none legible), one holding a placard marked cryptically "ANNEX I, MINIMUM 40%, NO OFFSETTING" and "DEMAND CLIMATE JUSTICE." Over this the journalist commented, "But many of the activists in Copenhagen reacted with scepticism [to the EU package]. They doubted it would lead to a breakthrough. Some of the new funds pledged, they believe, are a repackaging of old aid commitments, and others warned that only new money would get a deal next week." There was no reference at all to who these "activists" were, and none were interviewed, but it has subsequently emerged that their claim about re-hashed aid money had some truth to it.[5]

ITN coverage on the same day was equally brief, also using the EU package as a hinge for commentary. But after a preamble on the EU's aid initiative, the visuals showed a solitary protester being surrounded by numerous policemen and wrestled to the ground. It then cut to policemen vigorously using their batons on other protesters, one of whom falls to the ground. The over-dub was, "At the end of the critical first week at Copenhagen summit, and passions are on display." There was a cut to exactly the same footage of a sedate march and the vigorous red-flag-waver seen on BBC, but followed by more policemen pushing protesters and arresting one, who is seen being bundled into a police van. The voice-over was, "Protesters are accusing rich countries of avoiding tough choices, and behind police lines the real work is being done by delegates trying to ensure that this does not become history's most expensive and most futile gathering." The reference to "real work" could be considered to be somewhat disparaging, but with no further elaboration on protest aims, the item moves back to a description of the EU aid package.

In terms of context, significantly, at no point were any of these "activists" interviewed to camera on either channel. In fact, only one protester was interviewed in the *whole* of the coverage assessed. This was a Danish man who figured on BBC (12 December), and he did not speak about the issues being protested, the motivation of the activists, nor their rationale for being there, only registering a complaint about repressive police actions. Furthermore, like all the protest footage before and after 12 December, at no point were any of the activists ascribed an organizational or group affiliation. This is a feature which, Bennett et al. (2004) suggest, commonly undermines the credibility and authority of activists. But, importantly, it would also have impaired viewers' efforts to seek to follow up on the report on the web, in order to find out more about what the protesters were about. They would, in this instance, have had difficulty knowing where to start.

But the association with disorder, police activity, and criminality in these sequences is also of general significance, since many researchers suggest that this is a common contextual feature of protest coverage—a "protest paradigm" (McLeod & Detenber, 1999; Smith et al., 2001; Gavin, 2007b; Gavin, 2010). This is a persistent structure, featuring heavy emphasis on criminality, violence or disorder, often portrayed as premeditated on the protesters' part. There is often little commentary on the protest rationale, or the aims and motivations of those involved, with few interviewed. The structure also allows limited emphasis on the peaceful dimensions of protests and tends to over-use disparaging terms to describe their activity. As we have seen, this structure seems to have been in evidence in coverage on 11 December, but it surfaced again on the two other occasions where climate protesters figured prominently—on 12 and 16 December.

ITN's coverage on 12 December was, as we noted earlier, very brief, focusing on arrests and scuffles. The corresponding BBC headline had, "Nine hundred climate protesters arrested in Copenhagen as tens of thousands take to the streets," over jerky footage of two policeman subduing a thrashing protester. After footage of a large demonstration, the story continued "Tens of thousands of protesters descended on the Danish capital . . ." with "descent" the same questionable term used by the BBC on 11 December. And " . . . It all started good-humoured . . . But police say they rounded up six or seven hundred people, when some of the activists, masking their faces, threw cobblestones through the windows of the former stock exchange and the Foreign Ministry buildings." Over jerky images of two policeman subduing a thrashing protester, aerial and ground-level footage of protesters sat in long columns, surrounded by police officers, pictures of a police cordon, and a protester being led to a police van, the reporter said, "Many of the protesters detained said they had done no wrong, but they had been captured under Denmark's controversial new hooligan law, designed to prevent potential trouble." Later, after footage of conference developments, the commentary notes, "The protesters arrived at the conference itself this evening, but by then any potential troublemakers had been weeded out." After asking if such protests make a difference, the reporter concluded that they send a powerful message to politicians that people care. However, he ends " . . . that heaps on pressure to get a result, as if there weren't enough pressure already," a comment that seems to imply an unhelpful contribution to the proceedings.

On 16 December, the coverage also revolved significantly around violence, and its capacity to disrupt the conference. The BBC's headline was, "Chaos in Copenhagen as protesters clash with police at the climate summit," the succeeding commentary suggested the protest " . . . meant that delegates, including Gordon Brown, were locked inside the conference centre for a period." Over footage of violent clashes between police and protesters, the overdub noted, "With the eyes of the world on Copenhagen, Denmark does not want these crucial climate talks disrupted." With more footage of police confronting demonstrators (again with batons in use), and one protester wrestled to the ground and handcuffed, the reporter notes, "By this stage of the proceedings the protester's goal of getting into the conference had failed." The subsequent story focused on a gloomy prognosis for the talks. But the item ended with scenes of later street demonstrations, flanked by a policeman, and a cordon of policemen with dogs. The reporter said, "This evening, more protests, this time in the city centre. The talks have not been affected, they're just not getting very far."

On ITN, on the same day, the headline focused on conference deadlock, not on protest. But the subsequent item had scenes of hundreds of demonstrators hemmed in by policemen and crash barriers (some being hit by baton-wielding policeman), protesters breaking through, being chased and intercepted, one protester being pinned down, and handcuffed. The commentary said, "Impatience with progress outside the conference centre turned violent. Danish police adopted tough tactics when protesters briefly broke through the security cordon around the centre. The scuffles which began in the morning lasted well into the afternoon."

It is quite significant that this reference to "impatience for progress" is one of a tiny number of allusions to the motivations and thought processes behind the protest's actions. Others were:

"Protesters are accusing rich countries of avoiding tough choices . . ." (ITN 11 December)

Protests were " . . . part of a day of global action urging world leaders to do more to combat climate change." (ITN 12 December)

Protesters were " . . . calling for what they say is climate justice . . ." and " . . . demanding tough limits on the emissions blamed by most scientists for accelerating climate change." (BBC 12 December)

And "Some . . . doubt that the capitalist system can deliver the amount of carbon cuts that are needed. Others want to work within the system." (BBC 12 December)

This was the sum total of the commentary on the motivations and rationale behind the protest, none of it delivered from the mouths of the protesters themselves. And likewise, there was only one solitary allusion to *peaceful* protest amidst the coverage: "The scuffles, though, were sporadic, and most of the protest went off entirely peacefully" (BBC 12 December).

Overall, then, what are we to make of the coverage of internationally organized protest at Copenhagen? As with an earlier coverage of *nationally* situated protests (Gavin, 2007b), it would be premature to jump too quickly to criticize television journalists for any perceived deficiencies. The lack of protester voices is a case in point. When such a kaleidoscope of organizations and individuals is involved—sometimes with complex, and occasionally competing aims—it would have been very difficult for reporters to find anyone who could be portrayed as representative of them all and draw from them their case. Likewise, the seemingly irresistible draw of footage accompanying violence, scuffles and disorder must be viewed in the context of a conference where occasional talking heads, or people milling around the conference precincts, were as scintillating as the visuals got. The visual medium of television can hardly be blamed for emphasis placed on the photogenic clashes the police and protesters served up for them. And finally, during a conference with such high drama, so many twists and turns, such complex developments and controversial dimensions (all of which needed to be incorporated in stories), there may not have been enough airtime *left* to cover the details of protests.

Nevertheless, this does not diminish the significance of the protest paradigm's prevalence. Its contours, it is suggested, tend to reflect poorly on protesters, diminishing their credibility, and obscuring their purpose and rationale. From this perspective, the broadcasters do not seem to have done their audience a service, certainly in terms of helping them understand the protest phenomenon covered. But the more militant protesters were at least partly complicit in the production of this confection and do not appear to have been aware (or did not care) they would get an unflattering press, as a result. But, as with other protests (Gavin, 2007b), the loose affiliation of groups and originations constituting the activist body were, by their very nature, just not suited to projecting a clear, unified case. They did not speak with a single voice and could therefore not put forward an authoritative, credible representative who could act as spokesperson—the very thing journalists need. The obvious question, though, is whether internationalized protest of this diversity will ever be in a position to overcome this sort of difficulty.

Finally, the focus on clashes and disturbance may also have had collateral impact. Mainstream NGOs were almost absent from sustained coverage, the exception being an Oxfam representative's contribution to a conference post-mortem (BBC, 20 December). Otherwise, they figured only very briefly indeed—for example, Oxfam delegates in polar bear outfits, carrying "POOR PEOPLE CANT BEAR IT" placards (BBC, 14 December); or two gate-crashers seen ejected from a dinner, unfurling a "POLITICIANS TALK, LEADERS ACT, GREEN-

PEACE" banner (ITN, 17 December). This perhaps underplayed their real contribution in Copenhagen (for good or ill), and there is a danger that footage of clashes involving direct action groups helped displace the activities of their more
conventional NGO counterparts.

Copenhagen protests on the web

We now have a clearer picture of how Copenhagen protests were covered on British
television, and it is not a terribly flattering one. But how did the web contribute?
This technology is thought to offer activists, and the under-resourced or politically marginalized, an alternative to the mainstream media, and an opportunity to publicize their activities (Rodgers, 2003: 128; Oates, 2008). Our study undertook to
assess its likely contribution to public appreciation of the Copenhagen protesters
and the political positions they held.

In doing this, an obvious issue is what to look for and how. One answer is to
use Google. This begs the question, search for what? "Google Trends" can help here.
It tracks terms used in Google searches.[6] Although it does not give their specific
number, importantly, it shows the *shape* of attention to particular topics, and changes
over time, giving results first for worldwide volumes of traffic, then breakdowns by
country. Searches on "climate protest," "Copenhagen protest" (even on "Global
Climate Campaign"), got the response "Your terms do not have enough search volume to show graphs." Evidently very few people *worldwide* were using these, presumably even fewer in Britain. However, Figure 1 shows people *were* using "climate
change" and "climategate." The peak is around the time the "climategate" story

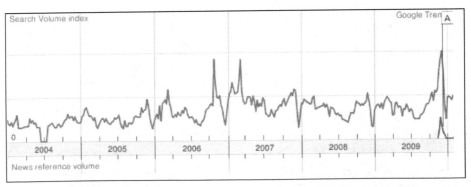

Figure 1: Google Trends searches on "climate change" and "climategate" by Britons, January 2004
to February 2010
Note: The "A" represents Google's attempt to tie spikes in searches to particular events, in this
case the UN IPCC criticizing the "climategate" affair; the lower, transitory spike in 2009 is for
"climategate."

broke, but there was still measurable traffic around Copenhagen. This justifies our approach, which was to conduct a search on "Copenhagen AND climate change" for each day of the conference.[7] The hits derived can be grouped into two categories: a) sites appearing consistently in almost every day's search, and b) those Google designated "News results," which were much more unstable from day-to-day. However, a second snapshot taken on each day suggested that b's overall *structure* did not change, though the content did.

In assessing this material, we were mindful that there is strong evidence that web users' attention rarely extends beyond the first page of search hits (Jansen & Spink, 2005, 2006; iProspect, 2008). So we paid particular attention to the first ten in both a and b categories, on each day–140 in each, and 280 overall. In category a, many sites made regular appearances: COP15's own site; "Copenhagen Climate Council," a business and science organization; and "Wattsupwiththat," an online climate sceptic blog, among them.[8] An item from *Time* magazine and Oxfam's site appeared, as did that of a climate science conference held in Copenhagen in early 2009. However, only three sites in group a carried significant material relating to Copenhagen protests and protesters: a BBC site, a Times Online story and a YouTube video clip originally from an early evening ITN bulletin.

The BBC site appeared on four different days after 12 December, with virtually identical content but various headlines, all related to arrests or detentions ("Police in Copenhagen in Denmark say nearly 1,000 protesters were detained after a huge climate change rally.")[9] This is significant as headlines constitute a signal concerning what, essentially, a story is about (Entman, 1993; Pan & Kosicki, 1993). The item also had many protest paradigm features, relying heavily on Danish police and government sources and laying emphasis on violence, disorder and arrests. Only one Copenhagen protester was given limited space ("This is the right time to shout out and let leaders know this is serious business for us all. Let's hope they listen") and was not given an affiliation. The only references to the Copenhagen protester's aims refer to them " . . . calling for decisive action on global warming" and arguing for " . . . legally binding agreement on emissions cuts to be signed by world leaders at the summit's conclusion at the end of next week."

The *Times* item appeared only once,[10] sketching a mixed picture, though erring on the side of unflattering. Like the BBC, it led with the crime angle ("Copenhagen summit: 600 arrested at climate change protest"), and much of its first half dominated by rioting, arrests and brick-throwing. It alluded to protesters highlighting the environmental impact of climate change and had exactly the same protester quote as the BBC. But there *were* three very brief references to peaceful demonstration, and some commentary on protest aims, and coming from participants themselves. A British couple said they had come " . . . to tell people about how climate change is biting hardest in developing countries. . . . Many people still don't realise that climate change affects people in poorer countries worst. . . . Things are getting worse and it is partly because of our Western way of life. . . . We need to do something about it." However, even this is not very much. It is also perhaps worth noting that in the space the newspaper made available for readers to comment on this story, strong and hostile climate sceptic messages (many highly critical of the demonstrators) outnumber the rest by nearly three to one.

The YouTube item from ITN also appeared only once.[11] It too had a mix of themes, although on balance, with more flattering than unflattering elements, but only just. It began with footage of a good-natured protest, the commentator referring to its multinational complexion. Then, "On the whole, a peaceful atmosphere, those wanting to influence political action on global warming, thought it best to keep their cool." Three demonstrators are interviewed, although they remained anonymous and were not given an organizational affiliation: "Unless they [the politicians] take the responsibility, nothing is going to change," "We need mass pressure to force leaders, to do the changes that we need," and "I want them to make a good deal for the world." But from here the tone changed, and over footage of a line of policemen facing red-flag-waving demonstrators and some teargas, we got "But as the afternoon wore on, the trouble that police had predicted started to emerge. Arrests were made after masked activists broke windows and threw bricks. A heavily policed cordon prohibited marchers from getting anywhere near the site of the summit." There then follows a brief interview with British Climate Secretary Ed Miliband on conference developments. However, we were soon back to the protests, and over footage of people watching a television we got, "As delegates watched the number of arrests grow outside, it's probably not a good idea to promise anything that can't be delivered." There was a brief reference to companion protest round the world. But then with pictures of a boulevard blocked by police confronting flag-waving demonstrators, policemen putting a person into place in a line of seated demonstrators, and angry demonstrators confronting policeman with batons raised, the story ends, "Protests are expected to intensify as the week goes on, especially if hopes of an agreement to cut carbon emissions start to fade. The real test for police and politicians is yet to come."

On the whole, then, the larger part of the more stable set of hits would have told web searchers next to nothing about the Copenhagen protests and protesters. The few that did touch on them bore the imprint of the protest paradigm and will have exposed browsers to climate sceptic messages. However, when we turned to the more variable "News results" hits in category b, some did deal with Copenhagen protests, but the vast bulk did not touch on them at all. Of those that did, six sites emerged across the two weeks but with only the very *briefest* of commentary. Amongst them was a Canadian Broadcasting Corporation News ("Immediate climate action needed, summit hears"), which appeared on seven different days but only mentioned activists.[12] Others included a *Sydney Morning Herald* article on Australian non-compliance with Kyoto and headed only by a picture of protesters detained by police ("Carbon Emissions Soar")[13] and an item in the *Taipei Times*,[14] both appearing only once.

Nevertheless, there *were* sites that took a more positive line on the protests,[15] or were more expansive. The latter were typically multimedia blogs, featuring embedded video and audio, and collating information from a number of sources, including protest organizations. One such was attached to the *Scotsman* newspaper's website.[16] It was written by a protest participant and spoke to the dominant self-image of protest organizations, their aims and their growing sense of a community. The other was a blog attached to the *Guardian* newspaper, carrying an audio file of a report from the protests from one of the *Guardian*'s correspondents in Copenhagen, plus links to other sites, including one offering a live stream from the protests.[17] Both were sympathetic to the protesters and their aims.

However, it is very important to put these sites into perspective. They were very few in number and were flanked by two other items which were hostile towards the protests and the protesters—from the *New York Times*[18] and the *Daily Telegraph*,[19] both manifesting many elements of the protest paradigm. The *Guardian* and *Scotsman* sites also have to be viewed in the context of the other 280 surveyed, many of which carried no reference at all to the protests. Of those that did, many carried only the briefest of allusions, some manifest elements of the protest paradigm, and others carried climate sceptic messages. This latter point is important, as the "News results" sites often expressed this sort of theme. Indeed, although formal assessment of the quantity of "contrarian" material contained within our *whole* sample has yet to be conducted, a provisional estimate suggests they featured much more prominently than did the activities of protesters.

Conclusions

What can we learn from this survey of television and the web at Copenhagen? This was the locus for internationally organized and coordinated action on a transnational issues, and we can say that television did take an interest. But its coverage will have done little to illuminate what the protesters were about. Understandably, it was preoccupied with the disruptive and violent dimensions of protests, footage of confrontation all but drowning out commentary on the (more numerous) peaceful protesters. And often bearing the imprint of the protest paradigm, this coverage will not have painted a particularly flattering picture of the people involved. Activist group structures, some protesters' deportment and their under-appreciation of the mediated dynamics of combative action, meant that perhaps the protests were always going to be vulnerable to this form of portrayal (see also Gavin, 2010). Moreover, protesters also do not appear to have been able to unlock the potential of new technologies (like hand-cams or cameras on mobile phones) to help shoehorn their *own* footage into the coverage (Allan & Thorsen, 2009).

Turning to the web, we found that it often reflects the output for the *conventional* media. Furthermore, relatively few sites dealt with protests or protesters, and of those that did, many had only the slimmest details. Sites that did carry substantial material could manifest elements of the protest paradigm or could be openly hostile to the protesters and their aims. So our survey of the web suggests that while it has *potential* to help protesters get their message across (or help them convey alternative points of view to the browsing public), this seems to have been unrealised at Copenhagen, as elsewhere (Gavin, 2010). Those arguing that the web has the potential to radically alter the balance of communicative power (Rodgers, 2003; Bennett, 2003b) may well be disappointed. Evidently the web can, potentially, contribute to the emergence of a truly international public sphere (Gavin, 2009), since nationally situated browsers can find themselves exposed to messages from across the globe and even contribute to this information flow. But our survey suggests the material that actually reaches the public will often bear the impression of the pressures and imperatives that govern the *conventional* media, and it will not necessarily reflect well on those engaged in protests. In addition, the web may leave browsers being exposed to a range of climate sceptic messages.

There is a danger that these forms of representation will "cultivate" an unflattering sense of what protesters are about (Gerbner et al., 1986; Miller, 2005), with negative repercussions for their image—especially for an audience that is dependent on the media for an understanding of what is gong on. Alternatively, the focus on disruption, violence or criminality may see these characteristics come to be the ones audiences associate with climate activism—a form of "second order" agenda-setting (McCombs, 2005; Weaver, 2007).

The lessons for activists are clear. The web may assist in mobilizing and organizing protest, galvanizing support within the activist community, and engendering a sense of collective identity therein. And protests may be a form of self-expression for those involved, contributing to participants' sense of well-being (Klar & Kasser, 2009). But these activities are refracted through the media (the web included), before reaching the wider public. Our survey suggests that disruptive or combative actions are highly likely to hog the limelight, with potentially unfortunate, but predictable consequences. The way this unfolds needs to be taken into consideration in any appreciation of tactics. Whether all protest organizations are fully in control of such developments does, however, remain to be seen.

Notes

1. "Carbon traders quit emissions market amid drop in demand" (*Guardian*, 25 January 2010).
2. http://gc-ca.org/
3. http://www.globalclimatecampaign.org/index.php?lang=en
4. However, an earlier bulletin did carry coverage, which found its way on to YouTube, as we will see in the next section.
5. "PM's pledged climate change cash will be syphoned from existing aid" (*Guardian*, 26 January 2010).
6. http://www.google.com/trends
7. Using "Copenhagen" almost exclusively gave sites of city tourist interest.
8. http://wattsupwiththat.com/2009/10/03/the-copenhagen-treaty-draft-wealth-transfer-defined-now-with-dignity-penalty/
9. http://news.bbc.co.uk/1/hi/world/europe/8409331.stm
10. http://www.timesonline.co.uk/tol/news/environment/copenhagen/article6954510.ece
11. Original video now unavailable but can still be found at the following: http://community.eco seed.org/_Copenhagen-climate-change-rally-leads-to-arrests/VIDEO/866622/29468.html
12. http://www.cbc.ca/world/story/2009/12/07/copenhagen-climate-change-open.html
13. http://www.smh.com.au/environment/carbon-emissions-soar-20091213-kqi2.html
14. http://www.taipeitimes.com/News/world/archives/2009/12/20/2003461353
15. http://www.etaiwannews.com/etn/news_content.php?id=1131773&lang=eng_news&cate _img=logo_taiwan&cate_rss=TAIWAN_eng
16. http://news.scotsman.com/world/Copenhagen-Climate-Change-Conference-blog.5907657.jp
17. http://www.guardian.co.uk/environment/blog/2009/dec/16/copenhagen-climate-change-protests-live
18. http://www.nytimes.com/2009/12/14/business/energy-environment/14iht-green 14.html?_r=2
19. http://www.telegraph.co.uk/earth/copenhagen-climate-change-confe/6797265/Copenhagen-climate-summit-descends-into-row-as-350-protesters-arrested.html

PART FIVE

Protesting Human Rights and Civil Rights

CHAPTER FIFTEEN

Open Source Protest

Rights, Online Activism
and the Beijing 2008 Olympic Games

ANA ADI AND ANDY MIAH

In a pre-Internet era, politicians, social movements and activist groups relied heavily on the mass media to amplify their messages. The Internet promised a new era of independent media with the potential to revolutionize the social and political world by redistributing the means of communication towards the masses, rather than the media monopolies. Its advantage would be to enable direct, two-way interaction between senders and receivers unmotivated by the drive to boost audience figures. For this reason, such authors as Grossman (1995) argued that the Internet could launch a third great era of democracy. As indication of this, today's social movements and activist groups, as seen in the cases of Wikileaks,[1] the Moldova Twitter Revolution,[2] the Iranian Elections,[3] and the Copenhagen environmental protests[4, 5] (Hodge, 2009; Parr, 2009) have utilized digital technology to bypass mainstream media channels both in accessing and distributing information (Russell, 2005). Yet, there is also considerable evidence to suggest that activist groups are very capable of getting their messages into mass media channels *as well* (Bennett, 2003a). As such, if the Internet can help activist groups and social movements circumvent traditional media, as well as gain its attention, then perhaps McCaughey and Ayers (2003) are right when claiming that more attention should be given to the Internet as a medium that is inextricable from *processes* of social change rather than just as a device to *provoke* discussions about change.

A prominent and recurrent platform where such transformative forces are apparent is the Olympic Games. Beyond being the biggest sports events in the world, the Olympic Games is frequently used as a platform where geopolitical and geo-commercial issues are played out by competing discourses between brand owners, media outlets, politicians and the public. We argue that recent Olympic Games demonstrate these mixed processes of media change, where both the largest gatherings of traditional media and independent media operate. In particular, we argue that activism is an *intrinsic* part of the Olympic Games experience and, by this, we mean that it is inevitable, necessary and even valuable. Olympic activism is shaped by a variety of intersecting factors, including the size and location of the Games, the geopolitical situation, and the local activist culture.

Using as a starting point McCaughey and Ayers' (2003) and Russell's (2005) arguments, according to which more attention should be given to the Internet as a medium that assists social change rather than provokes it, we discuss how international human rights advocacy groups, notably Amnesty International and Human Rights Watch, coordinated their Internet presence to reach the mass media, members of the public, critics and supporters of the Games alike during the Beijing 2008 Olympic Games. In making our case we provide examples of previous forms of protest in Olympic history, along with ethnographic data from Beijing 2008. We conclude that transnational activism, including Olympic-targeted activism, has entered a new stage to reveal a new wave of convergent media processes, characterized by integrated offline and online strategies. We also suggest that the Beijing 2008 Olympic Games confirms the need for social movements to receive media attention in order to further their causes and bring about social change. Thus, while online activism can help transcend local borders, it can be used both as an official medium to communicate information, as well as an alternative means through which to enable direct contact with members and supporters.

A brief history of Olympic protest

It is commonplace to think of activism and protest as a modern phenomenon. However, in the context of the Olympic Games, there is evidence of similar kinds of activity in antiquity, some as early as 364 BC. Then, Elian soldiers stormed the arena in Olympia in the middle of the most popular competition, wrestling, and started a battle against the Pisan organizers whom, according to Xenophon, had wrested the Games from the Elians, the traditional hosts. While the Elians lost the battle, their action secured the organization of the following Games (Perrottet, 2008). Even earlier, during 420 BC during the Peloponnesian War, Spartans were banned from the Games, although the sacred Olympic Truce worked as a cease-fire, granting safe passage to athletes and spectators during Games time. Twenty years later, the Spartans broke the truce by mounting a military campaign (Perrottet, 2008).

These ancient forms of Olympic activism were acts of defending honor in military terms, unlike modern Olympic activism, which has been mostly ideologically driven. On this basis, modern Olympic history has been marked by several instances where countries, communities or individuals have articulated their political positions via sports competitions. For example, Spain's People's Olympics of 1936, organized by its newly elected Popular Front government, was a way of opposing Hitler's Olympics in Berlin (Walters, 2006). Alternatively, the boycotts of Tokyo 1964 and the Montreal 1976 Games directed against South Africa's apartheid segregated system applied in sport are just some examples of government-initiated actions in support of political causes. Similarly, the case of international television networks and cinema newsreel companies' refusal "to pay royalties for the privilege of showing Olympic newsfilm on a delayed basis" (Wenn, 1993) during the Melbourne 1956 Games is the first to bring commercial, economic and ethical considerations under the same protest. On an individual athlete level, perhaps the most famous expression of activism undertaken by Olympic athletes is the "black power salute" delivered by USA representatives Tommie Smith and John Carlos. Sharing the 1968 Mexico Games medal podium with them was Peter Norman, an Australian athlete who although did not deliver the same salute supported the American athletes.[6]

Olympic activism in the 20th century utilized the Olympic Games as the locus of action–often by non-participation or boycott. In the 21st century, Olympic activism has thus far taken a different form, as boycotts are no longer considered effective by media, activists and think tanks (Schmemann, 2008). Instead, calls for the IOC to assume greater responsibility have surfaced, as they have aligned themselves with transnational corporate interests. Such concerns encompass human rights, environmental responsibilities, cultural legacies and impact on local communities. Thus, interest groups rather than nations have become the primary mechanism of Olympic activism. For example, the issues raised on the approach to the Sydney 2000 Games were about the diminishing resources of low-cost housing linked with the recognition of Aboriginal people's rights and media rights. Welfare groups threatened to set up a tent city to embarrass the authorities (ABC, 2000). Media activists set up their own media centre, the Sydney Independent Media Center, to counteract NBC's ban on uploading videos online before their airing in the USA (Lord, 2000).

At the Athens 2004 Games, a similar range of issues arose. Environmental and public space protection saw social resistance emerging at many different levels within the society (Portalious, 2008). The intensive working conditions in the construction sector, with the effective abolition of limits to working hours, led to daily accidents and a subsequent Games time protest in Athens' central square, Syntagma, on behalf of the 23 workers who had lost their lives during the construction of venues.

Beijing–the precedent

In the case of the Beijing 2008 Olympic Games, the Chinese organizers were under scrutiny as early as 1993, as the city first qualified to candidate status and ended up competing against Sydney for the Millennium Games. Some argued then that Beijing's loss by only two votes from Sydney was due to the international perception of China having a poor human rights record (Brownell, 2004; Ostbo Haugen, 2003).

Later, when Beijing's second bit was successful, the IOC's decision was subjected to various debates, such as those held by the US Congressional-Executive Commission on China (2003, 2008). Formal protests also took place. For example, the House Resolution introduced by US Congressman Dana Rohrabacher, the Ranking Member on the U.S. House of Representatives Foreign Affairs Subcommittee on International Organizations, Human Rights and Oversight, appealed to the government to boycott the 2008 Summer Olympic Games in Beijing ("Expressing the sense of the House of Representatives that the President should take immediate action to boycott the summer Olympic Games of 2008 in Beijing, China," 2007) being one of them. A similar call was also launched by the European Parliament to the European Union leaders (*New York Times*, 2008; Redorbit, 2008). Moreover, actress Mia Farrow and her son Ronan Farrow labelled the Beijing Games the "Genocide Olympics" on account of China's relationship with Darfur (Farrow & Farrow, 2007). Furthermore, protests from pro-Tibet activists and Burmese supporters calling upon people to boycott the Games were also visible throughout the preparation period preceding the Olympics.

China's temporarily instituted media legislation to allow greater freedoms for foreign journalists, which was implemented in January 2007, was also interrogated due to its ineffectual consequences. Additionally, just months before the Olympic Games started, the international leg of the Torch Relay was subject to numerous disruptions around the world. Part of the protests were sparked by China's reaction to the Tibetan uprising in March 2008, while others were triggered by more general concerns related to China's human rights record (Zizek, 2008; Jacobs, 2008). Finally, just days before the Olympic Games began, discussions about Internet and media censorship were still taking place, due to foreign journalists not being able to get access to the sites they wanted to use.

Thus, human rights received a lot of attention around the Beijing Olympics, notably in relation to freedom of speech, labor rights and forced evictions (Liu, 2007). In this respect, human rights advocacy groups and their sustained campaigns have contributed the primary forms of activism around Beijing. Consistent and constant communication undertaken by these groups emphasized the presence of a link between the Olympic fundamental principles and larger human rights and humanitarian concerns. Yet, of particular interest to us is what these activities reveal about how activist groups use the Internet to promote their causes.

For example in July 2001, when Beijing won the rights to host the 2008 Games, Human Rights Watch and Amnesty International, two of the most renowned human rights advocacy groups released major materials such as reports or press releases each about China's human rights situation. Other mentions of China's situation were made in specific reports as well such as Amnesty International's News for Health Professionals or Human Rights Watch's take on UN's Program of Action on Small Arms. Both groups used the Internet to distribute their documentation globally and aggregate information from their national sites. Both groups capitalized on international attention generated by the announcement of the 2008 Games host. Each of them sent out warning messages about China's potential impact on the spirit and values of Olympism. For example, Amnesty International issued a press release when Beijing's bid was announced as successful, which stated that "as host of the 2008 Olympic Games, China must improve its human rights situation and uphold principles enshrined in The Olympic Charter." In the same release, the group was suggesting that "the Chinese government must prove it is worthy of staging the Games (. . .) extending 'respect for universal fundamental ethical principles' to the people of China" (Amnesty International, 2001).

Alternatively, Human Rights Watch released more Olympics-oriented messages at key Olympic preparation landmarks. For example, on 10 July 2001, an opinion piece was published in the *International Herald Tribune* (print and online) calling to the IOC to request human rights guarantees from future candidate cities (Jones, 2001b). On the day of the winner's announcement, Human Rights Watch published in the same news section of its website another article emphasizing the burden "on the International Olympic Committee and the Games' corporate sponsors to make the Games a force for change in China" (Jones, 2001a). Finally, a week after Beijing was the known winner of the 2008 Games, a broader material, called a backgrounder, was made available under the same section. The document described China's freedom of expression and its Internet policy, discussing rules and regulations in place and arguing that the two elements needed drastic improvements (HRW, 2001).

In 2001, the messages of both advocacy groups were thus similar: that China's human rights record makes it unfit to organize an Olympic Games. Both suggested that the International Olympic Committee would request human rights guarantees from Olympic hosts in the same way it requires financial and environmental guarantees (Adi & Miah, 2008). Each organization claimed that human rights were inadequately addressed by the Olympic Movement generally and the Chinese government specifically.

From this, one may conclude that the media were the advocacy groups' main target in 2001 and the Internet just a support, or just another medium to disseminate their messages. The transmission of information both online and offline followed the same model of communication from one to many. A dramatic change in the use of digital media by HRW and Amnesty is apparent from 2001 to 2008.

Beijing and advocacy groups in 2008

The period from 2001 to 2008 marks a shift from using the Internet as a secondary tool for communication to a primary medium where activities are coordinated, protests are planned and high-quality information is publicized. Additionally, the Internet noticeably becomes an alternative medium of communication as well, one that enables activist groups to get in contact with their target audiences in a cost-efficient manner.

In 2008, Amnesty's main website, amnesty.org, remained the major source of information for its members, supporters and media. Most of the China and the Olympics-related content was uploaded under the news and updates area, where the public statements of the group were also published, as were their press releases and answer to articles published by traditional media outlets. However, for direct contact with the general public, a website dedicated to debating China and its human rights issues was launched. Hence, Amnesty's use of the Internet in a discriminatory way allowed it to publish different content to different websites it owned and reach other target audiences using the best-fit mechanisms, such as free platforms delivering specialized services. Moreover, having a differentiated communication strategy and multiple specialized presences online—such as the official website, campaign websites or a YouTube channel—Amnesty also created a better information distribution network relying on peer-to-peer transmission that transcended national borders.

The China Debate website was one such alternative, yet specialized, presence for Amnesty International, that aimed to promote dialogue and learn from the debates it initiated. As a web-presence requiring membership, Amnesty's China Debate website aimed to create as well as enable dialogue around the four-color coded human rights issues: repression of activists (pink), detention without trial (black), censorship (blue) and death penalty (green), which the organization prioritized as central to "upholding the Olympic value 'the preservation of human dignity'" (The China Debate). To these another "human rights legacy" was added. The topic was coded with yellow and according to website metrics it was the most commented and viewed issue, its "A promising Olympics" debate leading the online discussion. Within the same yellow coded content, other questions were also addressed such as "What is your view of the impact of the Olympics on human rights in China" and "How can the Chinese authorities deliver a lasting legacy for human rights". They were viewed more than 20,000 times and received over 90 comments. Links were also provided to related information and mechanisms of promotion suggested by Amnesty International, most often third-party websites known for their amplifying features: the social network Facebook, the social bookmarking websites Delicious, Digg and StumbleUpon, and the blogging search engine and blog popularity indexes provider Technorati. RSS (really simple syndication) updates and an email form entitled "Spread the Word" are also included within the "forwarding" features of the website.

These features emphasize Amnesty's objectives for the campaign: raising awareness and creating dialogue by amplifying the group's messages. A similar goal was sought through its presence on the video-sharing website, YouTube, where the group currently has over 4000 subscribers and registers more than one million total upload views since September 2006. In an online environment where interconnectivity is essential and viral effects are sought, the content-sharing strategy adopted by Amnesty aims to reach dispersed audiences united by unlimited access to the Internet.

Finally, polls were also used to assess public opinion and provide the group with more research-based information to support their claims. However, the disadvantage of such polls comes from the lack of background information on users, such demographic data or whether there were repeat votes from the same computer or IP address.

Human Rights Watch adopted a similar strategy to create a separate, China dedicated space. The website China.hrw.org entitled Beijing 2008. China's Olympian Human Rights Challenges followed HRW's official website structure, thus creating a different approach from Amnesty's distinct-looking website. Furthermore, HRW integrated information *sharing* with information *gathering* from online discussions, via its "join the discussion" section. This ensured coherence of information and responded to the information or dialogue needs that HRW's public might have. However, HRW's debate site is hosted by a link to a third party: the *Washington Post*'s Rights Watchers. This is a rather risky choice for a group that claims independence from other profit and non-profit, political and apolitical organizations and groups. Moreover, it has the potential to affiliate it with such organizations, by simple association with the *Washington Post*'s editorial policy as well as its sponsors and supporters. In this regard, it is important to note that there is very little research that indicates how users of web media interpret links and other spatial arrangements within sites, but one can assume that some principles that are apparent in traditional forms of advertising and product placement also apply in an online context. Alternatively, by including HRW's debate on a forum space of a media outlet, it is also possible to achieve more visibility for the group and thus help it reach more users with a more varied socio-economic-geographic background. Additionally, HRW's publicity is taken over by *Washington Post*, requiring less effort from HRW to distribute its information. Also, unlike Amnesty International, HRW places more emphasis on its opinion editorials, which their members of staff have secured in prominent media outlets such as the *International Herald Tribune*. Thus, HRW's communication strategy still heavily relies on the magnifying lens of traditional media and continues to use the Internet as a complementary medium.

In comparison with Amnesty International's site, the HRW Beijing Olympics dedicated page did not contain any other sharing options, apart from an "RSS feed" link which would enable subscribers to receive updates from the website as soon as they are made. However, both organizations make reference to similar groups including the Committee to Protect Journalists, Olympic Watch or Reporters Sans Frontières. As well, they both launch an appeal to action-taking. Among the actions suggested by HRW are: writing to the President of the International Olympic Committee, the Chinese Premier, or blogging for human rights in China while also finding ways to breach what the group calls "China's Great Firewall."

These two human rights advocacy groups have adopted quite differentiated strategies for their online communications. While Amnesty turned new media into its main medium using a lot of the web's social features, HRW remained focused on a traditional strategy where traditional media outlets give visibility, credibility, reputation and weight by magnifying a cause both in their traditional forms and via their online presences—websites, blogs, forums etc. In this respect, Amnesty intended to turn its campaign site members and its online visitors into online ambassadors of Amnesty's message by providing them with a variety of means of accessing its information as well as sharing it. However, when it comes to messaging, the two groups concentrate on the same topics.

Quiet, too quiet activism in Beijing

At the end of July 2008, just two weeks before the start of the Olympic Games, Amnesty International (2008a) was reporting that their websites were still blocked in China. Since the websites were spaces for sharing information both remotely from China and that could be reached by Internet users irrespective of their location, having the websites accessible during the Olympic Games was vital for both groups. However, it remains questionable as to why these groups focused their campaigns on China audiences, as a mechanism for promoting freedom of speech, since the groups' main targets were outside China. Moreover, since the information on the website is available only in English, French, Spanish and Arabic, it is further dubious as to whether the strategy to reach Chinese people was ever likely to be effective. Nevertheless, following successful campaigns aimed at lifting state censorship as a result of international media pressure, the two websites–together with others such as the BBC–were freely accessible in China during the Olympic Games.

This involved a mixture of online communications and traditional media relations, which resulted in a real-life pressure on Olympic authorities. Yet, it was exceptional and there was no apparent increase in communication in support for human rights promotion during the Beijing Olympic Games undertaken by human rights advocacy groups. Indeed, we consider that their activity was decreased drastically with official communication taking place only around key dates of the Games–such as the opening and closing ceremonies–rather than constantly during the Games. During this time, Amnesty International sent out only four press releases and statements while HRW issued ten. Further, the protests that did take place in Beijing were neither inspired nor influenced by any of the two groups we studied but rather by smaller ones such as Students for a Free Tibet[7] or FreeTibet.org.[8]

Moreover, there was no direct indication of Amnesty or HRW staff members who expected to be present in Beijing during the Games, nor any continued efforts to engage the Olympic or the Chinese authorities in a dialogue that could further human rights in China. This might be because activists considered that, once the Games had started, there would be little that their communication could do to influence and inspire change. This proposal is supported by Amnesty's China Debate forum censorship talks that took place June-August 2008, hence during the Olympics as well (The China Debate). However, the questions posed during Games time received rather little attention (2000 views and five comments at most) compared to those asked in June 2008 (more than 10,000 views and 40 comments). Alternatively, the activists themselves may have feared reprisals were they to enter China, thus breaking the law.

Raising voices after Beijing

Beijing celebrated the last day of the Olympic Games on 24 August 2008. Two days earlier, HRW labeled the Olympics as a catalyst for human rights abuses:

The reality is that the Chinese government's hosting of the Games has been a catalyst for abuses, leading to massive forced evictions, a surge in the arrest, detention, and harassment of critics, repeated violations of media freedom, and increased political repression. (Human Rights Watch, 2008)

On the day of the closing ceremony, Amnesty published a concluding press release that emphasized China's need to learn from its Olympic mistakes and uphold human rights values (Amnesty International, 2008b). Both news articles were published on the groups' main websites. Shortly after the closing of the Games, Amnesty disabled the participatory/dialogical options offered by its forum. Nevertheless the website is still active online as proof of the talks about China that Amnesty initiated. A few months after the Games closed, HRW ceased posting new information on its China dedicated website, the last opinion editorial dating back to 31 October 2008. While the campaign websites were closed, the groups' activity continued, China and Olympics related communication resurfacing at dates relevant for either one of the parties. Furthermore, the groups' messages remained unchanged since August 2008, appeals for introduction of monitoring measures and human rights guarantees requirements from Olympic hosts being maintained.

While we cannot assess whether Amnesty's and HRW's campaigns were successful, we can confirm that the Internet was a major vehicle of communication for them. We may also conclude that, due to the particularities of China's firewall and of the Games time period where so much scrutiny took place, the Internet was central to achieving their goals. While the groups had different approaches to communicating online—Amnesty made social media its central point, while HRW focused on the traditional, partisan media's power to amplify their cause—the groups' overall strategies were similar. Additionally, their hard push prior to and post-Games and soft communication during the Games has inspired other activist groups around the world in their shaping of their online communications. At the Vancouver 2010 Olympic Winter Games, similar strategies were apparent by Canadian activist groups such as, No 2010[9] or Solidarity with Six Nations.[10] Both groups had an official web presence marked by a blog or official website and already acknowledge other resources and individuals that support their cause. This helped them build visibility and achieve momentum as well as take their cause further than the borders of British Columbia and the city of Vancouver. Finally, this shows once more that online activism can help transcend local borders and can use the Internet both as an official medium to communicate information as well as an alternative meant to enable direct contact with members and supporters.

Conclusion

In a global, digitally mediated world, there are various dimensions of contemporary protest culture that require our reconsideration. First, the expansion of communi-cation technology permits local concerns to reach a global audience with consid-erable immediacy who, in turn, may also actively shape their reception. A good example of this is the British celebrity Stephen Fry's[11] re-tweeting of content relat-ed to the Iran election concerns of 2009 (McElroy, 2009). In this case, a celebrity's sharing of content and active interpretation of what was taking place thus becomes a primary frame around the issue at hand. This is a clear example of a celebrity act-ing as an activist, cultural intermediary, and journalist.

An *open media* culture requires that some control over one's "brand" or agenda is devolved, thus permitting the community to own and shape its development. This transition presupposes a shared value system, against which people may act and, while it is not difficult to imagine there is common ground in some cases, such as the world economy or climate change, it will require considerable work to ensure that local concerns have the kind of relevance for a global audience that would lead to greater support rather than audience apathy. This may require local communi-ties to compromise on their issues for a wider audience in order to optimize the pro-file of their concerns. For example, a community protest about local housing policy injustice may seek an alliance with other such communities in other parts of the world.

Second, the rise of transnational concerns means that protests against the institutions that do business across borders will find themselves under greater scrutiny by even greater advocacy groups. Thus, the growing monopolization of global companies creates a series of tensions for both politicians and user commu-nities. Such challenges were reflected in the 2010 dispute between China and Google over uncensored search engines, which demonstrated that such a universal-ly shared view about media freedom and access to information is not yet apparent. The debacle gave rise to considerable acts of protest over China's Internet laws.

More familiar examples of transnational protests have arisen in the context of fair-trade or ethical trade products, or concerns about child labour. In the context of the Olympics, this has particular relevance, since its financial base is supported by some of the world's biggest brands, such as McDonald's, Visa, Lenovo, Coca-Cola, etc. From one perspective, the Olympic Games could function as a device to make such companies more publicly accountable—for example by adhering to the IOC's environmental policies—and so one may argue that the Olympics is an arbiter of activist concerns. Yet, the broader social concerns about how such companies may benefit from a mega-event that many members of the public believe should be free from corporate interests, deem that this mechanism of building greater corporate responsibility may not always be a primary value for the general public.

Finally, a global, digital era requires us to interrogate what counts as activism or protest. While we strongly advocate the idea that even the most minimal gesture online should qualify—such as sharing a website address via the social networking platform Twitter, which may require little more than two clicks of a mouse button—it will be necessary to consider strategically how different forms of activism lead to different results. Clearly, what arises from a Web 2.0 era of user-generated content is the capacity to build impact from the ground up. This is why a powerful web community can outperform a large transnational company in such terms as Google rankings and general visibility, as is typified by viral marketing campaigns. Yet, it remains to be seen whether digital activism—or hacktivism—can generate a significant impact without receiving attention from traditional media. Of course, as a campaign escalates, there comes a point where the traditional media become an integral part of the cycle of news syndication, so these are incredibly difficult phenomena to analyze in isolation. Nevertheless, further research may study the interaction of traditional and online journalism to better gauge how *convergence*—a term that was applied to media systems in the 1990s—has reached the level of protest culture. In the Olympics, we suggest that this is already apparent.

Notes

1. http://www.wikileaks.org/
2. On Twitter most of the messages related to Moldova were easily searchable due to the common accepted hashtag #pman
3. Messages from Iran and in support of Iranian protesters sent during the Iran Elections were usually sent out with the #iranelection hashtag. This enabled easy searches, both live and post-event.
4. http://cop15.panda.org/
5. http://www.timeforclimatejustice.org/
6. Few people remember the Olympic Project for Human Rights badge worn by Peter Norman, the third athlete on the podium with Smith and Carlos, and the second place winner in their race. As well, often forgotten are the black berets and salute of the winners of the 4x400 meter final, both gestures in sympathy and support of Smith and Carlos (Hartmann, 1996; Arbena, 2002). Alwyn Morris' eagle feather raised in recognition of his heritage while on the podium of the 1000-meter Canoe Sprint competition in 1984 in Los Angeles is also forgotten (Morris, 1999)
7. http://www.studentsforafreetibet.org
8. http://freetibet2008.org
9. http://no2010.com/
10. http://6nsolidarity.wordpress.com/
11. Comedian and writer Stephen Fry was one of the top-10 Twitter accounts until 2009, after which all ten positions were held by mass media organizations. Nevertheless, his use of Twitter led to its popularization in the mass media and his ongoing commentary on digital culture has engaged a number of audiences, including the UK's Digital Britain committee and iTunes festivals, at which he has given lectures on such issues as file sharing.

CHAPTER SIXTEEN

The 2008 Tibet Riots

Competing Perspectives, Divided Group Protests and Divergent Media Narratives[1]

CHEN LI AND LUCY MONTGOMERY

Introduction

Awareness of the power of the mass media to communicate images of protest to global audiences and, in so doing, to capture space in global media discourses is a central feature of the transnational protest movement. A number of protest movements have formed around opposition to concepts and practices that operate beyond national borders, such as neoliberal globalization or threats to the environment. However, transnational protests also involve more geographically discrete issues such as claims to national independence or greater religious or political freedom by groups within specific national contexts. Appealing to the international community for support is a familiar strategy for communities who feel that they are being discriminated against or ignored by a national government.

In the twenty-first century new technologies and increasingly mobile populations make it ever more likely that audiences will have access to global media perspectives on events taking place in their backyard. The ways in which global diasporas make sense of the competing claims presented by news sources reporting on trans-national protest movements intended to bring pressure on the governments of their homelands thus become an important point of potential tension, as stakeholders vie to ensure that their perspectives are communicated and issues are simplified into familiar media narratives by the news system, which may clash with the pre-existing world views, belief systems and values of audiences from different backgrounds.

This chapter[2] explores the contending interpretations of riots that took place in Lhasa, Tibet in the lead-up to the Beijing Olympics in 2008 as they were presented by the British elite television news and online newspapers and the Xinhua News Agency and China Central Television. The riots took place in the context of an international campaign by pro-independence activists intended to capitalize on international media interest in China associated with the Olympics.[3] News coverage of the riots themselves became the catalyst of trans-national protests against "western media bias," in which Chinese students studying overseas played a key role. In addition to Chinese and British media coverage of the protests, the chapter draws on focus-group interviews with forty one Chinese students and forty-three British students, all of whom were studying at British universities and living in the UK when the Tibet riots occurred.[4]

Historical and contextual background

As the year of the Beijing Olympic Games, 2008 saw the spotlight of international media attention focussed on China. Both the Chinese government and many ordinary Chinese citizens hoped that the attention associated with the Olympics might allow the image of a "new China" to be presented to the world, encouraging international recognition of the substantial achievements of "reform and opening up" and highlighting China's status as a rising member of the international community with a great deal to offer the world. However, groups both inside and outside China also saw the Olympics as an opportunity to draw the world's attention to the continued existence of adversity and injustice within the "new China." Human rights activists, suppressed minorities and campaigners for political reform viewed the Olympics as a chance to draw the world's attention to their concerns and in so doing to exert pressure for change on China's authorities.

It is not surprising, then, that when violence broke out in Lhasa, Tibet on 14 March 2008, the international media were confronted with sharp contrasts between the official version of events proffered by the Chinese authorities and accounts provided by exiled Tibetans. Further tension was created by the fact that Western journalists were denied access to Lhasa.[5] Although the Chinese authorities maintained that the move was made out of a concern for the safety of journalists, it was widely interpreted by the international media as an attempt to "cover up" what had really taken place. Protests by exiled Tibetans that disrupted the Olympic torch relay served as the final catalyst for the first-ever global protests by the overseas Chinese community. These protests focussed on the Western media's treatment of China, and Chinese students studying overseas played a major role in them.

As with other internationally controversial issues, tension over Tibet's political status is part of a continuing discourse which by its nature involves competing interpretative packages and explanatory themes (Gamson & Modigliani, 1989; Philo, 1990). Debates over Tibet's political status are dominated by two principal groups: those who support Tibetan independence and those who believe that Tibet is a legitimate part of the People's Republic of China (PRC). These two groups compete with one another for a voice in the international mediasphere, projecting opposing views of Tibetan history, sovereignty, identity and contemporary politics (Sautman & Dreyer, 2006: 4). Chinese Communist Party (CPC) leaders claim that Tibet has been a part of China since the Yuan Dynasty. According to the CPC Tibet was "peacefully liberated" from a backward system of serfdom by the People's Liberation Army (PLA) when it asserted formal control over Tibet in 1951, three years after the establishment of the PRC. It is argued that since 1951 the PRC has heavily subsidized infrastructure development in Tibet and provided preferential policies for Tibetan residents. This view of Tibet's legitimate place within the borders of the PRC, and of the Tibetan people as major beneficiaries of the PRC's investment in the region's infrastructure, education and services is reflected in the PRC's official media, as well as in the curricula taught in Chinese schools and universities.

The 14th Dalai Lama–Tenzin Gyatso, the political and spiritual leader[6] of the Tibetan nation prior to 1951–fled into exile in India following an abortive uprising against the CPC in 1959. The Tibetans who followed the Dalai Lama into exile, and many of those who remained behind, view Tibet's history and the current situation of its residents in very different terms. This group believes that Tibet was an independent state prior to 1951 and that its current political status is that of an occupied territory with a legitimate claim to independence. Furthermore, the Dalai Lama and his supporters claim that the CPC has overseen a regime of terror in Tibet, violating the human rights of Tibetans, employing torture to silence opposition to CPC authority and carrying out cultural genocide by suppressing religious and political freedoms.

With the help of some Westerners and well-educated members of the Tibetan elite, exiled Tibetans and the Tibetan diaspora have adopted modern Western media strategies to promote the cause of a "Free Tibet" since the early 1960s. The Free Tibet Movement has expanded developed extensive international support through grassroots organizations based in Western countries, such as the International Campaign for Tibet, as well as among high-profile academics, celebrities, political activists and publishers. In addition to raising international awareness of human rights violations in Tibet, the Free Tibet movement has been involved in educating the public about Tibetan culture and Buddhism, a strategy that has proven highly effective in capturing the imagination of international audiences (Schwartz, 1994; Powers, 2000, 2004; Sautman & Dreyer, 2006; Anand, 2007).

Origins of the riots: What really triggered the violence?

As mentioned earlier, the 2008 Beijing Olympics were understood as an important opportunity by both the Chinese government and Tibetan activists. Despite fears of potential difficulties associated with sensitive issues, the Chinese government regarded the Olympics as a golden opportunity to project a new image of itself as a modern, peaceful force through the world's media. For supporters of Tibetan independence the Olympics were seen as an important opportunity to draw international attention to difficulties in Tibet and human rights violations taking place under Chinese rule. International campaigns calling for a boycott of the 2008 Olympics were staged by exiled Tibetans and their supporters, employing new media platforms such as Facebook, as well as older methods such as rallies. However, for many Tibetans still living in Tibet, the situation was more complex. Concerns over the treatment of Tibetans by the Chinese authorities and calls for the return of the Dalai Lama were mixed with anger and frustration over Han immigration into the region and perceived inequities in access to economic opportunities between Han migrants and the ethnically Tibetan population. The extent to which each of these factors was represented as causing the 2008 riots became a key point of divergence in Chinese and international media reports of the events.

Despite BBC News Online's intensive pre-riot coverage and analysis of events leading up to violence in Lhasa, both its *Six o'clock News* and *Ten o'clock News* failed to mention the fact that the riots occurred during the anniversary of the 1959 Tibetan uprising against Chinese rule and the Dalai Lama's exile. The *ITV Evening News* and *ITV News at Ten* also omitted this fact. *Channel 4 News* alluded to the anniversary of the 1959 uprising: "mark[ing] anniversaries of uprising against Chinese rule ... [and] Chinese occupation" as an explanation for protests by exiled Tibetans in India but failed to mention protests by monks within Tibet at all. Given Tibet's complex political history, it is not immediately clear whether the monks who initiated the 2008 protests inside Tibet were calling for an independent Tibetan state. As Sautman (1999) and Powers (2000) both point out, although some Tibetan lobbyists have remained focused on calls for an independent Tibetan state, the positions of others, including the Dalai Lama, have changed over time, tending towards calls for the "genuine autonomy" of ethnographically Tibetan areas within the PRC, rather than a complete break from China (see, for instance, his recent interview, CNN, 26 February 2010).

During the same period, a short statement[7] issued by Xinhua News Agency on 14 March was broadcast by China Central Television (CCTV) and circulated through China's official media. The statement provided an official account of events and reiterated the Chinese government's position on the history of Tibet and Tibetan separatism. In its subsequent report on 16 March 2008, the Chinese government's official version of the history of Tibet's incorporation into the CPC was alluded to by Xinhua in order to highlight Dalai clique's[8] long-standing commitment to "splitting China" in order to "restore their privileges as serf-owners" (Xinhua News Agency normative report, 14 March 2008).

Initial protests led by monks were presented by Xinhua as attempts to "stir up trouble."[9] "Defiant" behaviour [such as hurling stones] towards government officers performing their duty was emphasized.[10] In so doing, the riot was explained as the escalation of attempts to provoke a reaction from the Chinese authorities, who had responded with professionalism and restraint:

> . . . the monks who intended to make trouble failed due to the civilised methods of law enforcement by government officers, and then the violence erupted. (Xinhua News Agency normative report, 17 March 2008; Trans. from Chinese, Xinhuanet.com, 30 March 2008)

How, then, was the transition from "peaceful" protests to violent riots accounted for in the British media? Different narratives of this transition emerged during the period studied for this chapter. However, the most prominent narrative was the theme of a "crackdown" by the Chinese authorities on a challenge to their power. This narrative is evident in ITV's reporting of the violence:

> Gunfire was heard in the capital as authorities used tear gas to *continue their brutal crackdown* on opposition to Chinese rule. (Intro, ITV Evening News, 14 March 2008–our italics)

In other words, according to ITV reports, Chinese authorities responded to initially peaceful protests with a "brutal crackdown," rather than only once the protesters had become violent, as Chinese official news sources had suggested. The rhetorical choice of "continue" and "brutal," not only echoed ITV's own report the day before: "China is cracking down hard on Buddhist monks" (Intro, ITV News at Ten, 13 March 2008) but also implied the possibility of violence by protesters as a response to the excessive use of force by authorities, a familiar narrative in reporting the escalation of peaceful protests into violent clashes for Western audiences. The familiarity of this narrative to Western audiences is evident in the responses of British participants in this study's focus groups. Their views of events in Tibet were based on information supplied by the mainstream media, as well as their own experiences of similar violence in other contexts. As a result, the "crackdown" narrative adopted by outlets such as ITV resonated with the existing knowledge system of British student,[11] which included a predominantly negative view of the

Chinese government's track record on human rights and a perception of the organized forces of authority as a likely source of the violence that triggered rioting.

As Wolfsfeld et al. (2008) point out, "one of the most common [journalistic] routines is to employ terms or descriptions that present actions as a reaction to the violence carried out by the other side." Here we are not suggesting that the opinions of the British students were derived directly from the ITV news bulletin, but rather that they were influenced by the familiar narrative representation of the causes of violence presented to them by the mainstream Western media, which served to reinforce an existing belief system. As Jamie Morgan (2004: 402) points out:

> . . . the [western] media's construction of images of China entails . . . imbu[ing] those events with an editorial flavour that emerges from the media's own value system.

This approach is evident in reports on the riots by *The Sunday Times*, which emphasized their predictability in the context of the familiar image of a Chinese regime that is intolerant of challenges to its authority and which served to fuel a cycle of violence that resulted in riots by an oppressed minority:

> A predictable and harsh response by the Chinese set off more protests by monks, then ignited popular rage among the ordinary inhabitants of Lhasa. (*The Sunday Times*/Times Online, 16 March 2008)

In contrast, James Miles from *The Economist* (the only foreign journalist with official permission to be in Lhasa), reported that "the violence was fuelled by *rumours of killings, beatings and detention of Buddhist monks* by security forces in Lhasa this week" (Economist.com, 14 March 2008; also in Radio 4 World at One, 14 March 2008).

As Wolfsfeld et al. (2008) note, the adoption of a "Defensive Mode" of reporting violent conflicts makes it possible for violence to be justified, allowing the weaker side in a conflict to attribute their violent actions to oppression by an enemy. But there was no evidence in our focus group interviews with British participants to indicate that the violence of rioters in Tibet had been legitimized in this manner, in spite of the group's overwhelming acceptance of the narrative of "Tibetan resistance against the Chinese oppression." Some did suggest empathy with rioters, suggesting that "they would feel justified in violent protest" and "there might be a lot of anger and frustration built up" (D, British Group 3). However, British focus group participants also pointed out that the only option for Tibetan activists hoping to achieve independence for Tibet is the pursuit of peaceful strategies, given the strength of the PRC's military power.

At the same time, the majority of the Chinese students interviewed for this study appeared poorly informed about the reasons for the initial protests and were unaware of the fact that the protests occurred on the anniversary of the 1959

Tibetan uprising. The Chinese students interviewed were focussed on the violent behaviour of ethnically Tibetan protesters during the riots which followed the first protests. Although not all of the Chinese students felt certain that the Chinese authorities had "cracked down" on protesters, many insisted that if the Chinese authorities had responded harshly it was a direct response to the violent behaviour of rioters.

Intertwining motivations

There was one common feature between Chinese official media reports of events in Tibet and those of some British media such as the BBC and ITV: attributing the cause of the violence to "the desire for independence" [in Chinese terms, as an attempt "to split China"]. By presenting the conflict as simply being between two entities, the BBC's news bulletins interpreted the motives of the rioters as being "against Chinese rule" (BBC Ten o'clock News, 14 March 2008). ITV News also presented the situation as a Tibetan-Chinese dichotomy, explaining the violence against Chinese authorities as action directed towards a group who had occupied their homeland. Although the legitimacy of China's claim to sovereignty over Tibet is a key aspect of the Tibet Question, the challenges facing ethnic Tibetans in the twenty-first century are multi-dimensional and include questions over access to economic opportunities, the impact of trans-migration and whether, as the Dalai Lama has suggested, it might be possible for Tibetan people to secure religious and cultural autonomy while remaining within the PRC.

In the case of the riot itself, the heterogeneity of participating groups and the relationship between economic factors and social dislocation as well as the ethnic identity of the groups towards whom physical violence was directed cannot be ignored. In addition to acts of defiance directed at the authorities, James Miles reported rioters "hurling chunks of concrete [both] at the numerous small shops run by ethnic Chinese" and "at those passers-by who appeared to be ethnic Chinese," as well as looting and arson[12] (*The Economist*, 14 March 2008; Miles, 15 March 2008). This could be explained by several possibilities. Feng and Xu (2009) point out this riot shared some of the features of the 1992 Los Angeles riots, including resentment of the rich and attacks on the business of the economically privileged. Channel 4 News considered this as a possible cause of the violence, stating:

> Many [ordinary Tibetans] resent the Han Chinese who have gone to live in Tibet and are doing well in business there. (Channel 4, 14 March 2008)

Another possible cause for this resentment, identified by James Miles, was high inflation in relation to "food and consumer goods imported into Tibet from the rest of China" (Economist.com, 14 March 2008). Although inflation of food prices, in particular, was a phenomenon impacting on the whole country[13] it was easily interpreted by Tibetans as price gouging by Chinese traders, particularly given the "strong sense of divide between ethnic communities[14]" (Radio 4 World at One, 14 March 2008; Hilsum, 2008). Moreover in view of targeted violence against the Han Chinese residents of Lhasa, the nature of this violence can be understood as a manifestation of racial conflict, inextricably intertwined with other elements such as socioeconomic pressure relating to the influx of Han migrants into Tibetan communities.[15] Heavy investment from the central government and local economic development including the growth of tourism have not been enough to insulate Tibet from problems caused by global economic events, trans-migration and associated cultural tensions.

The Western media's reporting of the Tibet riots reflects existing narratives of conflict and repression surrounding the nature of the CPC's authority and the struggle for spiritual and political freedom being waged by the Tibetan people. The images most commonly brought to mind by British focus group participants when presented with the words "Tibet" and "China" were "conflict," "occupation" and "tension." These images of the relationship between Tibet and China have undoubtedly been reinforced by high profile campaigns for a "Free Tibet,"[16] which are viewed as "popular and fashionable" by many British students.

However, an association between the "progressive" and "liberal" tendencies of university students and the popularity of the Tibetan independence movement is not a reflection of naivety about the complex nature of China, or the often simplistic narrative of reporting on China that dominates the British mainstream media. A significant proportion of British focus group participants believed that the Western media are, on the whole, biased in their reporting of China.[17] Focus group participants also felt that the British media tended to favour groups and individuals opposed to the Chinese regime.[18] The mainstream media's portrayal of Tibet and China as two separate states, rather than of Tibetan independence activists as a separatist movement within the Chinese state, was also noted by the focus group participants, and understood as a rhetorical device with the power to influence public opinion on the legitimacy of Tibet's claims for independence.[19] As one focus group participant commented "they present both sides but they very much play at this idea of the big military power versus the underdog" (E, British Group 3). Some referred to their own life experience in helping them to understand that the mainstream media provide vastly simplified coverage of highly complex realities "as you get older you realize that it's probably not even half of the story they're telling you" (C, British Group 1). This appreciation of the complexity of situations simplified for reporting purposes by the media was echoed by other participants.[20]

Some British students were also able to articulate possible reasons for the media's interest in adopting a critical position in relation to the Chinese government in reporting on the riots.[21] However, although the British focus-group participants were aware that a particular narrative or reporting line had been adopted by the mainstream press, they did not perceive this to be automatically in conflict with the role of the media: "I don't mind if they take a side as long as it's fairly obvious. . .I mean, present both arguments" (E, British Group 3). In Morley's terms, the British students interviewed were aware of the media's "preferring" mechanisms (Morley, 1980: 140). Some British students were more critical of the media's angle on the Tibet riots on the grounds that "there was not a reasonable balance," such as one commenting: "you don't hear anything negative about the Tibetans; you just hear them as victims" (C, British Group).

However, the views of the majority of the British focus group participants shared important similarities with the perspectives expressed in the Western media content surveyed, particularly in relation to the motivations of the protesters and the causes of the violence. The role of the media in informing these views was expressly acknowledged by some " . . . any assumption I would make would certainly be based on the media portrayal that has been shown to me" (D, British Group 3). Besides reflecting an overarching negative impression of the Chinese government and its motivations for its involvement in Tibet, the views expressed by British students also reflected a narrative of Tibetans as "victims of forced modernisation brought about by Chinese rule," one of what Anand (2007: 98) has identified as two dominant representations of Tibetans in the West.

The "cultural uniqueness" of Tibetans in the minds of the Western public, informed by the dominant image of Tibetan people and their place in the public discourse, has narrowed debates around Tibetan issues into a narrative of defence against any forces that might destroy this uniqueness. This defence is based either on subjective cultural assumptions such as "they don't need much, they just want happiness" or suspicion of economic development and industrialization as a force of assimilation in the popular imagination. However, even the Dalai Lama has repeatedly challenged this image of Tibetans, stating "all Tibetans want more prosperity, more material development" (quoted in Sautman & Dreyer, 2006: 5) and "we Tibetans want modernisation" (*Time*, 15 April 2006). The perceived need to protect the uniqueness of the indigenous culture of Tibet is heightened when British students consider China's actions alongside their understanding of the impact of colonialism on diversity in other, more familiar contexts, and when the richness of Tibetan culture is contrasted with popular portrayals of the brutal application of the communist ideal of "uniformity of identity," as in the popular Hollywood film, which starred Brad Pitt, *Seven Years in Tibet*.

For British students, educated within a system in which rights to self-determination, freedom of expression and religious pluralism are highly valued, the Tibetan desire for independence was understood as both natural and logical. This view was reinforced by an acceptance of claims that the PRC's seizure of power in Tibet in 1959 constituted an "invasion of an independent country." Even the two British students who were willing to consider whether or not Tibet should be considered part of the PRC insisted that "Tibetan people should be given a say"[22] in answering this question.

The interpretation by British students of the Western mainstream media's narrative of the riots is thus a result of complex interactions between individual "systems of beliefs and values," "public assumptions and sentiments" and information supplied by "news frames" as well as through cultural products that capture the public imagination, including films and documentaries. It might be argued, therefore, that the British students participating in this study had simply been more or less influenced by the ideological and media environment they operated within. However, this continuity between popular narratives of the relationship between Tibet and the Chinese authorities might also be understood as a demonstration of the claim made by Wolfsfeld et al. (2008) that "journalists construct news frames that resonate with public assumptions and sentiments," in a two-way process in which the news media reflect not only to events they are reporting, but also to the pre-existing world views and narrative expectations of its audience.

Chinese narratives: Social stability, national unity and beyond

This section takes a more detailed look at the belief systems and narrative frameworks that informed the responses of Chinese students who participated in this study's focus groups. Most of the Chinese students who elected to be involved in this project had been involved in the protests against the Western media's "biased" reporting of the Tibet riots that took place across the UK in 2008. This section, therefore, focuses on how the Chinese students involved in the study defined and understood Western media bias, and why they believed that the Western media had treated China unfairly. Given that the Chinese students who participated were all frequent users of both British and Chinese media sources, it is important to explore relevant explanatory frameworks within the Chinese media coverage in order to understand how this coverage conflicted with Western media perspectives.

Following the release official statement on events in Tibet by Xinhua News Agency[23] on 14 March 2008, Xinhua News released a series of reports which focussed on two aspects of the riots: its disastrous impact and the "Dalai clique's" responsibility. These narratives directly linked the number of casualties and extent of the damage. The "ruthless mob" of Tibetan separatist rioters was presented in dramatized and highly emotive terms. This strategy fits well with what has been called a "victim's mode of reporting" (Wolfsfeld et al., 2008) in coverage of casualties resulting from violent conflicts. The death of "innocent civilians" was highlighted and witness accounts were quoted, for example: "the mob attacked passers-by, not even sparing the women and children" (Xinhua News Agency, 15 March 2008a). In so doing, these reports appear to have been intended to increase the emotional impact of the event on audiences, invoking sympathy for and solidarity with the victims and encouraging condemnation of the brutality of the rioters. Accounts of deaths included personal details such as victims, names, ages and even the terrified postures in which they had died. Not all of the victims were Han Chinese, a fact which further reinforced the image of tragic, senseless loss of life and property as a result of the riots.

Photographs of victims' injuries were also juxtaposed against images of rioters burning the Chinese national flag or chasing passers-by with knives. These emotive strategies were effective in establishing a dominant image of the rioters as a violent mob, responding to incitements to violence from a politically motivated separatist movement and entirely lacking in compassion. This image of Tibetan protesters was reflected in the views of the Chinese students studying at British universities who took part in our study. Although the Xinhua news reports were careful to point out that ordinary Tibetans had also been victims of the violence, it was apparent that Han Chinese[24] migrants into Tibet and their shops had been targeted. The Chinese students interviewed for the study, most of whom were Han,[25] found it easy to identify with the victims of the violence and expressed their anger at the attacks. Some also complained that the racially targeted nature of the violence had not been emphasized enough in the western media's reporting of the riots.

Quotes from local Tibetan people, such as "We're living a good life now. Why did they riot?", which were included in Xinhua news reports, reiterated the familiar assumption held by many Chinese people that the PRC's presence in Tibet had brought the region prosperity and stability, deeply valued by Chinese citizens. The actions of protesters were understood as not only an act of senseless violence, but also as a threat to the nation's stability. Social and political stability is widely viewed within China as having been hard won over several generations and as something which must be protected and defended, in order to safeguard the lives of ordinary citizens and their rights to security and prosperity. The Chinese media's framing of the riot as "disturbance aiming to destroy the stability that has been sustained for 18 years" (Xinhua News Agency normative report, 15 March 2008b; Xinhua, 16 March 2008) thus resonated with deeply held values and fears of Chinese audiences.

The Chinese authorities appear to have been eager to employ emotive strategies in official media reports, in order to add to the persuasive power to official versions of events. These strategies were particularly evident in reports relating to the threat posed by the "Dalai clique." A tactic frequently employed by the Chinese official media in order to calm social unrest and to allow stability to be re-established quickly is to blame an identifiable group of "trouble-makers" for disturbances. By blaming a small number of "trouble-makers," it becomes possible for the authorities to publically deal with these individuals, separating their role in events from the role that broader social issues might have played. This strategy makes it possible for individuals deemed responsible for unrest to be punished, allowing the rest of the population to return to normal life.[26]

In this instance blaming the mob itself was not enough; the Chinese government had also to deal with protests and allegations by exiled Tibetans and their international supporters. By focusing on the "Dalai clique's" culpability in these events, the Chinese government was able to further discredit the Dalai Lama and his supporters in the minds of the Chinese public and to avoid drawing too much attention on other controversial issues related to its own policies within Tibet. In so doing, public anger at the mob, propelled by emotive reporting of violence in Tibet could be mobilized against the Dalai Lama and supporters of Tibetan independence. In addition to being framed as posing a threat to the nation's stability, Chinese official media stressed the Dalai clique's long-standing goal of "splitting China" and "restoring their [the Tibetan elite's] privileges as serf-owners."[27]

A significant majority of Chinese students interviewed for this study believed that groups opposed to the PRC, including Western countries, were responsible for the riots. Western opposition to China was understood as part of a broader effort to disrupt China's long-term stability and prevent its continued economic development. (C, Chinese Group 7, B & C, Group 10, etc.)

In contrast to the British students, who viewed the conflict as being between two distinct nations, all of the Chinese students involved in the focus groups strongly believed that "Tibet is a part of China."[28] As one of the pro-China student demonstration slogans puts it: "Tibet was, is and always will be a part of China." The Chinese focus-group participants understood this statement as axiomatic. This belief is deeply held and difficult to challenge. Chinese focus-group participants emphasized the patriotic nature of the Chinese official media[29] and expressed anger and intolerance towards representations of alternative viewpoints by the western media, which they regarded as both "biased" and factually incorrect.

Their initial standpoints were wrong, always being sympathetic towards the exiled Tibetans and supporting the Tibet independence. (E, Chinese Group 8)

Even students who had worked in the Chinese media industry strongly rejected alternative points of view and viewed the issue of "balanced reporting" as irrelevant [such as F, Chinese Group 11].

The "discontent" narrative

Tempting as it may be to interpret Chinese students' passionate criticism of the Western media's reporting of the Tibet riots as evidence of "unquestioning support of their government"[30] (see, for example, Forney, 2008), such a view is overly simplistic. In fact, a number of Chinese students interviewed did not subscribe to the official Chinese narrative that suggested that the riots were an attempt to "split China." Rather, they regarded the violence as an attempt by Tibetans to "express their *discontent* with the Chinese government."

The generation of young Chinese born in the 1980s have become increasingly familiar with the Chinese media's "discontent" narrative, partly due to the increasing numbers of "mass incidents" (protests) or "social riots" that have taken place across China recent years. Many of these "mass incidents" are a result of anger over local corruption, while others are a result of frustration over unequal access to resources and tensions associated with trans-migration. According to some of the students, as in the case of "mass incidents" in other parts of China, Tibetans "have no way to appeal to the government to sort out their problems and they have to take unusual actions" (D, Chinese Group 5; D, Chinese Group 7, etc.). Although the Chinese students were conscious of significant subsidies made available to Tibet from the central government, some nonetheless understood the sources of social unrest in economic terms, originating in unemployment or disparity between the rich and the poor, which had resulted in frustration and resentment that had lead to the riots.

A significant feature of this "discontent" narrative, familiar to the Chinese students interviewed, is its combination with an image of a group of trouble-makers who take advantage of a discontented group and "stir up trouble" in an already frustrated population: "more or less there are some discontented people that can be easily taken advantage of" (A, Chinese Group 6); "The poor can be easily incited" (B, Chinese Group 6). This "common tactic" is reiterated in official statements circulated by the media every time social riots occur in China. Stating that trouble was "stirred-up by a small few" is inevitably a precursor to the launch of a campaign to blame and punish a group of identifiable troublemakers.

The Role of Religion

British students who participated in this study valued religious tolerance and pluralism, views that are encouraged by British education and liberal narratives. They also considered Tibetan Buddhism to be a peaceful religion which had either a benign or positive impact on the lives of its followers. Chinese students, on the other hand, possessed less positive views of religion in general and Tibetan Buddhism in particular. Rather than understanding Tibetan Buddhism as a benign force, they tended to view it in terms that might be applied to a dangerous cult in the Western context. As such rioters were regarded as "religiously controlled by the Dalai Lama" (B, Chinese Group 1) or "brainwashed" (C, Chinese Group 2), with emphasis of the "evil" power of religion and its extremists.

Concluding remarks

As this chapter has discussed, the international media attention on China associated with the 2008 Beijing Olympic Games was understood as an important opportunity by both the Chinese government and groups who are critical of its policies. As Free Tibet activists and the Chinese government competed to ensure that their preferred perspectives on events taking place in Tibet were beamed into the living rooms and onto the front pages of audiences around the globe, the "Western" media became both the site of clashes between competing claims, and a source of anger and frustration for many members of the Chinese diaspora. The "Anti Western Media Bias" protests which took place around the world in the wake of the Tibet riots reflected the power of narrative expectations and belief systems in informing responses to international news coverage of transnational protests, as well as the patriotism of Chinese citizens who felt that their nation and its government had been unfairly attacked by a hostile Western media.

The Tibet riots also highlight an important tension between transnational protest movements in which exiled populations play a decisive role in calls for independence and the experiences and actions of local populations in disputed territories. Dichotomy frameworks leave little space for the complex realities that inform the actions of protesters, some of whom may be living within a disputed territory and only indirectly connected to the activities of exiled activists and their international supporters. In order to understand the role that the media play not only in reporting protests, but as a forum through which conflicting narratives of identity, nationalism and persecution are presented, and to which audiences themselves bring interpretive paradigms, it is therefore vital to move beyond simplistic frameworks of political struggle.

Notes

1. Special thanks to Professor Greg Philo for his invaluable comments and encouragement.
2. This chapter is keeping with a long-term research tradition within media studies. A number of attempts have been made by media studies scholars to explore how media coverage of controversial events and issues interacts with the understanding, beliefs and attitudes of different groups within a society (Halloran et al., 1970; Philo, 1990; Philo and Berry, 2004). A central feature of this literature is a consideration of how "encoding" interacts with "decoding" (Hall, 1973b; Morley, 1980) or, in other words, how journalistic assumptions interact with the "belief/knowledge system" of the audience (Philo, 1990). Gamson (1988, quoted in Price, 1992: 89) employed focus groups to explore the extent to which "elements of media discourse have become part of the public's tool kit for making sense of public affairs."
3. Here we should be clear that the event was not simply a protest that included some violent elements of the type that Halloran et al. (1970) studied. Rather it was a riot or violent protest that erupted in the wake of what were claimed to be "peaceful protests" led by monks.
4. In-depth interviews with students who possessed particular knowledge or experience were also conducted. These included four British students studying Chinese who had spent time living in China, three British-born Chinese students who belonged to the second or third generation of Chinese immigrants to the United Kingdom, and six Chinese students, studying journalism, with previous full time experience working for Chinese media organizations.
5. Except for James Miles from *The Economist*, who luckily was approved to enter Tibet before the riot broke out.
6. The other spiritual leader is Panchen Lama, the second highest ranking lama after the Dalai Lama.
7. The normative report is quite short, only consisting of three parts of short sentences: 1) rioting activities brought disastrous damage to people's life, with people killed and properties damaged, 2) it was instigated by the Dalai clique to split China and that has been condemned by people in Tibet, 3) the local authorities have taken proper steps to restore order.
8. "Dalai clique" is a term coined by the Chinese government and used to refer to the major political figures (and especially the Dalai Lama) in exiled Tibetans as well as political organizations firmly dedicated to promote the cause of "Tibetan independence" such as the Tibetan Youth Congress (TYC).
9. It's flawed for Moyo (2010) to argue Xinhua News Agency constructed a "nationalistic discourse" by distorting "the legitimate struggle for rights [protests as he refers to] by the Tibetans" as "riots, vandalism and arson." He misunderstood the riot itself as violent elements [of a protest] that have been exaggerated.
10. A detailed official Chinese account of the initial protests in Tibet did not turn up until September 2008, when it was claimed during a press conference that "those who were *detained for questioning* were some of those monks carrying the illegal snow lion flag and crying slogans of 'Free Tibet' and 'Long Live Dalai.'"
11. For instance, "I mean you very *rarely have riots that were organized beforehand*, do you know what I mean? *Peaceful protests become riots.*" (C, British Group 6) "Don't all protests start peacefully, in the sense that they can't just start?" (E, British Group 3) It should also be noted

that a few of the British focus group subjects observed the possibility of "trouble-makers" initiating the violence [e.g. B, British Group 7].

12. There is no evidence to show these media here to present those rioters as "peaceful demonstrators," as some Chinese accused [see Liu, 2008]. Rioting actions of "looting" and "setting fire" were all covered.

13. China then suffered a high inflation rise by 7.1 percent in January 2008, the highest level in more than a decade. See for instance BBC's report titled "Inflation tops China 2008 agenda": http://news.bbc.co.uk/1/hi/world/asia-pacific/7278450.stm

14. This is also confirmed by several Chinese students in our focus groups who have either been to Tibet or been living there for quite a long time. One British student also mentioned this, and he has been living in China for years and been to Tibet for several times.

15. See, for instance, similar analysis from Hu and Salazar (2006).

16. It has been reinforced by Facebook and email campaigns, as well as the adoption of the Tibet cause by Hollywood film stars and the portrayal of the unequal struggle between poorly armed Tibetans and the PLA depicted in *Seven Years in Tibet* starring Brad Pitt.

17. For example, one commented, "It's always biased, [it] always seems so." (B, British Group 9)

18. Taking the Free Tibet movement for example, one commented, "They used to put China down and big Tibet up." (B, British Group 1)

19. Such as B and D in British Group 3.

20. One commented, "Well, there are probably problems there that we don't know about because the media only portrays certain ones. So you might get the wrong idea and it just depends how they want you to think" (B, British Group 1).

21. Its aim has been pointed out, "to embarrass the Chinese before they have the Olympics by having all these pictures beamed around the world" (For example, A and E in British Group 3).

22. One (A, British Group 3) furthered this by presenting his impression that "Tibetans want to become independent", while the other student (A, British Group 11) is a student who has been living China for eight years and is married to a Chinese wife refused to give further comments.

23. Nan Zhenzhong, former editor-in-chief of Xinhua, pointed out in a speech, "Xinhua should present the voice of the government, with authorized exclusive rights to cover . . . politically sensitive events" (quoted in Xin, 2006)

24. If Chinese officials defined this riot with "ethnic conflict" element by highlighting Han-Chinese who were attacked, it would produce more controversial debates related to its own ethnic policies. It's easier for them to target who should be responsible for the riot by emphasizing its damage on social stability and national unity.

25. Other ethnicities include Mongolian, Manchu and Korean, etc.

26. It was also pointed out by British students studying Chinese (British Group 11) by giving the examples from Cultural Revolution and the Tiananmen Incident. In response to social riots in recent years, such tactic was also employed, such as the one in Weng'an; the local government targeted at a group of "gangland" who participated it.

27. In some sense it can be seen as "pull[ing] the debate back to the one about Tibet's historical status" (FitzHerbert, 2008) to avoid yielding any inconsistency with the construction of 'Chinese nation'. (See more about the construction of the Chinese nationhood at Li, 2006:

9–12). For this riot, Xinhua states, "This riot was instigated and masterminded by the Dalai Clique, and *coordinated by 'Tibetan separatists' both inside and outside China*" (Trans. from Chinese, Xinhuanet.com, 22 March 2008–our italics; 30 March 2008).

28. A few participants emphasized this by furthering the strategic and geopolitical role of Tibet as well as its rich mineral and natural resources.

29. Similar attempts have been seen as the revival of Chinese nationalism (e.g., Jia, 2005; Zhao, 2009), such as the anti-Japanese demonstrations around the Pinnacle Islands in 2005.

30. Shown by the empirical evidence, not only from our focus group, but other researchers such as Latham (2009) also found "opinions rarely fell into black-and-white categories." In other words, some of those critical of western media bias have also shown their strong criticism of the Chinese government's "dodge" policies, of Chinese own dysfunctional media, and even of mistreating the Dalai Lama.

CHAPTER SEVENTEEN

Resistanbul

An Analysis of Mediated Communication in Transnational Activism

ILKE SANLIER YÜKSEL AND MURAT YÜKSEL

Introduction

Toward noontime on 26 September 2009, a marching crowd, carrying a big banner proclaiming "we are all migrants," stopped in front of a building with barred windows in the *Kumkapi* neighborhood of Istanbul. Euphemistically called the "Foreigners' Guesthouse," the building is used by the Turkish Government to detain "illegal immigrants" who do not meet the legal requirements or possess the personal documents for entry until their deportation. Locked in that building and deprived of their basic human rights, these immigrants could be held in inhumane conditions indefinitely, waiting for their deportation from Turkey. Chanting protesters, demonstrating to confirm their solidarity with the immigrants who rose up against their inhumane conditions in the detention center to demand better treatment from the authorities, were gathered by a call for action made through the web site of *Resistanbul*.

Resistanbul, a transnational anti-capitalist action network, was started by a coalition of activists in May 2009 to mobilize and coordinate wide-scale, mass demonstrations against the International Monetary Fund (IMF) and the World Bank (WB) meetings scheduled to be held in Istanbul in October 2009. The name itself embodies both local and global dimensions of political activism through the use of a portmanteau word created from "resistance" and "Istanbul." Organized through a website (http://resistanbul.wordpress.com), *Resistanbul* is basically an umbrella protest network, an internetworked "hyper-organization" of anti-globalization. Although initially started to facilitate the mobilization and organization of a transnational protest action against the IMF and WB meetings, along the way it also rapidly responded to a number of local and national issues and threats against humanity. From its founding in May 2009 until the main anti-IMF and anti-WB demonstration, the activists of *Resistanbul* organized about 20 public demonstrations, including the one in Kumkapi.

In this chapter we explore the ways in which *Resistanbul*, a transnational activist network, communicates both among its active members and with the public it seeks to influence. For that purpose we analyze different means of communication *Resistanbul* utilizes, by looking first at its use of the Internet to mobilize people and organize protest actions, and second at its attempts to attract mass media attention. We argue that in order to achieve the passage from micro to mass media, *Resistanbul* also organized various local protest campaigns on issues not directly related to their main cause, including the Kumkapi demonstration.

The new transnational activism and the new media

One of the most important types of social and political activism in the 21st century is transnational movements. Today the world is full of various transnational contentious mobilizations, demonstrations, and movements initiated by various NGOs, INGOs, and/or transnational advocacy networks devoted to a number of issues, including but not limited to human rights, the environment, women's rights, peace and justice, and development (Smith et al., 1997; Tarrow, 1998, 2005a; Keck & Sikkink, 1998; della Porta & Tarrow, 2005a; Reitan, 2007; della Porta et al., 2006; della Porta & Kriesi, 1999). Social movement scholars Donatella della Porta and Sidney Tarrow have recently depicted these transnational collective mobilizations as "the most dramatic change we see in the world of contentious politics" (2005a: 6). This dramatic change asserts itself not only in the frequency of interactions across national borders but also through frames of identification; adaptability to rapidly changing events; the complexity of protest campaigns and the density and design of movement networks; the fluidity of alliances that bring together a wide range of issues, actors, targets and perspectives; repertoires of action; and the boldness, assertiveness, and creativity of demands, claims (Reitan, 2007) and, more importantly, means of communication.

Many scholars have argued that the increase in transnational contention and activism has coincided with the spread of "neoliberal capitalist globalization" (Smith & Johnston, 2002; Gills, 2000; Gill, 2003). As a matter of fact, mobilizing resistance against the agents of the new neoliberal capitalist world order constitutes the major mobilizing framework for most transnational activism. Based on her extensive interviews with many transnational activists, Reitan (2007: 8) observes that:

> the enemy goes by many names, but almost always entails the global spread, and perceived mounting failures, of specific neoliberal policies, or institutions, and/or global capitalism overall: "structural adjustment," "the IMF," "World Bank," "Multilateral Agreement on Investment (MAI)," "WTO," "NAFTA," "FTAA," "multinationals" or "transnational corporations (TNCs)," "neoliberalism," "this kind of capitalism," or "capitalism" in general are the common culprits.

Other scholars, however, caution against assuming that there is a causal link between neoliberal capitalist globalization and the transnationalization of contention (Tilly, 2004; Tarrow, 2005a). As Tarrow (2005a) argues, it would be a mistake to see all transnational activism merely as a reaction against global neoliberalism. Nor should we assume that all transnational social movements are composed of activists with a global vocation. Many of the participants of transnational movements are still deeply rooted in domestic and local civil society. Many forms of transnational activism, such as human rights, immigrant rights, humanitarian aid, and justice against large-scale local, national, and regional infringements on humanity, may have little or nothing to do with capitalist globalization and much more to do with dictatorship, democracy and the abridgment of human rights. What we are witnessing, according to Tarrow, is, rather, a fusion between local and global activism as well as a fusion of local and transnational issues. Even as they make transnational claims, transnational activists draw on the resources, networks, opportunities, and issues of the societies in which they are embedded. The most distinguishing characteristic of the new transnational activism, therefore, is how it connects the local and the global (Tarrow, 2005a). Globalization, nonetheless, has facilitated these fusions and diffusions by providing local activists various means and opportunities to frame their claims in global terms, to connect with like-minded activists in other parts of the world, to internationalize their campaigns, and more.

One thing that old and new transnational social movements have in common is that they both heavily depend on technologies of communication. This is also true for more conventional local and national social movements. Since their invention, technologies of communication have always been vital tools of mobilization for modern social movements (Langman, 2005: 43). Whatever their origins, agendas, orientations or targets are, all social movement mobilizations depend heavily on communication media. This has obliged social movements to seek the communication strategies that are most suitable for satisfying their constituencies as well as for increasing support and sympathy from the general public. While social movements of earlier periods depended on the printing press, telegraph, radio, and even television, the prospects of new local as well as transnational social mobilizations depend not only on these, but also on new media, such as the Internet, cell phones and other digital media.

In a highly influential work, W. Lance Bennett (2005; also 2003a, 2003b) distinguishes between what he calls first-generation, NGO advocacy networks (Keck & Sikkink, 1998; Smith et al., 1997) and second-generation, direct activism social justice networks. According to Bennett, the first-generation, NGO advocacy model is characterized by limited, policy-oriented campaigning aimed at governments. In contrast, with its polycentric structure of mass activism, second-generation transnational activism is characterized by inclusive organizational models that favor diversity by linking issues through horizontal networks. They adopt social technologies that facilitate greater autonomy and leaderless networks and provide political capacities for communication.

Bennett (2003b) further argues that digital media, especially the Internet, are changing global activism in many important respects. The new media make loosely structured networks crucial for communication and coordination among activists; weaken the identification of local activists with the movement as a whole by allowing greater scope for the introduction of local, regional, and national issues into movement discourse; reduce the influence of ideology on personal involvement in social movements; diminish the relative importance of bounded, durable, resource-rich local and national organizations as bases of social movement activism; increase the strategic advantages of resource-poor organizations within social movements; promote the creation of permanent campaigns with rapidly shifting immediate targets; and combine face-to-face performances with virtual performances. Nevertheless, Bennett concludes that these very same features may also cause new communication-based transnational social movements to be vulnerable to age-old problems of decision-making, control, and collective identity. Following up on these potential problems that Bennett self-reflexively outlines, while acknowledging the advantages of the digital media for rapid and extensive mobilization, Charles Tilly (2004) casts doubt upon the political capacity of loose multi-issue internet-worked movements to generate the commitment, coherence and persistence of action required to produce significant social and political change. He argues that, despite their ability to mobilize large numbers of people rapidly, digitally networked protest action cannot necessarily be identified with collective action and politics that are produced by unified and sustained social movements (Tilly, 2004; also McAdam et al., 2001).

Our observations on the *Resistanbul* network mostly support Bennett's assertions. However, although it had most of the characteristics that Bennett associates with second-generation transnational activism, *Resistanbul* was far from being a pure type of second-generation direct activism network. It is also difficult to consider

Resistanbul as an example of a fully-fledged, sustained social movement, able to produce significant social and political change.

Resistanbul: A network of networks

As they have done since the Seattle meeting of 1999, opponents started to get ready for protest action as soon as it was announced in May 2009 that the next round of annual meetings of the IMF and WB were scheduled to be held in Istanbul on 6–7 October 2009. Various activist groups in Turkey, ranging from feminists, anarchists and eco-pacifists to anti-neoliberals and LGBTs, got together under the main theme of anti-globalization and global social justice and formed an umbrella organization, a "network of networks" called *Resistanbul,* to organize and coordinate wide-scale transnational protests against the IMF and WB, which they perceive to be the main agents of the new global neoliberal capitalist system. The organization labeled itself as "Resistance Days Coordination against the IMF and World Bank."

In experiences ranging from Seattle to Porto Alegre, from Genoa to simultaneous multi-city anti-war protests, the use of the Internet and other digital media has been fundamental in the organization of contentious mobilizations, transnational or otherwise. Since the "Battle in Seattle" in 1999, the Internet has been extensively used by ever-increasing numbers of transnational organizations and activists for multiple purposes: to communicate information, mobilize potential participants, form alliances and coalitions, attack enemy's high-tech resources, etc.

Resistanbul is no different in that regard. Without the use of the Internet, it would have been impossible for *Resistanbul* to reach thousands of activists from around the world, mobilize them in such a short period of time, and coordinate numerous mass demonstrations. For that aim, the first action that founders of *Resistanbul* took was to launch a website (http://resistanbul.wordpress.com/) in mid-July 2009, with a call to raise an "international voice against global capital." As framed by its members, the objective of the website, and hence of *Resistanbul,* was to support activist organizations and individuals in and through the Internet, and to contribute to the enhancement of global social justice, through the creation of a social forum which would facilitate and coordinate direct political participation on issues like human rights, economic inequalities, environment, and other related problems caused by neoliberal capitalist globalization. As the site's final report makes clear, *Resistanbul* advocated for and strove to create a new form of social movement which is highly flexible and consists of loose organizational structures: "In an age when life is being colonized and controlled by the power-holders, ways of resistance are being multiplied through the development of imagination, courage and solidarity. For this reason creation of a horizontal network of all different social struggles and connection of all resistances will be the goal of social movements for the coming years" (http://resistanbul.wordpress.com, accessed on 13 November 2009).

The role of the Internet in *Resistanbul*'s activism

In this section, we employ the model developed by della Porta et al. (2006) to analyze *Resistanbul*'s website through different categories of functions that the Internet has played in the movement. Although della Porta et al. (2006: 94) list those functions as instrumental, symbolic and cognitive, in our analysis we find that the most distinctive contribution of the Internet to *Resistanbul* is instrumental and cognitive rather than symbolic, which is also consistent with Diani's findings (2000). For the sake of the analysis, we divide the instrumental function into two subcategories: logistical and organizational. By logistical function we mean the Internet's ability to produce effective and fast communication, thus easing the coordination of protest and keeping affiliated groups and individuals continuously networked. Organizational function refers to the opportunities that the Internet provides for individual members to participate in the decision-making process and thus its potential to transform the organizational structure of the network. Cognitive function denotes the dissemination of information to members, the general public, and sometimes the media themselves concerning important issues that are either poorly covered or completely disregarded by mainstream media, thereby raising individual consciousness and sensitizing public opinion (della Porta et al., 2006; Warkentin, 2001).

More than anything else, *Resistanbul*'s use of the Internet seems to have played a crucial *logistical function* for coordinating the anti-IMF and anti-WB protests in Istanbul. Its website included a detailed map of Istanbul with meeting points, a calendar of the activities planned for the days of the protests, press releases, pictures of the demonstrations (as they were taking place), documents detailing the operations of the IMF and the WB, and an activist's cookbook. The latter document provides information on the nuts and bolts of preparation for protest action, transportation routes, legal rights and police station support in case of an arrest, proper dressing for protest, and definitions of roles during the demonstrations. Another important piece of information in the cookbook concerns gear that might be needed in case of an emergency, such as gas masks and lemons to protect against tear gas, enough water and proper documentation, and important telephone numbers such as that of Human Rights Association of Turkey. Also, through the website activists coming from outside of Istanbul had the chance to find a place to stay, most of the time free of charge as a sign of solidarity.

The website operates in two languages: Turkish and English. But the most important documents such as the manifesto and invitation to the demonstrations are available also in other languages, including Hungarian, Hebrew, Kurdish, Belarusian, Bulgarian, Czech, Macedonian, Greek, French, German, Italian, Portuguese, Spanish, Arabic and Catalan. The multi-language character of the website is also consistent with its transnational orientation.

As for *organizational function*, since the Internet provides relatively cheap and rapid communication opportunities, the website operated as a networking arena for activists to interact with each other through forums and posts. Members of *Resistanbul* used different computer-mediated communication (CMC) channels and interactivity options such as e-mail exchanges and posts on the website. Through the website, activists from all around the world were able to discuss and negotiate various organizational and tactical strategies. The resulting organizational structure of the demonstrations that *Resistanbul* initiated was the outcome of these interactions and negotiations amongst individual members of the network. In addition to facilitating logistical support for activists, then, these features of the website provided important organizational functions at both internal and external levels. That is to say, *Resistanbul*'s website turned out to be an organizational force that shaped and transformed both the relations among its members and the organizational structure of the movement itself. The adaptation of open communication networks transformed *Resistanbul*'s organizational structure by allowing information exchanges among its members (Bennett, 2003b).

As for its *cognitive function*, we observed *Resistanbul*'s website made wide use of the opportunities presented by the Internet to generate unmediated flows of information. The website became an alternative channel in providing information about operations of neoliberal transnational institutions and offering alternative solutions to the general public.

The use of the Internet as a multipurpose and open platform, which facilitates the dissemination of ideas, and at the same time the distribution of different formats of media produced at very low costs but with very high quality, has provided communication power to the activists (Castells, 2009). In the case of *Resistanbul*, in addition to being a valuable source of textual information and a forum of discussion, the website was also used as a stage for sharing audio and video documents freely by sidestepping copyright regulations. For example, the content of a video shared, with a title of "Riot Time," included IMF, WTO and WB operations, historical background on effects of globalization and statements on global inequalities. Therefore it is not only a call for resistance but also a major opportunity to disseminate information to the public on important issues.

By having a decentralized organizational structure, adopting a multi-issue, multi-campaign agenda, employing a variety of protest activities, widely using

CMC strategies both outside and inside the organization, and trying to raise public awareness, *Resistanbul* clearly belonged to the new generation of transnational activism. Nevertheless, although successful in utilizing the Internet to disseminate information, as we will show in the next section, members of *Resistanbul* still had to attract more mass media coverage in order to maximize their outreach, as many other social movements before them have done (i.e., Wright, 2004; Rucht, 2004).

Capturing media attention: Extending the action repertoire from anti-globalization to human rights

Connected rapidly and cheaply over the Internet, *Resistanbul* mobilized people for many causes from the day it started until the end of the anti-IMF and WB resistance week of October 1–8. By extending their action repertoire and raising public awareness, activists of *Resistanbul* tried to attract mainstream media coverage with colorful actions whose mission was to empower and support affiliated sectors and individuals (della Porta et al., 2006) in order to promote global justice, environmental sustainability and human rights. For example, they organized a "not money, but food" event against global capitalism and gentrification in the Tarlabasi neighborhood in Istanbul, giving out food that was recycled from organic and local markets. Another interesting campaign was a "party crashing" at the opening night of 11th International Istanbul Biennial. Activists read a press release and played and sang songs afterwards. Their main message was to artists, whom they urged not to attend the biennial, which is sponsored by both Turkish and global capitalists.

Since mainstream media outlets are crucial actors in agenda-setting, activists of *Resistanbul* organized a protest around a human rights abuse case that was already receiving mass media attention, with the hope of "careful strategic 'manipulation' of the media through spectacular activities" (Diani, 2000: 389). Hence, when the immigrants' protests in the Kumkapi detention center hit the news headlines, *Resistanbul* immediately organized a street demonstration to be held on 26 September 2009 to show their support for the immigrants who were held in the detention center against their will.

On 20 September, the 550-bed Kumkapi detention center, the so-called "Foreigners' Guesthouse" accommodating immigrants awaiting deportation, was the scene of immigrants' protests against their detention conditions. About a hundred immigrants broke the barred windows of the four-storey building in which they were kept and threw their beds, blankets, brooms, plastic plates and bottles out of the windows to push for administrative action. Some immigrants set fire to blankets and sheets, screaming that they did not want to stay there. They also hung a sheet on the window with a message demanding access to their countries' representatives in Istanbul.

The immigrants shouted their problems from the windows to the members of the press, claiming that they were not given food. The police were reluctant to intervene because a governor's order was legally required for intervention. The police surrounded the building with a security line so that nobody would be able to approach the detention center. The migrants ended their protest after a while. This wasn't the first time that detention centers made the news for their bad reputation because of their poor management and mistreatment of detainees.

According to numerous human rights reports (i.e., HCA, 2007; Içduygu & Biehl, 2008; AI, 2009) and news reports, the conditions of migrants in detention centers in Turkey are not very promising. The Kumkapi Foreigners' Guesthouse, in particular, is notorious for its harsh treatments of migrants. This has resulted in several protests by the migrants, including hunger strikes and suicides. Although international guidelines for the protection of refugees and asylum seekers prohibit deportation to a home country where the migrant's basic human rights might be violated, human rights advocacy groups (HCA, 2007; AI, 2009) and researchers (Mannaert, 2003; Içduygu & Biehl, 2008) agree that Turkey often violates irregular migrants' basic rights. Violations often start at the borders where migrants are prevented from applying for asylum. Many migrants detained at the airport transit zones in Turkey reported that they were denied their right to apply for asylum and were immediately deported (HCA, 2007: 31).

Moreover, those migrants who are able to enter into Turkey can face detention if they are caught by security forces upon illegal entry or exit, when they are waiting for removal, or while they are waiting for their asylum application to be processed. In most cases, once they are detained, their procedural rights and/or their basic human rights are usually violated. Detained migrants also face obstacles when applying for asylum, including concealment information about asylum procedures and refusal by the police to receive their asylum applications. The ones who are able to apply for asylum can also face detention rather than being transferred to one of the satellite cities where they are supposed to stay until their applications are processed. Many of these failures to provide access to asylum procedures have resulted in unlawful repatriations (HCA, 2007; AI, 2009; Mannaert, 2003; Içduygu & Biehl, 2008).

The detained refugees and asylum seekers are generally not informed of the reasons for their arrests or of their rights in detention. Many have to deal with assaults from the police when they ask for this information. They also lack information about the probable length of their detention, which leads to hopelessness and fear among the detainees. Besides the lack of basic information, detainees have only irregular access to lawyers. NGO representatives or human rights advocates are not allowed to visit detention centers. Especially the ones who are detained in transit zones have no access to lawyers, the UNHCR or other national and international NGOs at all.

According to human rights advocacy reports, many migrants also report substantial deficiencies regarding conditions in overpopulated detention centers. Overcrowding frequently causes detainees to sleep on the floor without sufficient bedding. Operating at overcapacity also worsens ventilation conditions, particularly in areas where smoking is permitted. Adults, minors, and convicted criminals are often accommodated in the same areas. Only men and women are separated from each other. Unhygienic living areas and lack of pest control further contribute to unhealthy conditions. Most of the time detainees have to buy their own cleaning supplies to clean up their living areas. Detainees often have to pay for their own toiletries and towels at excessively high prices. Access to hot water is also minimal. The meals provided in the centers are often deficient in nutritional value and no food is served on the weekends. Detainees have to get their drinking water at their own expense. Generally, recreational activities and reading materials are not made available to detainees. Medical services and facilities available in detention centers are insufficient. In addition to denial of access to medical service, high cost of treatment and medication and the inadequacy of available interpreters are among the obstacles for receiving proper health care. Detainees also report problems with communicating with the outside world. They are not allowed to receive calls and public phones are too costly. Visitor access is minimal. The major problem, however, is the use of verbal and physical aggression by police. Many detainees state that they were beaten up by police in detention centers.

The harsh treatment of immigrants and inhumane conditions in detention centers are the main reasons of the detained migrants' protests on 20 September 2009. As we recounted earlier, members of *Resistanbul* organized a demonstration on 26 September to show their solidarity with the detained migrants and to generate public awareness about the issue. The mission statement of *Resistanbul*'s demonstration framed their cause as fighting against the deprivation of detainees' basic rights. It called for closing down of the detention centers and ending the deportation of migrants. During the demonstration, they expressed their claims through slogans such as "No Border, No Nation, Stop Deportation," "Nobody is illegal!" "Without a reason, no one flees," and "We are all migrants."

Activists of *Resistanbul* also tried to link their detention center protests with their main networking purpose. They were not only trying to show their solidarity with the detained migrants, but they also used this opportunity to turn their action into a cry for global justice. According to the activists, policies imposed by supranational institutions such as NATO, World Trade Organization, International Monetary Fund and World Bank are causing hunger, drought, poverty, and conflict in many parts of the world. Many people who are affected by these policies are left with no option but to escape from their home countries. The protests of immigrants are thus framed as resisting immigration policies imposed by both individual states and international institutions on a global scale. In the global arena, Turkey has become a major junction for transnational migration from Africa, Asia and the Middle East into Europe, since many European countries have increasingly been adopting stricter measures to prevent illegal migration across their borders. Furthermore, as part of Turkey's accession process, the European Union has intensified pressure on Turkey to prevent the movement of immigrants, asylum seekers and refugees into Europe. According to HCA (2007), "as a result of Turkey's efforts to limit irregular migration flows, thousands of foreign nationals without travel documents, refugees among them, are detained while attempting to enter or exit the country illegally."

According to della Porta et al. (2006: 147) "the movement for globalization from below is faced with the eternal strategic dilemma between disruptive action, which is good for grabbing media attention but risks stigmatization by public opinion, and more conventional forms of action, which enhance legitimization but lower visibility and the capability of mobilizing activists." Consistent with this observation, *Resistanbul*'s peaceful demonstrations in support of the immigrants in Kumkapi detention center failed to attract the mass media's attention. It was covered as news only in *Birgün*, a left-wing newspaper and on *Bianet.org*, an alternative news website that aims at promoting co-operation among the local media and establishing a new channel for alternative journalism. For the rest of the media, peaceful protests against the "guesthouses" turned out to be an issue that hardly makes the news. This brings us to the difficulty of carrying the message from micro to mass media.

Passage from micro to mass media

Ranging from pacifist and good-humored to defensive and aggressive, from high-tech and global to low-tech and localized, a number of creative tactics have successfully been employed by members of *Resistanbul* in their campaigns: Internet-diffused calls for action for global protests, street reclaiming, and civil disobedience actions. In many of their demonstrations they tried to create a carnival atmosphere with samba marching bands.

Towards the later phases of the anti-IMF and WB protests, however, the action repertoire of *Resistanbul* activists also incorporated more aggressive tactics. Many activists attempted to break through police barriers to physically shut down official meetings of the IMF and the WB. Furthermore, Black Bloc, suddenly cutting into a *Resistanbul* cortege, started to throw stones at the windows of commercial banks and tossed Molotov cocktails at the police. Although Black Bloc was not a formal part of *Resistanbul*, in subsequent mass media reports its actions were attributed to all anti IMF and WB protesters.

In order to understand the portrayal of the anti-globalization protests and the protesters in the mass media, we collected news items from the period 6–8 October 2009 from eight mainstream Turkish newspapers.[1] This produced a data set of 69 news stories. While only five of these stories employed more balanced language, 64 of them portrayed protesters as violent actors and "criminals." In the dominant media discourse the protests were generally framed as a major law-and-order case and a threat to the nation's security. Our observations concur with what other researchers (Bennett, 2003b; della Porta et al., 2006) point out: that traditional mass media coverage of transnational activism tends to focus more on law and order problems than on the substantive proposals of activists, and "the passage from micro to mass media is problematic" (della Porta et al., 2006: 117).

Conclusion

As we write these words in February 2010, *Resistanbul* still existed but only as a virtual network. After the anti-globalization demonstrations in October were over, it has not been able to produce any other transnational or local collective action. According to a member of the movement who wants to remain anonymous, *Resistanbul* has not been dissolved but is in a passive phase awaiting for further opportunities to attack the enemy.[2] Whether or not that is going to happen is hard to tell, but our observations on *Resistanbul*, its members, organization, website, and activities point toward the fact that, with its strengths and vulnerabilities, it belongs to a class of phenomena that many researchers have been referring to as the new transnational activism.

As in other instances of this new type of transnational activism, *Resistanbul* heavily depended on CMC technologies, especially the Internet. The use of the Internet has affected the whole course of the protests that *Resistanbul* organized in terms of their size, multitude, and spontaneity. That, however, does not mean that it is only the technology of communication which determined the nature and success of the movement. The Internet is certainly a powerful tool of connection, mobilization, and information dissemination. Nevertheless, we believe that many of the features of new transnational activism result from changes in their social and political contexts rather than from technological innovations.

Despite the various advantages that the new media provided, *Resistanbul* still needed to combine online mobilization with face-to-face mass activism in order to be effective in achieving its goals. For that purpose it needed the mass media to get public support and visibility, without which it cannot create the commitment necessary to sustain itself and increase its political capacity. That's why the members of *Resistanbul* responded to various local issues, including the immigrants' protests in Kumkapi, through which they believed they could get mass media attention. Although our analysis of *Resistanbul*'s Kumkapi campaign shows that the passage from micro to mass media can be quite problematic, it still provides important clues about the potential of new transnational social activism for successfully connecting local and global issues.

Notes

1. The circulation of these eight newspapers (*Hürriyet, Milliyet, Zaman, Aksam, Radikal, Sabah, Referans, Habertürk*) comprised 61 percent of total newspaper circulation in Turkey in October 2009.
2. Personal communication, January 8, 2010.

CHAPTER EIGHTEEN

Political Protest and the Persian Blogosphere

The Iranian Election

NAZANIN GHANAVIZI

"Technology never brings true reform; only people do."

(ANTONY LOEWENSTEIN, 2008: 58)

On 15 June 2009, more than four million people took Tehran's streets in protest against the result of the presidential election on 12 June. This was the biggest demonstration since the 1979 Islamic revolution. Given the tight controls of the Iranian public sphere by the Islamic state, it is crucial to examine the facilities that Iranians deployed to rise up against their social and political status. In the last five years, the online sphere, and blogging in particular, has become important to Iranians as a space in which self-expression occurs, thereby linking the Internet with democratic politics and the privileges of democratic speech and inclusion. In this respect it is interesting to examine the ways in which the Internet has contributed to a public space as a forum for more democratic deliberation in comparison with what is possible in the Iranian physical sphere. Certainly, if a government makes space for its people to access a range of media through which to discuss and communicate their interests, this can also support more democratic political forms. But democracy is only achievable when a people know their rights and have sufficient capacity to understand and debate their common needs and interests. The specific history and shape of the Internet in Iran provide an example through which we can consider the association between blogs, free speech and protest and the new salience of the Internet in relation to public reasoning and social protest.

In this chapter, I examine the role of new media in improving public reasoning in countries where people have limited opportunities for publicly sharing and publishing their socio-political views. While there are discussions surrounding the idea of the Internet as a public sphere (Bohman, 2004), I argue that at least for a country like Iran, the Internet and blogging in particular have contributed greatly to the formation of public opinion. In order to develop this argument, I address the case of the Iranian presidential election because it amply demonstrates the ways Iranians behaved and stood up for their civil rights. While there is much debate about the democratic credentials of the Internet, the case of Iran underlies the fact that the democratic credentials are highly context dependant.

Due to the suppression of free speech in Iran and the tight state control of the press and other broadcast media industries over the last three decades, in recent years blogging has provided Iranians with a unique chance to express themselves. Although one of the crucial issues in "Internet Studies" is consideration of the limitations of Internet access and the skills needed for both Internet use and blogging, in the Iranian case these limitations are slight compared to the tight control of other forms of media in relation to the articulation of individual and community interests.

Media and Internet in Iran

The media, in particular the press, are an integral piece of unfolding modernity tied to concepts like "the public sphere" and "freedom of speech." Despite Iran's image and even its declared allegiances at different times in its history, the media have played an important modernizing role. Well aware of the importance of the role of media in Iran since the Constitutional Revolution in 1905 and into the present day, from its inception the Islamic government of Iran took steps to implement control over all forms of media from the beginning of its ascendancy. During the first years of the reformist Mohammad Khatami's presidency, there was an opening up of avenues for expression. and the media and the press in particular flourished as restrictions on expression of diverse ideas eased.

After experiencing many forms of suppression and even direct attacks on all forms of the press, including bookshops and the editorial offices of some magazines, Iranians welcomed a new freedom for the press and the perceived luxury of writers and intellectuals being able to freely express their views and ideas. Because the Islamic Republic of Iran Broadcasting (IRIB), responsible for the management of radio and television, has always been directed and controlled by the conservatives, the people who really needed media that could function as a platform for their voices, and who responded most enthusiastically to the new press, were the reformists. Even though the IRIB filled its television networks with new Hollywood movies and European football matches, the people preferred to rely on the press, deeming it to be a form of media less controlled and censored by conservatives (Keddie & Richard, 2003: 269).

The conservatives' complete control of the IRIB is a key issue in the ongoing power struggles for representation in Iran. It has resulted in the people failing to trust the state broadcasting system, preferring instead to access news from other sources. Alternative sources have always been sought by Iranians, from the first indications of censorship. During the first two decades of the Islamic Revolution, when access to the Internet was not available, many citizens preferred to get their news from foreign radio stations like BBC or Radio Israel and satellite television networks. Given that there are no other countries where a large proportion of the population speaks Persian, access to alternative media in Iran is very limited. The rise in the number of Persian satellite television networks to 37 at the time of writing provides a compelling example of popular distrust of state broadcasting that, in turn, produces an audience for alternative television (Alikhah, 2008: 109).

An augmenting wave of shutdowns and the censorship imposed by the conservatives on the reformist media increased again after the sixth parliamentary election in 2000. The conservatives banned the activities of the Iranian news agencies and imprisoned some reformist leaders. As Rahimi stresses, it seems that "the conservatives were determined to block the reformist attempts to challenge the establishment via the mass media" (Rahimi, 2008: 45).

While the origins of Iranian Internet access date back to 1987, the explosion of Internet use follows the official emergence of an internal data network in 1993, linked to the Telecommunication Company of Iran (TCI). Although the first public access in Iran, as in other countries, belonged to an academic space in 1993, the Internet was by this time deemed to be a strategic development for the country as a whole. Thus, unlike many other electronic devices, such as video players and satellite television networks, the Internet was generally received as of possible use to the state and thus acceptable to Islamic Iran.

ISPs opened for business in Iran in 1994, establishing organized systems for providing Internet connections. After just one decade, in its March 2004 report, TCI claimed that there were 648 active ISPs serving five million Internet users in 331 cities in Iran (TCI Annual Report, 2003).[1] The Internet access that ISPs were offering was appreciated by almost all sectors of society but in different ways. Business people, students, academics, intellectuals, and everyday people soon started to include the Internet in their daily lives. One of the most dramatic and visible signs of this inclusion was the integration of computer skills into widespread systems already in place for learning English. The high speed of the Internet in Iran at the time of its inception, together with its low price, were key factors underpinning its popularity. Interestingly, blogging in Iran became very popular in 2004, the year that many scholars call "the year of blogs" throughout the world (Bruns & Jacobs, 2006; Driscoll, 2008). The number of Internet users in Iran grew at an extraordinary pace at an average annual rate of approximately 48 percent, increasing from under one million Internet users in 2005 to around 23 million in 2008.[2]

Crucial factors affecting Iranians' appreciation of these new technologies are the nation's fairly high rate of literacy—77 percent—and high education levels. As university students, members of Iran's youth population are provided with Internet access and personal email addresses at their universities. Free participation in online chat rooms in university computer labs proved a strong starting point for the rise in the number of computer-literate, educated young people. This particular demographic is also often unemployed, due to economic problems that include US sanctions and Iran's limited political and economic relationships with developed countries. During the Internet boom period in Iran, increasingly educated and computer-literate young people with a lot of free time on their hands sought platforms for expression of their ideas, not the least of which was growing criticism of the social and political as well as economic failures of the Iranian government. Another crucial point contributing to escalating Internet use in Iran, one which also results from the higher education rate, is the fact that many Iranian university students who were not originally from the big cities return to their home towns after finishing their education (Rahimi, 2008: 41). Most of these graduates, who become accustomed to using the Internet during their student days, attempt to remain connected to the Internet. In addition, they introduce the people of their communities to possibilities that the Internet offers.

As has been observed in many other countries, the Internet has provided Iranians with an opportunity to express their political views free from many of the restrictions which affect them in "real" or offline life. Iranian people around the world participate in this virtual public space in order to find a broader scope and audience for expression of their ideas. Given that public conflict and even debate between the reformists and conservatives has always been suppressed by the Islamic state (and before the Islamic state), the relative difficulty in censoring the Internet continues to add immense value and opportunity to the political lives of everyday Iranians.

The first groups of Iranians to participate in such online debate were journalists and writers, who started writing about issues that they could not discuss in other public media or even often at private gatherings. Pro-reformist journalists like Akbar Ganji and Omid Memarian were among the first writers to join the Iranian blogosphere in 2002, while they were still working in more traditional media industries within Iran. While this does not mean they were never censored, even censorship was not wholly a limitation on this form of publishing.

It is crucial at this point to acknowledge the extent of existing Internet Studies literature on cyber democracy. Many scholars (Sunstein, 2007) have debated whether virtual public space can be understood as providing, at least potentially if not innately, grounds for democratic participation. Barry Hague and Brian Loader (1999: 38) argue that ICTs have clear potential to positively impact on democratic practice in a society that already has the "seeds of strong democracy."

Hacker and Todino (1996: 79) discuss the possibility that extending "the boundaries of political debate" to "the disempowered" can make "enfranchisement into the system of political discourse easier, make political discourse more rational and informative, and bring citizens closer to interaction with centers of power." While it is certainly possible to effectively meet such a goal through arenas for debate in the offline world, the blogosphere offers particular potential for such empowerment. Bruns discusses the potential of blogs for the participatory production of ideas in online discussions. He states:

> The production of ideas takes place in a collaborative, participatory environment which breaks down the boundaries between producers and consumers and instead enables all participants to be users as well as producers of information and knowledge—frequently in an inherently and inextricably hybrid role where usage is necessarily also productive: participants are producers. (Bruns, 2007:101)

Since one of the main focuses of this chapter is the important role of online media in offering Iranians a chance at inclusive decision-making regarding their own social and political futures, it is crucial to stress the question of accessibility raised by many critiques of the concept of the Internet as an example of a public sphere. Here I rely on Mitzi Waltz's specific comparison of the Internet with traditional media in terms of accessibility. She argues that even traditional media have never been accessible to everyone and do not offer total inclusion:

> Those mass-media products traditionally seen as influential opinion leaders and sites of public debate–primarily newspapers of record such as the *New York Times* and major broadcast news operations like the BBC–have historically been much less accessible to the majority of the world's population than the Internet is today. Until recently, they were usually available only to those who were geographically located in specific areas. (Waltz, 2005: 89)

Before further exploring the significant example provided by the 2009 presidential election in Iran, it is worth looking at ideas of the public sphere and the ways in which an online sphere might improve public reasoning and the formation of a rational public. In this case it is inevitable that we consider concepts that are linked to collectivity and the political activity of citizens.

Public sphere and formation of public opinion

Many of the iconic spaces around which notions of "the public" have formed, such as the ancient Greek agora, the local church, the coffeehouse, and even the street corners that have been arenas for discussion of public affairs and society are no longer prominent venues for political debate and action. Jürgen Habermas argues that public spaces constitute an aspect of civil society by providing citizens with opportunities for the formation of critical reason which promote free speech and other democratic rights. This element of civil society is also predominantly seen as counter to hegemonic interests. Mark Poster (2006: 63) states that the Habermasian public sphere "is formed within civil society that fosters resistance to formal institutes of the state." In the modern world, classic forms of the public space have largely been replaced by different forms of space, including media, that arguably isolate citizens from each other rather than bringing them together. However, the same degree of isolation is not applicable to all modes of modern media. If television and radio diminish critical reasoning by their unidirectional dissemination of news and information, the Internet, at least in part and in potential, provides its users with spaces for interaction that may support the formation of critical reason. Although Habermas does not consider the example of the Internet, he suggests that "the symbolic structures of every lifeworld are reproduced through three processes: cultural tradition, social integration, and socialization" (Habermas, 1984: 102), and such symbolic structures can certainly be deployed to consider the relations between the Internet and the "public sphere."

Theorists like Downey and Fenton argue that the public sphere cannot be considered as a public media arena, rather it is series of overlapping spaces for the dissemination, diffusion and deliberation of information (Downey & Fenton, 2003). Mitzi Waltz (2005: 89) also argues that the Internet is such a space because it connects its users to websites and discussion groups which provide them various webs of information.

Contemporary democratic political theory has been closely engaged with the crucial question of how power is organized and disseminated across different aspects of social life. Although the public sphere—as influentially described by Habermas—never included everyone, and by itself did not determine the outcome of all political actions, it contributed to the spirit of dissent found in a healthy representative democracy. Those political theorists considered to be most democratic, including Habermas, have been cautious if not fearful of governance by the uninformed masses. Nevertheless, from "classical democrats" to "participatory democrats," almost all trajectories in contemporary democratic political theory have encouraged political participation by the public, not only because it advances political efficiency but also because it is perceived as encouraging the emergence of a well-informed and intelligent public capable of striving for the common good.

The cyber public sphere, as a plural sphere, provides its users with a broad range of publics which expose them to greater social diversity. The Internet makes moving from one public to another easy, fast, and cheap for participants, and this inclusion improves the propensity of participants to engage in discussions in different publics. It also seems to satisfy the need for multiple public spaces through which participants can engage in different publics that are convergent to their interests. It matters as well, here, that no participant in online discussion is restricted to only one interest, one community or one public and the potential to focus on different interests further encourages engagement with multiple publics. Another important factor that helps to improve engagement in cyber publics is the absence of any physical dimensions in personal interaction. In other words, while participants may not actively participate in certain offline publics due to social, political, economic and spatial restrictions, they might participate online more freely—encouraged both by the openness that anonymity allows, the degree to which social placement by appearance and demeanor is limited online, and the cheap rates for communication over spatial distance.

The Habermasian public sphere, which is based on the dialogic articulation of ideas and interests, establishes the ground for the formation of public opinion. Shared ideas form as interacting private individuals search for recognition. Richard Sennett maintains that the agonistic give and take of the public sphere is the essential tool for the formation of public opinion which results in democracy (see Sennett, 2006). I suggest that cyberspace provides its participants with more or less fair conditions for this kind of interaction. It moreover provides participants with the information they need to evaluate the validity of claims made in the course of this interaction. And it gives them the opportunity to participate anonymously, with limited fear of social or political threat. In fundamentalist societies in particular, as in the example of Iran, cyberspace provides its users with more reliable and significant means of participation in the formation of public opinion. In light of the fact that fundamentalism seeks to react against elements of the Enlightenment or "modernity," the deliberative processes and consensus formation that result in democratic decision-making represent a tool which individuals can utilize to resist fundamentalist values. In countries where the state controls almost every social act, the Internet can emerge as a sphere in which participants have important opportunities to deliberate and perhaps act in concert. The nature of democratic elements such as elections in authoritarian regimes, like those recently held in Iran, increase to an even greater extent the significance of the inclusion and deliberation that the Internet provides. It is crucial to consider that in authoritarian regimes the state's setting of eligibility rules for candidates often creates "divided structures of contestation." This means that not all politically qualified candidates are able to find ways to run for office, and even those who do run may not enjoy equal opportunities in terms of campaigning and media coverage. Kenneth Greene (2007: 5) states that,"Dramatic resource advantages allow the incumbent to outspend on campaigns, deploy legions of canvassers, and, most importantly, to supplement policy appeals with patronage goods that bias voters in their favor." In this respect, the opportunity for deliberation and inclusion facilitated by cyberspace plays a necessary role in improving public awareness. In the next section I will examine the effectiveness of some of these theoretical propositions by approaching the particulars of the Iranian 2009 election and the consequences of popular awareness and actions against its result.

Presidential election 2009

For the first time since the Islamic Revolution in 1979 more than 80 percent of Iranians participated in the presidential election on 12 June 2009. While a great number of people did not show any interest in voting in 2005, this time most people were convinced that they had to participate in an election in order to take Ahmadinejad, the incumbent, out of office. Not only were the majority of people fed up with his international strategies, they also did not trust his domestic plans. Despite his promises for economic development and social freedoms, his hardline government tightened control of such freedoms more than ever. A great number of those who did not vote in 2005 still believed that their vote would bring about no change, but the candidateship of Mir-Hossein Mousavi and Mehdi Karoubi and their reformist promises increased hope that change was possible. From the beginning of the presidential campaign, both reformist candidates started websites and blogs which evaluated all speeches and gatherings and recorded the passionate reception of the candidates' speeches in different cities. More than anything else, like President Khatami before them, both reformists promised freedom of speech and thought. This was something that Iranian society has been particularly deprived of during the presidentship of Mahmoud Ahmadinejad. The issues surrounding the use of the Internet in regard to the Iranian presidential election provide a telling example of the ways in which online discussions can improve deliberation and public reasoning. In the case of Iran, blogs started discussions over the importance of participation in the election and had a great impact upon the public participation rate. Translations of texts on political history, sociological and political theory started by Iranian students and intellectuals outside the country were one of the most useful contributions of bloggers and greatly enhanced the quality and depth of online political discussion.

The visible contribution of the two reformist candidates within an online sphere was a crucial factor in their success in receiving support from young Iranians and intellectuals. Their supporting groups on Facebook and Twitter attracted a huge number of followers, and it could be argued that this exposure also pulled them up in online polls. Soon after Mr. Mousavi appeared in a campaign wearing a green shawl, an Islamic symbol for those who are descended from the Prophet Mohammad, Mousavi's supporters chose the color green as a symbol for their support. It was no more than a few hours later that many of his supporters colored their blogs, Twitter feeds and Facebook profile pictures green. This was the origin of what came to be known as the "Green Movement," a gesture of solidarity that started online, but quickly spread to the physical sphere. From this point on, all Mousavi supporters made a green gesture, through their clothing or online expression, in order to show their support.

As I discussed earlier in this chapter, public reasoning and the formation of rational public opinion are something that requires deliberation and exchange of ideas. It is also something that, as such, cannot be achieved in a short period of time. In the case of Iran, it seems that the Internet has for some time provided Iranians with an arena for deliberation and discussion. From 2004, with the growing popularity of the Internet and the rise of blogging, Iranians started to discuss various aspects of their socio-political life. In this respect, what the world witnessed in Iran during and after the June 2009 election was the product of at least five years of active deliberation of ideas. During the presidential campaign, the number of blogs grew and Iranians started recording and discussing campaign news from both sides. The transnational nature of the online sphere meant that discussions and news of the Iranian campaigns by blogs and other online venues transcended geographical boundaries, and this inspired large number of expatriate Iranians to participate in 2009 election.

As the government realized the social impact that the daily use of the Internet provided, their attempts to control it increased. At the same time as a grass-roots blog movement was developing, the government provided a budget to start 10,000 blogs and employed members of the revolutionary guard, Basij Members, to blog daily and spread their support for conservatism and hardliners like Ahmadinejad. Basij Members were also used to monitor and report what happened in the Iranian blogosphere. During this time approximately five million websites, social networks like Facebook and blogs were filtered, and many dissident bloggers were imprisoned. However, as I will discuss later, filtering did not work effectively after the election.

After over 80 percent participation by Iranians both inside and outside Iran in the 2009 election, Ahmadinejad's declared win was a big shock to the Iranian public. Soon after the official declaration of the election result people took to the streets in protect, expressing their concern that the election has been rigged. On

Monday 15 June 2009 more than three million people were reported to have demonstrated on Tehran's streets. Iran's defeated presidential candidate, Mir-Hossein Mousavi, called for demonstrations on his website, and this request circulated throughout cyberspace at a rapid pace. Within a few minutes, with the help of Iranian link-sharing websites hosted by Iranians outside Iran, such as Balatarin.com and Gooya.com, many Iranians were made aware of the planned protests. The large number of people who showed up at demonstrations, despite the fact that there was previously no official plan to protest, was a tremendous outcome of Iranian Internet activity around the time of the election. Given that the Internet was the only media that Mousavi had access to, the circulation of the notion of a popular protest on Monday 15 June was conducted almost solely online. Once the idea of a protest was released and disseminated online, it then circulated by word of mouth and via mobile text messages.

Although the demonstration on 15 June was a silent rally, the government did not tolerate it, and Basij militias attacked people on streets and arrested a great number of protesters. The majority of international journalists were expelled from the country at the beginning of this conflict, and the rest were forced to leave in the following days. Official Iranian media did not make mention of the demonstrations and attacks by police, and even President Ahmadinejad claimed that the great number of people who came to the streets were there to celebrate his success. At this stage, something extraordinary started developing in Iran for the first time. Citizen journalism became commonplace. The efforts of Iranians at a time when no international or reformist journalist could report the events complies with Kaid and Holtz-Bacha's definition of citizen journalism as "a move toward openness of information; horizontal structure of news gathering and news telling; blurred lines between content production and use; and diffused accountability based more on reputation and meaning than on structural system hierarchies" (2008: 105). While Iranians were quite active online before the election and during the presidential campaign, it now reached a new ascendancy as it became the only reliable source for international media seeking information regarding protest activities in Iran. With the high levels of telecommunication activity in Iran, especially the large number of Iranians who own mobile phones, it was possible for citizens to document what was happening on streets. This recorded information was then broadcast online. From 16 June, all demonstrations, police and militias' behavior, and reformist leaders' declarations were recorded and distributed to the international community as vlogging (video blogging) became popular. A crucial result of this activity was that citizen documentation of events added credibility to blog discussion of what was happening in Iran in the first days after the election and provided international media with credible sources.

The circumstances surrounding the dreadful death by militia gunshot of an innocent protester named Neda during protest action on Tehran's streets on 20 June circulated around the world within an hour. Neda's shooting and subsequent death were recorded on a mobile phone video camera and quickly uploaded online. International news channels reported this in detail, and it became a major headline. After the Iranian government claimed that the video was the product of a dramatic made-up event planned by British agents, Iranian citizens put further videos online that presented the same scene from another angle, one that also showed the shooter. Further to this, another citizen filmed and uploaded the shooter's identity card after people followed and attacked him. This evidence confirmed that the shooter belonged to the revolutionary guards' post. As soon as images of the shooter's identity card went online, people recognized him, found his contact details and home address. This was a curious reversal of power relations, as it transformed the fear that the government was trying to impose on people, turning it back onto those who encouraged fear in citizens. This example demonstrates but one way that Iranian citizen journalism carried international importance in 2009. For the first time in history, Iranians outside Iran united with those still living on home soil and helped them with their demonstrations in various online forms.

Following this, the Iranian government increased Internet filtering, in the hope that this would impede news providers, both within Iran and in the wider international community, gaining access to information about events in Iran. At the same time that CNN and other major international news channels were reporting on the conflict in Iran, Iranian television was filled with foreign TV serials and movies in an effort to keep the rest of the society uninformed about the reality of what was happening on Iran's streets. However, the head of IRIB declared that the rate of official Iranian radio and television audiences decreased dramatically after the June election. This was quite evidently because people turned to online media and satellite televisions, as these media provided information that citizens could not access through domestic media.

One of the main obstructive factors to media freedom, however, has remained the sophisticated filtering employed by the Iranian government. Iran is second only to China in the amount of filtering that it imposes upon its citizens, not to mention the arrest of online dissidents. Soon after the Iranian government started blocking access to certain websites and blogs, both Iranians and non-Iranians living outside of Iran started to design proxies that were able to break through filters. One example is Psiphon, an online censorship avoidance tool designed by researchers at the University of Toronto, that gave Iranians access to sites that the Iranian government has gone to great lengths to ban—including Facebook, Iranian opposition sites and international news networks. A further example of the transnationality of recent protests is the organization of simultaneous demonstrations by Iranians and non-Iranians all around the world, planned to occur on the same days as protests inside Iran. Posters, chants and banners were exchanged online, and there was a move to create a united message worldwide. In this way, not only did the Iranian diaspora join Iranians still at home, but non-Iranians, including famous figures such as Noam Chomsky and Jürgen Habermas, as well as celebrity artists and politicians, showed their support, using the Internet to post videos and statements of support. Since YouTube and other such websites are filtered in Iran, expatriate Iranians converted such videos into other formats and posted them on their blogs and websites, so that they would be available for Iran's residents to access. In general terms, the Internet helped to blur geographical borders and as a consequence of such, varied gestures of support and unity crossed into Iran, from first aid instructions to help a wounded or shot person and information about self-defense, to socio-political analysis of the situation in the country. Another example of the transnational nature of this movement is the way in which Twitter was used by those invested in the Iranian situation during and immediately after the election. With a 140-character limit that encourages micro-blogging, Twitter was an extremely effective way for activists to post rapid-fire updates on the situation on the ground in Iran. The significance of Twitter as an important communication tool in Iran was so great that the site's founders delayed prescheduled maintenance during this time.

Conclusion

It is worth building upon the analysis undertaken in this chapter with some recent facts about the Iranian online public and the ways the state continues to attempt to suppress it. As I argued throughout this chapter the Internet has innovative potential for sustaining a critical and democratic mode of deliberation that is not limited to spatial and temporal boundaries. The example of the Iranian 2009 presidential election is a telling indicator of the Internet's potential for the circulation of critical reasoning and the provision of access to less censored resources and more reliable arguments—a facilitation that, in the Iranian case, resulted in the formation of a self-aware public that rose for its rights.

As the unrest in Iran still continues at the time of this writing, it is amazing that even in the face of repression and violence people seem to detect the possibilities for protest and dissent. The Green Movement remains strong, and both reformist candidates and their supporters have joined in support of the need for reform. No doubt the main reason for the sustained existence of a Green Movement lies in the sustenance and power of the public reasoning that first raised the need for reform. As discussed in this chapter, the Internet must be counted as the principal tool employed by the Iranian public as they improved their collective reasoning and awareness, and continues to facilitate such awareness in the present.

The effectiveness of Iranians' online activities in terms of political effects can be also understood in the light of the state's treatment of online activists. At the time of writing two of those who were arrested during protests have been executed, and nine are sentenced to death only for their participation in demonstrations after the election. The state is not only suppressing online activists, journalists, and even the family members of the activists but also targets both Iranian and non-Iranian websites hosted outside Iran for diffusing videos and news about unrest in Iran. The so-called "Iranian cyber army" hosted by the Iranian state and conducted by IT experts employed by the state has hacked both Twitter and China's most popular search engine, Baidu. This indicates that the state has shifted its view of the online sphere from being a politically neutral facility to a definite threat, if not in itself then through its provision of channels for exchange of information and critical deliberation. With only a few days left until what is predicted to be one of the biggest demonstrations against the Iranian election result, the Iranian state is threatening the public, not only by setting foot armies on the streets but more than ever by spreading fear through its attempted control of cyberspace and the wider telecommunications sphere, through control of text messages exchanged by mobile phones.

Notes

1. See Middle East Internet Users, http://www.Internetworldstats.com/stats5.htm#me, and Telecommunication Company of Iran, "TCI at a Glance," http://www.tci.ir/eng.asp?sm=0&page=18&code=1 (accessed 16 June 2008)
2. Internet world Stats available at: http://www.internetworldstats.com/stats.htm

CHAPTER NINETEEN

The Global Human Rights Regime and the Internet

Non-Democratic States and the Hypervisibility of Evidence of Oppression

JAMES STANYER AND SCOTT DAVIDSON

Human rights abuses have never been so visible. Whereas once repressive acts in distant places were exposed to a mass audience intermittently or not at all, now such material is routinely posted online, made visible to a global audience of Internet users. What is emerging, this chapter suggests, is a new interconnected online space where a wide range of activists, media and civil society organizations, continually uncover, raise awareness and campaign for action on human rights abuses. It is a space that is importantly underpinned by codified global human rights norms. The interconnected websites and blogs form a permanent record of transgressions of these norms that can be easily accessed by an international audience that takes transgressions seriously. The evidence presented on these sites serves as the basis for campaigns to pressurize liberal democratic states and IGOs, such as the United Nations, to take action. The clusters of blogs and websites play a critical role in the emergence of what has been described as global human rights regime but a role that has not so far been fully documented (Brysk, 2002).

This chapter examines the emergence of a global human rights surveillance network, one that monitors, gathers and publicizes human rights abuses online. It starts by contextualizing the online sphere in relation to the rise of codified human rights norms, before elaborating on the monitoring, gathering and publicizing of human rights abuses. The chapter draws on empirical research by the authors that maps the clusters of human rights blogs and websites in relation to two non-democratic states, Burma and Zimbabwe (see Stanyer & Davidson, 2009). It aims to reveal the different advocates in these clusters, the type of evidence that is disclosed on their blogs and websites, and the interconnections between these blogs and websites.

The emergence of the global human rights regime

The emergence of the global human rights regime starts with the Universal Declaration of Human Rights in 1948 (Brysk, 2002; Sikkink, 2002). Before the Second World War only states had rights under international law, after the Universal Declaration rights were extended to individuals for the first time (Ignatieff, 2001). In the intervening years human rights have found their way into international treaties, declarations, programs of action, and are embodied in institutions such as the United Nations (UN), and have trickled down into the legal structure of most states (Khagram et al., 2002). Schaffer and Smith observe that there have been sixty human rights treaties, declarations and conventions in the postwar period (2004). The postwar spread of human rights has been given a further boost by the end of the Cold War and the subsequent process of democratization (Keck & Sikkink, 1998). Today human rights have become "settled norms," principles that are widely accepted as authoritative and could be said to have reached a consensual status at least amongst democratic states (Frost, cited in Donnelly, 2003: 23). Human rights norms provide a moral framework in which most states are bound and if not they need to pay attention (for a synoptic account of human rights norms, see Risse & Sikkink, 1999).

This normative regime is underpinned by sanctions of various kinds. These range from international sanctions to indictments by international criminal tribunals. International interventions on human rights grounds have gained precedent in recent years (Ignatieff, 2001). Liberal democratic states and other actors respond to violations because they are an affront to their values and policies and because they feel "a compassion for the fate and well being for unknown distant others" (de Oliveira and Tandon, cited in Schechter, 1999). This potential for action of various kinds underlies and reinforces the normative moral framework of human rights.

In the context of this chapter we want to suggest that a key aspect of the human rights regime involves a systematic monitoring and publicizing of transgressions of these norms and calls for action by a range of well-resourced rights NGOs, news media, and host of other groups and actors. It is hard to imagine that until the 1960s there were no systematic procedures for monitoring and publicizing human rights violations (Clark, 2001). Since then there has been a revolution in monitoring and disclosure led by western-based NGOs and it is this we want to turn to next.

The global human rights regime:
Monitoring and disclosure of violations

We live in a world of increased systematic monitoring of adherence to and publicizing of transgressions of human rights norms. International NGOs have been at the forefront of this process. Their numbers have grown, one estimate suggests that globally there are now 295 registered human rights NGOs, half forming after 1979 (Ron et al., 2005). Such groups are not the only actors involved. There are a growing number of actors who investigate and verify claims, compile annual surveys and reports and publicize transgressions. International human rights NGOs have been joined by inter-governmental organizations (IGOs). The office of the UN Commissioner for Human Rights, for example, now regularly monitors and reports on the activities of oppressive states (Ignatieff, 2001). In addition, there are indigenous social movements, NGOs, churches, academic experts, trade unions, and sometimes Western governmental actors (see Keck & Sikkink, 1998). Many of these groups have worked with international NGOs to investigate norm transgressions and alert Western governments to them (see Keck & Sikkink, 1998). In addition, news media outlets in developed liberal democratic states have been keen to disclose information on certain abuses to their audiences (Ovsiovitch, 1993). Large highprofile news outlets, such as the BBC, embark on their own investigations. Journalists are sent undercover to report on events in certain non-democratic states. Indigenous and regional media have also played a similar role. Sonwalker and Allen observe, in the context of India, that national media exposure of human rights abuses by the army brought pressure to bear on the Indian government to change existing laws (2007).

We can identify several systematic processes at work in the global human rights regime which have so far been alluded to. First, the monitoring and gathering of evidence. This well-established process has often used trained monitors or has relied on the testimony of victims or witnesses. The victim's or witness's story is now as much apart of this evidence presented by reports or in news bulletins. The use of testimonial evidence pioneered by rights NGOs is now widespread (Schaffer & Smith, 2004). In addition, there is a range of technological developments, such as cameras and recording devices, which allow the easier recording of transgressions (Weyker, 2002). Photographs and video footage of events often complement witness testimony, although they are sometimes used as evidence in their own right.

Second, after monitoring and gathering, the evidence is then disclosed to audiences. Importantly, disclosure is taken to mean the revealing of evidence of human rights abuses to an international audience, namely, one that resides in liberal democratic states and one that is aware of human rights norms. The act disclosure therefore involves a *cross border* publicizing of various forms of evidence and involves campaigning activities (see Keck & Sikkink, 1998).

The motive behind the publicizing of transgressions of international human rights norms is to force a response from the wider international community. As Weyker observes, "participants in movements try to influence those in power by tapping into the potential power of bystander reference groups in other countries (2002: 116–7). As noted, the global human rights regime is underpinned by sanctions of various kinds. The point is not to get into when and why bystanders may or may not respond but simply to suggest that there is pressure from a range of actors for some kind of robust response by states and IGOs even if considered second best by some. This pressure is direct but also emerges from a general outrage amongst publics in western democracies when confronted with the evidence of transgressions. With the disclosure of human rights abuses, elite and mass audiences not only learn that something has happened or is happening, but they also learn about something happening which they disapprove, which transgresses laws and norms which they hold as important. Revelations exist, therefore, in tandem with an opprobrious discourse in which a range of actors report, publicize and criticize human rights abuses. It should be noted that acts by violators to cover up the first transgression as a direct response to international publicity, may lead to a second-order transgression of norms and provoke further disapproval, shock or outrage.

The Internet and the global human rights regime

There is little sense in the wider literature of what role the World Wide Web plays in the bigger global human rights regime. All the actors and organizations identified earlier in this chapter have a presence on the World Wide Web. Together these websites play a crucial role in the monitoring, documenting and publicizing of evidence of human rights abuses and in the carrying of reaction. The thousands of websites and blogs present a large amount of evidence of abuse, including witness testimony, film, photographs, audio reports or second-hand reports or allegations (see Block, 2001). Often the information and imagery are combined in written reports/documents. This material is highly accessible and easily searchable. Websites such as hurisearch.org, a human rights search engine, allow detailed searches of an estimated 5000 websites. The nature of the web creates other opportunities for publicity. Evidence can be connected by so-called hyperlinks (Van Aelst & Walgrave, 2004). These are contained in posts made on different blogs and websites and through prominently displayed lists of hyperlinks to other blogs and websites. Websites can connect to other websites and blogs containing evidence leading visitors towards particular evidence. At the same time the number of websites and blogs is increasing. The rapid spread of the Internet means that nearly anyone, whether dissidents in an authoritarian state or NGOs and campaigners outside, as long as they have the ability to connect to the web can set up a site of their own, and connect to each other. Further, in the last five years the emergence and widespread availability of specialist easy-to-use software have meant that publicizing abuses no longer requires the production of a website. What has emerged online is a series of interconnected blogs and websites documenting and continually publicizing evidence of particular human rights atrocities.

The online visibility of repression in non-democratic states

One focus of the dense networks of human rights actors that cross the globe are human rights transgressions by non-democratic states. Giddens observes that in the contemporary world authoritarian states can no longer hide from the gaze of the global community (2000). Some authors have noted that the proliferation of the web especially in higher-tolerance authoritarian regimes, has presented new avenues for internal opponents to express their views on such contraventions and expose state activities (see Kalathil & Boas, 2003). Kalathil and Boas note that the Falun Gong movement in China and the opposition groups in Burma have used the websites to publicize regime's actions to an international audience (2003). The activities of non-democratic states are continually scrutinized, and their abuses made visible online. Audiences in western democracies are reminded of a state's actions and reputation and of the need to take action which will lead to change in behaviour. Keck and Sikkink are right to suggest that non-democratic states immune to internal pressures from their own citizens are vulnerable to external pressure triggered by exposure (1998). The online network of websites and blogs form an elaborate store of information and imagery which render an oppressive regime's activity almost permanently visible to an international audience. For the first time the actions of some of the world's most oppressive states are subject to a permanent surveillance. The next section looks at this in more detail, mapping the networks that emerge and documenting their content.

Researching networks that seek to pressure authoritarian regimes

This section focuses on the visibility of human rights transgressions by two non-democratic states, Burma (Myanmar) and Zimbabwe. Burma and Zimbabwe are both governed by what can be clearly described as oppressive regimes. Both countries feature in Freedom House's *The Worst of the Worst: the Worlds Most Repressive Societies 2008*. In the 2008 report both attained an overall status of "not free" and the worst possible scores for political rights and civil liberties. In addition, according to the voice and accountability index of World Bank's *Worldwide Governance Indicators* report, which ranks all countries according to the extent they allow their citizens to voice their opinions and select a government, Burma and Zimbabwe came at the bottom; Burma was in fact bottom with a score of 0 (see Kaufmann et al., 2007).

This section elucidates the structure of the networks of human rights actors that document abuses in both countries, using network visualization software, and examines the types of evidence of rights transgressions that are made public on websites (see Rogers, 2008).

Findings

In Figures 1 and 2, a node's size is an indication of the relative distribution of a site's status or recognition within the network. The cluster diagrams show that the websites belonging to *Amnesty International, Human Rights Watch, the International Labor Organization, International Confederation of Free Trade Unions*, the *VOA, CNN* and the *BBC* were present on both networks although their centrality to each varied. Figure 1, the cluster diagram produced by the analysis of sites concerned with

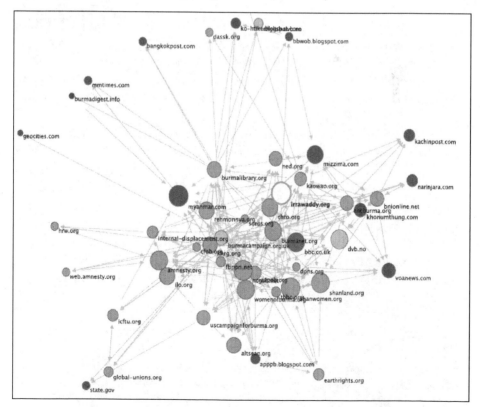

Figure 1: Cluster map of Burma blogs and websites, crawled 17 March 2008

Burma in March 2008, shows closer connections between regional websites and the international NGOs. In the left-central area of the main cluster are sites associated with international labor rights and laws such as the *International Labor Organization* (ILO), *International Confederation of Free Trade Unions* (ICFTU) and global-unions.org.

Within the well-defined central cluster are regional media such as *Irrawaddy* and *Mizzima* News. Regional NGOs, including those that promote the rights and claims of ethnic groups within Burma's borders, such as Shanland.org, also have a clear presence within this cluster. There is also the *Burma Library* website which provides considerable reference resources on most aspects of the historical and political situation in Burma.

The cluster map for Zimbabwe, Figure 2, shows a different pattern, with two major clusters visible. The top and left hand side of the map shows a cluster of IGOs. These include *UNICEF, UNDP, WTO, World Bank*, and *World Health Organization*. Below and to the left of this cluster there is a looser cluster of international human rights NGOs. These include the sites of *Front Line Defenders, Redress* and the *International Committee of Jurists*. The international NGOs are linked to other clusters through the shared hub of *Irinnews*. This is the website of the UN Office for the Coordination of Humanitarian Affairs—its remit is to supply news for the "humanitarian community." *IRIN News* also takes a number of links from Zimbabwean NGOs and blogs. Also connecting the international NGO cluster to other clusters are the site of the *Media Institute of Southern Africa* and the African news portal site of *AllAfrica.com*.

The second major cluster towards the centre and bottom of the map is dominated by a number of indigenous Zimbabwean and Southern African websites. This cluster consists of the websites of some of the main Zimbabwean newspapers and a mixture of regional and indigenous NGOs, pro-democracy and human rights groups and the occasional independent blog. A key point is the separation of the regional network and the international network of NGOs, not seen in the case of Burma. *SW Radio Africa* clearly holds a strong position within this second cluster. It is an independent radio station broadcasting on short wave. It received over 600 links from the analyzed sample but was also linked itself to other regional and indigenous NGOs, blogs and news sites, suggesting a good level of credibility and connectedness.

Also important in this discernible regional cluster is *Sokwanele*, this describes itself as a peoples' movement, embracing supporters of all pro-democratic political parties, civic organizations and institutions in Zimbabwe. The site includes the *This Is Zimbabwe* blog. Alongside is the *Kubatana Trust*—which aims to strengthen the use of email and Internet strategies in Zimbabwean NGOs—this is an important regional hub for NGOs, civil society groups and independent bloggers. Overall,

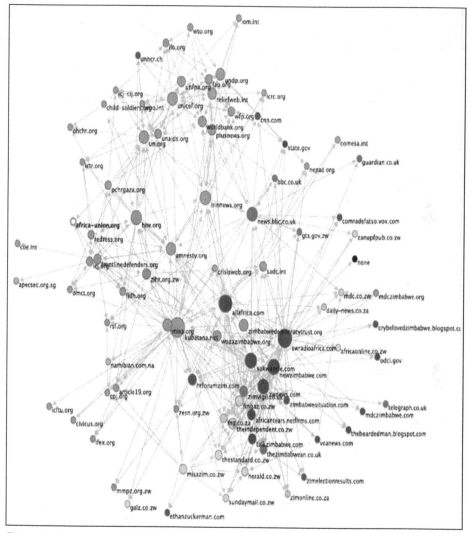

Figure 2: Cluster map of Zimbabwe blogs and websites, crawled 3 April 2008

Figure 2 suggests a strong regional dimension in the cluster concerned with the situation in Zimbabwe.

In sum, there are clearly similarities and differences between the online clusters. In terms of the patterns of interconnection, both clusters exhibited a scale-free pattern, with hub and periphery websites and blogs. Both online networks tend to be dominated by indigenous and regionally based/focused actors, especially indigenous and regionally based/focused news organizations and NGOs. Often these included main opponents to the regime. A range of international NGOs and IGOs were involved in documenting transgressions in both countries, but only four such groups appeared on both networks (*Amnesty International, Human Rights Watch, International Labor Organization*, and the *International Confederation of Free Trade Unions*). That said, there were some differences. In the case of Burma, the network was characterized by a single central hub of international and local/regional media and NGO websites. In the case of Zimbabwe, the chart showed there were two clusters: one mainly comprised of international NGOs and IGOs and a second formed of locally and regionally based and focused NGOs and news media. The significance of this difference might point to the importance of local and regional NGOs and media in the struggle against the Mugabe regime (see Lindgren, 2004).

The location of evidence

The study also examined a mixture of nearly 70 websites and blogs that were found in the key clusters generated above. The analysis sought to understand more about the type of evidence posted on each website and blog and the subject matter of each reported transgression.

Tables 1 and 2 show that, in both Burma and Zimbabwe, the websites of indigenous NGOs and international NGOs/ IGOs and those of locally/regionally based and focused news media outlets provided most evidence of regime oppression—these sites accounted for over 70 percent of all documented evidence of transgressions in respect to Burma and 83 percent for Zimbabwe. Many of the hubs of the networks identified above were evidence-rich websites. Those blogs by individual political actors, NGOs and journalists provided very little evidence of regime norm transgression.

Table 1: The number of pieces of evidence relating to Burma on blogs and websites by actor type

		Frequency	Percent
Type of actor	NGO/IGO website	147	40.7
	Local/ regional media website	110	30.5
	Opposition group website	41	11.4
	Individual political actors blogs	29	8.0
	Western Media website	22	6.1
	Media actor blogs	9	2.5
	NGO blogs	3	.8
	Total	361	100.0

Table 2: The number of pieces of evidence relating to Zimbabwe on blogs and websites by actor type

		Frequency	Percent
Valid	Local/ regional media website	130	47.3
	NGO/IGO website	99	36.0
	Individual political actors blogs	25	9.1
	Western Media website	16	5.8
	NGO blogs	5	1.8
	Total	275	100.0

Types of evidence publicized

Tables 3 and 4 identify different ways in which evidence featured on blogs and web-sites. On Burma and Zimbabwe, evidence was most commonly presented in the form of a report. Although reports varied in length, they often contained a mix of evidence types. Reports largely by NGO/IGO and media outlets accounted for 45 percent of all evidence of abuses in Burma and 50 percent in relation to Zimbabwe (see Tables 3 and 4).

The research was also interested in determining the presence of different types of stand-alone evidence. Tables 3 and 4 show that in websites and blogs on Burma there were 36 instances of witness testimony being used, and 26 in Zimbabwe. However, while witness testimony was the most frequently documented piece of stand-alone piece of evidence, when examining the websites there was a striking use of audiovisual material. Indeed, when combined, photographs, audio material and film footage were present more frequently than witness testimony.

Often where sites and blogs did not post evidence of regime abuses they either linked to evidence provided elsewhere or tended to copy it through a simple cut-and-paste. In terms of links to reports, there were a total of 37 links to NGO commissioned reports on Burma and 19 in relation to Zimbabwe. The cut-and-paste news reports, partial or in their entirety, were more frequent. In websites and blogs on Burma there were 69 examples of cut-and-paste and 58 in sites on Zimbabwe.

The issues

The study was also interested in ascertaining the nature of the reported human rights abuses committed by each state (see Tables 5 to 6). In the blogs and websites

Count

Table 3: The type of evidence of regime oppression in Burma, documented on blogs and websites by actor type (figures show the number of pieces of evidence)

		Type of evidence					
		Witness testimony only	Photos	Audio	Reports (written)	Evidence in press release form	Film	Total
Type of site	NGO/IGO website	8	14	1	52	21	18	114 (45%)
	Local/ regional media website	17	11	0	45	0	6	79 (31%)
	Western Media website	4	3	0	9	0	5	21 (8%)
	Opposition group website	2	0	0	7	3	6	18 (7%)
	Individual political actors blogs	4	6	0	2	1	4	17 (6.5%)
	Media actor blogs	0	1	0	1	1	2	5 (2%)
	NGO blogs	1	0	0	0	0	0	1 (0.5%)
Total		36 (14%)	35 (14%)	1 (0.5%)	116 (45.5%)	26 (10%)	41 (16%)	255

Count

Table 4: The type of evidence of regime oppression in Zimbabwe documented on blogs and websites by actor type (figures show the number of pieces of evidence)

		Type of evidence					
		Witness testimony only	Photos	Audio	Reports (written)	Evidence in press release form	Film	Total
Type of site	Local/ regional media website	8	7	4	66	0	1	86 (43.5%)
	NGO/IGO website	1	7	10	32	30	2	82 (41.5%)
	Western Media website	12	0	0	0	0	4	16 (8%)
	Individual political actors blogs	4	3	1	1	0	2	11 (5.5%)
	NGO blogs	1	1	0	0	0	1	3 (1.5%)
Total		26 (13%)	18 (9%)	15(7.5%)	99(50%)	30(15%)	10(5%)	198

examined, evidence of human rights abuses was greater than other kinds of oppression—accounting for 61 percent of all evidence in the case of Burma and 55 percent for Zimbabwe. Tables 5 and 6 show the majority evidence posted on human rights abuses in both countries focused on a similar range of abuses: torture/intimidation of opponents, internal displacement, and the incarceration of political opponents.

Table 5: The type of human rights abuse by the regime in Burma exposed on blogs and websites (figures show number of pieces of evidence)

		Frequency	% of all
Issue	Intimidation/detention/disappearance/ torture of opponents	56	15.5
	Displacement (refugees)	40	11.08
	Political incarceration	37	10.2
	Persecution of ethnic minorities and / or religious minorities	31	8.6
	Forced labour/ child labour	22	6.09
	Restrictions of media freedom/ free speech	14	3.9
	Child soldiers	9	2.5
	Persecution of citizens (general)	6	1.7
	Rape and violence against women	4	1.1
	Other human rights violation	1	.3
	Total	220	61.0

In sum, what seems to stand out is the centrality of regional NGOs and indigenous and regionally based and focused news organizations in exposing state human rights abuses. These organizations focus almost entirely on the actions of the governments in question and contain a large amount of evidence. This evidence is mostly in the form of reports, but stand-alone forms of evidence such as witness testimony and audio visual are also present. In fact these websites act as so-called hub sites. The other blogs and websites connect to them, publicizing the presence of evidence or recycling it through cut-and-paste.

Table 6: The type of human rights abuse by the regime in Zimbabwe exposed on blogs and websites (figures show number of pieces of evidence)

		Frequency	% of all
Issue	Intimidation/detention/disappearance/ torture of opponents	69	25.0
	Displacement (refugees)	18	6.52
	Political incarceration	17	6.2
	Restrictions of media freedom/ free speech	16	5.8
	Restrictions on Freedom of Assembly	11	3.99
	Persecution of citizens (general)	9	3.26
	Rape and violence against women	8	2.90
	Other human rights violation	2	.72
	Persecution of ethnic minorities and / or religious minorities	1	.36
	Total	151	54.8

Transnational monitoring and action on human rights

It is clearly possible to view the interconnected websites and blogs that centre themselves on the human rights situations in non-democratic states such as Burma and Zimbabwe as virtual clusters that engage in the documentation and exposure of the activities of oppressive states. At the centre of such clusters are relatively well-resourced hub websites. In our research these belonged to regional NGOs and indigenous and regionally based and focused news organizations, although in other instances they may well belong to western NGOs or media outlets who are equally highly motivated to expose transgressions of human rights norms. These hub sites regularly gather and publicize evidence of atrocities, often linking to other sites. They present a wide variety of primary evidence ranging from, at one extreme, highly credible material to less credible evidence. On the periphery of the clusters are individual blogs and websites of organizations perhaps not solely concerned or focused on these specific countries. The analysis showed that there are discernible groups of websites and blogs that echo and amplify information and images found on those hub sites, sometimes adding their own comments and reactions. These sites help further publicize the events that occur, carrying reactions and condemnations. Together, the cluster of websites and blogs form both an elaborate store of information and imagery and a means of publicizing it. These sites have proved popular. Tables 7 and 8 show the top 10 most popular websites which specifically focused on Burma and Zimbabwe. Table 7 shows, in the case of Burma, that six out of the top 10 most visited sites were indigenous/regionally based/focused news media websites, including the four most popular. Table 8 shows that in Zimbabwe, indigenous/regionally based/focused news media websites accounted for nine of the top 10 sites, including the five most popular.

Table 7: The top 10 Burma-focused websites by total monthly visitors 20 May–20 June 2008

		Total visits over 1 month
Web sites	Irrawaddy.org	357,700
	Mizzima.com	130,300
	Myanmar.com	127,700
	Narinjara.com	75,500
	UScampaign forburma.org	50,500
	Burmalibrary.org	47,600
	Burmadigest.info	28,400
	Burmacampaign.org.uk	23,300
	Foundationburma.org	21,200
	Burmanet.org	13,800
	Source: Trafficestimate.com	

Table 8: The top 10 Zimbabwe-focused websites by total monthly visitors 20 May–20 June 2008

		Total visits over 1 month
Web site	Newzimbabwe.com	341,300
	Zimbabwesituation.com	222,300
	Zimonline.co.za	140,200
	Zwnews.com	122,800
	Swradioafrica.com	114,400
	Sokwanele.com	109,700
	theZimbabwean.co.uk	104,200
	Talkzimbabwe.com	95,400
	Sundaymail.co.zw	80,300
	Thestandard.co.zw	43,600
	Source: Trafficestimate.com	

Conclusion

As mentioned earlier in this chapter, the way the Internet is being used to expose human rights abuses has not been fully investigated, although quite a few authors have remarked on the potential of new communication technologies to empower human rights activists and civil society organizations (Brophy & Halpin, 1999; Halpin & Hick, 2000). It would be naïve to assume that the cluster of interconnected blogs and websites documenting atrocities is *alone* responsible for the reaction of the international community or the implementation of sanctions. But, the continuous exposure of norm-transgressions and publicizing online builds on the visibility generated through traditional sources such as the news media. Stored records and a steady supply of new evidence publicized via the clusters of blogs and websites help maintain and strengthen campaigns for action. Clusters operate in a world where pressure can be applied by states and international bodies in response to highlighted abuses (Baek, 2008). In the case of oppressive governments, they are already under pressure to change, and the ubiquity of online evidence of their repression helps show whether they are changing and may maintain or intensify pressure to change. Evidence of human rights and other abuses no longer vanishes from the screens or ends up in library archives, it is stored and publicized, made easily accessible for bystander audiences on the web. These virtual clusters are an increasingly important part of the global human rights regime which doubly ensure, in Rosneau's words, that "the misdeeds of human rights violators no longer pass from human kind's conscience" (2002: 149).

PART SIX

Transnational Protests and the Media

Toward Global Civil Society?

CHAPTER TWENTY

Transnational Protests and the Media

Toward Global Civil Society?

LIBBY LESTER AND SIMON COTTLE

#G20. One minute ago. Subway stations are still closed in Toronto. Office workers at windows wave peace signs at passing protesters. Naomi Klein, on huffingtonpost.com, criticizes the G20. Marchers enter Queens Park chanting, "Whose city, Our city." Shireen defends her previous tweet, "I never said. . . ." Laura tries to find Nick in the park. No horses. Protesters chant, "We don't want a police state." Citizens and police walk together. A protester holds up a sign, "Anyone up for scrabble later?" A photo of another sign, "Peaceful protest is not a crime." And seconds ago: "It's been 3 days. Give it a rest, go home. . . ."

This is the protest about the protests in Toronto. There has been violence on the streets of the city over the previous two days as the G20 has met, issued its final communiqué and dispersed. Toronto, as one newspaper notes, has been left with a black eye. Spectacular, yet familiar, images of the clashes have appeared in media around the world, sometimes anchored by stories and analysis, sometimes only captioned. More than 600 have been arrested, and the fresh results appearing almost every second on the hashtag, #G20, connect to video blogs and testimonials from protesters and those arrested, questioning police tactics. Police will later apologize.

This final protest is peaceful–it settles the city. Yet, the activity on Twitter and on the pages and screens of mainstream media suggests not all is settled. The meanings of this protest and events of the previous two days are now being debated and negotiated. Asks one protester as he walks slowly towards the university, "What is this protest about?" On the Internet, we watch the answers appear.

Four weeks earlier, we watched another debate over the meanings of protest. On one hand, the Gaza-bound flotilla and its cargo of aid was a "symbolic gesture," a "publicity stunt," an "attention-grabbing exercise." On the other hand, nine people were dead, killed rather than being allowed to complete their voyage. We watched as media commentators, newspaper editorials and partisan pundits struggled to reconcile the two. Again, we were directed to eyewitness accounts, to footage on YouTube, to statements from government sources on official websites. Here, media roles became a principal focus of this interconnected debate: the quantity and content of images and words circulating on and through the range of transnational platforms were called upon to "prove" the claims of both protest organizers and the Israeli government, even a new era of "uncensored truth" was emerging; the absence of others "proved" that media were selectively and strategically being "used," and that control had never been tighter.

Protest seeks our attention. It is a statement or act of disagreement, of dissent, but one to which the attention of others must explicitly be drawn if it is to have political impact. However, in seeking our attention, protest asks us to do more than merely notice. Located within the space of political and social conflict, the meanings of protest will always be contested, challenged and debated. Protest's locale, after all, is civil society, whose spirit is restless and dynamic, changing and adapting in response to other spheres and to its own internal conflicts and compromises (Alexander, 2006: 552–3; Keane, 2005: 288). Thus, protest is attention seeking in that it makes us notice its displays of dissent but also engages us in continuing debates about its meanings, its roles and its outcomes.

That this now occurs in new forums that cross old boundaries is evident. But how those transnational forums and flows potentially change the meanings we attribute to protest, even our capacity to attribute meaning, and invariably connect with the aims and enactment of protest in its many forms, have been key concerns of this book. Increasingly, academic attention has turned towards ideas of the cosmopolitan, global civil society, and a global public sphere, spaces in which distant voices can be heard, responded to and acted upon. Without question, protest has a central role to play in levering dissenting and/or marginalized voices into these evolving social and political spaces that exist within and beyond the local and national. Yet, how it achieves such leverage–and whether it will continue to do so–depends in no small part on its capacity to be interpreted and understood in and across an ever-increasing range of cultural and geo-political contexts and scales.

In many ways, protest is better prepared than many political actions or institutions to function in such a transnational space and to take a place at the heart of a global civil sphere. It is conditioned to speak to the distant. The US civil rights movement could only succeed by seeking the attention of a distant American public. The largely fearful, disinterested or oppositional news media of the south limited the movement's access to symbolic power at the physical site of its struggle: they needed to be bypassed in order to speak to the north. The movement was able to do so, as Jeffrey Alexander writes, by "proving itself to be a master of the translating craft," carrying messages to northern media, which, in turn, interpreted them for the civil society for which it was a stand-in (2006: 304). The main task for the movement was to relocate the particulars of the black movement in the south to the contexts and understandings of the north, that is, to translate to the distant. Highly symbolic, dramaturgical framing allowed protests to be understood by an American public removed from the site of conflict (see also Cottle, Chapter 2, this volume).

Likewise, the fledgling contemporary environment movement could only win if it too successfully managed meanings as they traveled into distant locales. In Australia, a conservative local news media in the southern island state of Tasmania needed to be side-stepped also if the protest movement was to capture the attention of mainland voters and politicians, who might be encouraged to stop the damming of the remote Franklin River. Spectacular and theatrical displays against a backdrop of wilderness offered symbolic touchstones for those distant from the river and the protest action. While always for the cameras, these protests were also necessarily displays of commitment, of passion, of threat, and each day organizers worked to ensure journalists included such frames in their stories so distant readers and viewers could interpret and understand the protest in terms likely to incite political action.

Nevertheless, neither movement could afford to ignore or dismiss the local. Protest, as authors in this volume remind us, creates communities (della Porta & Piazza, 2008), and the local "community" remains an important site for mobilization and political opportunity that, with the right conditions, will be sustained to a greater and more effective degree than either national or global "communities." Thus, while on the one hand the civil rights movement invoked universally understood dramatic frames in order to invoke a political response from the distant north, it also needed to manage meanings of its actions within local and particular contexts. Martin Luther King was doing both when he described Rosa Parks as "one of the finest citizens in Montgomery," while his mobilization of the southern black leadership was vital in forming a powerful collective identity to help counter local news frames of "defiance," "anarchy," "paid agents," and "vagrants" (Alexander, 2006: 307–326). With the civil rights movement as inspiration, leaders of the Australian environment movement invoked the idea of "wilderness" and called upon an array of internationally known scientists and other public figures to lend legitimacy to their actions in a local context, and to complicate local journalists' accusations of disorder and disobedience (Lester, 2007: 44–65).

In both cases, the meanings of protest and political dissent were being debated and negotiated within a framework of 'civility', of what it meant to be a good citizen, to behave orderly and in a civilized fashion within a civil space, and this was occurring across many disparate sites and boundaries. A key task for these protest movements was to manage such debates. Their political sites were the streets and busses, the bush and rivers; their political acts were symbolic drama and performance. How these connected to ideas of civility, of democratic deliberation and reason, needed to be translated across multiple spaces, and here they only ever succeeded in part. Local news media continued with accusations that the politics of the street and the wilderness trivialized and threatened the politics of the state.

Thus, even within the primarily national bounds of these earlier protest movements, the distinct differences in understandings of the rights and responsibilities of protest posed major challenges. And herein lies a central issue for protest as it engages more fully with the transnational opportunities offered by today's interpenetrating media ecology and communication networks. Protest is conditioned to speak to the distant, and it is also conditioned to speak to and through media. Its political success relies on a complex negotiation about meaning that occurs on both a local level and in new forums and across multiple media platforms to a far greater and diverse 'distant' than ever before. As various contributors to this volume make clear, transnational protest needs to mean something across many levels to achieve cultural power and political efficacy.

What is also clear is that the transnational and its relationship to the local are not only a space for such negotiations but the subject. As we noted in the Introduction, protests and demonstrations now commonly bring into being an ethico-political imaginary and collective political action around the transnational–if only briefly. The transnational becomes an aspiration, instantiated in displays of dissent that may be firmly entrenched in a local place or issue yet seeking international audiences and intervention or involving massive and cohesive actions in dozens of countries but seeking a national or localized response. New social movements, coalitions of opposition and internationally coordinated pressure might be produced and, in some cases, sustained. Thus, the transnational becomes a tension and a site of contest in itself as political actors seek to harness and control the new networks and flows that potentially disrupt the strategic and symbolic power that has come to be associated with mass media and the national boundaries from which they emerged.

As contributing authors have argued, new forms of transnational protest and their enactment in and through today's media and communications ecology exhibit considerable complexity. Here are forces of media containment as well as progressive opportunities. It is not an either/or proposition. Print and broadcast news platforms and their online presences may frame protest in ways that potentially contain the symbolic power that protest organizers have attempted to strategically harness to transfer and translate meanings, yet traditional news coverage remains an ambition, a prize worth fighting for among many activist groups. Social networking and other forms of Internet-based communication may provide new means to participate, new styles of protest and new ways to mobilize support, but they cannot fully relocate the mediated politics of dissent away from mass media news platforms. All political actors are now present in both the 'old' media and what Manuel Castells calls the 'networks of mass-self communication' (2007: 257), and all undoubtedly will continue seeking to find bridges between the two.

These bridges are built upon the links and interconnections that send us from Facebook to huffingtonpost.com or from the *New York Times* to YouTube, upon the emails that ask us to donate money to buy advertising in influential international markets, upon the media releases that send journalists to footage of protest violence on MySpace. They can be strategically constructed bridges, such as when social networking becomes a tool for gaining international news coverage. They can also be casually formed, as, for instance, when a marcher tweets to friends. Such communications may be local in their intent, even intimate, but they are also now invariably transnational.

How the meanings and understandings of protest are carried, managed and translated across local and national boundaries will rest in no small part on future opportunities for such bridges to develop between existing and still emerging media sites and platforms. The world of protest is changing, and these media interconnections and networks provide an important means to interpret and negotiate the political aims and implications of protest across a diversity and scale not before seen. Here, we can debate ideas of protest and civility, of social responsibility and political dissent, in global but also highly local contexts. "What is this protest about?," someone asks from the strect in Toronto. From a distance, we can now more easily contribute to an answer.

Afterword

Media and the Arab Uprisings of 2011

SIMON COTTLE

As *Transnational Protests and the Media* moved into production the world witnessed a series of tumultuous events in North Africa and the Middle East that soon became known as the Arab uprisings. Mass protests first in Tunisia, followed by Egypt and a succession of other Arab states, including Morocco, Algeria, Yemen, Oman, Bahrain and Libya, as well as Syria, Iran and Lebanon and, more tentatively in Saudi Arabia, all challenged the repressive, anti-democratic nature of these regimes (ICG, 2011). They called for an end to corruption, improved employment opportunities, the institution of democracy and the protection of human rights. When Mohammed Bouaziz set fire to himself in the Tunisian town of Sidi Bouzid in December 2010—a desperate act of defiance following his denied attempts to work as a street vendor to support his family—he lit a flame that soon burned in capitals and cities across much of the Arab world. The scenes of his self-immolation captured by passersby and posted on YouTube as well as those of the mass protests that followed his funeral soon circulated in Tunisia and beyond.

New social media, YouTube, Twitter, Facebook, along with online bloggers and mobile telephony, played a central role in communicating, coordinating and channeling this rising tide of opposition and variously managed to bypass state controlled national media as they propelled images and ideas of resistance and mass defiance across the Middle East and North Africa. The startling and dramatic scenes from

Egypt of the 'Day of Anger' (25th January) followed by the 'Day of Rage,' culminating in the 'March of the Millions' (1st February), that forced Hosni Mubarak's departure, also pulsed through satellite and international news coverage. Foreign correspondents in Tahrir Square not only helped to focus world attention on these momentous events but also gave them a human face. Mass uprising on the streets of Egypt now appeared less distanced, less humanly remote. Visceral scenes and emotional testimonies elicited on the street brought home to watching millions something of the protestors' everyday despair and democratic aspirations as well as their extraordinary courage in confronting, by non-violent means, repressive state violence. Some, we know, lost their lives.

As the world's news media and new social networks communicated these dramatic images of mass opposition from across much of the Arab world, so Western democracies practiced in the ways of doing business with authoritarian regimes as well as oppressive states skilled in the means of coercive power looked on and must have wondered what these shocking events could mean for them. A seismic shift in the world's political tectonic plates was taking place, comparable perhaps to 1989 but as then, no one could foresee how far, how deep or at what pace this opening fault-line of democracy would continue to run. It took a rupture in the earth's geological tectonic plates off the coast of Japan (March 11, 2011) and the resulting earthquake, tsunami, nuclear meltdown and financial turmoil (also captured in real-time by a variety of media) to dislodge the Arab political earthquake from its centre position on the world news stage.

At the time of writing it is too early to say how these popular uprisings will eventually play out and whether they will manage to win regime change, improved social justice and the democratization of state and civil society. Zine al-Abedine Ben Ali in Tunisia and Hosni Mubarak in Egypt have both been ousted, and interim authorities have promised elections and thorough-going reforms, though military and conservative forces could yet reassert themselves. Protests meanwhile continue elsewhere in the Arab world and have variously been met with brutal violence, promises of reform and, as in Saudi Arabia, cynical bribes seeking to buy-off discontent. The iron fist in the velvet glove is barely disguised. Saudi Arabia and the United Arab Emirates have sent military forces to intimidate and help squash the peaceful protests in Bahrain, and video scenes of shocking state violence and reports of abduction and torture across many Arab states circulate widely.

In Libya popular mass mobilization had initially liberated much of the country from Muammar Gaddafis' 42-year grip on power, but from his stronghold in and around Tripoli he unleashed mercenaries and military forces against his own people, winning back rebel towns and plunging the country into bloody civil war. At first the world watched as governments procrastinated and debated the possibilities of military and humanitarian intervention, before finally the UN Security

Council agreed to a no-fly zone and authorized member states to 'take all necessary measures' to 'protect civilians and civilian populated areas under attack.' (UN Resolution 1973, 18ᵗʰ March).

What is striking about these uprisings is not only their historical momentousness and stunning speed of replication across so many countries but also the different ways in which media and communications have become inextricably infused *inside* them. Indeed some have been so bold as to label them as the 'Twitter Revolutions' or 'Facebook Revolutions' in recognition of the prominent part played by new social media, whether in the co-ordination of mass protests, communication of real-time images and up-to-date information, or processes of contagion across the Arab region. This, however, is to do less than justice to both the political *and* media complexities involved or their mutual interaction moving through time. In time a more considered, in-depth and comparative analysis of these events will necessarily have to attend to different structures of state power, the role of the military, and the organization of political opposition in each of these countries preceding the uprisings, as well as how media systems and communication networks have variously entered into their different trajectories.

Scholars and researchers, some hopefully close to the events concerned, will need to address how media and communications, both old and new, entered *temporally* into the unfolding political struggles within different countries and *spatially* extended their reach and repercussions across different political jurisdictions. Today's media ecology and communication networks, in keeping with the findings and discussion of this book, have performed an integral if multifaceted part in building and mobilizing support, coordinating and defining the protests within different Arab societies as well as *transnationalizing* them across the Middle East, North Africa and to the wider world.

The following provides a preliminary inventory only of some of the different ways in which media and communications were deployed, entered into and communicatively transacted the Arab uprisings in the early months of 2011. Ten different forms of media and communication inscription are observed, and together these point to the complex ways in which today's media systems and communication networks have become infused within such momentous events, their political unfolding and transnationalization. Mass protests and political uprisings do not simply erupt or appear from nowhere, of course, even if the 'event orientation' of news and authorities 'in denial' may suggest otherwise. Demonstrations and protests, no matter how spontaneous or seemingly unplanned arise from somewhere and are informed by preceding grievances and ambitions for change. Flash mobs have a political home. And so too can major protests and demonstrations continue to live on in the collective memories and political (re)actions of the reconfigured political field that is left behind, sometimes long after the news cameras and foreign correspondents have moved on. A symbolic down payment of sorts, deposited in the future political account.

Today's media ecology has powerfully and complexly become infused within the Arab uprisings, and this stretches across the period of growing discontent and opposition that precipitated the uprisings, the period of the revolts themselves, and the continuing processes of revolutionary consolidation, state reforms or ongoing repression and resistance that now characterize the situation in different Arab countries. Over these interlinked moments of political struggle and change, media and communications have played an inextricable part in extending their scope and sending visible shock waves like a political tsunami through the Middle East and North Africa and beyond to register on different national, regional and global shores. Ten ways, then, in which media systems and communications networks have powerfully become inscribed inside the Arab uprisings and complexly entered into their unfolding political trajectories.

1. *State controlled Arab media, blind Western media.* Though it is tempting to focus in on the role of media and perhaps new social media specifically in the immediate events of the Arab uprisings, a more politically contextualized approach would need to inquire first into how state-run Arab media have sought to legitimize their political regimes over preceding years and how also outside mainstream news media have played a less than critical role when reporting on many of them. This includes the Western media's conspicuous silence toward the everyday suppression of political dissent, human rights abuses and earlier emergent protests whilst uncritically reporting on their own government's trade and arms initiatives and conciliatory diplomatic relations that help bolster such regimes in power. If Western media had performed a more independent and critically engaged role, is it conceivable that the Arab uprisings of 2011 though surprising in terms of their speed and scale could nonetheless have been better understood and contextualized within a preceding narrative of growing political disenchantment and despair?

2. *Media, consumerism and democracy.* Though Western news media have played less than a democratizing role in the political run-up to the uprisings of 2011, the globalizing culture of consumerism and normative outlooks of Western democracies arguably form an unspoken backdrop in Western entertainment conglomerates and its satellite news channels. This, no doubt, has contributed to the globalization of the values and tenets of economic individualism and liberal democracy. Media-rich societies can no longer be hermetically sealed from this global culture of valorized consumption nor the communication flows that now transverse the globe providing symbolic referents for democracy and its emulation.

Noticeably the general democratic impulse expressed within the Arab uprisings surprised many in the West, confounding expectations post-9/11, post-Afghanistan and Iraq, that Islam and anti-Western sentiments would play a more prominent steering role in processes of regime change. The youthful composition of Arab populations and their broad-based demographics more generally have no doubt played an important part in defining the political ambitions and secular nature of the uprisings as well as their human rights focus. Kristian Ulrichsen and his colleagues, amongst others, for example observes how: '65% of the population of the Middle East is under the age of 30 and are increasingly technology-savvy and adept at using new forms of communication to bypass state controls and mobilize around common issues or grievances' and 'Bloggers in Egypt and Tunisia were instrumental in publicizing and spreading accounts of torture and human rights violations by the security services' (Ulrichsen et al., 2011). Young people plugged into Western media and immersed in wider cultural flows that normalize democratic practices and civil rights as well as conspicuous consumption have become an established communications backdrop in much of the Arab world notwithstanding the tensions and contradictions this poses to 'embattled' religious authorities and patriarchal structures of domination.

3. *Media conviviality in everyday life.* Media and communications in the Arab world not only convey images and ideas that are circulated and consumed more widely in today's globalizing communication flows, they also enter into the everyday via new social media, becoming part of the mundane sociability and conviviality of modernity. Though not necessarily enacting elevated forums for 'high' political debates about 'Democracy', the popular uptake of social media within everyday life proves 'democratizing' nonetheless. New social media help to bring into being a new space for group recognition, social inclusivity and pluralized participation as well as different forms of political conversation and engagement. This everyday conversation and conviviality entered into via new social media help to instantiate moments of social connectedness and interaction in which identities and interests, rights and responsibilities, can become recognized and performed and even produce new templates for the conduct of civil society beyond the virtual world.

According to a recent research report documenting the uptake and use of new social media across different Arab countries published in the immediate aftermath of the Tunisian and Egyptian uprisings, 'the Arab world has witnessed the rise of an independent vibrant social media and steadily increasing citizen engagement on the Internet that is expected to attract 100 million Arab users by 2015.' It concludes, 'These social networks inform, mobilize, entertain, create communities, increase transparency, and seek to hold governments accountable' (Ghannam, 2011). The new tools of sociability and conviviality can thus prove to be 'democratizing' in both the sense of facilitating pluralized interaction and intercourse in everyday life as well as providing the means for organizing for system change and the political establishment of 'Democracy' (See Ghanavizi, chapter 198, Sreberny and Khiabany, 2010)

4. Facilitating/communicating protest. New social media, including YouTube, Facebook, Flickr and Twitter, as well as mobile telephony distributing SMS (short message service) messages, images and live video streams, and Internet bloggers, have all played a key role in the recent uprisings though in differing permutations across the different countries concerned. Inflated claims about the power of new social media to foment protest and revolution lend themselves to the charge of media centrism and technological determinism that obfuscate the preceding social and political forces at work as well as the purposive actions of human beings prepared to confront state intimidation and violence in pursuit of political change. But, equally, claims that simply deny the important role of new media in coalescing broad-based, non-hierarchical political movements and coordinating and channeling their demographic weight into real democratic power, fail to understand the changed nature of today's media and communications environment or how this can now be harnessed by activists and protestors and creatively infused *inside* political struggle. The argument, therefore, is not so much about whether new social media did or did not perform a determining role in the events in question but rather how exactly did media systems and new communication networks complexly interact, enter into and shape them.

A Tunisian blogger, Sami Ben Ghabia, maintains, for example, that much of the content about the revolution in the mainstream media originated from Tunisians using Facebook, but this was then collected, translated and reposted on the website Nawaat, an independent blog set up for dissenting Tunisian voices and then passed on via Twitter for mainstream journalists. Each uprising, easily accessed by their different hashtags (Tunisia #SidiBouzid, Egypt #Jan25, Bahrain #Feb14, Libya #Feb17, Saudi Arabia #Mar20), effectively collects constantly updated information and links to crowd-sourcing maps, providing journalists and others with an accessible if not always strictly verifiable overview picture of what was occurring on the ground. 'If content had remained strictly on Facebook,' it is argued, 'its audience would have been limited to those who are members of certain groups, and would not likely have been disseminated in ways that proved pivotal to the media coverage' (Ghannam, 2011, p. 16).

In other words, new social media and mainstream media appear to have often performed in tandem, with social media variously acting as a watchdog of state controlled national media, alerting international news media to growing opposition and dissent events and providing raw images of these for wider dissemination. International news media, in turn, including Al-Jazeera, have distributed the flood of disturbing scenes and reports of the uprisings now easily accessed via Google's YouTube and boomeranged them back into the countries concerned. Mainstream newspapers and news broadcasters in their online variants increasingly incorporate direct links to these new social media, effectively acting as a portal to their updating communication flows direct from the protests themselves. This moving complex of interpenetrating communication flows and their political efficacy in respect to the different uprisings and their unfolding political dynamics deserves careful documentation and comparative analysis.

Generalizations about the role of news social media in the uprisings, for the present at least, must desist: 'the importance and impact of social media on each of the rebellions we have seen this year', concludes one media observer, 'has been defined by specific local factors (not least how people live their lives online in individual countries and what state limits were in place). Its role has been shaped too by how well organized the groups using social media have been' (Beaumont, 2011, p. 2). Even more fundamental in this respect is the varying penetration of these new technologies and their daily use within and across different Arab societies, recently documented in the research report *Social Media in the Arab World* (Ghannam, 2011).

5. Facilitating repressive state responses. It is not only activists who have become increasingly media-savvy in recent years, deploying new social media to organize and coordinate protests and distribute tactical information and so on but also repressive regimes. The Arab uprisings produced numerous instances of regimes trying to censor and contain the flow of images and information by 'pulling the plug' on the Internet, monitoring telecommunications and disrupting the work of foreign journalists through personal intimidation, targeting particular foreign news bureaus or simply refusing journalists access to the country. Mubarak's government as well as Gaddafi has also sought to rally pro-government supporters in particular locations at particular times by ordering mobile service providers to send text messages; a tactic that has also been used to dupe protesters into arriving at particular locations, dispersing them and/or positioning them to be picked up by the security forces.

As Evgeny Morozov (2011) elaborates in *The Net Delusion*, the Internet is not solely the preserve of the democratically inclined. Repressive regimes around the world now deploy sophisticated digital censorship and monitoring capabilities and engage in pernicious cyber attacks and the targeting of media activists and dissidents —and have done so for some time. And needless to say, state-controlled media, whether press, television or radio, will be put to full propaganda purposes when repressive regimes are challenged. Rather than seeing the authoritarian use of the Internet as a knockout blow in the argument against so-called 'cyber-utopians' and their medium-centric enthusiasm for the Net's democratizing possibilities, this is better conceived as an inevitable part of all political struggles when conducted in, through and on the media and communications battlefield. Historically this is neither new nor surprising and remains contingent upon the weighting of political forces and their respective capacities to exert control and creatively innovate in the communications field.

Repressive states do not have all the technological trump cards in their hand, and, increasingly, media-savvy activists swap and share theirs to help protesters circumvent attempted controls and gain the communications initiative. When states have sought to deny Internet access to particular websites by blocking servers, activists have made use of 'proxy' international servers and 'ghost servers' disguising the networks involved. When Mubarak turned off the Internet and SMS services on January the 28th, for nearly a week, an Al-Jazeera producer notes how within days 'clandestine FTP (File Transfer Protocol) accounts were set up to move videos out to international news outlets', and 'while accredited members of the media struggled to communicate and coordinate, street protestors were using landlines to call supporters, who translated and published their accounts on Twitter for an international audience hungry for news . . . ' (Ishani, 2011). Views of the Internet and new social media as either democratically benign or essentially open to repressive state appropriation and control, generally fail to recognize and interrogate the dynamic play of power and constantly updating war of technological maneuver that informs the battle for communication power.

6. *Media contagion.* There is a reticence by most scholars of media to entertain the ideas of media contagion and even more so when invoked in the context of political uprisings. Behaviorist claims about the media contagion of urban riots in 1960s America and 1980s Britain, for example, as well as the term's pathological connotation, tend to render the political motivations involved literally meaningless and thereby encourage conservative interpretations of collective violence. The breathtaking wave of uprisings and their rapid spread from one Arab country to another nonetheless points to the evident ways in which contemporary communication of dissent can help to embolden others, provide templates for action and thereby help to release pent-up political forces of change. The way images of political dissent and protest spill over national borders or leap frog across entire countries or even regions to impact political struggles waged elsewhere points once again to the transnationalizing nature of global protest communications as well as their capacity to help build and sustain feelings of political affinity and solidarity.

It is not only the demonstration of people power, however, that is 'contagious' and communicated via media and communication networks, lending hope and inspiration to those embarked on similar struggles elsewhere, or even the replication of protest tactics such as the symbolic occupation of central city squares or extreme acts of self-immolation by 'martyrs' to the cause like Mohammed Bouaziz.

Also 'contagious' are the constantly evolving communication tactics and creative adaptations of the same communicated around the world by media activists seeking to evade and counter media censorship and imposed media controls. In the years and months before the uprisings, media activists in Egypt and elsewhere, for example, were actively studying the tactics of networked opposition conducted elsewhere, including Iran's Green Movement and the communications tactics developed in the mass protests challenging the June 2009 post-election (Ishani, 2011).

7. International recognition and protest legitimation. Media and communications also enter the frame of political uprisings and mass protests in terms of how they become defined and deliberated in the international arena, especially as mass demonstrations appear to destabilize the regimes in question. Whereas Western governments at first seemed to be wrong-footed by the surprise and speed of the Arab revolts and equivocated about their possible causes, demographic composition and legitimacy (especially in respect to their foremost Middle East ally, Egypt), the news media in the UK in contrast, and possibly more widely, appeared to grant early recognition to the protesters' aims, sense of grievance and cause. In other words Western news media helped to grant them legitimacy in advance of elite political statements. Only as the political efficacy of the protests was grasped and the demise of the regimes such as Mubarak's Egypt anticipated, did official pronouncements begin to move toward a more supportive position toward the demonstrators, their civil rights and legitimate claims for democracy.

Contrary to established models of elite indexing, this finding seemingly suggests that mainstream media can, on some occasions, adopt a more independent and critically informed news stance even when political elites exhibit a relatively uniform front in terms of their expressed views on the political contention in question. Part of the explanation for this more independent and sympathetic media representation probably resides in today's global news ecology. This now includes the radical cross-fertilization of different communication flows from around the world and the influence particularly of 24/7 satellite channels such as CNN, BBC World and Al-Jazeera (the latter increased its market share exponentially during these events). It is also located in those up-close and personal scenes and testimonies collected by correspondents 'embedded' in the crowds, witnessing and possibly feeling their collective hopes, hurt and vulnerability in the face of an increasingly desperate political regime. Stories and sentiments that are now also vividly captured via new social media and media monitoring services such as BBC Monitoring that survey round-the-clock, TV, radio, press, Internet and news agency sources worldwide and available to newsrooms back home.

Activists and protesters on the ground can also be acutely aware of the need for international media recognition and clamor for opportunities in front of mainstream news cameras to put their case across to international audiences and governments. Attending to the public performances, symbols and dramaturgy involved as well as the master narrative of democracy mobilized in and by media deserves careful attention (See Juris, Chapter 7, Alexander, 2006, Alexander et al, 2006). How exactly this was conducted through today's overlapping media flows and communication networks is fertile ground for future research.

8. Media and the global village of repressive states. Just as repressive regimes confronting political opposition and dissent inside their borders will tighten their grip on media and double their efforts to censor, monitor, dupe and target their opponents, so repressive regimes around the world are also predisposed to do likewise when confronting the potentially toxic infusion of images and ideas of resistance from afar. They will also seek to learn lessons from the communication struggles waged elsewhere and seek to implement or adapt these when required. Both China and Iran, for example, sought to control the tide of images and information of the Arab uprisings coursing through the global news networks and Internet. The Chinese authorities clamped down hard after calls for a 'Jasmine Revolution' modeled on the pro-democracy protests surging through the Middle East and detained suspected activists and censored online calls to stage protests in Beijing, Shanghai and 11 other major cities. The reverberations that flow from Arab uprisings further underline the intensification of communications within today's political geography as their impacts circulate outwards as powerful ripple effects to repressive regimes and democracies with vested interests around the world.

9. Human rights surveillance and calls for R2P. As protestors came up against state repression and military violence, images and accounts of human rights abuses began to course through available media and confound the efforts of authorities to censor and impose a communications blackout. When Libya banned journalists from entering Libyan territory in the initial days of the uprising and military crackdown, images soon circulated on YouTube that were incorporated into mainstream news media that documented attacks on rebel forces by Libyan heavy armor. Dubbed 'The Global YouTube News Bureau', vivid images bearing witness to human rights abuses and impending humanitarian catastrophe circulated despite the absence of foreign correspondents on the ground. As they did, so calls were increasingly heard for those responsible to be pursued and prosecuted in the International Criminal Court.

In the context of the Libyan dictator's refusal to concede power and his preparedness to use military force, including heavy weaponry and military aircraft against his own people, the world's media increasingly gave vent to the calls for humanitarian and/or military intervention. A period of governmental procrastination ensued before the United Nations' Security Council eventually agreed to a no-fly zone and the necessary military measures to protect civilians. Though a far cry from a simplistic 'CNN model' of media causality, how these scenes and calls became communicated in the news media and registered on the international political stage warrants serious attention. This is all the more so in the context of the United Nations' proclaimed acceptance of the 'Responsibility to Protect' (R2P) doctrine and the establishment of political precedents that may yet have consequences for future humanitarian interventions.

Precedents established in Libya, as elsewhere, therefore, can influence future events, international policy responses and even the self-interested calculations of autocratic dictators when contemplating violence and genocidal actions against their own populations in the future. Though Western media have given some time and space to the issues of humanitarian response and a no-fly zone rarely have they sought to contextualize this debate in respect to the evolving world acceptance of the 'Responsibility to Protect' (R2P) doctrine, formally recognized since the UN World Summit in 2005, and how it requires a reconceptualization of ideas of national sovereignty.

The key point here, however, is that the media can indeed perform a necessary and possibly influential role in alerting world opinion to repressive and potentially prosecutable acts of inhumanity following in the wake of mass uprisings and can serve moreover as a public forum for deliberating the moral dilemmas and practical difficulties involved. Ideally these same media could yet perform a more educative role in informing publics around the world about the existing Responsibility to Protect framework and how this obliges the world's governments to intervene to protect human lives when sovereign states manifestly fail to do so or, worse, when they deliberately target their own citizens.

10. *New media systems maintaining democratic momentum.* And finally, the role of media and communications in maintaining the democratizing momentum of political movements for change in the immediate post-uprising phase and longer term will inevitably continue to have deep significance for the reconstruction of civil society and the pace of democratic advance. In countries such as Tunisia and Egypt this will require new systems of media regulation and governance and institutional reforms as well as shifts in professional practices and cultural outlooks on the part of those media workers and organizations closely associated with the former regimes. And so too will new media organizations and media forms be required to better express established and emergent constituencies of political, social and religious interests competing to steer processes of reform and civil society reconstruction.

In Libya it was interesting to observe how almost immediately following the the liberation of Benghazi, the stronghold town of opposition to Gaddafi's regime, a new daily newspaper simply called *Libya* quickly emerged, carrying on its masthead a picture of the national flag before Gaddafi took power and carrying the words 'We do not surrender—we win or die'—the rallying call of a Libyan resistance leader during the Italian occupation. 'Radio Free Libya from the Green Mountain', a new radio station, also sprung up. New forms of political communication often come into being and flourish when there is a felt need for them; they perform a vital function in maintaining the political momentum and constituting the public sphere(s) for its societal deliberation. Media and communications necessarily will form no less an inextricable and essential part in the continuing political struggles for regime change and the democratization of state and civil society across the Middle East and North Africa as they have in the uprisings themselves.

In each of these ten different ways, media and communications have variously enabled and enacted, performed and propelled, represented and resisted the Arab uprisings of 2011, and they will continue to do so and in no less complex and consequential ways in the years ahead. Together they point to how today's overlapping and interpenetrating media systems and communication networks now enter into revolutionary political struggles and can transnationalize them as they unfold over time, across space and politically reverberate around the globe.

Acknowledgment

This discussion draws on a forthcoming article in *Journalism: Theory, Practice and Criticism*, 2011, volume 11, both written in the immediate aftermath of the Arab uprisings.

References

ABC (2000). Tent City Housing Protest Threatens Sydney's Olympic Image. The 7:30 Report, ABC. http://www.abc.net.au/7.30/stories/s142537.htm (accessed 10 September 2009).

Adi, A., & Miah, A. (2008). Framing Beijing's Olympic Bid. Human Rights Advocacy Groups and International Media. Paper prepared for *Changes and Challenges: China Media Today* conference. Westminster.

Aitchison, Guy, 2009. 'An Open Letter to the BBC', Open Democracy, [Online] Updated 21 May 2009) Available at http://www.opendemocracy.net/blog/ourkingdom-theme/guy-aitchison/2009/05/21/an-open-letter-to-the-bbc [Accessed 8 September 2009].

Aitchison, G. (2009b, 8 September). The BBC and Their G20 Police Coverage. *Open Democracy*, http://www.opendemocracy.net/blog/ourkingdom-theme/guy-aitchison/2009/09/08/the-bbc-and-the-g20 (accessed 10 September 2009).

Alexander, J. (2006). *The Civil Sphere*. Oxford: Oxford University Press.

Alexander, J., Giesen, B., & Mast, J. (Eds.). (2006). *Social Performance: Symbolic Action, Cultural Pragmatics and Ritual*. Cambridge: Cambridge University Press.

Alikhah, F. (2008). The Politics of Satellite Television in Iran. In M. Semati (Ed.), *Media, Culture and Society in Iran: Living with Globalization and the Islamic State*. London: Routledge.

Allan, S., & Thorsen, E. (Eds.). (2009). *Citizen Journalism: Global Perspectives*. New York: Peter Lang.

Allan, S., Sonwalkar, P., & Carter, C. (2007). Bearing Witness: Citizen Journalism and Human Rights Issues. *Globalization, Societies and Education*, 5(3), 373–389.

Altheide, D. L., & Snow, R. P. (1991). *Media Worlds in the Postjournalism Era*. New York: Aldine de Gruyter.

Altman, M. (2002). Prospects for e-Government in Latin America: Satisfaction with Democracy, Social Accountability, and Direct Democracy. *International Review of Public Administration,* 7(2), 5–20.

Amnesty International. (2001, 12 July). China: Human Rights and the Spirit of Olympism. Amnesty.org. http://www.amnesty.org/en/library/info/ASA17/023/2001 (accessed June 2010).

Amnesty International. (2008a). Amnesty International Website blocked at Olympic Venue. Amnesty.org. http://www.amnesty.org/en/news-and-updates/news/amnesty-international-website-blocked-at-olympic-venue-20080728 (accessed 28 July 2008).

Amnesty International. (2008b). Olympics: China and IOC must learn from mistakes and uphold human rights values. amnesty.org. http://www.amnesty.org/en/news-and-updates/olympics-china-and-ioc-must-learn-mistakes-and-uphold-human-rights-values-200808 (accessed 24 August 2008).

Amnesty International. (2009). *Iki Arada Bir Derede: Türkiye'deki Mültecilere Koruma Saglanmiyor.* Istanbul.

Anand, D. (2007). *Geopolitical Exotica: Tibet in Western Imagination.* Minneapolis and London: University of Minnesota Press.

Anderson, A. (1997). *Media, culture and the environment.* London: UCL Press.

Anderson, B. (1991). *Imagined Communities: Reflections on the Origin and Spread of Nationalism.* London: Verso.

Angus, I. (2000). *Primal Scenes of Communication.* Albany: SUNY.

Appadurai, A. (1996). *Modernity at Large: Cultural Dimensions of Globalisation.* Minneapolis: University of Minnesota Press.

Arbena, J. L. (2002). Hosting the Summer Olympic Games: Mexico City, 1968. In J. L. Arbena & D.G. LaFrance (Eds.), *Sport in Latin America and the Caribbean.* Wilmington: Jaguar Books.

Arquilla, J., & Ronfeldt, D. (Eds.). (2001). *Networks and Netwars: The Future of Terror, Crime, and Militancy.* Santa Monica: Rand.

Arquilla J., & Ronfeldt, D. (2001). The advent of netwar (revisited). In J. Arquilla & D. Ronfeldt (Eds.), *Networks and netwars: The future of terror, crime, and militancy.* Santa Monica: Rand.

Arsenault, A., & Castells M. (2008). Switching Power: Rupert Murdoch and the Global Business of Media Politics. *International Sociology,* 23(4), 488–513.

Artz, L. (2007). The Corporate Model from National to Transnational. In L. Artz and Y. Kamalipour (Eds.), *The Media Globe: Trends in International Mass Media.* Lanham, Maryland: Rowman and Littlefield.

Asen, R. (2004). A Discourse Theory of Citizenship. *Quarterly Journal of Speech,* 90(2), 189–211.

Assadourian, C. S., Bonilla, H., Mitre, A., & Platt, T. (1980). Minería y espacio económico en los Andes. *Siglos,* XVI-XX. Instituto de Estudios Peruanos, Lima, Perú.

Atton, C. (2003). Reshaping Social Movement Media for a New Millennium. *Social Movement Studies,* 2(1), 3–15.

Badiou, A. (2001). *Ethics.* New York: Verso.

Baek, B. S. (2008). Economic Sanctions Against Human Rights Violations. *Cornell Law School LLM Paper Series,* Paper 11.

Ball-Rokeach, S. (1985). The Origins of Individual Media-System Dependency: A Sociological Framework. *Communication Research,* 12(4), 485–510.

Bakhtin, M. (1984). *Rabelais and His World*. Bloomington: Indiana University Press.

Bandy, J. and Smith, J. (2004) 'Factors Affecting Conflict and Cooperation in Transnational Movement Networks,' pp. 231–249 in Bandy, J. & Smith, J. (eds), *Coalitions Across Borders: Transnational Protest and the Neoliberal Order*. London. Rowman & Littlefield.

Barham, B. & Coomes, O. (1994). The Amazon Rubber Boom: Labor Control, Resistance, and Failed Plantation Development Revisited. *Hispanic American Historical Review*, 74(2), 231–257.

Barthes, R. (1981). *Camera Lucida*. New York: Hill and Wang.

Baudrillard, J. (1987). *The Evil Demon of Image*. Sydney: Power Institute of Fine Arts.

Baudrillard, J. (1994). *Simulacra and Simulation*. Michigan: University of Michigan Press.

Baudrillard, J. (2000). Photography, or the Writing of Light. *Ctheory.Net*, 1–6.

Bauman, R. (1977). *Verbal Art as Performance*. Rowley, Mass: Newbury House Publishers.

Bauman, Z. (2007). *Liquid Times*. Cambridge: Polity.

Bayat, A. (2005). Islamism and Social Movement Theory. *Third World Quarterly*, 26(6), 891–908.

BBC News. (2009, 1 April). Police clash with G20 protestors. http://news.bbc.co.uk/1/hi/7977489.stm (accessed 2 April 2009).

BBC News. (2009, 7 April). Footage shows G20 death man push. http://news.bbc.co.uk/1/hi/england/london/7988828.stm (accessed 7 April 2009).

BBC News. (2010a, 22 March). Metropolitan Police admit unlawful G20 arrests. http://news.bbc.co.uk/1/hi/uk/8580344.stm (accessed 22 March 2010).

BBC News. (2010b, 22 March). Alleged victim fails to attend G20 police trial. http://news.bbc.co.uk/1/hi/england/london/8580211.stm (accessed 22 March 2010).

BBC News. (2010, 31 March). G20 police office Delroy Smellie cleared of assault. http://news.bbc.co.uk/1/hi/england/london/8597217.stm?(accessed 7 May 2010).

BBC News Online. (2008, 14 March). Eyewitness: Monk "kicked to floor." http://news.bbc.co.uk/1/hi/world/asia-pacific/7296134.stm (accessed 10 August 2009).

Beaumont, P. (2011). The Truth about Twitter, Facebook and the Uprisings in the Arab World' *The Guardian*. Friday 25 February. (http://www.guardian.co.uk/world/2011/feb/25/twitter-facebook)

Beck, U. (1999). *World Risk Society*. Cambridge: Polity.

Beck, U. (2006). *Cosmopolitan Vision*. Cambridge: Polity.

Beck, U. (2009). *World at Risk*. Cambridge: Polity.

Becker, H. (1967). Whose Side Are We on? *Social Problems*, 14(2), 239–248.

Bennett, W. L. (1990). Towards a Theory of Press-state Relations in the United States. *Journal of Communication*, 40(2), 103–25.

Bennett, W. L. (2003a). New Media Power: The Internet and Global Activism. In N. Couldry & J. Curran (Eds.), *Contesting Media Power: Alternative Media in a Networked World*. Oxford: Rowan and Littlefield.

Bennett, W. L. (2003b). Communicating Global Activism: Strengths and Vulnerabilities of Networked Politics. *Information, Communication and Society*, 6(2), 143–168.

Bennett, W. L. (2003c). *News: The Politics of Illusion*. New York: Longman.

Bennett, W. L. (2005). Social Movements Beyond Borders: Understanding Two Eras of Transnational Activism. In D. della Porta and S. Tarrow (Eds.), *Transnational Protest and Global Activism*. Oxford, UK: Rowman & Littlefield.

Bennett, W. L., Breunig, C., & Givens, T. (2008). Communication and Political Mobilization: Digital Media Sse and Protest Organization among Anti-Iraq War Demonstrators in the U.S. *Political Communication*, 25 (3), 269–89.

Bennett, W. L., & Givens, T. (2006). Communication and Political Mobilization: Digital Media Use and Protest Organization among Anti-Iraq War Demonstrators in the US. Unpublished manuscript from personal communication.

Bennett, W. L., & Iyengar, S. (2008). A New Era of Minimal Effects? The Changing Foundations of Political Communication. *Journal of Communication*, 58, 707–731.

Bennett, W. L., Pickard, V. W., Iozzi, D. P., Schroeder, C. L., Lagos, T., & Evans Caswell, C. (2004). Managing the Public Sphere: Journalistic Construction of the Great Globalization Debate. *Journal of Communication*, 54(3), 437–455.

Berglez, P. (2008). What Is Global Journalism? Theoretical and Empirical Conceptualisations. *Journalism Studies*, 9(6), 845–858.

Berton, J. (2009, 16 April) Catching up with . . . Julia Butterfly Hill. *San Francisco Chronicle*. http://articles.sfgate.com/2009–04–16/entertainment/17192543_1_julia-butterfly-hill-social-change-hip-dysplasia (accessed June 2010)

BID (Banco Internacional de Desarrollo). (1992). Amazonía sin mitos. Informe del Programa de las Naciones Unidas para el Desarrollo, Tratado de Cooperación Amazonica. Washington DC.

Bimber, B. (2001). Information and Political Engagement in America: The search for Effects of Information Technology at the Individual Level. *Political Research Quarterly*, 54. 53–67.

Bimber, B. (2003) *Information and American Democracy: Technology in the Evolution of Political Power*. Cambridge. Cambridge University Press.

Blair, T. (2007, 12 June). Full Text: Blair on the Media. BBC News. http://news.bbc.co.uk/1/hi/uk_politics/6744581.stm (accessed 30 October 2009).

Block, D. (2001). Broadcast and Archive: Human Rights Documentation in the Early Digital Age. Paper presented at the Florida State University Conference on Human Rights, 1–3 November.

Bohman, J. (2004). Expanding Dialogue: The Internet, the Public Sphere and Prospects for Transnational Democracy. In N. Crossley & J. M. Roberts (Eds.), *After Habermas: New Perspectives on the Public Sphere*. Oxford: Blackwell.

Bolter, J., & Grusin, R. (1999). *Remediation*. Cambridge: MIT.

Boyd-Barrett, O., & Rantanen. T. (Eds.). (1998). *The Globalization of News*. London: Sage.

Boyle, M. P., McCluskey, M. R., McLeod, D. M., & Stein, S. E. (2005). Newspapers and Protest: An Examination of Protest Coverage from 1960 to 1999. *Journalism & Mass Communication Quarterly*, 82, 638–53.

Bray, D., & Storch, H. v. (2008). *CliSci2008: A Survey of the Perspectives of Climate Scientists Concerning Climate Science and Climate Change*. Geesthacht: GKSS.

Brophy, P., & Halpin, E. (1999). Through the Net to Freedom: Information, the Internet and Human Rights. *Journal of Information Science*, 25(5), 351–364.

Brownell, S. (2004). China and Olympism. In J. Bale & M. K. Christensen (Eds.), *Post-Olympism? Questioning Sport in the Twenty-first Century*. Oxford, Berg.

Bruns, A. (2007). *The Ecclesial Self: Stanley Grenz, Postmodernism, and Community*. Chicago: North Park University.

Bruns, A., & Jacobs, J. (2006). *Uses of blogs*. New York: Peter Lang.

Bryant, R., & Bailey, S. (1997). *Third World Political Ecology*. London: Routledge.

Brysk, A. (ed.). (2002). *Globalization and Human Rights*. Berkeley, CA: University of California Press.

Brzezinski, Z. (2004). *The Choice: Global Domination or Global Leadership*. New York: Basic Books.

Burnett, R. (2005). *How Images Think*. Cambridge, MA: MIT.

Calhoun, C. (2001). Putting Emotions in Their Place. In J. Goodwin, et al. (Eds.), *Passionate Politics*. Chicago: University of Chicago Press.

Cammaerts, B. & Van Audenhove, L. (2005). Online Political Debate, Unbounded Citizenship, and the Problematic Nature of a Transnational Public Sphere. *Political Communication, 22*, 179–196.

Campbell, M. (2004, 30 January). Pirate chic. *The Age* http://www.theage.com.au/articles/2004/01/30/1075340827447.html?from=storyrhs (accessed 28 November 2009).

Canetti, E. (1962). *Crowds and Power*. New York: Farrar Straus Giroux.

Carey, J. (1989). *Communication as Culture*. Boston: Unwin Hyman.

Carroll, W., & Hackett, R. (2006). Democratic Media Activism Through the Lens of Social Movement Theory. *Media, Culture & Society, 28*(1), 83–104.

Carruthers, S. L. (2000). *The Media at War: Communication and Conflict in the Twentieth Century*. Basingstoke: Macmillan.

Carter, N. (2009). Can the UK Reduce its Greenhouse Gas Emissions by 2050? In A. Giddens, S. Latham, & R. Liddle (Eds.), *Building a Low-Carbon Future: The Politics of Climate Change*. London: The Policy Network.

Castells, M. (1996). *The Rise of the Network Society*. Oxford: Blackwell.

Castells, M. (1997). *The Power of Identity*. Oxford: Blackwell.

Castells, M. (2000). *The Rise of the Network Society*. 2nd edn. Oxford: Blackwell.

Castells, M. (2001). *The Internet Galaxy*. Oxford: Oxford University Press.

Castells, M. (ed.). (2004a). *The Network Society: A Cross-Cultural Perspective*. Cheltenham: Edward Elgar.

Castells, M. (2004b). *The Power of Identity*. 2nd edn. Malden, MA: Blackwell.

Castells, M. (2004c). Informationalism, Networks, and the Network Society: A Theoretical Blueprint. In M. Castells (Ed.), *The Network Society: A Cross-Cultural Perspective*. Cheltenham: Edward Elgar.

Castells, M. (2007). Communication, Power and Counter-Power in the Network Society. *International Journal of Communication, 1*, 238–266.

Castells, M. (2008). The New Public Sphere: Global Civil Society, Communication Networks, and Global Governance. *The Annals of the American Academy of Political and Social Sciences, 616*(1), 78–93.

Castells, M. (2009). *Communication Power*. Oxford: Oxford University Press.

Castells, M., Fernandez-Ardevol, M., Linchuan Qiu, J., & Sey, A. (2007). *Mobile Communication and Society: A Global Perspective*. Boston: MIT.

Castree, N., (2004). Differential Geographies: Place, Indigenous Rights and "Local" Resources. *Political Geography, 23*, 133–167.

Chadwick, A. (2006). *Internet Politics: States, Citizens and New Communication Technologies*. Oxford: Oxford University Press

Channel 4 News. (2008). Tibet Rebellion, 14 March [News video].

Chesters, G., & Welsh, I. (2006). *Complexity and Social Movements: Multitudes at the Edge of Chaos*. London: Routledge.

China Debate, The. (n.d.). Amnesty International. http://thechinadebate.org (accessed 30 July 2008).

Chomsky, N. (2002). Journalist from Mars: How the 'War on Terror' Should be Reported. *Extra!*, 15, 10–16.

Chouliaraki, L. (2006). *The Spectatorship of Suffering*. London: Sage.

Clark, A M. (2001). *Diplomacy of Conscience: Amnesty International and the Changing Human Rights Norms*. Princeton, NJ: Princeton University Press.

Clausen, L. (2003). *Global News Production*. Copenhagen: Copenhagen Business School Press.

CNN. (2010, 26 February) Dalai Lama: China denies problem in Tibet. http://www.cnn.com/2010/WORLD/asiapcf/02/22/tibet.dalai.lama.lkl/index.html (accessed 27 February 2010).

Cockburn, C. (2003). Why (and Which) Feminist Antimilitarism? Paper presented at Annual General Meeting of the Women's International League for Peace and Freedom Nantwich. http://cynthiacockburn.typepad.com/Blogfemantimilitarism.pdf (accessed 18 December 2007).

Cohen, A., Levy, M., Roeh, I., & Gurevitch, M. (1996). *Global Newsroom, Local Audiences: A Study of the Eurovision News Exchange*. London: John Libbey.

Collins, R. (2001). Social Movements and the Focus of Emotional Attention. In J. Goodwin, J. M. Jasper & F. Polletta (Eds.), *Passionate Politics*. Chicago: The University of Chicago Press.

Corcoran, F., & Fahy, D. (2009). Exploring the European elite sphere. *Journalism Studies*, 10, 100–113.

Cottle, S. (1998). Analysing Visuals: Still and Moving Images. In A. Hansen, S. Cottle, R. Negrine, & C. Newbold (Eds.), *Mass Communication Research Methods*. Basingstoke: Macmillan.

Cottle, S. (2000). Rethinking News Access. *Journalism Studies*, 1(3), 427–448.

Cottle, S. (ed.). (2003). *News, Public Relations and Power*. London: Sage.

Cottle, S. (2006). *Mediatized Conflict: New Developments in Media and Conflict Studies*. Maidenhead: Open University Press.

Cottle, S. (2008). Reporting Demonstrations: The Changing Politics of Media Dissent. *Media, Culture & Society*, 30(6), 853–72.

Cottle, S. (2009). *Global Crisis Reporting: Journalism in the Global Age*. Maidenhead: Open University Press.

Cottle, S., & Nolan, D. (2007). Global Humanitarianism and the Changing Aid-media Field: "Everyone Was Dying for Footage." *Journalism Studies*, 8, 862–878.

Cottle, S., & Rai, M. (2008). Global 2/7 News Providers: Emissaries of Global Dominance or Global Public Sphere. *Global Media and Communication*, 4, 157–181.

Couldry, N. (2003). Beyond the Hall of Mirrors? Some Theoretical Reflections on the Global Contestation of Media Power. In N. Couldry & J. Curran (Eds.) *Contesting Media Power: Alternative Media Power in a Networked World*. Lanham, Maryland: Rowman and Littlefield.

Crack, A. M. (2008). *Global Communication and Transnational Public Spheres*. New York: Palgrave Macmillan.

Craig, G. (2002). The Spectacle of the Street: An Analysis of Media Coverage of Protests at the 2000 Melbourne World Economic Forum. *Australian Journal of Communication*, 29(1), 39–52.

Cubitt, S. (2005). *EcoMedia*. Amsterdam: Rodopi.

Dahlberg, L. and Siapera, E. (2007). *Radical Democracy and the Internet*. Houndmills, Basingstoke: Palgrave.

Dahlgren, P. (2009). *Media and Political Engagement: Citizens, Communication and Democracy*. Cambridge: Cambridge University Press.

Davis, A. (2000). Public Relations, News Production and Changing Patterns of Source Access in the British National Media. *Media, Culture and Society*, 22, 39–59.

Davis, A. (2003). Public Relations and News Sources. In S. Cottle (Ed.), *News, Public Relations and Power*. London: Sage.

Deacon, D., & Golding, P. (1994). *Taxation and Representation*. London: John Libbey.

Dear, J. (2008) NUJ Submission to the Parliamentary Committee on Human Rights—Policing and Protest. http://www.nuj.org.uk/getfile.php?id=662 (accessed 22 May 2009).

Debord, G. (1983). *Society of the spectacle*. Detroit: Black & Red.

de Jong, W., Shaw, M., & Stammers, N. (eds.). (2005). *Global Activism, Global Media*. London: Pluto.

della Porta, D. (2005). Multiple Belongings, Tolerant Identities, and the Construction of "Another Politics": Between the European Social Forum and the Local Social Fora. In D. della Porta & S. Tarrow (Eds.), *Transnational Protest and Global Activism*. Lanham, MD: Rowman & Littlefield.

della Porta, D. & Piazza, G. (2008). *Voices of the Valley, Voices of the Straits: How Protest Creates Communities*. New York: Berghahn Books.

della Porta, D. & Tarrow, S. (2005a). Transnational Processes and Social Activism: An Introduction. In D. della Porta & S. Tarrow (Eds.), *Transnational Protest and Global Activism*. Lanham, MD: Rowman & Littlefield.

della Porta, D. and Tarrow, S. (eds.). (2005b). *Transnational Protest and Global Activism*. Oxford: Rowman and Littlefield.

della Porta, D., Andretta, M., Mosca, L., & Reiter, H. (2006). *Globalization from Below: Transnational Activists and Protest Networks*. Minneapolis, London: University of Minnesota Press.

della Porta, D., & Kriesi, H. (1999). Social Movements in a Globalizing World: An Introduction. In D. della Porta, H. Kriesi, & D. Rucht (Eds.), *Social Movements in a Globalizing World*. London: Macmillan.

DeLuca, K. (1999). *Image Politics: The New Rhetoric of Environmental Activism*. New York: The Guilford Press

DeLuca, K. M. (2003). Meeting in a Redwood: Wilderness on the Public Screen. *Situation Analysis*, 2 (Spring), 32–45.

DeLuca, K. M., & Peeples, J. (2002). From Public Sphere to Public Screen: Democracy, Activism and the "Violence" of Seattle. *Critical Studies in Media Communication*, 19 (2), 125–151.

Derrida, J. (1973). *Speech and Phenomena*. Evanston, IL: Northwestern University Press.

Derrida, J. (1976). *Of grammatology*. Baltimore: The Johns Hopkins University Press.

Derrida, J. (2002). Artifactualities. In J. Derrida & B. Stiegler (Eds.), *Echographies of Television*. Boston: Polity.

Deuze, M. (2003). The Web and Its Journalisms: Considering the Consequences of Different Types of News Media Online. *New Media and Society*, 5(2), 203–226.

Diani, M. (2000). Social Movement Networks: Virtual and Real. *Information, Communication & Society*, 3(3), 386–401.

Diani, M. (2001). Social Movement Networks: Virtual and Real. In F. Webster (Ed.), *Culture and Politics in the Information Age: A New Politics?* London: Routledge.

Diani, M. (2005). Cities in the World: Local Civil Society and Global Issues in Britain. In D. della Porta & S. Tarrow (Eds.), *Transnational Protest and Global Activism*. Lanham, MD: Rowman & Littlefield.

Doherty, B., Plows, A., & Wall, D. (2003). "The Preferred Way of Doing Things": The British Direct Action Movement. *Parliamentary Affairs*, 56(4), 669–86.

Doherty, B., Plows, A., & Wall, D. (2007). Environmental Direct Action in Manchester, Oxford and North Wales: A Protest Event Analysis, *Environmental Politics*, 16(5), 805–25.

Donk, W., Loader, B., Nixon., P. and Rucht, D. (eds.). (2004). *Cyberprotest: New Media, Citizens and Social Movements*. London: Routledge.

Donnelly, J. (2003). In Defense of the Universal Declaration Model. In G. M. Lyons & J. Mayall (Eds.), *International Human Rights in the 21ˢᵗ Century: Protecting the Rights of Groups*. Lanham, MD: Rowman and Littlefield.

Downey, J. (2007). Participation and/or Deliberation? The Internet as a Tool for Achieving Radical Democratic Aims. In L. Dahlberg and E. Siapera (Eds.), *Radical Democracy and the Internet: Interrogating Theory and Practice*. Basingstoke: Palgrave Macmillan.

Downey, J., & Fenton, N. (2003). New Media, Counter Publicity and the Public Sphere. *New Media & Society*, 2, 187.

Driscoll, C. (2008). This is not a Blog: Gender, Intimacy, and Community. *Feminist Media Studies*, 8 (2) 198–202.

Earl, J. (2000). Methods, Movements, and Outcomes. *Social Movements, Conflicts, and Change*, 22, 3–25.

Economist, The. (2008, 14 March). Fire on the Roof of the World. http://www.economist.com/daily/news/displaystory.cfm?story_id=10870258&source=login_payBarrier (accessed 10 December 2009).

Edwards, R., et al. (2009, 2 April). G20 protests: demonstrator dies and 87 arrested following clashes with police. *Telegraph Online*. http://www.telegraph.co.uk/finance/financetopics/g20-summit/5091795/G20-protests-demonstrator-dies-and-87-arrested-following-clashes-with-police.html (accessed 2 April 2009).

Entman, R. M. (1993). Framing: Towards Clarification of a Fractured Paradigm. *Journal of Communication*, 43(4), 51–58.

Entman, R. (2004). *Projections of Power: Framing News, Public Opinion and Foreign Policy*. Chicago: University of Chicago Press.

Entman, R. M., & Page, B. I. (1994). The news before the Storm: The Iraq War Debate and the Limits to Media Independence. In W. L. Bennett & D. L. Paletz (Eds.), *Taken by Storm: The Media, Public Opinion, and US Foreign Policy in the Gulf War*. Chicago: University of Chicago Press.

Environmental Audit Committee. (2007). *The EU Emissions Trading Scheme: Lessons for the Future*. London: House of Commons.

Environmental Audit Committee. (2009). *The Role of Carbon Markets in Preventing Dangerous Climate Change*. London: House of Commons.

Epstein, C. (2008). *The Power of Words in International Relations: Birth of an Anti-whaling Discourse*. Cambridge: MIT Press.

Etzioni, A. (1970). *Demonstration Democracy*. New York: Gordon and Breach

Falk, R. A. (2002). Testing patriotism and citizenship in the global terror war. In K. Booth & T. Dunne (Eds.), *Worlds in Collision: Terror and the Future of Global Order*. London: Palgrave.

Fang, Y-J. (1994). "Riots" and Demonstrations in the Chinese Press: A Case Study of Language and Ideology. *Discourse and Society*, 5(4), 463–481.

Farrow, R., & M. Farrow. (2007, 28 March). The "Genocide Olympics." New York: *The Wall Street Journal*.

Featherstone, D. (2008). *Resistance, Space and Political Identities*. Chichester: Wiley-Blackwell.

Featherstone, M., & Lash, S. (eds.). (1999). *Spaces of culture: City, Nation, World*. London: Sage.

Feng, Y., & Xu, M. (2009). The Hatred for the Rich Complex and the Tibet Riot 2008. Paper presented at the annual meeting of the ISPP 32nd Annual Scientific Meeting, 14 July, Trinity College, Dublin, Ireland. http://www.allacademic.com/meta/p305323_index.html (accessed 20 December 2009).

Finke. R., & Stark, R. (2005). *The Churching of America: Winners and Losers in our Religious Economy*. New Brunswick: Rutgers University Press.

Fisher, D. R., Stanley, K., Berman, D., & Neff, G. (2005). How Do Organizations Matter? Mobilization and Support for Participants at Five Globalization Protests. *Social Problems*, 52, 102–121.

FitzHerbert, G. (2008, 18 June). Why Care about Tibet? *The Times Literary Supplement*. http://entertainment.timesonline.co.uk/tol/arts_and_entertainment/the_tls/article4164090.e ce (accessed 18 January 2009).

Fleras, A., & Elliott J. L. (1999). *Unequal Relations: Race, Ethnic and Aboriginal Dynamics in Canada*. Scarborough, Ontario: Prentice Hall Allyn & Bacon.

Forney, M. (2008, 15 April). China's Loyal Youth. *The New York Times*. http://www.nytimes.com/2008/04/15/opinion/15iht-edforney.1.12004110.html (accessed 28 August 2009).

Frazer, N. (2007). Transnationalizing the Public Sphere: On the Legitimacy and Efficacy of Public Opinion in a Post-Westphalian World. *Theory, Culture & Society*, 24(4), 7–30.

Frazer, N., & Honneth, A. (2003). *Redistribution of Recognition?* London: Verso.

Friedman, T. (2005). *The World is Flat*. New York: Farrar, Straus and Giroux.

Gamson, W.A. (1988). Political Discourse and Collective Action, *International Social Movement Research* 1, pp. 219–46.

Gamson, W. A., & Modigliani, A. (1989). Media Discourse and Public Opinion on Nuclear Power: A Constructionist Approach. *The American Journal of Sociology*, 95 (1), 1–37.

Gamson, W., & Wolfsfeld, G. (1993). Movement and Media as Interacting Systems. *Annals of the American Academy of Political Science*, 528, 114–125.

García Pérez, A. (2007, 28 October). El síndrome del perro del hortelano. *El Comercio*, http://elcomercio.pe/edicionimpresa/html/2007–10 28/el_sindrome_del_perro_del_hort. html (accessed June 2010).

Garrett, R. K. (2006). Protest in an Information Society: A Review of Literature on social movements and ICTs. *Information, Communication & Society*, 9, 202–24.

Gavin, N. T. (2007a). Global Warming and the British Press: The Emergence of an Issue and Its Political Implications'. Paper presented at the 'Elections, Public Opinion and Parties' conference, Bristol University, September.

Gavin, N. T. (2007b). *Press and Television in British Politics: Media, Money and Mediated Democracy*. London: Palgrave/Macmillan.

Gavin, N. T. (2009). Addressing Climate Change: A Media Perspective. *Environmental Politics*, 18(5), 765–80.

Gavin, N. T. (2010). Pressure Group Direct Action on Climate Change: The Role of the Media and the Web in Britain—A Case Study. *British Journal of Politics and International Relations*, 12 (3) 459–75.

Gensuikyo. (2003, 5 August). Declaration of the International Meeting from The World Conference Against Atomic and Hydrogen Bombs. http://www10.plala.or.jp/antiatom/html/e/eWC/e03wc/intl-meeting/e-dec.htm (accessed 12 December 2007).

Gerbner, G., Gross, L., Morgan, M., & Signorielli, N. (1986). Living with Television: The Dynamics of the Cultivation Process. In J. Bryant & D. Zillman (Eds.), *Perspectives on Media Effects*. Hilldale, NJ: Lawrence Erlbaum Associates.

Ghannam, J. (2011). *Social Media in the Arab World: Leading up to the Uprisings of 2011*. Washington, D.C.: Center for International Media Assistance.

Giddens, A. (1990). *The Consequences of Modernity*. Cambridge: Polity Press.

Giddens, A. (1991). *Modernity and Self–identity: Self and Society in the Late Modern Age*. Stanford: Stanford University Press.

Giddens, A. (2000). *Runaway World: The Reith Lectures Revisited*. Lecture 5: Democracy. http://www.lse.ac.uk/Depts/global/ (accessed 5 May 2009).

Gill, S. (2003). *Power and Resistance in the New World Order*. New York: Palgrave Macmillan.

Gillan, K. (2008). Diverging Attitudes to Technology and Innovation in Anti-War Movement Organisations. In T. Häyhtiö & J. Rinne (Eds.), *Net Working/Networking: Citizen Initiated Politics*. Tampere: Tampere University Press.

Gillan, K., & Pickerill, J. (2008). Transnational Anti-war activism: Solidarity, Diversity and the Internet in Australia, Britain and the United States after 9/11. *Australian Journal of Political Science*, 43 (1) 59–78.

Gillan, K., Pickerill, J., & Webster, F. (2008) *Anti-War Activism: New Media and Protest in the Information Age*. Basingstoke: Palgrave Macmillan.

Gills, B. (ed.). (2000). *Globalization and the Politics of Resistance*. New York: St. Martin's Press.

Gitlin, T. (1980). *The Whole World Is Watching: Mass Media in the Making and Unmaking of the New Left*. Berkeley: University of California Press.

Glasgow University Media Group. (1985). *War and Peace News*. Milton Keynes: Open University Press.

Gobierno del Perú. (2010). Informe Final de la Comision Especial para investigar y analizar los sucesos de Bagua. Lima, Perú.

Goddard, P., Robinson, P., & Parry, K. (2008). Patriotism Meets Plurality: Reporting the 2003 Iraq War in the British Press. *Media, War and Conflict*, 1(1), 7–27.

Goggin, G. (2003). Digital Rainbows: Inventing the Internet in the Northern Rivers. In *Belonging in the Rainbow Region*. Lismore: Southern Cross University Press.

Goggin, G. (2004). Antipodean Internet: Placing Australian Networks. In G. Goggin (Ed.), *Virtual Nation: The Internet in Australia*. Sydney: New South Wales University Press.

Goodwin, J., Jasper J. M., & Polletta, F. (eds.). (2001). *Passionate Politics*. Chicago: University of Chicago Press.

Gootenberg, P. (1993). *Imagining Development*. Berkeley: University of California Press.

Gould, D. (2001). Life During Wartime. *Mobilization* 7(2), 177–200.

Gourevitch, A. (2001, 29 June). No justice, no contract: The Worker Rights Consortium leads the fight against sweatshops. *The American Prospect Online*. http://www.prospect.org/cs/articles?article=no_justice_no_contract (accessed June 2010).

Gowing, N. (2009). *"Skyful of Lies" and Black Swans: The New Tyranny of Shifting Information Power in Crises*. Oxford: Reuters Institute for the Study of Journalism, University of Oxford.

Greene, K. F. (2007). *Why Dominant Parties Lose: Mexico's Democratization in Comparative Perspective*. London: Cambridge University Press.

Greenpeace Australia Pacific. (2003,19 December). John Butler Trio Singer Visits Global Rescue Station in Styx Forest. Media release.

Greenpeace Australia Pacific. (2004a, 15 January). "Working Class Man" Lends a Hand to Styx Campaign. Media release.

Greenpeace Australia Pacific. (2004b, 12 March). Thousands Expected at Rally for Tasmania's Forests. Media release.

Greenpeace Australia Pacific. (2004c, 7 April). Styx Campaign Shifts from Tree-Sit to Ballot Box. Media Release.

Grossman, L. K. (1995). *The Electronic Republic: Reshaping Democracy in America*. New York: Viking.

Gunning, T. (1999). Embarrassing Evidence: The Detective Camera and the Documentary Impulse. In J. M. Gaines & M. Renov (Eds.), *Collecting Visible Evidence*, London: University of Minnesota Press.

Habermas, J. (1974). The Public Sphere. *New German Critique*, 3 (Autumn), 49–59.

Habermas, J. (1984). *The Theory of Communicative Action*. Boston: Beacon Press.

Habermas, J. (1989). *The Structural Transformation of the Public Sphere: An Inquiry into a Category of Bourgeois Society*. Cambridge, Massachusetts: MIT Press.

Habermas, J. (1996). *Between Facts and Norms: Contributions to a Discourse Theory of Law and Democracy*. Cambridge: Polity Press.

Hacker, K. L., & Todino, M. A. (1996). Virtual Democracy at the Clinton White House: An Experiment in Electronic Democratisation, *Javnost/the Public*, 3(1), 71–86.

Hackett, R. A., & Zhao, Y. (1994). Challenging a master narrative: Peace Protest and Opinion/Editorial Discourse in the US Press during the Gulf War. *Discourse & Society*, 54(4). 509–41.

Hafez, K. (2007). *The myth of media globalization*. Malden, MA: Polity.

Hague, B. N., & Loader, B. (1999). *Digital Democracy: Discourse and Decision Making in the Information Age*. London: Routledge.

Hall, S. (1973a). A World at One with Itself. In S. Cohen & J. Young (Eds.), *The Manufacture of News: Social Problems, Deviance and the Mass Media*. London: Constable.

Hall, S. (1973b). *Encoding and Decoding the TV Message*. CCCS mimeo: University of Birmingham.

Hall. S., Chritcher, C., Jefferson, T., Clarke, J., & Roberts, B. (1978). *Policing the Crisis, Mugging, the State and Law and Order.* London: Macmillan.

Hallin, D. (1986). *The "Uncensored War?" The Media and Vietnam.* New York: Oxford University Press.

Hallin, D., & Mancini, P. (1992). The Summit as Media Event: The Reagan/Gorbachev Meetings on US, Italian, and Soviet Television. In J. Blumler, K. E. Rosengren, & J. McLeod (Eds.), *Comparatively Speaking: Communication and Culture across Space and Time.* Beverly Hills: Sage.

Halloran, J., Elliott, P., & Murdock, G. (1970). *Demonstrations and Communication: A Case Study.* London: Penguin.

Halpin, E. F., & Hick, S. (2000). Information: an Essential Tool for Human Rights Work. In S. Hick, E. F. Halpin, & E. Hoskins (Eds.), *Human Rights and Internet.* Basingstoke: Macmillan.

Hames, R. (2007). The Ecologically Noble Savage Debate. *Annual Review of Anthropology,* 36, 177–190.

Hamilton, J. M., & Jenner, E. (2004). Redefining Foreign Correspondence. *Journalism,* 5(3), 301–321.

Hannerz, U. (2004). *Foreign News: Exploring the World of Foreign Correspondents.* Chicago and London: The University of Chicago Press.

Hansard. (2009, 1 April). http://www.publications.parliament.uk/pa/cm200809/cmhansrd/cm090401/halltext/90401h0005.htm (accessed 23 May 2009).

Hansen, A. (ed.). (1993). *The Mass Media and Environmental Issues.* Leicester: Leicester University Press.

Harcourt, W., & Escobar, A. (2002). Women and the Politics of Place. *Development,* 45, 7–14.

Hardt, M., & Negri, A. (2000). *Empire.* Cambridge: Harvard University Press.

Harper, M. (2009). Saving the Franklin: The Environment Takes Centre Stage. In M. Crotty & A. Roberts (Eds.), *Turning Points in Australian History.* Sydney: University of New South Wales Press.

Hartley, J. (1992). *The Politics of Pictures.* New York: Routledge.

Hartmann, D. (1996). The Politics of Race and Sport: Resistance and Domination in the 1968 African American Olympic Protest Movement. *Ethnic and Racial Studies,* 19, 548–566.

Harvey, D. (1989). *The Condition of Postmodernity.* Cambridge: Blackwell.

Hay, P. (1991–1992). Destabilising Tasmanian Politics: The Key Role of the Greens. *Bulletin of the Centre for Tasmanian Historical Studies,* 3(2), 60–70.

Hayes, D., & Guardino, M. (2010). Whose Views Made the News? Media Coverage and the March to War in Iraq. *Political Communication,* 27, 57–87.

Held, D. (2004). *The Global Covenant.* Cambridge: Polity.

Helsinki Citizens' Assembly (HCA). (2007). *Unwelcome Guests: The Detention of Refugees in Turkey's "Foreigners' Guesthouses."* www.hyd.org.tr/staticfiles/files/rasp_detention_report.pdf (accessed 17 November 2009).

Her Majesty's Inspector of Constabulary (HMIC). (2009). Adapting to Protest: Inspecting Police in the Public Interest. http://www.hmic.gov.uk/SiteCollectionDocuments/PPR/PPR_20090706.pdf (accessed 10 September 2009).

Herman, E. S. (2000). The Propaganda Model: A Retrospective. *Journalism Studies,* 1(1), 101–112.

Herman, E. & Chomsky, N. (2008). *Manufacturing Consent: The Political Economy of the Mass Media.* London: The Bodley Head.

Hetherington, K. (1998). *Expressions of Identity*. London: Sage Publications.

Hilsum, L. (2008, 19 March). The Truth about Tibet. *New Statesman*. http://www.newstatesman .com/asia/2008/03/dalai-lama-china-chinese-tibet (accessed 10 August 2008).

Hjarvard, S. (2001). News Media and the Globalization of the Public Sphere. In *News Media in a Globalized Society*. Goteborg: Nordicom.

Hodge, N. (2009). Inside Moldova's Twitter Revolution. *Danger Room: What's Next in National Security*. Wired.Com. http://www.wired.com/dangerroom/2009/04/inside-moldovas/ (accessed 15 January 2010).

Holbert, R. L., Garrett, R. K., & Gleason, L. S. (2010). A New Era of Minimal Effects? A Response to Bennett and Iyengar. *Journal of Communication*, 60, 15–34.

Home Office. (2009, 18 August). Circular 012/2009: Photography and Counter-Terrorism Legislation. http://www.homeoffice.gov.uk/about-us/publications/home-office-circulars/circulars-2009/012-2009/ (accessed 10 September 2009).

House of Commons Home Affairs Committee. (2009, 15 December). Policing of the G20 Protests: Government's Response to the Committee's Eight Report of Session 2008–09–First Special Report of Session 2009–10. http://www.parliament.thestationeryoffice.co.uk/pa/cm200910/cmselect/cmhaff/201/201.pdf (accessed 22 March 2010).

House of Representatives. (2007). Expressing the Sense of the House of Representatives That the President Should Take Immediate Action to Boycott the Summer Olympic Games of 2008 in Beijing, China. http://www.govtrack.us/congress/bill.xpd?bill=hr110–628 (accessed June 2010).

Hu, W. (2010, 27 April). In New Jersey, a Civics Lesson in the Internet Age. *New York Times*.

Hu, X., & Salazar, M. A. (2006). Market Formation and Transformation: Private Business in Lhasa. In B. Sautman & J. T. Dreyer (Eds.), *Contemporary Tibet: Politics, Development, and Society in a Disrupted Region*. New York and London: M. E. Sharpe.

Human Rights Watch. (2001). Freedom of Expression and the Internet in China: A Human Rights Watch Backgrounder.

Human Rights Watch, (2008). China: Hosting Olympics a Catalyst for Human Rights Abuses. IOC and World Leaders Fail to Challenge Great Leap Backward for Rights in China. china.hrw.org. http://china.hrw.org/press/news_release/china_hosting_olympics_a_catalyst_for_human_rights_abuses (accessed 22 August 2008).

Hutchins, B., & Lester, L. (2006). Environmental Protest and Tap-dancing with the Media in the Information Age. *Media, Culture & Society*, 28(3), 433–51.

Içduygu, A., & Biehl, K. (2008). *Living Together Programme. Migrant Cities Research: Istanbul*. http://www.britishcouncil.org.tr/LivingTogether/migrantcitiesreports/Istanbul.pdf (accessed 17 November 17).

Ignatieff, M. (2001). *Human Rights as Politics and Idolatry*. Cambridge, MA: Harvard University Press.

Independent, The (2009, 19 June) Images of "Amazon's Tiananmen"—Peru Accused of Cover-up after Indigenous Protest Ends in Death at Devil's Bend. Article by Guy Adams, *Independent World News Americas*. http://www.independent.co.uk/news/world/americas/images-reveal-full-horror-of-amazons-tiananmen-1708990.html (accessed June 2010).

International Crisis Group. (2011) *CrisisWatch*, No.91. March. (http://www.crisisgroup.org/)

iProspect. (2008). *iProspect Blended Search Results Study*. www.iprospect.com/about/research-study_2008_blendedsearchresults.htm (accessed February 2010).

Irish Examiner. (2003, 13 November). Greenpeace in Treetop Fight to Save Hardwood Forest. *Irish Examiner* http://archives.tcm.ie/irishexaminer/2003/11/13/story610614766.asp (accessed 9 January 2008).

Ishani, M. (2011). 'The Hopeful Network' *Foreign Policy*. (http://www.foreignpolicy.com/ articles /2011/02/07/the_hopeful_network)

ITV Evening News. (2008). At least two people are reported to be killed in the most violent clash between the police and protesters in Tibet for nearly twenty years, 14 March [News video].

ITV News at Ten. (2008). China is cracking down hard on Buddhist monks, 13 March [News video].

Iyengar, S. (1991). *Is Anyone Responsible?: How Television Frames Political Issues*. Chicago, IL: University of Chicago Press.

Jacobs, A. (2008). Battered Olympic Tour to Continue, but IOC Chief Rebukes China. Beijing. http://www.nytimes.com/2008/04/10/world/americas/10iht-torch.4. 11878506.html?scp=1&sq=Battered%20Olympic%20tour%20to%20continue,%20but%20I OC%20chief%20rebukes%20China&st=cse (accessed August 2008).

James, D. (2000). Ten Ways to Democratize the Global Economy. In K. Danaher & R. Burbach (Eds.), *Globalize This: The Battle Against the World Trade Organization and Corporate Rule*. Monroe, ME: Common Courage Press.

Jameson, F. (1984). Postmodernism, or the Cultural Logic of Late Capitalism. *New Left Review*, 146, 53–92.

Jansen, B. J., & Spink, A. (2005). An Analysis of Web Searching by European AllltheWeb.com Users. *Information Processing Management*, 41(2), 361–81.

Jansen, B. J., & Spink, A. (2006). How Are We Searching the World Wide Web? A Comparison of Nine Search Engine Transaction Logs. *Information Processing Management*, 42(1), 248–63.

Jenkins, H. (2006). *Convergence Culture: Where Old and New Media Collide*. New York: New York University Press.

Jha, S. (2008). Why They Wouldn't Cite from Sites: A Study of Journalists' Perceptions of Social Movement Web Sites and the Impact on Their Coverage of Social Protest. *Journalism*, 9, 711–32.

Jia, Q. (2005). Disrespect and Distrust: the External Origins of Contemporary Chinese Nationalism. *Journal of Contemporary China*, 14(42) February, 11–21.

Jones, S. (2001a). China: Now It's Up to the Olympic Sponsors. HRW.org.

Jones, S. (2001b). China: Require Rights Guaranteed from Olympic Hosts. *International Herald Tribune*.

Journalist. (2009). Up against the Law. May/June 2009, 14–17.

Juris, J. S. (2005a). The New Digital Media and Activist Networking within Anti-Corporate Globalization Movements. *The Annals of the American Academy of Political and Social Science*, 597, 189–208.

Juris, J. S. (2005b). Violence Performed and Imagined. *Critique of Anthropology*, 25(4), 413–432.

Juris, J. S. (2008a). Performing Politics: Image, Embodiment, and Affective Solidarity during Anti-corporate Globalization Protests. *Ethnography*, 9(1), 61–97.

Juris, J. S. (2008b). *Networking Futures*. Durham, NC: Duke University Press.

Kaid, L. L., & Holtz-Bacha, C. (2008). *Encyclopedia of Political Communication*, Volume 1. London: Sage.

Kalathil, S., & Boas, T. C. (2003). *Open Networks Closed Regimes: The Impact of the Internet on Authoritarian Rule*. Washington, DC: Carnegie.

Kaldor, M. (2003). *Global Civil Society*. Cambridge: Polity.

Kaldor, M. (2007). *Human Security*. Cambridge: Polity.

Kapchan, D. A. (1995). Performance. *Journal of American Folklore*. 108(430), 479–508.

Karp Toledo, E., & Tucker, L. L. (eds.). (2003). *El tema indígena en debate–Aportes para la reforma constitucional*. Despacho de la Primera Dama de la Nación. Lima, Perú.

Katz, C. (2001). On the Grounds of Globalization: A Topography for Feminist Political Engagement. *Signs*, 26, 1213–1234.

Kaufmann, D., Kraay, A., & Mastruzzi, M. (2007). *Governance Matters VI: Governance Indicators for 1996–2006*. http://www.worldbank.org/reference/ (accessed 1 February 2008).

Keane, J. (2003). *Global Civil Society*. Cambridge: Cambridge University Press.

Keane, J. (2005). Global Civil Society. In J. A. Hall & F. Trentmann (Eds.), *Civil Society: A Reader in History, Theory and Global Politics*. Basingstoke: Palgrave Macmillan.

Keck, M. E., & Sikkink, K. (1998). *Activists Beyond Borders: Advocacy Networks in International Politics*. Ithaca: Cornell University Press.

Keddie, N.R. and Richard, Y. (2003). *Modern Iran: Roots and Results of Revolution*. New Haven: Yale University Press.

Kellner, D. M. (1992). *The Persian Gulf TV War*. Boulder, CO: Westview.

Kellner, D. (2003). *Media Spectacle*. London: Routledge.

Keohane, R., & Nye, J. (2000). Globalization: What's New? What's Not? (And So What?) *Foreign Policy* (spring), 104–119.

Khagram, S., Riker, J. V., & Sikkink, K. (2002). From Santiago to Seattle: Transnational Advocacy Groups Restructuring World Politics. In S. Khagram, J. V. Riker, & K. Sikkink (Eds.), *Restructuring World Politics: Transnational Social Movements, Networks and Norms*. Minneapolis, MN: University of Minnesota Press.

Kitzinger, J. (2000). Media Templates: Patterns of Association and the (Re)construction of Meaning over Time. *Media, Culture & Society*, 22(1), 61–84.

Klar, M., & Kasser, T. (2009). Some Benefits of Being an Activist: Measuring Activism and Its Role in Psychological Wellbeing. *Political Psychology*, 30(5), 755–77.

Klein, N. (2001). Reclaiming the Commons. *New Left Review*, 9, 81–89.

Kolb, F. (2005). Mass Media and the Making of ATTAC Germany. In D. della Porta & S. Tarrow (Eds.), *Transnational Protest and Global Activism*. Lanham, MD: Rowman & Littlefield.

Koopmans, R. (2004). Movements and Media: Selection Processes and Voluntary Dynamics in the Public Sphere. *Theory and Society*, 33, 367–391.

Laclau, E., & C. Mouffe (1985). *Hegemony and Socialist Strategy*. Verso: London.

Langman, L. (2005). From Virtual Public Spheres to Global Justice: A Critical Theory of Internetworked Social Movements. *Sociological Theory*, 23(1), 42–74.

Lanier, J. (2010). *You Are Not a Gadget*. New York: Knopf.

Latham, K. (2009). Media, the Olympics and the Search for the "Real China." *China Quarterly*, 197, 25–43.

le Grignou, B., & Patou, C. (2004). ATTAC(k)ing Expertise: Does the Internet Really Democratize Knowledge? In W. van de Donk, B. D. Loader, P. G. Nixon, & D. Rucht (Eds.), *Cyberprotest: New Media, Citizens, and Social Movements*. New York: Routledge.

Lester, L. (2006). Lost in the Wilderness? Celebrity, Protest and the News. *Journalism Studies*, 7(6), 907–921.

Lester, L. (2007). *Giving Ground: Media and Environmental Conflict in Tasmania*. Hobart: Quintus.

Lester, L. (2010). *Media and Environment: Conflict, Politics and the News*. Cambridge: Polity.

Lester, L., & Cottle, S. (2009). Visualizing climate change: television news and ecological citizenship. *International Journal of Communication*, 3, 920–36.

Lester, L., & Hutchins, B. (2009). Power Games: Environmental Protest, News Media and the Internet. *Media, Culture & Society*, 31, (4) 579–95.

Leung, L. (2009). Mediated Violence as "Global News": Co-opted "Performance" in the Framing of the WTO. *Media, Culture & Society*, 31, 251–269.

Levi, M., & Murphy, G. H. (2006). Coalitions of Contention: The Case of the WTO Protests in Seattle. *Political Studies*, 54(4), 651–670.

Levin, J. (1960). *The Export Economies: Their Pattern of Development in Historical Perspective*. Cambridge MA: Harvard University Press.

Lewis, J., Inthorn, S., & Wahl-Jorgensen, K. (2005). *Citizens or Consumers? What the Media Tell Us About Political Participation*. Buckingham: Open University Press.

Lewis, J., Williams, A., & Franklin, B. (2008). A Compromised Fourth Estate? UK News Journalism, Public Relations and News Sources. *Journalism Studies* 9(1): 1–20.

Lewis, P. (2010, 25 March). I feared the crowd, says G20 policeman charged with baton assault. *Guardian Online*. http://www.guardian.co.uk/uk/2010/mar/25/g20-smellie-fisher-assault-trial (accessed 25 March 2010).

Lewis, P., & Taylor, M. (2009, 6 November). Scotland Yard riot squad faces calls to end "culture of impunity." *Guardian Online*. http://www.guardian.co.uk/politics/2009/nov/06/police-scotland-yard-riot-squad (accessed 7 November 2009).

Lewis, S., & Reese, S. D. (2008). What Is the War on Terror? Exploring Framing through the Eyes of Journalists. In *Association for Education in Journalism and Mass Communication*. Chicago, Illinois.

Li, C. (2006). *A Policy Approach to Ethno-Cultural Diversity, Cultural Politics and Audiovisual Media within China*. MA Dissertation. University of Leeds. http://129.11.76.45/pg%20study/ma%-20showcase/Chen_Li.doc.

Lindgren, B. (2004). *Power and Counter Power in Zimbabwe: Political Violence and Cultural Resistance*. The Nordic Africa Institute. http://www.nordiskaafrikainstitutet.com (accessed 30 April 2008).

Liu, J. (2008). The Western Media Hegemony: The Case of Tibet Riot [in Chinese]. *Li lun wen ge*, March, 60–63.

Liu, J. H. (2007). Lighting the Torch of Human Rights: the Olympic Games as a Vehicle for Human Rights Reform. *Northwestern Journal of International Human Rights*, 5, 213–236.

Loewenstein, A. (2008). *The Blogging Revolution*. Melbourne: Melbourne University Publishing.

London Summit, The. 2009. (2009, 2 April).Global Plan for Recovery and Reform (02/04/2009). http://www.londonsummit.gov.uk/resources/en/news/15766232/communique-020409 (accessed 5 October 2009).

Lord, C. (2000, 7 August). General News Online. *Olympics 2000. The Times*.

Luft, O. (2010, 24 March). Paul Lewis: Police Tried to Discourage our Story. *Press Gazette* http://www.pressgazette.co.uk/story.asp?sectioncode=1&storycode=45224&c=1 (accessed 28 March 2010).

Luther, C. A., & Miller, M. M. (2005). Framing of the 2003 U.S.-Iraq War Demonstrations: An Analysis of News and Partisan Texts. *Journalism & Mass Communication Quarterly*, 82(1), 78–96.

MacLean Stearman, A. (1994). "Only Slaves Climb Trees": Revisiting the Myth of the Ecologically Noble Savage in Amazonia. *Human Nature*, 5(4), 339–357.

Macnaghten, P., & Urry, J. (1998). *Contested Natures*. London, Sage.

Maguire, S. (1998, 7 March). Alone up a Tree, Linked to the World. *The Mercury*.

Mannaert, C. (2003). *Irregular Migration and Asylum in Turkey*. Report prepared for United Nations High Commissioner for Refugees.

Manning P. (2001). *News and News Sources: A Critical Introduction*. London: Sage.

Manuel, G., & Posluns, M. (1974). *The Fourth World: An Indian Reality*. Collier Macmillan Canada, Ontario.

Martain, T. (2003, 13 November). Global Eco-Activists Get the Message Out. *The Mercury*.

Mauss, M. (1973). Techniques of the Body. *Economy and Society*, 2(1), 70–88.

McAdam, D. (2000). Movement Strategy and Dramaturgic Framing in Democratic States: The Case of the American Civil Rights Movement. In S. Chambers & A. Costain (Eds.), *Deliberation, Democracy and the Media*. Oxford: Rowman and Littlefield.

McAdam, D., Tarrow, S., & Tilly, C. (2001). *Dynamics of Contention*. New York: Cambridge University Press.

McCaughey, M., & Ayers, M. D. (2003). *Cyberactivism: Online Activism in Theory and Practice*, New York: Routledge.

McCombs, M. E. (2005). A Look at Agenda-Setting: Past, Present and Future. *Journalism Studies*, 6(4), 543–57.

McElroy, D. (2009). Iran Protest News Travels Fast and Far on Twitter. Telegraph.co.uk. http://www.telegraph.co.uk/news/worldnews/middleeast/iran/5549955/Iran-protest-news-travels-fast-and-far-on-Twitter.html (accessed 15 January 2010).

McFadden, R. (2003, 16 February). From New York to Melbourne, cries for peace. *New York Times*. http://www.nytimes.com/2003/02/16/international/16RALL.html (accessed June 2010).

McFarlane, C. (2009). Translocal Assemblages: Space, Power and Social Movements. *Geoforum*, 40(4), 561–567

McGee, M. (1975). In Search of the People: A Rhetorical Alternative. *Quarterly Journal of Speech*, 61(3), 235–249.

McLeod, D. C., & Detenber, B. H. (1999). Framing Effects of Television News Coverage of Social Protest. *Journal of Communication*, 49(3), 3–23.

McLuhan, M. (1964). *Understanding Media: The Extension of Man*. New York: McGraw-Hill.

McNair, B. (2006) *Cultural Chaos: Journalism, News and Power in a Globalised World*. London: Routledge.

Meister, M., & Japp, P. M. (eds.). (2002). *Enviropop: Studies in Environmental Rhetoric and Popular Culture*. Westport: Praeger.

Melluci, A. (1996). *Challenging Codes: Collective Action in the Information Age*. Cambridge: Cambridge University Press.

Memou, A. (2010). "When It Bleeds, It Leads": Death and Press Photography in the Anti-Capitalist Protests in Genoa. *Third Text*, 24(3), 341–351.

Metropolitan Police. (2009). Photography Advice. http://www.met.police.uk/about/photography.htm (accessed 7 July 2009).

Metropolitan Police. (2010). The Investigation into the Death of Blair Peach. http://www.met.police.uk/foi/units/blair_peach.htm (accessed 17 May 2010).

Metropolitan Police Civil Rights Panel. (2010). Responding to G20 (Final Draft). http://www.mpa.gov.uk/downloads/committees/mpa/100325–06-appendix01.pdf (accessed 22 March 2010).

Meyrowitz, J. (1985). *No Sense of Place*. New York: Oxford University.

Miles, J. (2008, 15 March). They stopped attacking the boy when I rushed forward. *The Times*. http://www.timesonline.co.uk/tol/news/world/asia/article3556473.ece (accessed 10 December 2009).

Miller, K. (2005). *Communications Theories: Perspectives, Processes, and Contexts*. New York: McGraw-Hill.

Milne, K. (2005). *Manufacturing Dissent: Single-Issue Protest, the Public and the Press*. London: Demos.

Morgan, J. (2004). Distinguishing Truth, Knowledge, and Belief: A Philosophical Contribution to the Problem of Images of China. *Modern China*, 30(3) July, 398–427.

Morley, D. (1980). *The Nationwide Audience: Structure and Decoding*. London: BFI.

Morozov, E. (2011). *The Net Delusion: How Not to Liberate the World*. London: Allen Lane.

Morris, A. (1999). The Olympic Experience: An Aboriginal Perspective. In T. Taylor (Ed.), *The First International Conference on Sports and Human Rights*. Sydney, Australia, University of Technology, Sydney.

Moyo, L. (2010). The Global Citizen and the International Media: A Comparative Analysis of CNN and Xinhua's Coverage of the Tibetan Crisis. *The International Communication Gazette*, 72(2), 191–207.

Murdock, G. (1973). Political Deviance: The Press Presentation of a Militant Mass Demonstration. In S. Cohen & J. Young (Eds.), *The Manufacture of News: Social Problems, Deviance and the Mass Media*. London: Constable.

Murdock, G. (1981). Political Deviance: The Press Presentation of a Militant Mass Demonstration. In J. Young & S. Cohen (Eds.), *The Manufacture of News—Deviance, Social Problems and the Mass Media*. London: Constable.

Murray, C., Parry, K., Robinson, P., & Goddard, P. (2008). Reporting Dissent in Wartime: British Press, the Anti-war Movement and the 2003 Iraq War. *European Journal of Communication*, 23(1), 7–27.

Nagtzaam, G., & Lentini, P. (2008). Vigilantes on the High Seas?: The *Sea Shepherds* and Political Violence. *Terrorism and Political Violence*, 20(1), 110–33.

Nah, S., Veenstra, A. S., & Shah, D. (2006). The Internet and Anti-War Activism: A Case Study of Information, Expression and Action. *Journal of Computer-Mediated Communication*, 12(1), http://jcmc.indiana.edu/vol12/issue1/nah.html (accessed 5 December 2006).

Neales, S. (2008, 1 November). Bartlett's Forestry Balancing Act. *The Mercury*.

New York Times. (2008, 10 April). Parliament Urges EU Leaders to Boycott Olympic Opening Ceremony. http://www.nytimes.com/2008/04/10/world/europe/10iht-brown.4.11878547.html (accessed 8 August 2008).

Nichols, B. (1994). *Blurred Boundaries: Questions of Meaning in Contemporary Culture*. Bloomington and Indianapolis: Indiana University Press.

Norris, P. (2002). *Democratic Phoenix: Reinventing Political Activism*. Cambridge: Cambridge University Press.

Oates, S. (2008). *An Introduction to Media and Politics*. London: Sage.

Ofcom. (2007). *New News, Future News: The Challenges for Television News After Digital Switch-Over*. London: Ofcom.

Office of Public Sector Information. (2000). Terrorism Act 2000. http://www.opsi.gov.uk/acts/acts2000/ukpga_20000011_en_6 (accessed 28 March 2010).

Office of Public Sector Information. (2008). Counter-Terrorism Act 2008. http://www.opsi.gov.uk/acts/acts2008/ukpga_20080028_en_9#pt7-pb3-l1g76 (accessed 28 March 2010).

Oliver, P., & Maney, G. M. (2000). Political Processes and Local Newspaper Coverage of Protest Events: From Selection Bias to Triadic Interactions. *American Journal of Sociology*, 106, 463–505.

O'Neill, K. (2004). Transnational Protest: States, Circuses, and Conflict at the Frontline of Global Politics. *International Studies Review*, 6, 233–251.

Opel, A., & Pompper, D. (eds.). (2003). *Representing Resistance: Media, Civil Disobedience and the Global Justice Movement*. Westport, Connecticut: Praeger.

Ostbo Haugen, H. (2003). The Construction of Beijing as an Olympic City. *Department of Sociology and Human Geography*. University of Oslo.

Ovsiovitch, J. S. (1993). News Coverage of Human Rights. *Political Research Quarterly*, 46(3), 671–689.

Owens, L. & Palmer, L.K. (2003) Making the News: Anarchist Counter-Public Relations on the World Wide Web. *Critical Studies in Media Communication*, 20 (4), 335–361.

Padovani, C. (2010). Citizens' Communication and the 2009 G8 Summit in L'Aquila, Italy. *International Journal of Communication*, 4, 416–439.

Pan, Z., & Kosicki, G. M. (1993). Framing Analysis: An Approach to News Discourse. *Political Communication*, 10(1), 55–75.

Parr, B. (2009). HOW TO: Track Iran Election with Twitter and Social Media. Mashable.com. http://mashable.com/2009/06/14/new-media-iran/ (accessed 15 January 2010).

Paterson, C. A. (2001). The Transference of Frames in Global Television. In S. D. Reese, O. H. Gandy Jnr, & A. E. Grant (Eds.), *Framing Public Life*. Mahwah, NJ: Erlbaum.

Peet R., & Watts, M. (2004). *Liberation Ecologies: Environment, Development, Social Movements*. New York: Routledge.

Perlmutter, D., & Wagner, G. (2004). The Anatomy of a Photojournalistic Icon: Marginalization of Dissent in the Selection and Framing of a "Death in Genoa." *Visual Communication*, 3(1), 91–107.

Perrottet, T. (2008, 12 April). Beware of Greeks Bearing Placards. *New York Times*. http://www.nytimes.com/2008/04/12/opinion/12perrottet.html (accessed 12 April 2008).

Peters, J. (1999). *Speaking into the Air*. Chicago: University of Chicago Press.

Peterson, A. (2001). *Contemporary Political Protest*. Aldershot: Ashgate.

PGA (People's Global Action). (1998). Organising Principles. http://www.nadir.org/nadir/initiativ/agp/cocha/principles.htm (accessed 12 December 2005).

Phillips, R. S. (2009). Bridging East and West: Muslim-identified Activists and Organisations in the UK anti-war movements. *Transactions of the Institute of British Geographers,* 34, 506–520.

Philo, G. (1990). *Seeing and Believing: The Influence of Television.* London and New York: Routledge.

Philo, G., & Berry, M. (2004). *Bad News from Israel.* London and Ann Arbor, MI: Pluto Press.

Pickerill, J. (2003). *Cyberprotest: Environmental Activism Online.* Manchester: Manchester University Press.

Pickerill, J. (2007). "Autonomy on-line": Indymedia and Practices of Alter-globalisation. *Environment and Planning,* A 39.

Pickerill, J. (2009). Symbolic Production, Representation, and Contested Identities: Anti-war Activism Online. *Information, Communication and Society,* 12 (7), 969–993.

Plows, A., Wall, D., & Doherty, B. (2004). Covert Repertoires: Ecotage in the UK. *Social Movement Studies,* 3(2), 199–219.

Portalious, E. (2008). Social Resistance Movements against the Olympic Games 2004, in Athens. *Non/De/Re-regulation: Limits, Exclusions and Claims.* International Network for urban research and action (INURA).

Poster, M. (2006). *Information Please: Culture and Politics in the Age of Digital Machines.* Durham: Duke University Press.

Powers, J. (2000). The Free Tibet Movement: A Selective Narrative. *Journal of Buddhist Ethics* 7. http://www.buddhistethics.org/7/powers001.html?referer=www.clickfind.com.au#3 (accessed 10 January 2010).

Powers, J. (2004). *History as Propaganda: Tibetan Exiles versus the People's Republic of China.* New York: Oxford University Press.

Price, V. (1992). *Public Opinion.* Newbury Park: Sage.

Radio 4 World at One. (2008, 14 March). A British journalist in Lhasa describes the tense mood. http://news.bbc.co.uk/player/nol/newsid_7290000/newsid_7296700/7296722.stm?bw=bb& mp=rm&asb=1&news=1&bbcws=1# (accessed June 2010).

Rahimi, B. (2008). The Politics of the Internet in Iran. In M. Semati (Ed.), *Media, Culture and Society in Iran: Living with Globalization and the Islamic State.* London: Routledge.

Rai, M., & Cottle, S. (2007). Global Mediations: On the Changing Ecology of Satellite Television News. *Global Media and Communication,* 3(1), 51–78.

Rapley, J. (2004). *Globalization and Inequality: Neoliberalism's Downward Spiral.* Boulder: Lynne Rienner.

Record, J. (2003). *Bounding the Global War on Terrorism.* Carlisle, PA: Strategic Studies Institute, U.S. Army War College.

Redorbit. (2008). Mini-Boycott of Olympics Urged. RedOrbit.com. http://www.redorbit.com/ news/display/?id=1302557 (accessed August 2009).

Reese, S. D. (2001). Understanding the Global Journalist: A Hierarchy-of-Influences Approach. *Journalism Studies,* 2, 173–187.

Reese, S. D. (2004). Militarized Journalism: Framing Dissent in the Persian Gulf Wars. In S. Allan & B. Zelizer (Eds.), *Reporting War: Journalism in Wartime.* New York: Routledge.

Reese, S. D. (2008). Theorizing a globalized journalism. In M. Loeffelholz & D. Weaver (Eds.), *Global Journalism Research: Theories, Methods, Findings, Future.* London: Blackwell.

Reese, S. D. (2010a) Finding Frames in a Web of Culture: The Case of the War on Terror. In P. D'Angelo & J. Kuypers (Eds.), *Doing News Framing Analysis: Empirical, Theoretical, and Normative Perspectives*. New York: Routledge.

Reese, S. D. (2010b). Journalism and Globalization. *Sociology compass*.

Reese, S. D., & Buckalew, B. (1995). The Militarism of Local Television: The Routine Framing of the Persian Gulf War. *Critical Studies in Mass Communication*, 12, 40.

Reese, S. D., & Lewis, S. (2009). Framing the War on Terror: Internalization of Policy by the U.S. press. *Journalism: Theory, Practice, Criticism*, 10(6), 777–797.

Reeve, S. (2000). *One Day in September: The Full Story of the 1972 Munich Massacre*. New York: Arcade Publishing.

Reitan, R. (2007). *Global Activism*. New York: Routledge.

Resistanbul. (n.d.). http://resistanbul.wordpress.com (accessed 13 November 2009).

Rights Watchers. (n.d.) Discuss Crises around the World. . . *Washington Post*. http://www.washingtonpost.com/wp-srv/community/groups/index.html?plckForumPage=Forum&plckForumId=Cat%3aa70e3396–6663–4a8d-ba19-e44939d3c44fForum%3adc3a3115–503a-4666–836e-c654abd1a2ce (accessed 30 October 2008).

Risbey, J. S. (2008). The New Climate Discourse: Alarmist or Alarming. *Global Environmental Change*, 18(1), 26–37.

Risse, T. and Sikkink, K. (1999). The Socialization of International Human Rights Norms into Domestic Practices: Introduction. In T. Risse, S. C. Ropp, & K. Sikkink (Eds.), *The Power of Human Rights: International Norms and Domestic Change*. Cambridge, UK: Cambridge University Press.

Robertson, A. (2010). *Mediated Cosmopolitanism*. Cambridge: Polity Press.

Robertson, R. (1990). Mapping the Global Condition: Globalization as the Central Concept. In M. Featherstone (Ed.), *Global Culture*. London: Sage.

Robinson, P. (2001). Theorizing the Influence of Media on World Politics: Models of Influence on Foreign Policy. *European Journal of Communication*, 16(4), 523–44.

Robinson, P., Goddard, P., Parry, K., & Murray, C. (2009). Testing Models of Media Performance in Wartime: UK TV News and the 2003 Invasion of Iraq. *Journal of Communication*, 59 (3), 534–63.

Robinson, P., Goddard, P., Parry, K., & Murray, C. (2010). *Pockets of Resistance: British News Media, War and Theory in the 2003 Invasion of Iraq*. Manchester: Manchester University Press.

Rodgers, J. (2003). *Spatializing International Politics: Analysing Activism on the Internet*. London: Routledge.

Rogers, R. (2008). Issue Crawler Web Network Mapping Software and Allied Tools. http://www.govcom.org/publications/full_list/rogers_issuecrawler_context.pdf (accessed 30 April 2008).

Rojecki, A. (2002). Modernism, State Sovereignty and Dissent: Media and the New Post-Cold War Movements. *Critical Studies in Media and Communication*, 19(2), 152–171.

Rojecki, A. (2004). Media Discourse on Globalization and Terror. *Political Communication*, 22, 63–81.

Ron, J., Ramos, H., & Rodgers, K. (2005). Transnational Information Politics: NGO Human Rights Reporting, 1986–2000. *International Studies Quarterly*, 49(3), 557–588.

Rosie, M., & Gorringe, H. (2009). What a Difference a Death Makes: Protest, Policing and the Press at the G20. *Sociological Research Online*, 14(5), http://www.socresonline.org.uk/14/5/4.html (accessed 18 January 2010).

Rosneau, J. M. (2002). The Drama of Human Rights in a Turbulent, Globalized World. In A. Brysk (Ed.), *Globalization and Human Rights*. Berkeley, CA: University of California Press.

Routledge, P. (1994). Backstreets, Barricades, and Blackouts. *Environment and Planning*, D 12, 559–578.

Routledge, P. (1997). The Imagineering of Resistance. *Transactions of the Institute of British Geographers*, NS 22, 359–376.

Routledge, P., & Cumbers, A. (2009). *Global Justice Networks: Geographies of Transnational Solidarity*. Manchester: Manchester University Press.

Rucht, D. (2004). The Quadruple "A": Media Strategies of Protest Movements since the 1960s. In W. van de Donk, B. D. Loader, P. G. Nixon, & D. Rucht (Eds.), *Cyberprotest: New Media, Citizens and Social Movements*. London: Routledge.

Russell, A. (2005). Myth and the Zapatista Movement: Exploring a Network Identity. *New Media & Society*, 7, 559–577.

Salter, L. (2003). Democracy, New Social Movements, and the Internet: A Habermasian Analysis. In M. McCaughey & M. D. Ayers (Eds.), *Cyberactivism: Online Activism in Theory and Practice*. New York: Routledge.

Sautman, B. (1999). The Tibet Issue in Post-summit Sino-American Relations. *Public Affairs*, 72(1), 7–21.

Sautman, B., & Dreyer, J. T. (eds.). (2006). *Contemporary Tibet: Politics, Development, and Society in a Disrupted Region*. New York and London: M. E. Sharpe.

Scalmer, S. (2002). *Dissent Events: Protest, the Media and the Political Gimmick in Australia*. Kensington: University of New South Wales Press.

Scarce, R. (1990). *Eco-warriors*. Chicago, IL: Noble Press.

Schaffer, K., & Smith, S. (2004) *Human Rights and Narrated Lives: The Ethics of Recognition*. New York: Palgrave Macmillan.

Schattschneider, E. E. (1960). *The Semisovereign People*. New York: Holt, Rinehart, Winston.

Schieffelin, E. L. (1985). Performance and the Cultural Construction of Reality. *American Ethnologist*, 12, 707–724.

Schlesinger, P. & Tumber H. (1994). *Reporting Crime*. Oxford: Clarendon Press.

Schechter, M. G. (1999). Globalization and Civil Society. In M. G. Schechter (Ed.), *The Revival of Civil Society: Global and Comparative Perspectives*. New York: Macmillan.

Schmemann, S. (2008). Olympic Flames, Then and Now. *New York Times*. http://www.nytimes.com/2008/04/27/opinion/27iht-edserge.1.12372194.html (accessed 27 April 2008).

Scholte, J. (2006). Global Civil Society. In R. Little & M. Smith (Eds.), *Perspectives on World Politics*. London: Routledge.

Schudson, M. (2005). Four Approaches to the Sociology of the News. In J. Curran & M. Gurevitch (Eds.), *Mass Media and Society* (fourth edition). New York: Hodder Arnold.

Schuldt, J. (2005). ¿Somos pobres porque somos ricos? Recursos naturales, tecnología y globalización. Fondo Editorial del Congreso de la República del Perú, Lima.

Schwartz, R. (1994). *Circle of Protest: Political Ritual in the Tibetan Uprising*. London: Hurst & Company.

Sea Shepherd. (2007, 8 February). Whalers Activities Disrupted by Sea Shepherd. Sea Shepherd news. http://www.seashepherd.org/news-and-media/news-070208–2.html (accessed 28 November 2009).

Sea Shepherd. (n.d.). Sea Shepherd's Mission Statement, http://www.seashepherd.org/who-we-are (accessed 10 December 2009).

Sennett, R. (2006). *The Culture of the New Capitalism.* New Haven: Yale University Press.

Serra, S. (2000). The Killings of Brazilian Street Children and the Rise of the International Public Sphere. In J. Curran (Ed.), *Media, Organization and Society.* London: Arnold.

Shaw, M. (1996). *Civil Society and Media in Global Crises.* London: St Martin's Press.

Shaw, M. (2005). *The New Western Way of War: Risk—Transfer War and Its Crisis in Iraq.* Cambridge: Polity.

Sikkink, K. (2002). Restructuring World Politics: The Limits and Asymmetries of Soft Power. In S. Khagram, J. V. Riker, & K. Sikkink (Eds.), *Restructuring World Politics: Transnational Social Movements, Networks and Norms.* Minneapolis, MN: University of Minnesota Press.

Sikkink, K. (2005). Patterns of dynamic multilevel governance and the insider-outsider coalition. In D. della Porta & S. Tarrow (Eds.), *Transnational Protest and Global Activism.* Lanham, MD: Rowman & Littlefield.

Smith, J., & Bandy, J. (2004). Coalitions Across Borders: Transnational Protest and the Neoliberal Order. In J. Bandy & J. Smith (Eds.), *Coalitions Across Borders: Transnational Protest and the Neoliberal Order.* Lanham: Rowman and Littlefield.

Smith, J., & Johnston, H. (eds.), (2002). *Globalization and Resistance: Transnational Dimensions of Social Movements.* Lanham, MA: Rowman & Littlefield.

Smith, J., Chatfield, C., & Pagnucco, R. (eds.). (1997). *Transnational Social Movements and Global Politics: Solidarity Beyond State.* Syracuse: Syracuse University Press.

Smith, J., McCarthy, J. D., McPhail, C., & Augustyn, B. (2001). From Protest to Agenda Building: Description Bias in Media Coverage of Protest Events in Washington, DC. *Social Forces,* 79 (4), 1397–1423.

Smith, N. (2001). Hector the Protector. In H. Gee (Ed.), *For the Forests.* Hobart: The Wilderness Society.

Smith, P. (2005). *Why War?: The Cultural Logic of Iraq, the Gulf War, and Suez.* Chicago: University of Chicago Press.

Snow, D. A. & Benford R. D. (1992). Master Frames and Cycles of Protest. In A.D. Morris, & C.M. Mueller (Eds.), *Master Frames and Cycles of Protest.* New Haven, CT: Yale University Press.

Solnit, R. (2003). *River of Shadows.* New York: Viking.

Sontag, S. (1977). *On Photography.* New York: Farrar, Straus, and Giroux.

Sonwalker, P., & Allen, S. (2007). *Citizen Journalism and Human Rights in North-East India.* http://www.wacc.org.uk (accessed 30 April 2009).

Sparks, Colin. (2007). What's Wrong with Globalization? *Global Media and Communication,* 3, 133–155.

Sreberny, A. and Khiabany, G. (2010). *Blogistan: The Internet and Politics in Iran* London: I.B. Tauris.

Stanyer, J., & Davidson, S. (2009). *The Internet and the Visibility of Oppression in Non-democratic States: The Online Exposure of Human Rights Violations and other Repressive Acts.* Paper delivered at the Annual Meeting of the International Communication Association Conference, Chicago, IL, May 20–25.

StWC. (2003). With the Palestinian and Iraqi Resistance—Against Capitalist Globalization and US Hegemony. The Second Cairo Declaration. http://www.stopwar.org.uk/article.asp?id= 141203 (accessed 12 December 2007).

Sun, Y., & DeLuca, K. (2009). Framing China: US Media, Global Warming, and the Chinese "Threat." Paper presented at the international conference "Global Warming and Climate Change," June 17–19. Lingnan University, Hongkong.

Sunstein, C. R. (2007). *Republic.com 2.0*. Princeton: Princeton University Press.

Tagg, J. (2009). *The Disciplinary Frame: Photographic Truths and the Capture of Meaning*. London and Minneapolis: University of Minnesota Press.

Tarrow, S. (1998). *Power in Movement: Social Movements and Contentious Politics*. Second Edition. Cambridge: Cambridge University Press.

Tarrow, S. (2001). Transnational Politics: Contention and Institutions in International Politics. *Annual Review of Political Science*, 4, 1–20.

Tarrow, S. (2005a). *The New Transnational Activism*. Cambridge: Cambridge University Press.

Tarrow, S. (2005b). Rooted Cosmopolitans and Transnational Activists. Prepared for a special issue of Rassegna Italiana di Sociologia. Available at http://falcon.arts.cornell.edu/Govt/faculty/Tarrow%20docs/rooted%20cosmopolitans.pdf (accessed 14 June 2007).

Tarrow, S. (2006). *The New Transnational Activism*. Cambridge: Cambridge University Press.

Tarrow, S., & McAdam, D. (2005). Scale Shift in Transnational Contention. In D. della Porta & S. Tarrow (Eds.), *Transnational Protest & Global Activism*. Oxford: Rowman and Littlefield.

Telecommunication Company of Iran: Annual Report 2003, Accessed July 2009, http://www.tci.ir/s1_6/p_2.aspx?lang=En

TeleSur. (2009, 8 June). TeleSur/TV Peru. Edited excerpts from http://www.youtube.com/watch?v=He41YLgm28k&feature=related (accessed June 2010).

The Sunday Times/Times online. (2008). Fears of another Tiananmen as Tibet explodes in hatred. *Sunday Times* [Internet], 16 March. Available from: <http://www.timesonline.co.uk/tol/news/world/asia/article3559355.ece> [Accessed 10 December 2009].

Thompson, E. P. (1991). *The Making of the English Working Class*. London: Penguin Books.

Thompson, E. P. (1993). *Customs in Common*. London: Penguin Books.

Thompson, J. B. (1995). *Media and Modernity*. Cambridge: Polity.

Thompson, J. B. (2005). The New Visibility. *Theory, Culture & Society*, 22(6), 31–51.

Thussu, D. K. (2000). *International Communication: Continuity and Change*. London: Arnold.

Thussu, D., & Freedman, D. (Eds.). (2003). *War and the Media: Reporting Conflict 24/7*. London: Sage.

Tilly, C. (2004). *Social Movements, 1768–2004*. Boulder, CO: Paradigm.

Tilly, C. (2005). *Popular Contention in Great Britain, 1758–1834*. Boulder, CO: Paradigm.

Time. (2006, 15 April). Dalai Lama: Tibet Wants Autonomy, Not Independence. http://www.time.com/time/world/article/0,8599,1184009,00.html.

Tomasulo, F. P. (1996) "I'll see it when I believe it": Rodney King and the Prison-House of Video. In V. Sobchack (Ed.), *The Persistence of History: Cinema, Television and the Modern Event*. London and New York: Routledge.

Tumber, H., & Webster, F. (2006). *Journalists Under Fire: Information War and Journalistic Practices*. London: Sage.

Turner, G. (2004). *Understanding Celebrity*. London, Sage.

Turner, V. (1986). *The Anthropology of Performance*. New York: PAJ Publications.

Tyler, P. (2003, 17 February). Threats and Responses: News Analysis. A New Power in the Streets. *New York Times*. http://query.nytimes.com/gst/fullpage.html?res=9902E0DC1E3 AF934A25751C0A9659C8B63 (accessed 13 December 2007).

Ubaquivel. (2009). 90 Segundos–Alberto Pizango llega a Nicaragua. Channel 4 Nicaragua. http://www.youtube.com/watch?v=EDk9H1EBu-U (accessed June 2010).

Ulrichsen, K., Held, D, and Brahimi, A. (2011) 'The Arab 1989?' Open Democracy (http://www.opendemocracy.net/kristian-coates-ulrichsen-david-held-alia-brahimi/arab-1989)

Urry, J. (2003). *Global Complexity*. Cambridge: Polity.

Van Aelst, P., & Walgrave, S. (2004). New Media, New Movements? The Role of the Internet in Shaping the "Anti-globalization" Movement. In W. van de Donk, B. Loader, P. G. Nixon and D. Dieter (Eds.), *Cyberprotest: New Media, Citizens and Social Movements*. London: Routledge.

Vandermeer, J., & Perfecto, I. (2005). *Breakfast of Biodiversity—The Political Ecology of Rainforest Destruction*. Oakland, CA: Food First Books.

Verhulst, J., & Walgrave, S. (2010). Politics, Public Opinion, and the Media: The Issues and Context behind Demonstrations. In S. Walgrave & D. Rucht (Eds.), *The World Says No to War*. Minneapolis: University of Minnesota Press.

Volkmer, I. (1999). *News in the global sphere: A study of CNN and Its Impact on global communication*. Luton: University of Luton Press.

Volkmer, I. (2003). The Global Network Society and the Global Public Sphere. *Development*, 46(1), 9–16.

Volkmer, I. (2007) Governing the "Spatial Reach"? Spheres of Influence and Challenges to Global Media Policy. *International Journal of Communication*, 1, 56–75.

Waddington, D. (1992). Media Representation of Public Disorder. In D. Waddington (Ed.), *Contemporary Issues in Public Disorder* London: Routledge.

Walgrave, S., & Verhulst, J. (2003). The February 15 Worldwide Protests against a War in Iraq: An Empirical Test of Transnational Opportunities. Outline of a Research Programme. Paper from International Workshop on Contemporary Anti-War Mobilizations, Corfu, Greece. http://nicomedia.math.upatras.gr/conf/CAWM2003/Papers/Verhulst.pdf (accessed 19 December 2007).

Wall, M. (2003). Social Movement and the Net: Activist Journalism Goes Digital. In K. Kawamoto (Ed.), *Digital Journalism*. London: Rowman and Littlefield.

Walters, G. (2006). *Berlin Games: How Hitler Stole the Olympic Dream*. London: John Murray.

Waltz, M. (2005). *Alternative and Activist Media*. Edinburgh: Edinburgh University Press.

Warkentin, C. (2001). *Reshaping World Politics: NGOs, the Internet, and Global Civil Society*. Lanham, MD: Rowman and Littlefield.

Warner, M. (2010, 30 April). For corn syrup, the sweet talk gets harder. *New York Times*.

Waterman, P. (2004). The Global Justice and Solidarity Movement and the WSF: A Backgrounder. In A. Sen et al., (Eds.), *The World Social Forum: Challenging Empires*. New Delhi: Viveka Foundation.

Watson, P. (2008, 23 January). I'm proud to be a pirate. *The Guardian*. http://www.guardian.co.uk/commentisfree/2008/jan/23/japan.australia (accessed 29 November 2009).

Weaver, D. (Ed.). (1998). *The Global Journalist: News People around the World.* Creskill, NJ: Hampton.

Weaver, D. H. (2007). Thoughts on Agenda Setting, Framing, and Priming. *Journal of Communication,* 57(1), 142–47.

Wenn, S. R. (1993). Lights! Camera! Little Action: Television, Avery Brundage and the 1956 Melbourne Olympics. *Sporting Traditions, The Journal of the Australian Society for Sports History,* 10, 38–54.

Weyker, S. (2002). The Ironies of Information Technology. In A. Brysk (Ed.), *Globalization and Human Rights.* Berkeley, CA: University of California Press.

Whipple, T. (2009, 3 April). Why did the police punish bystanders? *Times Online.* http://www.timesonline.co.uk/tol/news/politics/G20/article6025481.ece [accessed 4 April 2009].

Willetts, P. (1996). From Stockholm to Rio and Beyond: The Impact of the Environmental Movement on the United Nations Consultative Arrangements for NGOs. *Review of International Studies,* 22 (1), 67–70.

Wolf, M. (2004). *Why Globalization Works.* New Haven: Yale University Press.

Wolfsfeld, G. (1997). *Media and Political Conflict: News from the Middle East.* Cambridge: Cambridge University Press.

Wolfsfeld, G., Frosh, P., & Awabdy, M. T. (2008). Covering Death in Conflicts: Coverage of the Second Intifada on Israeli and Palestinian Television. *Journal of Peace Research,* 45 (3), 401–17.

Wood, L. J. (2004). Bridging the Chasms: The Case of People's Global Action. In J. Bandy & J. Smith (Eds.), *Coalitions Across Borders: Transnational Protest and the Neoliberal Order.* Lanham: Rowman and Littlefield.

Wright, S. (2004). Informing, Communicating and ICTs in Contemporary Anti-capitalist Movements. In W. Van de Donk, B. D. Loader, P. G. Nixon and D. Rucht (Eds.), *Cyberprotest: New Media, Citizens and Social Movements.* London: Routledge.

Xin, X. (2006). A Developing Market in News: Xinhua News Agency and Chinese Newspaper. *Media, Culture & Society,* 28 (1), 45–66.

Xinhua News Agency. (2008). Sabotage in Lhasa masterminded by Dalai clique, Tibet regional government says [both in Chinese and English] [Internet], 14 March. Available, for instance, from: <http://news.xinhuanet.com/newscenter/2008-03/15/content_7792268.htm> and <http://english.people.com.cn/90002/93607/6378542.html> (accessed 10 July 2009).

Xinhua News Agency. (2008). Dalai-backed violence scars Lhasa [Internet], 15 March (a). Available, for instance, from: <http://news.xinhuanet.com/english/2008-03/15/content_7792827.htm > (accessed 10 July 2009).

Xinhua News Agency. (2008). Lhasa calm after riot, traffic control imposed [Internet], 15 March (b). Available, for instance, from: < http://www.chinadaily.com.cn/china/2008-03/15/content_6539180.htm> (accessed 10 July 2009).

Xinhua News Agency. (2008, 22 March). The Truth of "14 March" Lhasa Riot [in Chinese]. http://news.xinhuanet.com/newscenter/2008–03/22/content_7837535.htm (accessed 10 July 2009).

Xinhua News Agency. (2008, 30 March). Dalai Clique Instigated and Masterminded the Lhasa Riot [in Chinese] http://news.xinhuanet.com/newscenter/2008–03/30/content_7884185 .htm (accessed 10 July 2009).

Yánez, C. (ed.). (1998). Nosotros y los otros: Avances en la afirmación de los derechos de los pueblos indígenas amazónicos. Defensoría del Pueblo, Lima, Perú.

Yashar, D. J. (1998). Contesting Citizenship: Indigenous Movements and Democracy in Latin America. *Comparative Politics*, 31(1), 23–42.

Zhao, Y. (2009), New Students, Old Loyalties: Re-examining American Views of China's New Nationalism. Honours Thesis. University of Michigan. http://deepblue.lib.umich.edu/handle/2027.42/63958 (accessed 29 January 2010).

Zizek, S. (2008, 30 May). Who are the good guys? *New York Times*. http://www.nytimes.com/2008/05/30/opinion/30iht-edzizek.1.13344398.html (accessed August 2008).

Contributors

Ana Adi is a doctoral researcher in the Faculty of Business and Creative Industries at the University of the West of Scotland, where she investigates the framing of the Beijing 2008 Olympic Games by public relations practitioners, online non-accredited media outlets and online readers.

David Archibald teaches in the Department of Theatre, Film and Television Studies at the University of Glasgow. He has written for numerous newspapers and magazines (*Financial Times, Guardian,* etc.) and is currently Convenor of the University's Film Journalism Masters program.

Adam Bowers is a Communication and Public Information Officer at the International Labour Organization. He has previously worked as a Senior Press Officer for UK-based NGO Voluntary Service Overseas. He holds a Masters in Mass Communication from Leicester University and a Bachelor in Politics from the University of Sheffield.

Simon Cottle is Professor of Media and Communications and Deputy Head of the School of Journalism, Media and Cultural Studies at Cardiff University. His latest books are *Mediatized Conflict* (2006)and *Global Crisis Reporting* (2009), and he is Series Editor of the Global Crises and the Media Series for Peter Lang Publishing.

David Crouch did his Masters research at the University of Queensland and completed his PhD at the University of Melbourne, where he currently teaches in the School of Culture and Communication. His research interests encompass literary, cultural and media theory.

Katarina Damjanov (MA Belgrade, PhD Melbourne) has research interests in global cultural and media studies, particularly in the context of the world's Global Commons (the ocean, Antarctica and outer space). She currently teaches in the School of Culture and Communication at the University of Melbourne.

Conny Davidsen is an Assistant Professor of Environmental Policy and Governance at the University of Calgary, Department of Geography. Her research focuses on the processes behind changing environmental policies from a political ecology perspective, especially global-local linkages between governance, power and communication.

Scott Davidson is a Senior Lecturer in Public Relations and Media at De Montfort University. He researches the impact of new technology on activism and brings professional experience from a career in public affairs campaigning to his work. He has also published on how strategic political communications are responding to population ageing.

Kevin Michael DeLuca, Communication Department, University of Utah, explores how humanity's relations to nature are mediated by technology. Besides the book *Image Politics: The New Rhetoric of Environmental Activism*, DeLuca has published dozens of essays on media, activism, and social theory and is currently lost in China. He creates media productions under AiTu Media.

Neil Gavin, Senior Lecturer in Politics, University of Liverpool, researches the media coverage of climate change, energy security and the economy. He is author of *Press and Television in British Politics* (2007) and editor of *The Economy, Media and Public Knowledge* (1998).

Nazanin Ghanavizi is a postgraduate research student in the department of Political Science at the University of Toronto. Her research areas include deliberative democracy, citizen journalism and public reasoning. She has published articles on new media and social movements.

Kevin Gillan is a Lecturer in sociology at the University of Manchester. He has published a number of articles on movement theory and on uses of technology by activists and, in 2008, a book-length study of anti-war activism with Jenny Pickerill and Frank Webster.

Peter Goddard is Senior Lecturer in the Department of Communication and Media at the University of Liverpool. His research interests include broadcasting history and regulation, journalism and documentary. He is co-author of *Public Issue Television: World in Action, 1963–98* (2007).

Brett Hutchins is a Senior Lecturer in Communications and Media Studies at Monash University, Melbourne. His research investigates the effects of the shift from analogue-print to digital-convergent media systems. His latest publications appear in *Television & New Media, International Journal of Communication*, and *Convergence.*

Jeffrey S. Juris is an Assistant Professor of Anthropology in the Department of Sociology and Anthropology at Northeastern University. He is the author of *Networking Futures: The Movements of Corporate Globalization* (2008) and is currently writing a book on media activism and autonomy in Mexico.

Libby Lester is Associate Professor of Journalism, Media and Communications at the University of Tasmania. She has also worked as a journalist for a number of leading Australian newspapers and magazines. Her most recent book is *Media and Environment: Conflict, Politics and the News* (2010).

Chen Li is a PhD candidate and part-time researcher at Glasgow University Media Group (GUMG). His research interests focus on the news media, audience reception and Information Communication Technologies.

Tom Marshall has completed undergraduate studies in International Politics at Aberystwyth University and will be returning to do a Masters and PhD in International Relations.

Andy Miah is Chair of Ethics and Emerging Technologies in the Faculty of Business & Creative Industries at the University of the West of Scotland. He has published extensively on digital culture and the Olympic Games, most recently developing the concept of 'ambush media' to characterize tactical media practice.

Lucy Montgomery is a Research Fellow of the ARC-funded Centre of Excellence for Creative Industries and Innovation at Queensland University of Technology. She holds a QUT Vice Chancellor's Research Fellowship (2010–2013) and is the author of *China's Creative Industries: Copyright, Social Network Markets and the Business of Culture in a Digital Age* (2010).

Craig Murray is chief media analyst with the Norwegian media monitoring company Opoint. He has a PhD from the Queensland University of Technology in Brisbane, Australia.

Katy Parry is a Research Associate in the Department of Communication and Media at the University of Liverpool, working on the AHRC-funded project, 'Media Genre and Political Culture'. Her research interests include political communication, photojournalism and conflict. She is a co-author of *Pockets of Resistance: British News Media, War and Theory in the 2003 Invasion of Iraq* (2010).

Jennifer Peeples is an Associate Professor of environmental rhetoric in the Department of Languages, Philosophy and Speech Communication at Utah State University.

Jenny Pickerill is a Senior Lecturer in Human Geography at Leicester University. She has published three books and more than twenty academic articles. Her work focuses upon the interrelationships between society and technology. It explores the rhetoric, aims, practices and outcomes of the quest for environmental protection and social justice.

Stephen D. Reese is Jesse H. Jones Professor of Journalism and Associate Dean for Academic Affairs in the College of Communication at the University of Texas. His research has been widely published in the sociology of news, the framing of political issues, and, most recently, the effects of globalization on journalism.

Piers Robinson, Senior Lecturer in International Politics, University of Manchester, researches the relationship between communications and world politics. He is author of The *CNN Effect: The Myth of News, Foreign Policy and Intervention* (2002) and *Pockets of Resistance: British News Media, War and Theory in the 2003 Invasion of Iraq* (2010).

Andrew Rojecki is Associate Professor of Communication at the University of Illinois, Chicago. His principal research interests are the politics of dissent and race. He is author of *Silencing the Opposition* (1999) and co-author of *The Black Image in the White Mind* (2000).

James Stanyer lectures in Communication and Media Studies at Loughborough University. His research focuses on developments in political communication in advanced industrial democracies. His work has appeared in a wide range of academic journals, and he has also authored two books, *The Creation of Political News* (2001) and *Modern Political Communication* (2007).

Ye Sun, Communication Department, University of Utah, is interested in the social-psychological processes through which media messages influence individuals' various behavioral decisions and has published in many top journals. Her research currently focuses on health information campaigns and environmental activism in China.

Frank Webster is Professor of Sociology and Head of Department, City University London. He is author or editor of many books, including *Theories of the Information Society* (3rd edition, 2006) and *Journalists under Fire* (with Howard Tumber, 2006).

Ilke Sanlier Yüksel is Assistant Professor in the Communication Sciences Department at Dogus University, Istanbul. Her research interests include media reception, the representation of immigrants in mainstream media and its role on diasporic cultures as well as transnational politics through mediated settings.

Murat Yüksel is Assistant Professor of Sociology at Koc University, Istanbul. He received his PhD from Columbia University. His research interests include state-society relations, social and political movements, and forced migration in the post-imperial Middle East.

Index

B

U